WALTER BENJAMIN
An Aesthetic of Redemption

Benjamin in 1927, at the age of 35. (PHOTO: SUHRKAMP VERLAG)

WALTER BENJAMIN

An Aesthetic of Redemption

RICHARD WOLIN

Columbia University Press
New York   1982

Thanks to Harcourt Brace Jovanovich for permission to reprint from Benjamin's *Illuminations* (New York, 1969) and *Reflections* (New York, 1978).

To New Left Books for permission to reprint from Adorno's *Aesthetics and Politics* (London, 1977) and from Benjamin's *Understanding Brecht* (London, 1977) and *Charles Baudelaire: A Lyric Poet in the Era of High Capitalism* (London, 1973).

Suhrkamp Verlag for permission to reprint from Benjamin's *Briefe* (2 vols., Frankfurt am Main, 1966) and *Gessemelte Schriften* (6 vols., Frankfurt am Main, 1972–   ).

Methuen, Inc. for permission to use Brecht's poem, "On the Suicide of the Refugee W. B." From *Berthold Brecht: Poems, 1918–1956* (New York, 1976).

Columbia University Press
New York   Guildford, Surrey

Clothbound editions of Columbia University Press books
are Smyth-sewn and printed on permanent and durable
acid-free paper.

Library of Congress Cataloging in Publication Data

Wolin, Richard.
    Walter Benjamin, an aesthetic of redemption.

    Bibliography.
    Includes index.
    1. Benjamin, Walter, 1892–1940—Criticism
and interpretation.   I. Title.
PT2603.E455Z96   838'.91209   81–21791
ISBN 0–231–05422–X   AACR2

For my parents,
Harold and Merle Wolin,
with love and gratitude

CONTENTS

PREFACE

Like a shipwrecked man who keeps afloat by climbing to the top of a mast that is already disintegrating. But from there he has a chance to signal for his rescue.

—*Walter Benjamin (1931)*

The life of the German-Jewish literary critic and philosopher Walter Benjamin was marked by a series of failures and misfortunes, from the rejection of his *Habilitationsschrift* in 1925 to his death by suicide on the Franco-Spanish border in September 1940. Once he was denied an academic career he was forced for the remaining fifteen years of his life to pursue a hand-to-mouth existence as a free-lance writer, first in Germany, and then, following Hitler's seizure of power in 1933, in Paris. His life seemed dominated by a perpetual wanderlust; seldom would he remain in any of his favorite European haunts for longer than a few months at a time. He possessed a lifelong fascination for modern city life and published accounts of his forays into the urban landscapes of Naples, Moscow, and Marseille. Benjamin, the admirer and translator of Proust, recorded in the 1930s a series of reflections on his childhood experiences. He also kept a record of his experiences with hashish and mescaline which he hoped one day to use as the basis for a study on the subject of drug-induced intoxication.[1] However, this study, not to mention the major project of his later years, his *Paris, the Capital of the Nineteenth Century* or *Passagenarbeit* (Arcades Project), was never completed. Much has been made of Benjamin's fascination with "ruins"[2] (especially with reference to his failed *Habilitationsschrift* on seventeenth-century German *Trauerspiel*), and in many ways Benjamin's lifework itself remains a ruin. Aside from a collection of aphorisms (*One-Way Street*) the only book he published in his lifetime was *Ursprung des deutschen Trauerspiels* (1928). His literary estate comprises scores of essays and reviews, miscellaneous fragments, two volumes of correspondence, and hundreds of pages from the ill-fated Arcades Project.

He remained virtually a nonentity in the field of German letters until a two-volume selection of his *Schriften* appeared in 1955, edited jointly by Theodor and Gretel Adorno. Since then he has become a bona fide phenomenon; the most recent and comprehensive bibliography of secondary literary on Benjamin now lists 430 entries,[3] and there is no reason to suspect that this profusion of posthumous interest will abate in the near future. The unorthodox character of his life and literary legacy is surely in part responsible for the Benjamin enthusiasm of the last two decades. Benjamin, as certain critics would have it, should be viewed as a twentieth-century anachronism, the last representative of a vanishing species: the authentic European *homme de lettres,* someone for whom philosophy and literature are not mere parlor games, but for whom these serve as the focal point, the raison d'être of life. Benjamin, the ill-fated, twentieth-century Wandering Jew, was born into the wrong era, we are told. He was "The Last Intellectual."[4]

Benjamin's intellectual odyssey, which culminated in such tragic fashion, was certainly unconventional. Unfortunately, however, much secondary literature on the American side of the Atlantic has taken this aura of unconventionality as its point of departure without probing much deeper; and thus it has been the idiosyncratic side of Benjamin, as a personality, as an intellectual, which has captured the imagination of so many American interpreters and critics.[5] To be sure, it is difficult to come to terms with his thought; one reason is that it possesses a magical quality, an originality of focus and vision, such that those select traditions with which he actively came into contact appear—once absorbed through the prism of his work—transformed to the point of being unrecognizable. Yet, once this aura of unconventionality is pierced, one realizes that as a theorist Benjamin was preoccupied with fundamental and relevant issues concerning the nature of art and philosophy, their point of intersection—criticism—and the sociohistorical matrix from which they emerge.

Hence, if there remains no simplistic, unifying theme to which the totality of his *oeuvre* might be reduced, there nevertheless exists a set of underlying problems and recurring motifs which lend that *oeuvre* a continuity much greater than one would initially suppose. It is precisely these problems and motifs that I have sought to bring to the fore in my presentation; while at the same time I attempt to avoid the all-too-seductive temptation of becoming immersed in the labyrinthine structure of Benjamin's arguments to the point of emerging with greater perplexity than one had before the original descent. Nevertheless, Benjamin self-consciously opted for a hermetic and forbidding mode of discourse, further compounding the difficulties of reception by steadfastly refusing in most cases to supply outright the meta-theoretical bases of his conceptual train. The latter were to emerge of their own accord, unforced, from the thing itself. There is no question that this procedure greatly laid itself open to the misunderstandings, confusions, and condemnations to which his works so often fell victim; or to the seemingly more benign epithet of "unconventionality." Yet, it must be said in Benjamin's favor that during the period of his intellectual maturation circa World War I, the established models of his theoretical discourse—whether neo-Kantianism, *Lebensphilosophie,* or positivism—all presented themselves as equally inauthentic; and so he was compelled to probe elsewhere, but also to invent on his own. As Adorno has remarked, Benjamin's thought often takes on the form of a rebus;[6] his discourse becomes a collage of images which, like a work of art that kindles one's fascination, beseeches interpretation or decipherment. And for these reasons, the moment of interpretation occupies a prominent position in the present work.

Upon reviewing the secondary literature on Benjamin, what struck me initially was the lack of any English-language attempt to consider his work as a totality or systematically. To be sure, there are strong reasons against attempting to judge his work in systematic fashion. First of all, his work has an intentionally a-systematic, fragmentary nature. As has been previously suggested, Benjamin has not left an integral, coherent *oeuvre* over which posterity might marvel, but rather a series of fragments. Although he was not without admiration for the main exponents of systematic philosophy, his thinking must be classified among those partisans of an anti-systematic spirit within philosophy. Moreover, not only is his *oeuvre* a series of fragments, but it is also itself fragmentary: since the Arcades Project, on which Benjamin labored from 1927 until his death in 1940, not only remains unfinished, but also in a large measure unpublished, it would perhaps seem advisable at this point to withhold final judgment on the status of his work as a whole. In addition, his professed "Janus-face," which compelled him to oscillate between metaphysical concerns and Marxist interests, represents another factor which speaks against the presumptive attempt to deal with his work in any unified or comprehensive fashion. As a result, the very real barriers to defining any fundamental, overarching intentions in Benajmin's thought have predictably encouraged a plethora of contributions to the feuilleton sections of many a newspaper and journal, but few serious attempts at systematic study.

I have attempted to refrain from violating the fundamentally a-systematic character of Benjamin's work by refusing to confer on it an external, artificially contrived unity for the sake of narrative consistency. Where tensions or irreconcilable contradictions crop up in his development, I have made no attempt to resolve them in intellectually pleasing but spurious unities. Instead, I have taken the position that the tensions and oppositions within his theoretical orientation often represent those tendencies which are most vital and enduring in his thought as a whole—in accordance with the Hegelian maxim that contradiction need not inherently indicate a deficiency on the part of the reasoning subject, but may at times more accurately reflect the inner tensions of the object itself.

However, it would be an even greater distortion to suggest that these disunities would be in some way symptomatic of a methodological approach that was in the least disorganized or haphazard, as if to imply that the various theoretical directions pursued by Benjamin were totally devoid of teleological determinacy. The erroneousness of such a claim can be demonstrated most clearly in terms of the first phase of his intellectual development, which spanned the years 1916 to 1925. These years correspond more or less to what has been commonly referred to as Benjamin's metaphysical or theological period. It is a phase which in secondary literature has suffered somewhat from neglect, largely because the German Benjamin revival of the 1960s saw as its first priority the rehabilitation of the "materialist" Benjamin, in keeping with the political climate of the decade. It is my contention that Benjamin's work from the 1916 essay "On Language as Such and on the Language of Man" through the 1925 *Trauerspiel* study can be read as an integral whole. I have characterized Benjamin's method during this period as one of "redemptive criticism" (*rettende Kritik*) following the lead of Jürgen Habermas; and I have tried to penetrate the veil of hermeticism which surrounds this phase of his work and which accounts for the noticeable diffidence of many critics when confronted with the unequivocally formidable hermeneutic difficulties it presents.[7]

The second phase of Benjamin's work is not so easily definable. Though it can by no means be said to have suffered from critical neglect, the treatment of it has nevertheless been extremely one-sided. In this phase, one learns, the metaphysically inclined Benjamin of the early period has reached maturity. The esoteric, speculative guise of his theoretical stance of the *Trauerspiel* book phase has been cast aside in favor of an orthodox yet innovative materialist approach to the study of cultural phenomena. This view of the later Benjamin consequently accords programmatic status to the 1936 essay on "The Work of Art in the Age of Mechanical Reproduction" and related studies. At this stage, the problem of *reception aesthetics* preoccupies Benjamin; his interest in bourgeois autonomous art is relinquished in favor of an understanding that concentrated on the material conditions of the production and reception of works of art. Indeed, following Benjamin's lead in this field, there has been considerable focus in postwar German criticism on reception aesthetics and the "posthistory" (*Nachgeschichte*) of the work of art; an emphasis which stands in opposition to the exclusive stress in bourgeois aesthetics (from the German Romantics, to *l'art pour l'art*, to the new criticism) on the autonomous, a-social dimension of works of art.

I would not begin to call into question the sincerity of Benjamin's commitment to developing the principles of a materialist aesthetic; nor do I view it fitting to denigrate the important advances he has made in this direction, most notably in the aforementioned "The Work of Art" essay. There are those (e.g., Gershom Scholem) who have viewed the materialist side of Benjamin's Janus-face with nothing but suspicion, and who perceive his affiliation with Brecht in 1929 as being responsible for the advent of a highly uncharacteristic and deleterious influence in his work. Though the result of this influence certainly led to a departure in many ways from an approach to criticism whose success had already been proven, Benjamin's involvement with the materialist world view should instead be viewed as a sincere response on the part of a radical intellectual to the political events and crises of his era, a fact demonstrated in an exemplary fashion by the work of Sandor Radnoti. That Benjamin sought to come to grips politically with the problems associated with the disintegration of Weimar and the rise of fascism, rather than, like so many other members of the German liberal intelligentsia, merely persist in feigning a state of blissful ignorance, was honest and commendable. Yet, once this political stance was translated into theoretical terms, the version of Marxism that resulted was often one that was extremely undialectical and simplistic; a problem which anyone sincerely interested in Benjamin's relevance for the legacy of historical materialism today is obligated to confront fully and not merely pass over in charitable reticence.[8]

At the same time, I wish to dispel the widespread misapprehension that Benjamin in his later years simply *abandoned* his earlier metaphysical concerns. Alongside of the better known materialist studies of this period are essays of a metaphysico-theological inclination which are integrally related to his former method of redemptive criticism—essays such as "On the Mimetic Faculty," and "Franz Kafka," and the seminal "Theses on the Philosophy of History." In light of this evidence, the standard practice in Benjamin criticism of neatly dividing his work into an early "theological period" and a later "materialist phase" would seem in need of substantial revision. Instead, if there is any overall sense of continuity to his work, it must be seen in terms of the definite persistence of Messianic motifs in his later work. In the later Benjamin, therefore, one notes a pronounced and baffling tendency to alternate between a Marxist and metaphysical frame of reference. Only in his final theoretical statement, the "*Geschicht-*

philosophische Thesen"—where Benjamin openly advocates that historical materialism take theology into its service if it wishes to be victorious—did he make an explicit and concerted attempt to unite these two diverse strands of his thinking. In the "Theses" there is no question that Benjamin, disillusioned by the Stalin–Hitler pact and the seemingly implacable rise of the Nazi war machine, confers on the theological side the upper hand.

My objective is to present a comprehensive, well-rounded account of Benjamin's work as a totality, while at the same time remaining sensitive especially to those aspects of his thought which remain relevant from a contemporary point of view. I have taken pains to avoid the predominant pitfalls of Benjamin scholarship, such as emphasizing one aspect or phase of his thought to the exclusion of all others, a practice which has resulted in some extremely one-sided and partial portraits of his accomplishments. The tendency to isolate either the Brechtian or theological dimension of his thinking, for example, is not in itself unwarranted or unfruitful; yet when these aspects are set in relief to the exclusion of the other moments, the intricacies, the breadth, and, to be sure, the contradictions of his *oeuvre* become suppressed in favor of a deceptively unitary image of his theoretical project. The continuity of Benjamin's lifework can only be discovered by way of its *discontinuities*. He combined in one lifetime the activities of the critic, the man of letters, the philosopher, the philologist, the religious thinker, the *Publizist,* and the historical materialist. He drew upon theoretical traditions as diverse as the Jewish Kabbalist Abraham Abulafia's theological philosophy of language and the Marxist playwright Bertolt Brecht's theory of epic theater. Yet, it is remarkable that among all the various accusations that have been leveled against his work over the years, the charge of "eclecticism" has rarely figured among them. His perpetual refusal to respect the traditional boundaries of the intellectual division of labor resulted in a work whose fusion of subtlety and scope would be nearly unthinkable under the climate of spiritual life today, where specialization reigns uncontestedly.

Nominally the subject of this study is Walter Benjamin, a European social philosopher and critic who lived from 1892 to 1940. At the same time, it is my sincere hope that the present work will prove relevant in a more universal sense, insofar as it simultaneously addresses themes concerning philosophy, aesthetics, social theory, and philosophy of history which remain of central importance from a contemporary standpoint. In many respects, Benjamin's reflections on these themes offer a type of privileged insight into the aporias of modern social life and thought.

Berkeley, March 1982

ACKNOWLEDGMENTS

The following individuals have in various ways provided invaluable assistance in the course of my research: Joe Polonsky, Rina Grafstein, Andrew Lichterman, Martin Jay, Leo Lowenthal, Steve Levine, John Sewart, Anna Haynes, Colin Chin, Elizabeth Arkwright, and Justin Simon. Leslie Bialler, my manuscript editor at Columbia University Press, deserves thanks. Detlev Holz, the chief archivist at the University of Muri, was always cooperative and available. I am especially grateful to Christian Lenhardt of York University, whose patience, advice, and generosity I consider myself most fortunate to have received. Last, but most importantly, I would like to express my gratitude and appreciation to Denise Wenner, whose unflagging care and sustenance over the last few years made my labors incomparably easier to bear.

A Note on the Translations

When an English translation of a German text has been altered, a reference to the German original is included in addition to the English reference.

A Note on Terminology

In the text the word "historico-philosophical"—from the German "*geschichtsphilosophisch*"—appears frequently. In German this term has a very specific meaning which might not be readily apparent to the unsuspecting English-speaking reader: it means from the standpoint or perspective of a given *philosophy of history*. It thus represents the adjectival form of the term "philosophy of history," for which there is no satisfactory English equivalent.

WALTER BENJAMIN
An Aesthetic of Redemption

Mein Flügel ist zum Schwung bereit,
ich kehrte gern zurück,
denn blieb ich auch lebendige Zeit,
ich hätte wenig Glück.

(My wing is ready for flight,
I would like to turn back,
For if I stayed timeless time,
I would have little luck.)

—Gerhard Scholem,
"Gruss vom Angelus"

Chapter One

ORIGINS

Childhood and Autobiography

WALTER BENJAMIN was born on July 15, 1892, in Berlin, a time when that city had truly begun to come into its own as a metropolis. His mother, Paula Benjamin (née Schönflies), came from a well-to-do family in East Prussia. Emil Benjamin, his father, worked as a merchant for a Berlin auction house which trafficked in antiques and oriental rugs. Walter Benjamin believed his family to be related to Henrich Heine through his great-grandmother on his father's side, whose maiden name, van Geldern, was the same as the German poet's mother. He had a younger sister, Dora, with whom he would share a room in Paris in the 1930s; and a younger brother, Georg, a communist doctor who ministered to working-class families in Berlin and eventually died in a Nazi concentration camp. Georg Benjamin's wife, Hilde, later became a minister of justice in the German Democratic Republic and achieved reknown as a vigorous prosecutor of former Nazis.

In stark contrast to his later years, the young Benjamin knew very little of material want. His autobiographical writings are a testament to the comfort of his parental home, and references to governesses and mandatory shopping expeditions, led by his mother, to the finer shops of Berlin abound. For Benjamin and other children of his class background comfortably ensconced in Berlin's West End, poverty was a phenomenon to be marveled at from a distance. "The poor?" he writes at one point; "they lived at the back of beyond."[1] As was the case at the time with so many German Jews of upper-middle-class origin, Benjamin came from an assimilated family and appears to have had little formal religious training. The Christmas tree that bedecked the Benjamin home at holiday time was by no means an uncommon sight in Jewish households of the day. His early educational experiences took place at institutions which, when measured against the rigid standards of the times, can only be considered "progressive": first, the Kaiser Friedrich School in Berlin, and subsequently, at the age of 13, the elite Friedrich-Wilhelm Gymnasium in Thuringia. It was there that he was first exposed to the educational philosophy of Gustav Wyneken, founder of the "Free School Community" and leading figure of the German Youth Movement, whose ideas would exercise a profound influence on Benjamin's life in the ensuing years.

Two volumes of Benjamin's childhood recollections have been preserved, *Berlin Chronicle* and *Berliner Kindheit um Neunzehnhundert,* both written in desultory fashion over a period of years in the 1930s. Yet, these collections of reminiscences are far from being autobiographical in the traditional sense; they in no way pretend to yield a portrait of the artist as a young man. Rather, traces of subjective interference in the descriptions are kept to an absolute minimum, in accordance with Benjamin's longstanding philosophical conviction that the movement of truth is objective.[2] Instead of a linear narrative, what emerges are isolated images—in essence, a series of snapshots-in-prose—which when juxtaposed to one another produce a montage-like effect. It is a literary technique which one observes at work time and again in his writings. The true subject matter of these ostensibly biographical works, then, is not Benjamin's youthful development per se, but, quite literally, a Berlin childhood in general. However, of equal importance is the unique mélange of specific sites and incidents which provide the stimulus for the unraveling of the mnemonic tapestry. The novelty of Benjamin's childhood reflections lies in the fact that in his narrative *space* acquires predominance vis à vis *time*. He expresses this idea as follows:

Reminiscences, even extensive ones, do not always amount to an autobiography. And these quite certainly do not, even for the Berlin years that I am exclusively concerned with here. For autobiography has to do with time, with sequence and what makes up the continuous flow of life. Here, I am talking of space, of moments and discontinuities.[3]

As one might surmise, the model and precursor to whom Benjamin looked in his labor of recollection was Marcel Proust: "What Proust began so playfully became awesomely serious. He who has once begun to open the fan of memory never comes to the end of its segments; no image satisfies him, for he has seen that it can be unfolded, and only in its folds does the truth reside."[4] The work of remembrance is in principle inexhaustible, for its key is not inscribed on the surface of the events of life themselves, but instead, is to be found in their interstices, in the *meanings* which attach to them; and these meanings themselves change in character as each subsequent event alters their position within the context of the whole of a life.

Through the impersonality of Benjamin's discourse a discerning eye can nevertheless recognize the shadow of Benjamin the adult. The childhood portrait that emerges is that of a lonely and brooding youngster: acutely sensitive to his immediate environment, hyper-reflective, alienated from his surroundings. He shows himself put off by the loutish behavior of his schoolmates as well as the compulsory treks into the heart of the city with his mother; for both deprived him of that solitude which, he concluded, was "the only fit state of man."[5] He speaks of the unclear vision of intellectuals which results from an innate tendency toward flight from reality; a tendency he claimed to have detected in himself at an extremely early age and which in his eyes manifested itself in his staunch refusal to form with others under any circumstance a united front—be it even with his own mother, whose wrath he would intentionally solicit by perpetually remaining a half step behind on walks. "My habit of seeming slower, more maladroit, more stupid than I am, had its origins in such walks, and has the great attendant danger of making me think myself quicker, more dexterous, and shrewder than I am."[6] Benjamin turned to the theme of childhood memories at a period of his life and in history when all possibilities seemed to be blocked. What he sought in these precious early experiences, however, was not a refuge from the onslaught of historical events, but instead, their *redemption*—for the sake of an unnamed future witness. What he attempted to capture in these reflections was, above all, *a capacity for lived experience* associated with an upbringing in Berlin at this time, whose last vestiges were in the process of being extinguished by the world-historical march of the forces of disenchantment. His reminiscences attempt to record for posterity the swan song of this capacity. They announce: this was a Berlin childhood as it revealed itself to me around 1900, Berlin as it existed once upon a time, as it will never appear again.

Youth Movement

The years of Benjamin's adolescence coincided with the blossoming of the German Youth Movement. It had begun in Berlin in 1901, as a hiking society for boys, and the rapidity with which it gained popularity throughout Germany was just short of phenomenal.[7] One of its chief convictions was the idea that youth was not merely a transitional phase on the way to adulthood, but a value in and of itself. Hence, its slogan "Youth among itself." As such, it soon took on the character of a massive protest against the decaying values of the older generation. Yet, it did not by any means conceive of itself as a future-oriented, progressive force. Instead, it remained overwhelmingly past-directed and Volkish. For this reason, it has been rightly discussed as an intellectual precursor of National Socialist ideology.[8] The ethic to which it appealed emphasized the values of Teutonic mythology: purity of the Nordic race, allegiance to the Germanic heritage, heroism, nature-worship, etc. In sum, it was a movement which sought to mobilize the values of nature and tradition against the evils of modern civilization. Its organization structure, the *Bund*, was thoroughly anti-democratic and elitist, with inordinate emphasis placed on the ideals of leader and leadership. This accentuation of the cult of leadership was in no small way a harbinger of the *Führerprinzip* of the Hitler years. With the start of World War I the Youth Movement came to an end (although a few of its currents lived on until the early 1920s) that was both tragic and ironic: in an orgy of patriotic zeal thousands volunteered to be sent to the front, where they would perish in a war that had been conceived of and staged by the same generation whose values they had unhesitatingly scorned right up until the eve of the war's outbreak.

As would prove to be the case with so many of his intellectual influences, Benjamin's relation to the Youth Movement remained highly personal and individualistic. Moreover, he belonged neither to the main wing of the Youth Movement, Wandervögel, (his ethnic background sufficed to rule out that possibility), nor to the Movement's Jewish branch, Blau Weiss. Instead, Benjamin joined the radical group around his former teacher, Gustav Wyneken, which pursued a course that was in several key respects markedly distinct from the main tendencies of the Youth Movement. Its members on the whole were of Jewish origin. Although Wyneken was in agreement with the ideal of a return to the lost purity of nature and with the condemnation of the ruinous effects which the modern ethos of scientific rationality had upon the substance of cultural life—both standard components of Wandervögel ideology—he found himself strongly at odds with the mainstream of the Youth Movement as to what these principles signified from a practical standpoint. Above all, Wyneken rejected as inauthentic the Wandervögel's call for a return to the racial values of Volk mythology. Instead, he believed that it was the ultimate destiny of "youth culture" to realize loftier spiritual ideals, whose end lay not in the sacrifice of the self for the sake of the Volk, but in the self-formation and cultivation of the individual. It was in the realization of these ideals on the part of individuals and not, according to Wyneken, the recourse to the crude values of blood and soil, that the Youth Movement would discover its true purpose and fulfilment. Consequently, Wyneken and his followers showed themselves extremely receptive to the highly individualistic innovations of Expressionist aesthetics, which in turn were quite naturally perceived as anathema by the Youth Movement at large, which embraced aesthetic values which were rigidly traditional and primitivist.[9]

The Wyneken faction, which centered around the journal Der Anfang, had fully absorbed the elitist implications of the Youth Movement. It, too, glorified the principle of the leadership. Benjamin was considered one of its most talented spokesmen, and there is little doubt about the passion and sincerity of his commitment. Yet, to conclude from this that the elitist orientations of these youthful experiences would play a determining role in his mature literary criticism, as does Bernd Witte,[10] would be to overlook the unique nature of Benjamin's participation in it—and, for that matter, the finality of his break with the Movement in 1914. For Benjamin's theoretical position within the Wyneken group as a whole was on the ethical left wing. He was forever wary of any attempts to force the group into a determinate practical or political direction that would compromise its position from an ethical point of view. In this connection, the source from which Benjamin drew his inspiration, and the one whose tone and substance informs the entirety of his youthful, prewar writings, was Kant's moral philosophy. For him, the significance of the Youth Movement lay in its value as *an Idea in the Kantian sense*: as an absolute end in itself unobtainable, which nevertheless serves as a binding guide for ethical conduct. For the collectivist ideology of the Movement as a whole, Benjamin had little use. Instead, he perceived the Youth Movement as a vehicle for *individual self-fulfillment,* for the attainment of a state of "solitude" in which self and Idea coalesce in a condition of pure communion. As he expresses this thought in a letter from the summer of 1913:

I believe that only in a community, in a community of the most sincerely faithful, can a person possess true solitude: a solitude in which the self raises itself up against the Idea, in order to come into its own. . . . the most profound solitude is that of the ideal man in relation to the Idea, which destroys his human characteristics. And this more profound solitude we can first expect from the true community."[11]

In another letter from the same period he asserts: "I renounce every reality which fails to accommodate itself to the Idea."[12]

Early on, tensions developed in Benjamin's relation to Wyneken's group as a result of the inordinately high ethical code against which, in his eyes, it was obligated to measure itself. Taking his bearings with unrelenting exactitude from the standpoint of Kant's Second *Critique*, he denounced on a priori grounds any attempt to consider the Movement as a means to an end rather than an end in itself. Specifically, as the jingoistic fervor of the prewar years began to reach an alarming level, Benjamin feared justifiably that the Youth Movement would become increasingly susceptible to manipulation on the part of nationalistic interests. Yet, this apprehension was merely the manifestation of a more fundamental conviction that political goals and ethical conduct were *mutually opposed realms of human endeavor*—a conviction to which he remained faithful even at the time of his initial exposure to communist ideals in the mid-twenties. In one of his earliest preserved letters, he speaks of a first awakening of Zionist sympathies.[13] However, only a few months later, in January 1913, he distances himself from the Zionist movement by explaining that for him politics remains forever "the choice of the lesser evil. The Ideal never appears in it, only the party."[14] In Zionism, the ethical substance of Judaism is consumed by nationalistic-political objectives. Thus, he concludes, it is the intellectual and literary element of Judaism which attracts his interest, not the political, propagandistic side.

Consequently, as Benjamin observed renewed efforts to channel the energies of the Youth Movement toward determinate practical goals, his association with it became increasingly tenuous. As he writes in a letter of September 1913:

This is what is most important: we must not commit ourselves to a determinate idea [*Gedanken*]; even the idea of youth culture should be for us only the illumination which draws the most distant spirit into effulgence. However, for many, even Wyneken and the *Sprechsaal*★ will become a "movement," they will have committed themselves; and they will no longer perceive the spirit where it appears more free, more abstract. This constantly pulsating feeling for the abstractness of pure spirit—that is what I would like to call Youth.[15]

One of the most compelling formulations of Benjamin's early, intensely ethical theoretical outlook is the essay "Der Moralunterricht," his first published work, which appeared in Wyneken's journal *Die Freie Schulgemeinde.* The essay represents an uncompromising confrontation of an orthodox Kantian moral standpoint, distilled from the *Groundwork of the Metaphysic of Morals,* with contemporary attitudes toward the question of moral

---

★ "Sprechsaal der Jugend": the Berlin student group organized by Wyneken in which Benjamin was active at this time.

instruction prevalent in Wyneken's "Free School Community." It is remarkable in its demonstration of Benjamin's radical allegiance to the Kantian viewpoint that all attempts to base ethics on whatever empirical maxims of necessity entail a compromise of the principle of moral freedom and, as such, represent a relapse into the faculty of "inclination" or "desire"—that is, the realm of moral heteronomy. For Kant, ethical conduct proceeds from respect for the pure *form* of the moral law alone;[16] and this is precisely the vantage point from which Benjamin seeks to censure the educational views of the school reform movement.

The cardinal error committed by the reform movement was its belief that there could exist something akin to an "educational science" of moral principles, that the question of moral education could be broached from the point of view of a "scientifically closed theory."[17] Benjamin feared that any attempt to subordinate such instruction to the particular aims of a given pedagogical movement would result in the sacrifice of the moral law to external, heteronomous ends. In sum, he was apprehensive about the likelihood of the *routinization* of the ethical ideal (to employ Weber's term) once it became objectified within a concrete institutional setting. In this connection the rigidly Kantian ethical stance upheld by the early Benjamin cannot help but call to mind Hegel's famous caricature of the "beautiful soul" in the *Phenomenology of Spirit*[18] (and how much more apropos would the Hegelian epithet appear only five years later as Benjamin in his dissertation explicitly took up the philosophy of Novalis, for whom the label was originally intended). In the spirit of Kant's ideal of a "kingdom of ends," he quotes the latter's remark in the *Groundwork of the Metaphysic of Morals* that, "It is not enough that what is morally good should *conform* to the moral law; rather, it must also occur *for the sake of the moral law*."[19]

For Kant, it was impermissible to classify as "moral" an act which, although ostensibly in agreement with the moral law ("Act only on that maxim through which you can at the same time will that it should become a universal law"), was actually undertaken with an ulterior motive in view (be it for the sake of personal happiness or whatever other merely contingent goal). In a similar vein, Benjamin argues that even if the school reform movement had possessed a perfectly legitimate aim in desiring to raise the standards of ethical conduct in the educational system, it was nevertheless guilty of betraying the moral law insofar as it acted out of regard for *determinate empirical ends,* and not out of respect for the moral law for its own sake. His summary verdict on the idea of moral pedagogy thus reads as follows: "since the process of ethical education is in principle incompatible with every rationalization and schematization, it can have nothing whatsoever to do with instruction of any kind."[20]

The moral law is not something that can be illustrated by recourse to individual practical examples or timely illustrations, insofar as it derives from a priori, universal grounds: "The guarantee of actually encountering the ethical will as such is not given to us under any individual empirical conditions."[21] As a result, the paradoxical judgment with which Benjamin confronts Wyneken's "Free School Community" is that *moral instruction in principle cannot be taught.* It cannot be recommended on the basis of specific empirical arguments, insofar as it is an Idea of reason—hence, of a nonempirical, intelligible nature—and on this account must be followed for the sake of its form alone.[22]

Although its intelligible character enters into contradiction with that world of causality in which our actions necessarily have their outcome, we are nevertheless obligated to act as if we were members of that intelligible world, or else relinquish the ground of our freedom which lies in the moral law alone. This is the well-known "antinomy of practical reason" of Kant's Second *Critique*[23]—a world of subjective freedom on the one hand and a world of objective necessity on the other—and there is little question on which side of the antinomy Benjamin elects to take his stand. In "Der Moralunterricht" Benjamin speaks from the standpoint of a Kantian "kingdom of ends." "The pure will, which does the good for the sake of the good, cannot be attained with the means of the educator."[24]

What is especially noteworthy about Benjamin's inflexible adherence to the Kantian position is the debilitating consequences which emerge from a practical standpoint when that position is followed to its logical conclusion. For the ethical individual can maintain his devotion to the transcendental principle embodied in the moral law only at the cost of an often fatal disregard for the actual results of his action (or, as is more often the case, his *inaction*) in the empirical world. Since, according to Kant, the consequences of our acts are subject to the realm of necessity, and thus, strictly speaking, beyond our control, the empirical world itself can lie in a shambles as far as the ethical individual is concerned, as long as he has fulfilled his duty by remaining faithful to the formal demands of the moral law.[25] Thus, a rigorous pursuit of the ethical standpoint leads either to an extreme quietism—in the case where the moral subject defensively retreats into the ivory tower of the pure will—or else to what is in effect an "unethical" disregard for the actual consequences of one's actions in the (subaltern) sphere of empirical life.[26]

Even at this extremely early point in Benjamin's intellectual development (he was 21 years of age at the time "Der Moralunterricht" appeared), one can already detect in his solidarity with Kant the incipient adumbrations of an ethical point of view that would later provide the foundation for his mature philosophy of history. Specifically, in the neo-Kantian dichotomy between the intelligible world and the empirical world, one can already glean the origins of the Benjaminian distinction between the iniquitous nature of historical time and the fulfilled time of the Messianic era, a distinction which remained essential for his world view through the writing of the *Origin of German Tragic Drama* (1925) and beyond. Nevertheless, one can also recognize at this early stage the first indications of a dissatisfaction on Benjamin's part with the limitations of a purely ethical standpoint and the attempt to provide a nonformal, substantive basis for it. As he remarks at one point in "Der Moralunterricht": "Whereas today one sees everywhere an increase in the number of people who consider ethical life and religion to be in principle independent of one another, for us it appears that it is only in religion—and in religion alone—that the pure will finds its content. The everyday of an ethical community bears a religious imprint."[27] The desire to discover a positive guarantee for the grounding of ethical consciousness which would escape the isolation of the Kantian moral subject led Benjamin in the ensuing years to an increasingly serious confrontation with the possibilities embodied in the idea of religious experience. For religion professes to offer something that the ethical point of view can in no way furnish: the possibility of salvation.

The dissolution of Benjamin's relation to the Youth Movement followed a predictable course given his sensitivity to its employment for practical ends. The first signs of a break occurred on the occasion of the scandal provoked by Max Reinhardt's staging of the Gerhart Hauptmann play *Festspiel in deutschen Reimen* in the Spring of 1913. The play was supposed to be written by Hauptmann to commemorate the 100th anniversary of Germany's emancipation from French dominion during the Napoleonic era. As such, at a time when talk about Germany's encirclement by hostile foreign powers was rampant, Hauptmann and Reinhardt were naturally expected to field a production which eulogized the virtues of patriotism and Prussian militarism. However, what the audience actually experienced on opening night, May 31, 1913, was something entirely different. Heroes of German nationalism such as Frederick the Great were mockingly portrayed as puppets. At the end of the drama, Reinhardt himself appeared on stage and summarily packed away the puppets in trunks. Then, addressing both puppets and audience, he concluded the play with the following words:

Du wackrer Graukopf, lieg an deinem Ort.
Was leben bleiben soll, das sei dein Wort.
Ich schenk es Deutschland, brenn es in sein Herz—
nicht deine Krieglust, aber—dein vorwärts!*

Vorwärts, of course, was the name of the leading Social Democratic paper. The audacity of the Hauptmann-Reinhardt production can only be fully appreciated when one takes into account that the public flaunting of pacifist sentiments in Wilhelmine Germany at the time was akin to high treason. Not surprisingly, the play was forced to close after only 11 performances.[28]

Benjamin's reaction to this series of events was swift and

---

* Brave old man, don't budge from your spot.
  Your motto should be: live and let live.
  I submit this to Germany, let it burn in her heart:
  not your love of battle, but your forward!

vehement. In letters to Wyneken, he immediately requested that the next number of *Der Anfang* be devoted to the issues that had been raised by the Hauptmann-Reinhardt play. He and his close friend, the poet Fritz Heinle, quickly drafted articles to appear in the forthcoming issue. Yet, Benjamin's attitude toward the chain of events which the play had set in motion can only be considered political in a roundabout way. What appears to have incited his wrath was not so much the question of militarism versus pacifism, but more specifically the attempt once again on the part of the older generation to foist its chauvinistic values on the cause of youth, thus nipping the latter's possibilities for spiritual self-development at the bud. The widely vaunted experience of the older generation, invoked to keep the eagerness of youth in its place, for Benjamin amounted to nothing but "years of compromise, impoverished ideas, and unimaginativeness,"[29] a mere ploy to prevent youth from dreaming its own dreams. Aside from his sincere appreciation of the bold act of defiance represented by the Hauptmann-Reinhardt production,[30] what concerned him most about the play's censure was that it constituted another oppressive attempt to smother the aspirations of youth under the weight of the stale, tradition-bound values of Wilhemine Germany; and thus that ultimately the promise of the Youth Movement would be fully assimilated amidst the fanatical outpouring of patriotic sentiment—a suspicion that would not prove unfounded.

In the summer semester of 1914, Benjamin was elected President of the Free Student League in Berlin and used his inaugural address as a platform from which to voice his rapidly mounting disillusionment over recent attempts to channel the direction of the Youth Movement toward political goals. His speech, "Das Leben der Studenten," reiterated in a sense many of the themes from "Der Moralunterricht." The tone of the address was stern and admonitory, insofar as he felt that the Movement had in many ways betrayed its original theme of "Youth among itself." Instead, he viewed a growing trend toward the perception of youth as a merely transitional stage in life, as a means to an end—adulthood—rather than an end in itself. Therefore, he criticized especially the tendency to look upon university education as a vehicle for career advancement and not as a value in its own right: "Where the predominant idea of student life is office and career, knowledge takes a back seat. A dedication to knowledge is something to be feared, insofar as it leads away from the path of bourgeois security."[31] In this statement one can already detect the seeds of Benjamin's later scorn for the necessity of choosing a bourgeois vocation; but here, too, one can already sense the conviction behind his life-long dedication to the pursuit of knowledge and truth.

The inevitable final break with the Youth Movement came in August of that year, when Wyneken, like the Social Democrats to whom he perhaps stood closest politically, delivered his followers to the German war machine. Benjamin, out of numbness and despair, contemplated enlisting, if only in order to remain with his friends. But then an event occurred which awakened him from his numbness and would leave a profound imprint on his life for years to come: the death of his young friend Heinle[32]— "a poet, and the only one of them all whom I met not in 'real life' but in his work"—[33] who, in an act of defiance over the foundering of the Youth Movement and the hideous triumph of the spirit of war enthusiasm throughout German society, committed suicide. In a letter to Wyneken in which he severed all ties with his former mentor, Benjamin fully acknowledged that Wyneken had been the first to lead him "in the life of spirit," and that breaking off relations was a way of remaining faithful to the principles for which Wyneken once stood. However, he continued reproachfully, "You have committed fearful, abominable treason against the women who love your students. You have ultimately sacrificed youth to the state, which has taken everything from you."[34]

The disintegration of the Youth Movement in the destructive frenzy of the war years only reinforced further Benjamin's innate distrust of politics as a solution to the failings of humanity. As such, the onset of war represented for him an occasion to retreat more deeply into the world of philosophy, literature, and letters.

Romantic Anticapitalism

In his 1962 Preface to *The Theory of the Novel* Georg Lukács coined the term "romantic anticapitalism" to refer to a cultural attitude widespread among the Central European intelligentsia at the time of World War I. This attitude was characterized both by a bitter resentment against the soulless world engendered by modern industrial capitalism and by a marked nostalgia for bygone epochs in which communal forms of life remained intact. Owing to a peculiar conjuncture of sociohistorical circumstances, for much of the nineteenth century the last rudiments of feudal society had not yet been fully vanquished in Germany, while at the same time the developing forces of capitalist industry were still insufficiently advanced to assert control over social life. This situation gave rise to a partial vacuum of power and status in German society—a vacuum members of the academic community were only too happy to fill. However, with Germany's remarkably rapid industrial growth in the latter third of the nineteenth century, the preeminent social position of the mandarin intellectual caste began to be threatened by an upstart class of successful entrepreneurs. It was this state of affairs that made Imperial Germany especially fertile soil for the growth of hostility toward the forces of modernization—particularly among the intellectual elite.[35]

Moreover, since German cultural life had already passed through a vigorous romantic phase early in the nineteenth century, a strong intellectual precedent had been established for the proliferation of such attitudes in the century's later years. One of the classical texts of this renewed antimodernist sentiment was Ferdinand Tönnies' *Gemeinschaft und Gesellschaft* (1887), in which the organic, personal, and direct character of traditional, communal social organization was favorably contrasted with the mechanical, impersonal, and calculating world of commodity production under capitalism. As such, the dualism that informs the title of Tönnies' work would become the watchword of classical German social theory from Dilthey to Simmel to Weber. Moreover, it found expression in an analogous terminological opposition which enjoyed increasingly widespread currency in German intellectual circles toward the latter years of the nineteenth century: the contrast between *Kultur* and *Zivilisation*, where *Kultur* symbolized a cultivated, aesthetic, spiritual, and organic relation to the world—a relation associated with traditional patrician German values—and where *Zivilisation* represented the superficial, materialistic, artificial, and commercial orientation of the decadent capitalist West. As Michael Löwy, quoting Fritz Ringer, has observed:

Traumatized by the social and cultural effects of capitalist domination, the academic intelligentsia reacted "with such desperate intensity that the spectre of a 'soulless' modern age came to haunt everything they said and wrote no matter what the subject"; all their thinking was marked by "their horror of a streamlined and, they will say, shallow and materialistic age."[36]

Needless to say, such resolutely antimodernist tendencies were often accompanied by pointedly reactionary convictions, such as the desire to stem the tide of progress by reasserting traditional, patriarchal feudal values. Nevertheless, in the same Preface Lukács observes another current in the intellectual tradition of romantic anti-capitalism, one which is characterized not so much by a static and unfruitful longing to find refuge in the past per se, but which instead remains future-oriented by virtue of a *utopian* vision which seeks to discover in the past forgotten semantic potentials relevant to the present needs of humanity. Speaking of this other current, in terms of which Lukács situates his own early writings, he adds, "We need only think of Ernst Bloch's *Geist der Utopie* (1918, 1925) and *Thomas Münzer als Theologe der Revolution,* of Walter Benjamin, even the beginning of Theodor W. Adorno, etc."[37]

Of course, in 1962 Lukács, speaking as a confirmed historical materialist, had long since renounced his pre-Marxist writings (not to mention *History and Class Consciousness,* the most significant treatise on dialectics to appear since Marx's day) and regards this tradition disparagingly. It aimed, he suggests, "at a fusion of 'left' ethics and 'right' epistemology (ontology, etc.);"[38] by which he means to imply that while its vehement ethical rejection of the capitalist world was essentially sound, its deficiency lay in its failure to make the leap Lukács himself made in the late twenties: the *total* abandonment of bourgeois philosophy in favor of dialectical materialism. However, the solution advocated by Lukács— based on an overly literal reading of the well-known eleventh of Marx's "Theses on Feuerbach"—is not only precipitate but also becomes a defeatism of reason in a historical situation in which the attempt to realize philosophy has not only miscarried, but has become, moreover, a new form of historical oppression.[39]

In this sense, the spirit of left-wing, romantic, anticapitalism, whose irrelevance the later Lukács prematurely celebrates, merits renewed consideration at the present juncture in history. As Paul Piccone, a leading American social theorist, has recently observed, "it is necessary to return preliminarily to the vision of the Lukács of *The Soul and the Forms,* the Gramsci of *La Città Futura,* or the Bloch of *The Spirit of Utopia* . . . [as] a broad existentialist critique of the Enlightenment and of bourgeois civilization."[40] The inclusion of Benjamin's name in the above list would have been entirely appropriate.

Thus, one can begin to situate Benjamin's philosophical project in the context of the like-minded theoretical efforts of Bloch and the young Lukács. Each attempted to combine a critique of the prosaic, dispirited world of capitalist rationality with a search for a qualitatively new Archimedean point from which the world could be not just changed, but apocalyptically transformed. It is a passionate and radical *will to transcendence* that unites the thinking of these three men in their early years, an obstinate, principled refusal to brook any compromise with the status quo. It is precisely the primacy of this will to transcendence which serves to differentiate the romantic anticapitalism of Bloch, Lukács, and Benjamin from that of conservative critics of culture such as Simmel or Weber, who deem present conditions a priori insurmountable and thus remain trapped at the level of a "tragic" view of life. Although each selected a different route, they shared a common goal. This is made evident by the guiding conceptual principles around which the theoretical endeavors turn in each case: utopia (Bloch), totality (Lukács), and redemption (Benjamin). In addition, both Lukács and Benjamin would ultimately become disenchanted with the esoteric, quasi-elitist formulations of their early work (only with Lukács was the break total) and turn to Marxism as a more generalizable, historically adequate solution to the problem of a regenerated humanity.

In the context of the intellectual climate of World War I Germany, the common enemy on the theoretical front for the utopia-oriented thought of Bloch, Lukács, and Benjamin was the reigning philosophical school of neo-Kantianism.[41] Their deeply rooted theoretical antipathy to Kantian thought was based on the latter's rigid epistemological ban on thinking the absolute; or the stigma with which it branded any thought that dared to overstep the boundaries given to us immediately in sensible intuition. To thinkers so radically devoted to questions of transcendence and the problem of rescuing an atrophied bourgeois world from the cataclysmic abyss toward which it seemed uncontrollably headed, the reverence with which neo-Kantian thought stood before the boundaries of empirical experience, a scientistic holdover from its Enlightenment origins, appeared as nothing less than traitorous vis-à-vis the true, utopian mission of thought.

In this connection, it is hardly coincidental that the thought of all three, Bloch, Lukács, and Benjamin, gravitated decisively toward the realm of art in their search for a resolution to the cultural crisis at hand. For if utopia was the objective, the profound longing for transcendence evinced in authentic works—their attempt to embody the idea of a nondegraded, unprofane spiritual totality—places them in the forefront of the utopian impulses of thought. Moreover, when viewed against the neo-Kantian intellectual backdrop of Germany at this time, works of art possess a salutory function as the living refutation of the Kantian proscription against meanderings in the intelligible realm, against his claim that the concepts of our understanding "would mean nothing were we not always able to present their meaning in appearances, that is, in empirical objects."[42] For works of art overreach the Kantian barrier of the "objects of possible experience" and present, nevertheless, meaningful and compelling judgments about the objective world—judgments which are in fact often more "valid" than the natural-scientific judgments Kant seeks to emulate. The following brief discussion of the early aesthetics of Lukács and Bloch is intended to bring the specificity of Benjamin's theoretical project into focus more clearly.

In his 1910 *Soul and Form,* Lukács's theme was the inability to form life, the incapacity of the forms of culture to realize themselves in a prosaic empirical world—a world that proves itself at every turn inimical to the higher demands of the world of spirit. At this stage in his development Lukács does not yet seek to provide a sociological account for this crisis of values, e.g., in terms of the phenomenon of "rationalization" or the transition from *Gemeinschaft* to *Gesellschaft*, as he would in his 1911 study on the *History of Modern Drama*. Instead the dichotomy between the world of values and the world of experience is viewed from a Kierkegaardian, existential standpoint, as an ontological "given."[43] There is no immanent way out of this cultural-historical impasse. Alienation, the separation of soul and empirical life, of creator from creation, reigns uncontested. In this basic motif one sees already at work a significant recourse to the problematic, which animated the entirety of classical German philosophy—the hiatus between subject and object. And it was the search for a resolution to this (Kantian) dichotomy between thought and being, ought and is, which became the driving force behind all of Lukács' intellectual activity in his early years. His conception of the network of universal alienation in which modern man finds himself inextricably embedded is expressed in the following passage:

once it has entered life, everything has its own existence independent of its progenitor and his purposes whether they be useful or detrimental, good or evil. . . . The life (of every work) separates itself from its originator and the aims he had in mind. It lives an independent life. As it grows it develops into directions not anticipated by him; it may even turn against him, annihilating that which it was supposed to ground and support. Means become ends, and nobody knows in advance or after the fact what sort of latent situational energy lie in wait in the things![44]

And in "The Metaphysics of Tragedy," the essay in *Soul and Form* which most influenced Benjamin, Lukács formulates the existential predicament of the modern era as follows:

Life is an anarchy of light and dark: nothing is ever completely fulfilled, nothing every quite ends; new confusing voices always mingle with the chorus of those that have been heard before. Everything flows, everything merges into another thing, and the mixture is uncontrolled and impure; everything is destroyed, everything is smashed, nothing ever flowers into real life. To live is to live something through to the end: but *life* means nothing is ever fully and completely lived through to the end.[45]

In the "Metaphysics of Tragedy" Lukács uses this diagnosis of the congealed state of modern culture as an argument for the *impossibility of tragedy* in the modern era. Life has become a universal leveling process whereby the higher is constantly brought down to the level of the lower. In contrast, ancient tragedy dealt directly with fates and destinies. The link between individual fortune and the destiny of humanity as a whole always appeared self-evident. It is precisely the *lack* of this self-evidence that defines the relation of the modern tragic hero to the rest of life. For the fate of each individual seems condemned to the narrowness of his own contingent, subjective particularity. The highest station that the individual can reach at present is insight into the nature of the irremediable antinomy between cultural forms and life, an act of recognition which confers a modicum of tragic dignity on an otherwise unfulfilled existence. Each of the essays in *Soul and Form* takes this antinomy as its theme. In the end there is no salvation for the individual, merely the empty consolation of recognition.

Of Lukács's pre-Marxist work, however, *The Theory of the Novel* (1914) was to have the greatest impact on Benjamin's thought. Subtitled "A Historico-philosophical Essay on the Forms of Great Epic Literature," *The Theory of the Novel* demonstrated convincingly the historical determinacy of literary genres, an approach that would become paradigmatic for Benjamin's analysis of *Trauerspiel*. Organic, rounded, totality-oriented works of art are appropriate to "integrated civilizations" such as classical Greece, Lukács argues, epochs where the "extensive totality of life" remains intact. Lukács then contrasts the world of the novel to such epochs, a world in which meaning seems to have flown from life, a thoroughly profane age of "transcendental homelessness." *The Theory of the Novel* omits a sociological analysis of the specific historical conditions which give rise this age, but relies on the Hegelian concept of "second nature" to account for a world become soulless and rigidified—"a charnelhouse of long-dead interiorities."[46] As Lukács remarks, "The novel is an epic in a world that has been abandoned by God."[47] *Demons* now inhabit the world. As such, the world of the novel is one in which the ideal is repulsed from the real, in which the ideal can never be lived. It is an antinomic, Kantian world characterized by the separation between subject and object, between "ought" and "is." Freedom exists only inwardly, subjectively; and against this freedom the subject finds itself confronted with an objectively meaningless cosmos of facts. Though this account of the prosaic state of empirical life is in many ways similar to the analysis in *Soul and Form,* it proves superior insofar as it recognizes this state as historically determined rather than an ontological absolute.

The Kantian dualisms which Lukács make use of are suggestive of the theological dualism between the sacred and profane orders of life, indicating similarities with the theological strains of Benjamin's thought. Yet, out of this dualism a solution emerges for Lukács—to be sure, one that is qualified and partial—a solution to which Benjamin, the more theologically oriented of the two, would never accede. For the absence of objective or immanent meaning in life compels the artist to posit or construct meaning subjectively (for Lukács, this is the source of the "irony" characteristic of the novelistic point of view). For the novelist confronts the meaningless cosmos of life as a *form-giver.*[48] He is the one who bestows order upon chaos by virtue of the regenerative powers of aesthetic form. Ironically, meaning is recaptured "precisely when the author goes all the way, ruthlessly, towards exposing its absence."[49] In this way, even though the category of totality remains absent from life, it can nevertheless be reasserted on the (subjective) plane of artistic form. "The immanence of meaning which the form of the novel requires lies in the hero's finding out through experience that a mere glimpse of meaning is the highest life has to offer, and that this glimpse is the only thing worth the commitment of an entire life, the only thing by which the struggle will have been justified."[50] For the hero of the novel, whose destiny never attains the dignity of the tragic hero, the resigned "glimpse of meaning" represents an (albeit weak) claim to superiority. Yet, the true hero of *The Theory of the Novel* is the artist himself, insofar as he re-creates the lost totality of meaning on the basis of his capacity as artist or form-giver.

Nevertheless, there remains a contradiction inherent in Lukács's reliance on the moment of aesthetic form to attain the formed totality, the unity of subject and object, which reified daily life denies. For a solution in terms of the ideal of "aesthetic culture" is one which ultimately leaves the rest of life and everything in it unchanged. Furthermore, by seeking an isolated and private, *aesthetic* solution to the cultural crisis, the artist himself withdraws into his own narrow, specialized field; and in this way the universal fragmentation of life wrought by the division of labor ultimately penetrates *l'art pour l'art*, the allegedly autonomous domain of aesthetic form. The artist is thus reduced to being merely one "specialist" among many in a society that takes pride in specialization. For Lukács:

the cultivation of interiority [*Innerlichkeit*] makes the aesthete a specialist of inner life, a passive, fragmented spectator of his own passing moods and fancies. The cultivation of interiority in fact severs him from any possible unity of culture, just as specialization exerts the same toll on any area of modern life.[51]

However, for the theologically oriented thought of Benjamin, the idea of re-creating the lost unity of subject and object through the methods of "aesthetic culture" becomes clearly illegitimate. For Benjamin there exists a crucial distinction between the "created totality" and the "formed totality." The created totality produces something out of nothing and as such remains the province of God.[52] At certain points in *The Theory of the Novel* Lukács speaks of the totality of the novel as if it were in actuality a created totality, that is, as if the novelist possessed the capacity to re-create life itself through art. However, the artist remains capable only of producing a formed totality: he projects order on chaos—and only an apparent, symbolic, aesthetic order at that. For Benjamin, the possibility of restoring harmony and order to the world, the possibility of redemption, rests with the redeemer or Messiah. The artist who thought it possible to bring about this end through purely aesthetic means would be guilty of hubris. The act of creation, when properly understood, is a divine act. Thus, Benjamin (e.g., in his *Elective Affinities* essay) makes a sharp distinction between the saint and the poet: whereas the life of the former represents a pure relation of humanity to God, the forms of the latter remain confined to the (profane) world of intersubjective relations among people. Thus, in Benjamin's eyes, works of art can at best be understood as *prefigurements* of reconciled life, and it becomes the task of the critic to make precisely this moment in them clear and manifest; no matter how avidly it strives to reach the absolute in and of itself, a work of art remains something that in the last analysis is merely man-made. For Benjamin the eternal paradox of human existence is the fact that its fulfillment or consummation ultimately lies beyond the immediate grasp of man himself.

As we have already suggested, Lukács position vis-à-vis this dilemma remains ambivalent. He seems to believe that the artist, because of his capacity as form-giver, is the only individual in modern society capable of restoring the lost totality of meaning. At the same time, he remains cognizant of the limitations of a solution that is confined to the realm of aesthetic culture, leaving the forms and institutions of life itself unaltered. Lukács, in 1914, seemed to see a leap of faith as the only way out of this dilemma. The transformation of mankind could not find a solid basis in this-worldly institutions, since, for the pupil of Simmel, the latter always develop according to their own uncontrollable, alienated logic, independent of the human subject who had first given form to them. In face of the irreconcilable dualism between "is" and "ought," Lukács, like Kierkegaard before him, was convinced of the necessity of transcending the ethical standpoint, insofar as the logically consistent moral actions of the ethical subject carried no guarantee of realization in an empircal world dominated by the laws of necessity. He believed he had discovered the embodiment of this superior, *pure* form of action in the "Russian Idea" as portrayed in the novels of Tolstoy and, even more so, in those of Dostoyevsky. As such, the heroes and heroines of Dostoyevsky's novels—Prince Myshkin, Sonia, and Alexei Karamazov—represent a *meta-ethical* standpoint; they represent the elect who, through the grace of God, alone remain capable of actually realizing divine ends in the realm of empirical life. They are incarnations of the concept of "goodness," and as such realize these superior ends by virtue of having in their acts transcended the tainted sphere of empirical necessity, a fact which lends their achievements a "miraculous" character.[53] For this reason in *The Theory of the Novel* Dostoyevsky enjoys a privileged position. His works push the novel form to its limits, to the point at which aesthetic culture passes over into the *spiritual regeneration of humanity*. As Lukács remarks, Dostoyevsky "belongs to the new world. Only formal analysis of his works can show whether he is already the Homer or the Dante of that world or whether he merely supplies the songs which, together with the songs of other forerunners, later artists will one day weave into a great unity: whether he is merely a beginning or already a completion."[54] In this sense, "The ideal for which Lukács was the spokesman . . . was that of Slavic culture and mystical thought as an alternative to the 'worldly asceticism' and 'goal-oriented' action of the bourgeois West."[55]

The philosophical affinities between Benjamin and Bloch are somewhat less direct, although Bloch was to play an influential role in shaping the development of Benjamin's political convictions in the early twenties. But the reason for this seemingly greater theoretical divergence is more a question of material focus than of fundamental outlooks. For in contrast to both Benjamin and Lukács, Bloch, in his great theoretical work of the 1910s, *Geist der Utopie,* concentrates in his discussions of aesthetics almost exclusively on music rather than literature. In many ways the utopian impulses which Benjamin and Lukács discover in literary works of art Bloch attributes to musical experience.

The central role Bloch assigns to music in *Geist der Utopie* derives from the antipositivist theory of experience to which he attempts to give shape. This theory takes the inauthenticity and blindness of the contemporary, unreflective mode of existence (*"das Dunkle des gelebten Augenblicks"*)[56] as its point of departure and appeals to a "turning-inward" (*Inwendigkeit*), a cultivation of the depths of subjectivity, in an effort to gain a superior concept of experience. As such, music occupies a preeminent position insofar as it is acknowledged as the most "subjectivized," least "sensuous" among the arts—a consideration Bloch undoubtedly takes over from Hegel's discussion of the hierarchy of the arts. Music's lack of corporality can be most clearly seen in its medium of expression: in contrast to painting, sculpture, and architecture, it exists in the dimension of time rather than space. Bloch proceeds from historico-philosophical presuppositions that are nearly identical to those of Benjamin and Lukács: presuppositions concerning the unbridgeable historical gulf separating lived existence in the here and now from the absolute or fulfillment. However, insofar as Bloch and Lukács both take their bearings from the philosophical tradition of German classicism, their thinking holds in reserve the category of *subjective mediation* as a principle capable of theoretically penetrating the opaqueness of the current crisis and offering some hope of meaning. The theological origins of Benjamin's thought know of no such mediation, and his concept of redemption remains therefore more of a pure posit or a regulative idea.

For Bloch, meaning at present can only be rediscovered through a radical turning away from the world, through a recourse to "inwardness." Music of all the arts fulfills this desideratum insofar as its disembodied character confers on it the greatest affinities with the powers of spirituality. Since it is the least socially mediated of all the arts, the least scarred by utilitarian constraints of social function, music is simultaneously the most "true." As the radical Other of society, music thus becomes a model of utopian anticipation, a way of thinking, acting, and existing that prefigures the contours of reconciled life. "The outstanding function of music, to embody, by virtue of its tonality and dynamic structure, the breach with the empirically existing, becomes the historical index of a complete subjectification of the locus (Topos) of truth."[57] In this sense Bloch relies on Schopenhauer's notion that music grasps things in themselves, that it gives expression to the inexpressible. We live, according to Bloch, in an age in which things and men are not yet identical with themselves, in which they fail to coincide with their essences or full potential. Music, like all the arts, and like all fantasy, serves as a spiritual anticipation of the ultimate *telos* of humanity. As such, it designates the threshold at which aesthetics passes over into religion.[58] The anagogic aspect of musical experience has frequently been pointed out, perhaps most notably by Augustine. For Bloch, "Music is the only subjective theurgy."[59] "[The] great work of art is a reflection, a star of anticipation and a song of consolation on the way home through darkness."[60]

The difference between Bloch's early aesthetic and that of Lukács is readily discernible. Whereas Lukács in his weaker moments confers on the work of art the autonomous status of a restored totality of subject and object, for Bloch works of art remain merely aesthetic, symbolic totalities that fulfill an essential *anticipatory* function in the re-creation of totality, but which can never embody the latter in and of themselves. They are for Bloch Messianic promises which explode in the dark and meaningless continuum of contemporary life to light the way toward the long sought after homeland ("*Heimat*"). However, he is careful to point out that as aesthetic symbols they remain only fictive, imaginary incarnations of this ideal, and thus are merely one aspect of a larger process of coming to self-consciousness on the part of the species, a process whose traces are equally discernible in the mystical and esoteric aspects of the great world religious systems, the tradition of Western metaphysics, daydreams, fantasy, etc. The spiritualistic emphasis Bloch gives to the problem of world-reconstitution in *Geist der Utopie* derives in part from what he perceives as the scientistic unsurpation of the legacy of historical materialism, a tendency already implicit in the productivist bias of Marx's original theory. In this sense, Bloch's 1918 critique of Marx astutely recognizes that scientific Marxism will more likely result in a mechanistic world where the "laws of necessity" remain fully predominant rather than in a historical leap into the "realm of freedom."

Perhaps the most distinct point of convergence between Bloch and Benjamin lies in their attempt to turn a historico-philosophical judgment into a theory of experience in which products of culture occupy a primary role. For both Bloch and Benjamin works of art represent alternative models of experience endowed with the capacity to break through the eternal recurrence of the "always-the-same" (Benjamin) or the "darkness of the lived moment" (Bloch). For Benjamin they are "now-times" (*Jetztzeiten*); for Bloch they serve as anticipatory images of utopia (*Vorscheinen*). Hence, for both thinkers it becomes the task of the theorist to resuscitate the memory of such phenomena so that they do not fall victim to the oblivion of forgetting. In this way, the cultural treasures of bygone ages assume an important function in the philosophies of both men.

Yet, Bloch assigns to works of art an ontological status to

which Benjamin would never accede. Bloch's gaze is directed toward the past for the sake of the future. For him, works of art are full-fledged incarnations of utopia in the sphere of aesthetic *Vorschein* and as such allegedly provide concrete and tangible signs of the path mankind must follow if it is to surmount the inauthentic realm of "prehistory." In this sense Bloch (and here he stands close to Lukács) attributes a specific and direct power of social change to art that runs the risk of subordinating aesthetic autonomy to the imperatives of "utopian praxis." In any event the path to real historical change for real, living men could be demonstrated by the methods of concrete sociohistorical analysis rather than by abstract appeals to the utopian spirit. Benjamin remains faithful to the Judeo-Marxian *Bilderverbot* by refusing to posit any immediate correlation between the now-time embodied in works of art and the utopian terminus. If significant works of art transcend the historical continuum of suffering and oppression and thereby yield affinities with a state of redeemed life, they nonetheless stop short of providing an ontological guarantee of this possibility. Benjamin's gaze is directed toward the past insofar as he, too, would like to safeguard the semantic potentials that have been sedimented in works of art from a fate of historical anonymity; yet for him this act represents merely the weak claim of redemptive criticism against the profane forces of history and remains incapable of ensuring any immediate and direct link with the utopian future of humanity—the strong claim of Bloch's philosophy of utopia.

But there is a more fundamental difference between Benjamin and Bloch. Benjamin, for all his forays into the arcane regions of Jewish mysticism, remains, first and foremost, a literary critic. Works of literature were the prisms he used to enhance his own powers of insight and intuition, the bridges he traversed on his way to philosophical or religious truth. Immanent criticism of the work of art was the *sine qua non* of his thought. Almost nowhere does Bloch engage in an *immanent* consideration of works of art. Rather, their individual status remained subaltern in face of their imputed cognitive function, that is, in face of their position in the spiritual procession of utopian projections.

Bloch, Lukács, and Benjamin all turn to the realm of aesthetic experience where, in the midst of the crisis of civilization triggered by the events of the First World War, an anticipation of transcendence might be glimpsed. Their shared emphasis on the cognitive value or truth content of works of art should be viewed, rather than as a flight into the irrational, as a well-conceived attempt both to address the unresponsiveness of the contemporary intellectual scene to the crisis, as well as ultimately to hasten the resolution of that crisis in practical life. For in an era in which traditional philosophical system-building had been discredited (by Marx and Nietzsche) and its legacy usurped by the positivist attempt to fashion philosophy according to the model of the natural sciences, Bloch, Lukács, and Benjamin took it upon themselves to probe to what extent truth had migrated from the realm of philosophy to that of art. The aesthetic consciousness as the guarantor of historical truth: this became the general framework in which Bloch, Lukács, and Benjamin sought to recast the mission of reason.

"It is just as absurd to fancy," remarks Hegel in the preface to his *Philosophy of Right,* "that a philosophy can transcend its contemporary world as it is to fancy that an individual can overleap his own age, jump over Rhodes." The logical correlate to this brief finds expression in the famous dictum which concludes the same preface, the claim that "The Owl of Minerva spreads its wings only with the falling of dusk." Hegel's first statement may well contain a large measure of truth. When the philosopher attempts to transcend his own age in thought he forfeits that touchstone of certainty—fidelity to the empirically existing—that has been the hallmark of scientific thinking in recent centuries. By emphasizing the ideal at the expense of the real, his thought always suffers from a certain implausibility in the eyes of its addressees who are accustomed to more tangible guarantees of validity. At the same time, however, a philosophy which remains narrowly wedded to the *post festum* theory of truth advocated by the later Hegel and others is guilty of surrendering the ultimate responsibilities of knowledge in a different sense. For above all, this theory of truth relinquishes the all-important *critical* capacity of knowledge, a capacity it upholds by refusing to accede to a premature identification of the "real" with the "rational," by refusing to let the object in its mere facticity establish the standard or criterion of truth, and by instead forcing the *object* itself to measure up to the truth of the *concept*. Rather than compelling thought to lower its standards to conform with the deficient reality of the object— thereby attaining an apocryphal unity between subject and object for the sake of the hollow, identitarian laws of formal logic—the tradition of speculative philosophy has proven its integrity and merit when it actively confronts the unreason of society with the reason embodied in the idea of philosophical truth; for it is precisely in the historically conditioned hiatus or *nonidentity* between these two dimensions that the relevance of the theory of knowledge resides today, a truth that simultaneously represents the point of departure for the will to emancipation. It is squarely within the contours of this dying philosophical legacy that the theoretical projects of Bloch, Benjamin, and Lukács may be situated. Though these projects are on many individual points at odds, they are united in their conviction that *philosophical contemplation must draw its strength as much from the hopes inspired by what has never yet been as from that which merely is.* For it is only by way of transcending the boundaries of empirical experience that theory proves capable of confronting life at present with the incriminating reality of the ideals it denies; and in this way thinking wins back the scope and relevance it abdicated when, as a result of the final stages of the dialectic of enlightenment, it reduced itself to the status of an obsequious handmaiden to the natural sciences. Perhaps in this way philosophical speculation attempts less to accomplish the impossible, to transcend its age in thought, than it seeks to provide that age with compelling reasons to transcend its own limitations and blindness. For Lukács, Bloch, and Benjamin, the owl of Minerva spreads its wings not at the twilight hour but at the initial glimmer of dawn.

Chapter Two

THE PATH TO
TRAUERSPIEL

IN HIS seminal study "Bewusstmachende oder rettende Kritik—Die Aktualität Walter Benjamins," Jürgen Habermas makes the important distinction between the notion of ideology critique—the confrontation of an illusory truth claim with the reality underlying it, thereby releasing an emancipatory potential encrusted in that illusion—employed by Theodor Adorno and Herbert Marcuse, and that of redemptive critique toward which the thinking of Benjamin inclined—a type of criticism that relates *conservatively* rather than *critically* to its object. Habermas provides a programmatic account of the nature of this distinction:

While Marcuse would like to prepare for the transformation of demystified material conditions of life through the analytical destruction of an objective illusion [in bourgeois works of art] and in this way accomplish the *Aufhebung* of culture (in which these conditions are stabilized), Benjamin does not see his task in an attack on art, which is already understood as being in a stage of decomposition. His criticism of art relates to its objects conservatively, whether it is a question of baroque *Trauerspiel,* Goethe's *Elective Affinities,* Baudelaire's *Fleurs du mal,* or Soviet film of the early twenties. It aims, to be sure, at the "mortification of the works";[1] however, criticism effects a mortification of the work of art only in order to transpose it from the medium of beauty to the medium of truth—and thereby *to redeem* it.[2]

The last sentence of the Habermas citation conveys most felicitously the quintessence of Benjamin's conception of art criticism. At issue is a *metaphysic of redemption,* whereby through the "mortification" of the work of art as an autonomous, independent entity accomplished by the philosophical insight of the critic, the "dead," historical, "material content" of the work is mediated to the point where its "truth content"—an idea in the Neo-Platonic sense—bursts forth and its link to the realm of redeemed life is thereby revealed. A significant account of this unique methodological self-understanding appears in the introductory remarks to Benjamin's 1922 essay on Goethe's *Elective Affinities*:

Material and truth content, united in the work's early period, become separated from one another in the course of time; for if the latter always keeps itself hidden, the former protrudes. As time goes on the interpretation of surprising and estranging elements, of the material content, consequently becomes a precondition for every later critic. One can compare this phenomenon with a paleographer before a piece of parchment, whose faded text is covered with traits of a more visible script related to it. Just as the paleographer must begin by reading the later script, so the critic can only begin by commentary [on the material content]. And from the outset, from it there originates for him an invaluable criterion for his judgment: only in this way can the fundamental question of criticism be posed: whether the appearance of the truth content is attributable to the material content or the life of the material content is attributable to the truth content. For in the measure that they dissociate themselves from one another in the work they determine its immortality.[3]

The distinction between "material content" and "truth content" concerns the paradoxical fact that works of art are objects that originate in a determinate, fleeting moment in time but transcend that limited, historical point of origin in order to reveal something suprahistorical: an image of truth. The constantly fluctuating historical relation between these two moments accounts for the enigma of every work of art with which the critic always finds himself confronted initially: the *Schein des Scheinlosen*, the appearance of that which cannot appear, the emergence of something infinite, the truth, from something that is man-made and finite, a work of art.

In a letter to Gershom Scholem in January 1930 Walter Benjamin announced his great hope: "to be considered the greatest German literary critic."[4] Yet, to interpret this seemingly straightforward remark in light of contemporary conceptions of the idea of literary criticism would be highly misleading. For according to Benjamin's profoundly fertile reconceptualization of the significance of this dying genre, criticism becomes, in no uncertain terms, *the metaphysical point of convergence between the domains of art, religion, and philosophy.* Though each of these spheres, from its own partial standpoint, ultimately treats of the same object, it is only from the sovereign perspective of the critic that the essential, indivisible unity of all three vantage points can be grasped. For if art concerns itself with life, if philosophy seeks out truth, and religion inquires into the meaning of God (or what is the same, the meaning of God for us: salvation), then criticism, beginning with art as its object and by way of the mediation of philosophical insight, establishes the ultimate link with that realm with which mere life in its immediacy can have no contact: *the realm of redeemed life.* It is a relentless desire for redemption which represents the inner drive behind the entirety of Benjamin's theoretical *oeuvre*— a drive which became all the more fervid the more the forces of history seemed to conspire against the realization of this goal. The *Trauerspiel* study, in magisterial fashion, embodies the fulfillment of his search for an object and critical methodology adequate to the sublime nature of this end point. For Benjamin *Trauerspiel* is much more than a literary genre as traditionally conceived. Under the transformative power of his critical gaze, it becomes an Idea.

Experience, Kabbalah, and Language

It was by way of an early confrontation with Kant's theory of knowledge and the correspondent concept of cognitive experience that Benjamin first came to formulate the outlines of his own philosophical project. "Über das Programm der kommenden Philosophie" (1918) shows Benjamin adhering to the (to be sure, short-lived) conviction that the tasks of philosophy could still be accomplished within the traditional framework of the philosophical system. The rehabilitation of the ideal of "philosophy as doctrine" is to be achieved through the critical transcendence of Kantian thought. As Benjamin states: "The central task of the coming

philosophy is, beginning from the most profound presentiments
that it borrows from its age and from the anticipation of its great
future, to allow these to accede to knowledge through an examination of their relation to the Kantian system."[5] His aim, then,
is the "epistemological establishment of a superior concept of
experience according to the typology of Kantian thinking."[6]

Like all great inquiries in the field of epistemology, Kant was
concerned with establishing the lasting, a-temporal value of
knowledge in face of the transient and temporal nature of its
objects—the objects of the empirical world. It was ultimately his
selection of this inferior object domain that, for Benjamin, proved
his undoing. For even if his end, providing a universal and necessary basis for the traditional concept of truth, *adequaetio intellectus
et rei*, has been achieved, the price of his triumph was a concept
of experience so hollow as to be nearly valueless: "That Kant
could commence his immense work under the sign of the Enlightenment means that it was undertaken on the basis of an experience reduced to a nadir, to a minimum of signification, so to
speak."[7] Kant's grave error was his uncritical acceptance of the
standard of "valid" cognitive experience of his epoch, the concept
of reality advanced by the natural sciences—"a reality of an inferior
rank."[8] Like most men of his age, Kant naturally considered the
only possible legitimate idea of experience to be one based on the
proven foundations of Newtonian physics. For Benjamin, the
world view of the Enlightenment which originated from these
foundations "was one of the most base experiences or views of
the world."[9]

For the ultra-skeptical philosophical consciousness of the Enlightenment ultimately backfires. Its initially progressive concern
with interrogating all dogma, superstition, and false absolutes
eventually supplants such illusions with one of its own: the belief
that the standard of true knowledge is empirically measurable
knowledge. If the speculative excesses of rationalism have been
laid low, the victory has simultaneously resulted in the banishment
from the scope of acceptable theoretical discourse of the ultimate
questions of human existence—those concerning the true meaning
of life, man's station vis-à-vis the absolute. Such questions were
traditionally the province of the now discredited field of meta-

physics. The death knell of metaphysics reverberates in the First *Critique*, when Kant formulates the central problem of theoretical reason in terms of the seemingly innocent question, "How is pure mathematics possible?"[10] The recent success of mathematics and natural science, Kant recommends, "should incline us, at least by way of experiment, to imitate their procedure, so far as the analogy which, as a species of rational knowledge, they bear to metaphysics will permit."[11] The reduction of the concept of "reason" to the status of a handmaiden to the natural sciences, the ban on utopian thinking, inasmuch as "ideas of reason" are relegated to the domain of dialectical illusion or the supersensible "intelligible world," are the impulses behind Benjamin's harsh characterization of Enlightenment thought as "one of the most base." The methodological inability of neo-Kantian thought to go beyond the given world of facts, the mood of impotent resignation with which it observed a world clearly headed for disaster (one need only think of Simmel's "tragedy of culture" or Weber's "iron cage") were for Benjamin the contemporary manifestations of this problematical heritage.

Another deficiency of the Kantian theory of knowledge in Benjamin's eyes was the radical subjectivism of its point of departure. Kant's belief in the sovereign nature of the transcendental consciousness contributes greatly to the impoverishment of his discussion of truth. In Benjamin's view, the richness and fecundity of our conception of truth diminishes profoundly if it is limited to something which is merely "subjectively constituted," as Kant argues in the Transcendental Analytic. For Benjamin, truth is something *objective* and *divine* in origin, and therefore ontologically superior to the abstract synthesizing activities of the transcendental subject. It is precisely the inviolable primacy of the transcendental subject in Kant which prevents him a priori from gaining insight into the essences of things themselves. The categories, with the help of their underlying basis, "the transcendental unity of apperception," mechanistically synthesize sensations received from a mechanistic natural world to produce a concept of experience which is predictably mechanistic in turn. Benjamin objects to the prejudicial selection of egoistic self-certainty as the starting point for the theory of knowledge, a problem which has plagued all post-Cartesian epistemological inquiries. Rather than deducing the world from the standpoint of the isolated, monadic, bourgeois individual, it is the standpoint of that individual itself which should be deduced from the world. It is the world in its objectivity that is ontologically prior to the epistemological subject of rationalism, not vice versa.[12] The self-defeating consequences of assuming a subjectivist point of departure for the theory of knowledge are illustrated by the typical theoretical impasses to which this position has historically fallen victim: skepticism (British empiricism), dogmatism (Leibniz), solipsism (transcendental phenomenology).

In sum, it is Benjamin's fear that the inordinate Enlightenment biases of Kant's theory of knowledge conspire to produce a concept of experience that remains hostage to the scientistic prejudices of his age; and that the highly rationalized concept of experience which results from this epistemological standpoint dovetails only too well with a streamlined modern world in which the values of technical reason reign supreme.[13] In this respect his 1918 critique of Kant bears marked affinities with that of Ernst Bloch in *Geist der Utopie*:

[Kant] asks how the formula of the attraction of masses is possible, in order to define the faculty of reason. One can with good reason doubt whether this positing of boundaries, this transcendental theory of the constitution of spirit, which remains faithful to Newton and oriented toward nothing else, would still be able to mean something within the greater phenomenological scope of consciousness. For it is clear that one can just as easily ask how Javanese dance rites, Hindu mysteries, and Chinese ancestor cults would be possible; or . . . how the sacrifice of Christ, predestination, the apocalypse, and certain other similar synthetic judgments would be possible.[14]

In refutation of Kant's thesis concerning the absolute primacy of the transcendental subject, Benjamin counters with the following examples culled from the domain of empirical experience itself, in language strikingly reminiscent of the Bloch passage just cited:

We know that primitive peoples, at the stage of so-called pre-animism, identify themselves with sacred animals and plants, and take their name from them; we know that madmen at times identify themselves in part with the objects of their perception, which are thus no longer "Objecta" standing before them; we know of sick persons who attribute the sensations of their bodies to beings other than themselves, and of visionaries who at least claim to be able to feel the perceptions of others as their own.[15]

Benjamin refers to these as examples of "mythologies of knowledge" and designates Kant's theory of knowledge, as well as likeminded modern approaches, as mythological in essence. By this characterization he implies that such forms of knowledge are equivalent insofar as they suggest equally *profane* conceptions of experience, conceptions similarly removed from contact with the absolute. As such they are not totally invalid, merely inferior, inasmuch as they fall short of the authentic and ultimate tasks of cognition. Benjamin desires a conception of knowledge that is not empirical, and thus nonmythological, but *transcendent* and *pure*. Once it has been attained, the other subaltern species of knowledge will assume their proper place in the hierarchy. Only when the supreme object of philosophical knowledge has been reached will an adequate conception of experience be restored. He discovers this object in the idea of God as the content of pure philosophical knowledge:

Thus the task of the coming philosophy can be understood as the discovery or creation of the concept of knowledge which, insofar as it relates the concept of experience *exclusively* to the transcendental consciousness, renders possible not only mechanical but also religious experience. Which is not to say that knowledge renders God possible, but rather that it first makes the experience and doctrine of God possible.[16]

Once philosophy takes religion as its proper object, the "concrete totality of experience"—which for Benjamin is distinguished from the "sum total of all experience"—becomes accessible to it, for this underlying unity is religious in origin. Kant's fatal error, and one repeated by the neo-Kantians, was to have supplanted the integral notion of a "concrete totality of experience" with the particularized ideal of "scientific experience." If the neo-Kantians actually attempt to preserve the idea of freedom from the mechanistic conception of social action espoused by positivism, their ready acceptance of the fragmentation of knowledge into separate disciplines remains incompatible with the idea of a higher, unified conception of experience.[17] Therefore, at this point in his development, in opposition to the heritage of the Enlightenment, Benjamin has recourse to a religious notion of truth in order to establish "a pure and systematic continuum of experience."[18] "What the Enlightenment lacked was authorities, not in the sense of something to which one would have to submit uncritically, but rather as spiritual powers which would have been capable of providing experience with a superior content."[19]

Prima facie, there is an inherently disquieting aspect about Benjamin's recourse to the sphere of religion in "Über das Programm der kommenden Philosophie" in his attempt to surpass Kant. For does such recourse not represent an instance of regression to precisely those dogmatic pre-Enlightenment standards which Kant struggled so admirably to refute throughout his life? However, in Benjamin's case such criticisms would be unjustifiable, insofar as it is not to a *positive* conception of religion that he appeals in the essay in question; instead, the concept of religion is employed as a regulative idea. With that idea, one can convict the radical iconoclasm of Enlightenment thought of having gone too far in its nominalist attack against fixed "standards" and thereby having forsaken the entirely legitimate concern of knowledge with the ultimate questions of life.

In the *Programm* essay, then, Benjamin's conception of what in fact would constitute a superior idea of experience is phrased only in the negative, in opposition to the dominant scientistic schools of thought. Only in the final paragraph does he advance a more determinate image of what it is that would differentiate his conception of religious knowledge from numerous other conceptions. But even these remarks remain highly allusive and in fact do not stand on their own. For Benjamin, the foundation of the coming philosophy in its search for religious truth is to be sought in terms of the *philosophy of language*:

The great transformation and rectification of the one-sided, mathematical-mechanical conception of knowledge can only be accomplished by relating knowledge to the philosophy of language. . . . Kant completely neglected the fact that all philosophical knowledge has its unique expression in language, not in formulas or numbers. . . . A concept of knowledge acquired by reflection on its linguistic essence will create a corre-

spondent concept of experience, that will also encompass the domains
whose true systematic arrangement Kant has failed to grasp. The highest
of these domains is called religion.[20]

Benjamin's theological philosophy of language can be said
to provide the *telos* of his notion of redemptive criticism. According to his religious interpretation, the secret of redemption
is encoded in language. At the same time, the philosophy of language remains one of the most recondite chapters of an *oeuvre* that
is not generally noted for its accessibility. For if it contains the
key to understanding the theological dimension of Benjamin's
thought, at the same time its origins are buried deep in the forbidden recesses of Kabbalist wisdom.

In 1930, Benjamin, on separate occasions, told both Adorno
and Max Rychner that only someone familiar with Kabbalah—
the sacred texts of the Jewish mystical tradition—would be able
to understand the notoriously difficult prologue to the *Trauerspiel*
study.[21] Moreover, in the dedication inscribed in Scholem's personal copy of the book, Benjamin wrote, "Donated to Gerhard
Scholem for the ultima Thule of his Kabbalah library"[22]—insin-
uating that its proper resting place would be in a library of books
on Kabbalah. The actual meaning of these remarks remains in part
a mystery even to Scholem, who, as the individual singularly
responsible for rescuing the lore of the Kabbalah from historical
oblivion, would seem the one most qualified to comment on
them.[23] Nevertheless, there exists an undeniable and essential link
between Benjamin's conception of an *Ursprache* (a pure, original,
and seamless totality of linguistic expression, the utopian *Ursprung*
toward which his thought inclines) and the central role of language
in the Kabbalistic interpretation of the biblical myth of creation
(which Benjamin seems to make his own with little alteration).

There appear to be two myths of Kabbalistic origin that resurface in Benjamin's thinking, which taken together prove essential for an understanding of his notion of "origin as the goal."[24]
The first concerns the myth of the Tree of Life and the Tree of
Knowledge, designed to explain the status of the Torah before
and after the fall of man from paradise, and also to provide an

image of the state of redemption to which life will return with the coming of the Messiah. The Tree of Life governs the world before the fall. It "represents the pure, unbroken power of the holy, the diffusion of the divine life through all worlds and the communication of all living things with their divine source. There is no admixture of evil in it, no 'shells' which dam up and choke life, no death, and no restriction." The Tree of Knowledge, on the other hand, governs the world once this original, unified stream of divine life has been sundered by the sin of Adam, and hence embodies a world of separation: the separation between good and evil, holy and unholy, pure and impure, etc. Before the fall, when the distinction between good and evil did not yet exist, there was no need of "knowledge" to differentiate between them. Corresponding to the Tree of Knowledge is the Torah of the Exile, which guides life in the unredeemed state in which it exists at present. It takes on a proscriptive and admonitory character insofar as the forces of evil permeate the world after the fall. Conversely:

Only the redemption, breaking the dominion of exile, puts an end to the order of the Tree of Knowledge and restores the utopian order of the Tree of Life in which the heart of life beats unconcealed and the isolation in which everything now finds itself is overcome. Thus the inner logic of this conception of the Dominion of the Tree of Knowledge as the legitimate form of revelation in an unredeemed world had to return home to Paradise where all things will again be in their true place.[25]

The Torah of Redemption presides over this state: in it the restrictions and prohibitions of the Torah of the Exile dissolve, and its allegorical, esoteric content, unable to show itself in an unredeemed world, is finally revealed.

Consequently, for the Kabbalistic idea of redemption, *origin is the goal*; that is, the return to the condition of universal harmony represented by the Tree of Life, usually envisioned in terms of a return to paradise or a restoration of the Davidic Kingdom. Though this idea can at times take the form of a static, purely restorative conception of redemption, quite often it is infused with radical and utopian elements: it need not imply the reestablishment of a pristine, original state of things; but according to a more dynamic reading, redemption signifies a return to a content merely *implicit* in the original paradisiacal state, whose ultimate, eschatological meaning will fully unfold only after the profane realm of history has been surmounted and the will of the Messiah realized. Origin is still the goal, but not as a fixed image of the past that must be recaptured *in toto*, but rather as the fulfillment of a potentiality which lies dormant in origin, the attainment of which simultaneously represents a quantum leap beyond the original point of departure. According to this conception, human activity can play a role in the realization of this goal, but since the realms of history and salvation are *antitheses*, human action can never have a *direct* effect in bringing it about; rather, its relation to the Messianic terminus always remains uncertain. This accounts in part for the seemingly fantastic speculation to which the Kabbalists were driven in their efforts to divine from the sacred texts of Judaism an indication of the utopian future. For since the Torah of the Exile and the Torah of Redemption are opposites, a reading of the former in order to gain insight into the latter can only be accomplished by way of a highly esoteric and anagogical approach to knowledge. To be sure, "knowledge" in the customary sense must be forsaken, since it is a profane operation of mind (corresponding to the rule of the Tree of Knowledge) flatly incommensurable with the transcendent nature of salvation.

By drawing attention to the mystical approach to scriptural exegesis practiced by the Kabbalists we are not suggesting any direct link with Benjamin's self-understanding as a literary critic. At the same time, if one is to lend any credence to his remarks concerning the importance of Kabbalah for understanding his work, there seem to be definite parallels between his conception of literary works of art as hieroglyphs of redeemed life and the Kabbalistic idea of a state of redemption whose nature can be intuited through a linguistic analysis of sacred texts. The latter idea was promoted by the thirteenth-century Spanish Kabbalist Abraham Abulafia and is the second current of Kabbalistic legend which finds its way into Benjamin's work.[26] Under the influence of Neo-Platonic doctrines, Abulafia sought a pure, unsullied path toward mystical communion with God. The chief obstacle to this goal, however, was man's contamination by the impure, finite world of the senses—rendering him unfit for any such transcendental experiences. Consequently, Abulafia looked for an object of meditation that would be capable of elevating the mystic above the world of sense, an object that would be sufficiently supramundane so as not to distract him from his higher spiritual pursuits. What he discovered were the letters of the Hebrew written alphabet:

Basing himself upon the abstract non-corporal nature of script, he develops a theory of mystical contemplation of letters and their configurations, as the constituents of God's name. For this is the real, and if I may say so, the peculiarly Jewish object of mystical contemplation: the Name of God, which is something absolute, because it reflects the hidden meaning of the totality of existence; the Name through which everything else acquires its meaning.[27]

Abulafia's theory, "the science of the combination of letters," is only the most radical expression of the long-standing Kabbalistic doctrine of language as the divine substance of reality. According to this doctrine: "all things exist only by virtue of their degree of participation in the Great Name of God, which manifests itself throughout the whole of creation."[28] Abulafia gives voice to a theme common to all Kabbalistic writings: that language is not simply a utilitarian means of communicating something, but is of an inherently divine nature, and as such represents the most direct link that mankind can have with God. For according to Kabbalistic doctrine, it is through language that God created the world. Hence, all existence has its ultimate origin and significance in the creative language of God. While human language retains close ties with divine language, it is merely *receptive* and *cognitive*; i.e., it is confined to the world of knowledge. Divine language, however, is *creative*; i.e., it has engendered the world and everything in it. This accounts for the Kabbalists' mystical fascination with language as the object in which the ultimate secret of creation is concealed. The name of God, the Tetragrammaton YHWH, is the chief object of mystical contemplation insofar as all earthly names have their origin in the creative power embodied in the divine name.

In a letter to Hugo von Hofmannsthal Benjamin asserts that:

every truth has its home, its ancestral palace, in language, that it is erected from the oldest *logoi*, and in face of a truth established in this way the insights of the individual sciences remain subaltern, as long as they, so to speak, nomadically here and there make use of the realm of language, preoccupied with that view of the sign-character of language whose irresponsible arbitrariness impresses itself on their terminology.[29]

The key to this philosophy of language follows directly from the Kabbalistic conception of language as the divine substance of reality. As Benjamin argues in the 1916 essay "On Language as Such and on the Language of Man," in communicating its "linguistic being," all reality indicates its ultimate "origin" in the creative word of God. He develops this conception by way of an interpretation of the first chapter of Genesis. There exists an important distinction, he notes, between the creation of man and that of all other reality. "The second version of the story of the Creation which tells of the breathing of God's breath into man, also reports that he was made from earth."[30] However, for the rest of creation, the following pattern holds: Let there be—He made (created)—He named. Thus, at the beginning and end of each act of creation ("Let there be" and "He named"), language, the word of God, plays an essential role: "With the creative omnipotence of language [Creation] begins, and at the end as it were assimilates the created, names it. Language is therefore both creative and finished creation, it is word and name. In God name is creative because it is word, and God's word is cognizant because it is name."[31]

Yet, since God does not create man from the word but in fact invests man himself with the power of language (though in man this power is merely cognitive and not creative) there exists a very special relation between the language of Creation and the language of man:

God did not create man from the word, and he did not name him. He did wish to subject him to language, but in man God set language, which had served *Him* as medium of creation, free. God rested when he had left his creative power to itself in man. This creativity, relieved of its divine activity, became knowledge. Man is the knower in the same language in which God is creator. God created him in his image, he created the knower in the image of the creator.[32]

As a result of the close relationship between divine language and human language, man, as it were, has been charged with the task of *completing* the process of creation. He accomplishes this by translating the imperfect, mute language of things into the language of names; that is, among creatures, man possesses a privileged status as *name-giver*. The objectivity of this process of translation is ensured by the affinity between the creative word, by virtue of which all things have come into existence, and the cognizing word of man. By bestowing names upon things man elevates them, grants them dignity, redeems them from a fate of speechless anonymity.

However, upon expulsion from paradise the pure language of man suffers degradation, resulting in the fragmentation of the original language into an impure plurality of languages: "The paradisiac language of man must have been one of perfect knowledge; whereas later all knowledge is again infinitely differentiated in the multiplicity of language, was indeed forced to differentiate itself on a lower level than creation in name."[33] The original language was a *pure language of names*; it did not yet know of the (profane) separation between word and thing; that is, it had no need of "knowledge" to produce artificially an identity of subject and object. This is the original, harmonious, precognitive form of cognition which serves as the *telos* for the "Erkenntniskritische Vorrede" to the *Trauerspiel* study. In his description of this original utopian condition of knowledge, as yet unrent by the subject–object split, Benjamin makes explicit reference to the Kabbalistic myth of the Tree of Knowledge (of good and evil):

For that the language of paradise would have been one of perfect knowledge, even the existence of the Tree of Knowledge cannot conceal. . . . the knowledge to which the snake seduces, that of good and evil, is nameless. It is null and void in the deepest sense. . . . knowledge of good and evil abandons the name, it is a knowledge from outside, the uncreative imitation of the creative word. Name steps outside itself in this knowledge: the Fall marks the birth of the *human word*, in which the name no longer lives intact, and which has stepped out of the language of names. . . . the word must communicate *something* (other than itself). That is really the Fall of language-mind. The word as something externally communicating, as it were a parody by the expressly mediate word of the expressly immediate, the creative word of God, and the decay of the blissful, Adamite language that stands between them.[34]

After the fall the original divine condition of language has sunk to the state of Kierkegaardian "gibberish" (*Geschwätz*), though at the same time the link between the existing plurality of impure languages and the divine *Ursprache* can still be dimly perceived. The oblique relation between the two, the conception of the latter as the distant horizon of a linguistic-critical method of literary exegesis, in which the lost paradisiac language of names contains within itself the hidden script of redeemed life, becomes the focal point of Benjamin's critical energies. The pure language of names is the "origin" that has become the "goal," inasmuch as its affinity to the divine language of creation lends it the greatest proximity to a state of redemption. For the Kabbalists the texts which revealed the most immediate contact with the word of God were those of Scripture. In Benjamin's quasi-secularized reinterpretation of this doctrine, not scripture alone, but also *literary works of art*, are legitimate objects of the exegetical quest for the key to redemption. The preeminent status he accords literary works of art follows, above all, from their *linguistic* nature. Consequently, when Benjamin announces in the *Programm* essay that the regeneration of philosophy is possible only under the condition that the problem of knowledge is placed in relation to the idea of language, and that the highest domain of knowledge is that of religion, he is referring to his theological philosophy of language as developed under Kabbalistic influences.[35]

Benjamin relinquished the idea that the rightful end of theoretical reflection lay in the form of the philosophical system in his dissertation of 1919, *Der Begriff der Kunstkritik in der deutschen Romantik*.[36] It was in this work, an interpretation of fragments from the aesthetic writings of Friedrich Schlegel and Novalis, that his method of redemptive criticism first crystallized. However, this method can already be seen at work in embryonic form in a 1917 essay on Dostoyevsky's *The Idiot*. The essay gives us a first-hand glimpse at the technique of redemptive criticism *in nuce*, and also prominently displays the attendant difficulties of this method.

In the essay Benjamin appeals to the concept of *immanent criticism* which was of paramount importance in the critical studies of the German romantics. As the name suggests, this concept condemned the heteronomous imposition of external criteria in the reading of literary texts. Instead, the latter were to be treated as autonomous, independent wholes; and it became the sworn duty of the critic to respect the principle of textual autonomy in his interpretative ventures. It was in precisely this vein that Benjamin objected to the fashionable contemporary practice of subjecting Dostoyevsky's novel to a psychological reading: "what is represented in the minds of our critics as a psychological problem is actually nothing of the sort: as if it were a question of the Russian 'psyche' or the 'psyche' of an epileptic. Criticism only justifies its right to approach the work of art insofar as it respects the terrain internal to the work, insofar as it refrains from trampling that terrain."[37]

Only a few lines later, he cites an observation by Novalis—later repeated verbatim in the dissertation itself—that could easily be considered the watchword of the romantic approach to criticism: "[This] novel, like every work of art, *rests on an idea*, 'has an Ideal a priori, a necessity in itself, to exist,' as Novalis says; and clearly, to demonstrate this necessity and nothing else is the task of criticism."[38] The Novalis citation is representative of the peculiar apotheosis of works of art practiced by the German romantics: an elevation of works of art, and especially literary works of art, to the status of objects containing privileged access to truth. Benjamin's endorsement of this conception of the virtues of literature is unequivocal. In accordance with it, the "Idea" on which the Idiot rests in his eyes is that of an "unforgettable, immortal life": "The immortal life is unforgettable, that is the sign under which we recognize it. It is the life that without monument, without memory, perhaps without witness, must remain unforgotten. It cannot be forgotten. . . . And to say 'unforgettable' means something more than that we are unable to forget it; it refers to something essential in the unforgettable itself through which it is unforgettable."[39]

Benjamin's comments of course refer to the main character of *The Idiot*, the epileptic Prince Myshkin. Outside of the brief timespan of the novel, we know merely the outlines of his life history. We first encounter Myshkin in the course of his departure from the asylum, and in the end we learn he has returned there in a state of near catatonia, little else. Yet, the interim period which the novel treats is so infinitely rich, the impact he has left on the lives of all who come into contact with him is so palpable, that in spite of the apparent oblivion to which his life has been consigned at this early age, it is unthinkable that the events which have transpired could ever fall entirely from memory. This is the reasoning behind Benjamin's attempt to link *The Idiot* with the idea of an "unforgettable, immortal life." For according to the strictures of the method of redemptive criticism, it falls due to the critic to immolate the anachronistic historical "material content" of the novel in order that the contemporary relevance of its "truth content" might shine forth all the more brilliantly. The act of redemptive critique is therefore a work of *remembrance*: it is a process of preserving the truth content or Idea of a work from the ever-threatening forces of social amnesia to which humanity has over the ages become inured. The manifest importance of the idea of *The Idiot* for the development of the technique of re-demptive criticism in Benjamin's own mind can be found some six years later, in "The Task of the Translator" (1923). There, he returns to the theme of an "unforgettable life" in language re-markably akin to that of the earlier work. Moreover, in the present context the 1923 essay takes on an added significance insofar as it represents in general a vehement and unmitigated reaffirmation by Benjamin of his 1916 position on the philosophy of language. For the main object of "The Task of the Translator" is to establish the original paradisiacal language of names ("the blissful, Adamite language") as the theological foundation of the ultimate kindred-ness of all languages, which should in turn provide the divine basis for the translation of any one language into another:

One might, for example, speak of an unforgettable life or moment even if all men had forgotten it. If the nature of such a life or moment required that it be unforgotten, that predicate would not imply a falsehood but merely a claim not fulfilled by men, and probably also a reference to a realm in which it is fulfilled: God's remembrance. Analogously, the translatibility of linguistic creations ought to be considered even if men should prove unable to translate them.[40]

The unforgettable nature of Prince Myshkin's life receives an a priori metaphysical guarantee, since, come what may, it will remain immortal in the eyes of *divine remembrance*. The hope of salvation for man, however, remains contingent on ensuring that this and similar immortal moments are preserved in historical memory, for they incarnate the nearest approximations of transcendence that we know. It is this function that becomes the imperative task of the critic in his reading of cultural history.

However, in the Dostoyevsky essay Benjamin does not consistently remain faithful to the precepts of the German romantic conception of "immanent criticism," and it is precisely this infidelity which gives rise to a problematical dimension in the literary criticism of his early years. Bernd Witte has identified this dimension in his work in terms of a tendency to present an *allegorical* rather than strictly immanent reading of literary texts, and on this account charges that Benjamin's critical method is victimized by an inherent arbitrariness.[41] Witte's contention would seem to be confirmed by Benjamin's concluding statement on the significance of *The Idiot*:

The pure expression for life in its immortality is, however: youth. That is Dostoyevsky's great lament in this book, the foundering of the movement of youth. Life remains immortal to youth, however it loses itself in its own light. In *The Idiot* Dostoyevsky laments the fact that Russia is unable to preserve its own immortal life—for these men are the bearers of the youthful heart of Russia—is incapable of giving it nourishment.[42]

This assessment of Dostoyevsky's novel is virtually unintelligible without some measure of prior knowledge concerning Benjamin's own youthful experiences. In any event it is in no way based on the notion of immanent criticism professed by the early romantics and emphatically endorsed by Benjamin earlier in the same essay. Prince Myshkin's "youth" (he is 24) is unquestionably incidental to the novel. At best it serves to enhance the idea of his purity, but it is certainly a fact on which Dostoyevsky himself placed no great emphasis. Benjamin's discussion of the significance of youth in its relation to immortality has a profoundly esoteric and personal basis. As Scholem demonstrates, Benjamin's claim concerning the "immortality of youth" is an unmistakable reference to his beloved boyhood friend, the poet Fritz Heinle, who took his own life in 1914.[43] Benjamin was deeply shaken by Heinle's death and, in response to Scholem's conjecture that the essay in question represented an allegorical reading of *The Idiot* in terms of Heinle's suicide, showed himself moved by his friend's keen powers of intuition. Moreover, the reference in the preceding citation to "the foundering of the movement of youth" is undoubtedly an allusion to Benjamin's own frustrated efforts to give direction and leadership to the Berlin student movement in the early 1910s. In sum, as Witte points out, there is an ever-present danger that the method of redemptive critique will pass over into "allegorical criticism," in which the being in itself of the textual object is ignored, in order that the critic might proceed thereby to affix his own subjective and arbitrary meanings.

There is little doubt that Benjamin's early aesthetics are marked by a distinct predilection for the esoteric. However, Witte's argument becomes invalid when he equates this predilection with an out and out arbitrariness on Benjamin's part, an arbitrariness which in effect vitiates, as Witte claims, the entirety of Benjamin's youthful output. To be sure, it was Benjamin's aversion to all superficiality, his radicality in the etymological sense of the word—his ceaseless desire to get to the root of things—that allows him in retrospect to tower above the other critics of his generation. Furthermore, Witte's accusation that Benjamin systematically makes blatantly gratuitous, extratextual allusions (as we have seen in the case of Benjamin's essay on *The Idiot* with reference to his boyhood friend Heinle), which in some way become the dominant tendency in his criticism, remains totally unfounded. In the relatively few instances where such practices do occur, they are consistently subordinated and marginalized vis-à-vis the main lines of Benjamin's interpretive framework. In the case of Witte's book, such objections undermine a work which otherwise, along with Rolf Tiedemann's *Studien zur Philosophie Walter Benjamins*, represents one of the few reliable book-length studies of Benjamin's work to date.[44]

Messianic Time Versus Historical Time

In an essay on Benjamin, Scholem suggests an important hermeneutic guide for the interpretation of his work: "Two categories above all, and especially in their Jewish versions, assume a central place in his writings: on the one hand Revelation, the idea of the Torah and of sacred texts in general, and on the other hand the Messianic idea and Redemption. Their significance as regulative ideas governing his thought cannot be overrated."[45]

Indeed, Benjamin's conception of the mission of literary criticism is intimately related with his vision of the realm of redemption. However, access to this realm must always be circuitous in the context of the profane world of history in which man finds himself at present. It is the concealed, nonmanifest content of redeemed life in the historical age, and not an infatuation with the arcane for its own sake, which accounts for the often elliptical and fragmentary character of his discourse.[46] The antithetical relation in which the realm of redemption stands to the historical world, such that in the latter we are provided only with the most fleeting and ephemeral traces of the path to salvation, explains Benjamin's peculiar philosophy of history and the special position in it accorded to works of art. For Benjamin, the philosophy of history becomes *Heilsgeschichte*, the history of salvation, and the task of the critic—or later, that of the historical materialist—is that of rescuing the few unique visions of transcendence that grace the continuum of history, the now-times (*Jetztzeiten*), from the fate of oblivion which incessantly threatens to consume them. Only in this manner can one prevent the fragile traces of salvation from being swallowed whole by the destructive power of unredeemed historical life, which Benjamin designates as the mythic, homogeneous, empty time of the "always-the-same" (*Das Immergleiche*). To preserve a record of such now-times, the function of historical remembrance, is the ultimate end of the method of redemptive criticism. Moreover, works of art present themselves as objects most ideally suited to this approach insofar as they embody, in manifest defiance of the Kantian "barrier," the utopian content of the intelligible world, though *within* the bounds of the world of experience—a fact acknowledged by Kant himself in the

Third *Critique*, where he designates aesthetic judgment as the mediatory link between the spheres of theoretical and practical reason.[47] That Benjamin seizes on this route in his *Aufhebung* of Kant—and it was hardly coincidental that he assimilated these views in the course of his dissertation on the early romantics— suggests strong affinities between his approach and the analogous *aesthetic* path to the supersensible pursued by Schiller and Schelling.

The later Benjamin, under the influence of historical materialism, refers to his method as a dialectic at a standstill (*Dialektik im Stillstand*). By this concept he intends a decisive break with the Enlightenment (and Social Democratic) notion of historical progress, which only recognizes an infinite series of empty, quantitative transitions, the homogeneous time of the always-the-same, and whose defining characteristic is the incessant piling up of "ruins upon ruins."[48] The method of *Dialektik im Stillstand* instead concentrates its energies on those focal points in history that are laden with now-time—just as Robespierre viewed ancient Rome as a "past charged with now-time that he blasted out of the continuum of history."[49] Benjamin remained faithful to this attitude toward cultural history over twenty-five years of literary activity (which belies the commonplace juxtaposition of the early "theological" to the later "materialist" Benjamin). This can be demonstrated by the comparison of two statements expressed at opposite ends of the spectrum of his creative life. The first is from his inaugural address to the Free Student League of Berlin in 1914. It commences with the following reflections on the idea of history:

There is a conception of history which out of confidence in the infinity of time discerns only the rhythm of men and epochs which, quickly or slowly, advances on the road of progress. . . . The following consideration leads, against this conception, to a determinate state in which history rests collected into a focal point, as formerly in the utopian images of thinkers. The elements of the end condition are not present as formless tendencies of progress, but instead are embedded in every present as endangered, condemned, and ridiculed creations and ideas. The historical task is to give absolute form in a genuine way to the immanent condition of fulfillment, to make it visible and predominant in the present. . . . however, it is only comprehensible in its metaphysical structure, like the Messianic realm or the idea of the French Revolution.[50]

The second is from his "Theses on the Philosophy of History" (1940), where he defines the idea of *Dialektik im Stillstand*:

Thinking involves not only the flow of thoughts, but their arrest as well. Where thinking suddenly stops in a configuration pregnant with tensions, it gives that configuration a shock, by which it crystallizes it into a monad. A historical materialist approaches a historical subject only where he encounters it as a monad. In this structure he recognizes the sign of a messianic cessation of happening, or, put differently, a revolutionary chance in the fight for the oppressed past. He takes cognizance of it in order to blast a specific era out of the homogeneous course of history— blasting a specific life out of the era or a specific work out of the life work.[51]

As in the 1914 address, he contrasts his quest for such instants of "messianic cessation of happening," monadic configurations charged with now-time, with the idea of historical progress, "which cannot be sundered from the concept of its progression through a homogeneous, empty time."[52] In the "Theses on the Philosophy of History" the project of a redemptive relation to the historical past becomes all the more urgent under the pressures of the struggle against fascism—which would shortly claim Benjamin as one of its victims. Only with the onset of National Socialism did the hitherto abstract and homogeneous continuum of historical time begin to assume a more determinate form in his work. In the later writings the struggle for redemption becomes almost a hand-to-hand combat with fascism, resonant with eschatological significance, over who will control the historical past as it lives on in the memory of humanity. As Benjamin implores: "every image of the past that is not recognized by the present as one of its own concerns threatens to disappear irretrievably."[53] It threatens to become a tool of the ruling classes used to perpetuate their self-serving illusions and deceits. "Historical materialism wishes to retain that image of the past which unexpectedly appears to man singled out by history at a moment of danger. . . . Only that historian will have the gift of fanning the spark of hope in the past who is firmly convinced that *even the dead* will not be safe from the enemy if he wins. And this enemy has not ceased to be victorious."[54]

Benjamin counterposes now-time, "which is shot through with chips of Messianic time," to the homogeneous time of the historical era, which he equates with the notion of eternal repetition or *myth*. Man stands under the domination of mythical fate when his powers of remembrance fail him: that is, he is condemned to repeat. The recurrence of myth in unredeemed historical life remains an object of theoretical attack throughout Benjamin's writings. In the *Programm* essay, he denigrates the impoverished, psychologistic character of Kant's theory of experience as "mythical." In his treatment of the historical basis of ancient tragedy, Benjamin sees its outstanding feature as its once-in-history struggle against the supremacy of myth, represented by the "speechlessness" of the tragic hero once he realizes himself superior to the fate ordained by the mythical gods he has challenged.[55] In his uncompleted *Passagenarbeit*, he understands Baudelaire's poetry as providing an "*ur*history of the modern:" That is, in its imagery of mid-nineteenth-century Paris, it uncovers a mythical compulsion to repeat under the guise of "modernization"—the representation of the always-the-same as the "new" which characterizes the consumption of commodities under capitalism. For Benjamin, "myth demonstrates that the human species, hopelessly depraved in its quest for a good and just life, is condemned to the cycle of the reproduction of mere life and survival."[56]

Under mythical justice, which Benjamin contrasts with divine justice, life is governed by a universal network of misfortune and guilt. This is the realm of *fate* which for Benjamin characterizes not only the pagan religious systems of prehistory, but remains predominant in the modern world under the order of *law*, where, under the guise of justice, misfortune and guilt are merely rendered abstract and take on the personalized form of "right." "Mistakenly, through confusing itself with the realm of justice, the order of law, which is only a residue of the demonic stage of human existence where legal statutes determined not only men's relationships but also their relation to the gods, has preserved itself long past the time of the victory over the demons."[57] Yet, the network of guilt which grips man under the domination of mythical fate fails to touch that part of man which is ultimately bound up with the divine realm of redemption: "It is never man but only the life in him that it strikes—the part involved in natural guilt and misfortune by virtue of illusion. . . . The guilt context is temporal in a totally inauthentic way, very different in its kind and measure from the time of redemption, or of music, or of truth."[58]

According to Benjamin, the sphere of natural life where mythical forces hold sway can be surmounted *only through death*. Death represents the overcoming of man's "natural," earth-bound life, and his elevation to a state of communion with divine life. "Fate leads to death. Death is not punishment but atonement, an expression of the subjection of guilty life to the law of natural life."[59] The idea of salvation through death is, particularly in his writings through the *Trauerspiel* study, the cornerstone of his method of redemptive critique. It appears in his 1917 essay on *The Idiot*: only through Prince Myshkin's death (albeit metaphorical), his return to exile in the asylum, can his life become immortal, can it be related to the sphere of redeemed life through the idea of its "unforgettableness." It is the basis for his understanding of the moment of redemption proper to Greek tragedy. There, the noble hero is sacrificed to the willfulness of the mythical gods in order that the national community might come to self-consciousness in face of its subjection to the irrationalism of mythical powers; and in this way the hero is immortalized or redeemed. Similarly, this view plays an essential role in Benjamin's interpretation of the redemptive function of allegory in *Trauerspiel*, whose stages revel in death-imagery, ruins, and corpses: for in these highly stylized dramas of seventeenth-century Counterreformation Germany, only a perspective which was utterly convinced of the wretchedness, profanity, and insignificance of all natural, earthly existence was deemed capable of rising above the ruins of mere life and gaining access to the realm of salvation. If the idea of redemption through death distinguishes the allegorical path to salvation characteristic of *Trauerspiel*, it provides, all the more so, the basis of Benjamin's own critical methodology, which echoes clearly in his claim that "Criticism means the mortification of works."[60] For the goal of criticism is, through the "mortification" of the transitory, historical, material content of works of art, to permit them to bask in the eternal light of truth, and thereby pave the way for their redemption:

The object of philosophical criticism is to show that the function of artistic form is as follows: to make historical content, such as provides the basis of every important work of art, into a philosophical truth. The transformation of material content into truth content makes the loss of effect, whereby the attractiveness of the earlier charms diminishes decade by decade, into the basis for a rebirth, in which all ephemeral beauty is completely stripped off, and the work stands as a ruin.[61]

Only when mortified, when stripped of all ephemeralness, does the work of art stand ready for transposition from the transitory medium of beauty to the sacred realm of truth.

Before the *Trauerspiel* study, this critical procedure was brought to fulfillment in Benjamin's long essay on Goethe's novel *Elective Affinities* (1921–22). It followed the dissertation on Schlegel and Novalis and is the study which stands closest to the concept of art criticism developed in that work. It is hardly coincidental that Benjamin happened to select Goethe's novel for this study. For the programmatic statement of the philosophy of art criticism of the early romantics was a similar essay by Schlegel on another Goethe novel, *Wilhelm Meister*.[62] The parallel was clearly present in Benjamin's mind. Both essays show themselves at pains to avoid the traditional method of aesthetic judgment based on the notion of external standards to which a work must make itself accountable (*Regelästhetik*) and the concept of the "genre" through which works of art were to be analyzed. Both proceed according to the idealist conviction that every authentic work of art contains the seeds of its criticism entirely within itself, thus rendering the use of external standards superfluous. Finally, both conceive of the vocation of criticism in terms of the interpretation of *individual* works of art and contend that it is in fact only through the medium of criticism that works of art attain *fulfillment* or *completion*. In retrospect, Benjamin comments on the methodological intention of his study: "In my essay 'Goethe's Elective Affinities,' I attempted to illuminate a work entirely on the basis of an internal reading [*aus sich selbst heraus*]."[63]

Benjamin's ostensible motive for writing the essay was the

appearance of Friedrich Gundolf's hagiographic Goethe biography in 1918. Indeed, the first few pages of the essay's second section contain a devastating attack on Gundolf's attempt to interpret the meaning of Goethe's work in terms of a mythologized vision of his life.[64] However, to confuse the external occasion for Benjamin's composition of the work with its more general *theoretical* import would be extremely unfortunate (In Benjaminian terms, it would amount to mistaking the material content of the essay—the polemic with Gundolf, whose relevance has obviously faded from a contemporary standpoint—for its truth content).[65] For these reasons, we shall discuss this essay primarily in terms of its conceptual significance for Benjamin's early development.

According to Benjamin, Goethe's novel (which was the subject of considerable controversy at the time of its appearance because of the illicit liaison that lies at its center) portrays the implacable retribution of mythical fate once the bounds of law have been transgressed—the instance of law in this case being the institution of marriage. The conspicuous absence of names in the novel is attributable to an order "whose members live under a nameless law, a fate, which fills their world with the dull light of a solar eclipse."[66] The elective affinities under whose spell Ottilie and Eduard fall are not of a spiritual but of a natural-scientific kind. The novel is filled with natural portents and omens which point the way toward disaster well in advance. For Benjamin, Goethe neither sings the praises of forbidden romance nor moralistically tries to demonstrate the ruinous fate that is sure to befall those who flout monogamous family life. "However, for the poet, the imprint of legality remained indispensable in this work. He did not want . . . to establish a basis for marriage, but rather to show those powers which proceed from its decline. However, these are, to be sure, the mythical powers of law."[67]

Goethe believes that the stability of marriage must ideally be found in the constancy of love rather than in legal or social norms (the position of Mittler's insensitive discourse on marriage). At the same time, when the light of love grows dim, there is nothing to fall back on but the powers of naked law. As Benjamin states, "It is only in the act of perishing that marriage becomes the juridical relation that Mittler cherishes"[68]—just as when society begins to disintegrate as an organism the state resorts to naked force to ensure social cohesion. In this way, Goethe touches on the thing-like character of marriage suggested by Kant's infamous definition in the *Metaphysics of Morals*.[69] In *Elective Affinities* the institution of marriage, as important as it is in the context of the novel, is used merely as an example of a larger theme: the mythical vengeance that lurks behind the civilized appearance of the legal sphere: "Marriage here is neither an ethical problem nor a social problem. It is not a bourgeois form of life. In its dissolution everything human becomes an appearance and the mythical alone remains as essence."[70]

Ottilie and Eduard are victims of the mercilessness of a fate that envelops the lives of men and women merely because they are participants in the order of unredeemed life: "Fate is the context of guilt of the living."[71] It is a context of guilt so powerful that it can be transmitted through heredity: conceived in a moment of thoughtlessness and desperation, Charlotte's infant son is doomed from the outset. Clearly, in the latter instance it cannot be a case of a *moral* error in judgment: for how could a newborn child stand accused of such an error? Rather, it is a question of *"natural guilt,"*

which befalls man not on account of action and decision, but through idleness and hesitation. When, failing to pay heed to the human, he falls under the power of nature, natural life, which in man preserves its innocence only as long as it is bound to a higher life, drags the latter down to its own level. With the disappearance of the supernatural life in man his natural life becomes laden with guilt, even if he commits no immoral act. For now it is in league with mere life, which manifests itself in man as guilt. . . . When man sinks to this level then life itself appears to gain the power of dead things.[72]

Benjamin's interpretation of Goethe's novel seems to coincide with his analysis of classical tragedy: in both cases he proceeds by way of the threefold schema of fate (myth), sacrifice (death), and atonement (redemption). Fate demands that the transgression of the bonds of matrimony be expiated; hence, Ottilie's sacrifice, her suicide. However, in death she finds her salvation. If the forces unleashed in the disintegration of the marriage are destined to triumph in the sphere of mere natural life, the latter sphere is transcended in the redemption represented by death. Thus, according to Benjamin, Ottilie's death can be best understood as a "mythical sacrifice"—the term he also uses to characterize the death of the hero in ancient tragedy. From the outset, the innermost tendencies of the mythical world of the novel demand this sacrifice in expiation for her sin: "In terms of the mythical world which the poet conjures up, expiation has always meant the death of the innocent. . . . Goethe has made myth the basis of his novel. The mythic is the material content of the book: its content appears as a mythical shadow-play staged in the costumes of Goethe's time."[73]

The hope we are left with at the novel's end is that the lovers will reawaken "not in a beautiful world . . . but in a blissful world."[74] Through death their sin has been expiated; they pass beyond the bonds of the natural, mythic world order, the prosaic world of convention they sought to transcend in life, only to attain salvation in the blissful realm of the afterlife—or so we are given to hope. It is those who have suffered most in life who shall (we hope) capture the fruits of the next. For after all, "Only for the sake of the hopeless are we given hope."[75] Goethe describes the ultimate fate of the lovers, who have been entombed in adjacent coffins, with the following words: "And thus the lovers lie side by side. Peace hovers about their abode, smiling angelic figures (with whom too they have affinity) look down upon them from the vault above, and what a happy moment it will be when one day they awaken together."[76]

For Benjamin, once the material content of *Elective Affinities* is stripped away—i.e., "the mythical shadow play staged in the costumes of Goethe's time"—the truth content emerges: the hope we hold out for the ultimate redemption of the lovers in the sphere of immortal life; the hope suggested by the sacrificial, expiatory death of innocents.

However, by viewing the lovers' deaths strictly as a "mythical sacrifice," a term that is reserved in the *Trauerspiel* book for the once-in-history struggle against myth characteristic of classical tragedy, Benjamin runs the risk of de-historicizing the usage of this category. In the *Elective Affinities* essay Benjamin himself warns strongly against the tendency to view the figure of Ottilie as in the least tragic or heroic: her meekness and inaction remain incompatible with any such attempt.[77] Nevertheless, his interpretation of the material content of the novel as essentially mythic points to a more far-reaching problem of his philosophy of history, based as it is on the rigid separation between the historical and the Messianic ages. For if one proceeds from this distinction, the historical era cannot help but appear as undifferentiated and uniform, as the homogeneous and empty time that Benjamin takes it to be. When history is interpreted on the basis of an a priori dichotomy between sacred and profane epochs, now-times must of necessity be *exceptions,* and the possibility of indicating general historical tendencies capable of leading to a state of reconciliation is foreclosed from the outset. Consequently, Benjamin's Messianic philosophy of history presents the danger of a political attitude that is decidedly quietistic and resigned; and it is not at all clear that the Messianic zeal carried over from this phase to his later acceptance of historical materialism provides a solution that is any more realistic. If Benjamin distinguishes correctly between the eras of history and tragedy—insofar as tragedy is concerned with the once-in-history transcendence of myth, and for this reason becomes a genre that is inappropriate to the post-mythical historical world—he regresses to an a-historical conception of history by attempting to comprehend *all* subsequent history in terms of the domination of myth and fate—as is evidence by his interpretation of *Elective Affinities* in terms of the "tragic" schema of myth, sacrifice, and redemption.

Outside of the "Theses on the Philosophy of History" the question of the relation of the historical to the Messianic age is addressed specifically by Benjamin in the "Political-Theological Fragment" (ca. 1920).[78] In the first paragraph of the "Fragment" Benjamin extols Bloch's *Geist der Utopie* for having "repudiated with utmost vehemence the political significance of theocracy."[79] For theocracy implies the endeavor to realize the Kingdom of *divine* ends within the *profane* context of this-worldly existence, a proposition manifestly incompatible with Benjamin's conception of the mutually exclusive relation between these two orders. The Messianic age is not the *culmination* of history, but rather its *ter-*

mination, a qualitative leap into a realm *beyond* history. As such, direct, organic movement from the one stage to the other is impossible. As Benjamin explains:

Only the Messiah himself consummates all history, in the sense that he alone redeems, completes, creates its relation to the Messianic. For this reason nothing historical can relate itself on its own account to anything Messianic. Therefore the Kingdom of God is not the *telos* of the historical dynamic; it cannot be set as a goal. From the standpoint of history, it is not the goal, but the end. Therefore the order of the profane cannot be built upon the idea of the Divine Kingdom, and therefore theocracy has no political but only a religious meaning.[80]

Benjamin then explains the mysterious connection that does in fact exist between the profane and Messianic orders. But since this explanation is itself affected by the dichotomy between rational cognition and its transcendent object, it can only be represented figuratively. After identifying the goal of history as the attainment of *happiness,* which he counterposes to the *blissfulness* represented by the realm of redeemed life, Benjamin provides an illustration of the hidden interrelation that exists between the two spheres:

If one arrow points to the goal toward which the profane dynamic acts, and another marks the direction of Messianic intensity, then certainly the quest of free humanity for happiness runs counter to the Messianic direction; but just as a force can, through acting, increase another that is acting in the opposite direction, so the order of the profane assists, through being profane, the coming of the Messianic Kingdom. The profane, therefore, although itself not a member of this Kingdom, is a decisive category of its quietest approach.[81]

It is with this conception of the mysterious and oblique relation between the historical and Messianic realms in mind that Benjamin claims some twenty years later that the task of the historical materialist is "to brush history against the grain."[82] It is in this sense, too, that the method of redemptive criticism, later characterized as *Dialektik im Stillstand,* searches against the flow of historical progress for those moments of "Messianic *cessation* of happening," the rare instances of monads, or now-time, into which images of reconciled life are compressed. Yet, because the precise nature of their relation to the Messianic order remains indeterminate, they are still merely a "category of its quietest approach."

Benjamin's Kabbalistically influenced conception of the philosophy of history helps to account for his preoccupation with fragmentary works of art as opposed to totality-oriented, classical art—works such as *Trauerspiel*, Baudelaire's *Fleurs du mal*, and Kafka's parables. For only such "profane" works of art undercut the illusory Enlightenment vision of cumulative historical progress and its concomitant myth of the infinite perfectability of man; and thus, by setting in relief the incorrigible depravity of the human condition, they refute the false semblance of reconciliation in fallen, historical life, in order to appeal all the more imperatively to the need for transcendence. In keeping with the taboo against graven images, fragmentary works of art stand in contrast to the semblance of reconciliation fostered by classical works of art; and it is in this sense that they can be said to brush the illusion of historical progress against the grain. For according to Benjamin, in certain historical ages when man's relation to the absolute has become enshrouded in darkness and uncertainty—e.g., medieval times, the baroque era, romanticism, and expressionism—the production of "perfect" works of art is given over to *epigones* and the creation of authentic works assumes the form of fragments or ruins. For these are ages "possessed of an unremitting will to art. This is true of all periods of so-called decadence. The supreme reality in art is the isolated, self-contained work. But there are times when the well-wrought work is only within reach of the epigone. These are periods of 'decadence' in the arts, the periods of artistic 'will.' "[83]

For Benjamin, the more manifestly historical life appears destitute of salvation, the more inexorably it presents itself as a ruin, the more it refers to that sphere *beyond* historical life where redemption lies in store. This sphere can only be reached through the utter *devaluation and mortification of all worldly values*. Just as the critical mortification of works of art points the way to their ultimate salvation, so, too, the *mortification of historical life serves as the negative indication of the path to redeemed life*. In this way Benjamin's historico-philosophical methodology appears analogous

to the exercises in *negative theology* in which the Kabbalists engaged. For if the Messianic age is deemed the absolute antithesis
of the historical age, the deepest insight into the most sacred truths
of the former realm are allegedly indicated, albeit *negatively,* by
the most thoroughly profane and forsaken aspects of the latter.
In other words, there exists a type of negative semiology whereby
the profane order, if reversed, can be shown to hold the key to
the sacred. A predominant motif in the Messianic literature of the
Kabbalah is that of the "birth pangs" of the Messianic age. It refers
to the anticipated series of natural disasters and catastrophes that
will herald the transformation of the era of history into the Messianic era, and emphasizes that there will be no smooth transition
from historical to redeemed life. It is not a question of the organic
transition from one realm to the next:

It is rather transcendence breaking in upon history, an intrusion in which
history itself perishes, transformed in its ruin because it is struck by a
beam of light shining into it from an outside source. The contructions of
history in which the apocalyptists (as opposed to the prophets of the
Bible) revel have nothing to do with modern conceptions of development
or progress, and if there is anything which, in the view of these seers,
history deserves, it can only be to perish. The apocalyptists have always
cherished a pessimistic view of the world. Their optimism, their hope,
is not directed to what history will bring forth, but to that which will
arise in its ruin, free at last and undisguised.[84]

There could be no more faithful formulation of Benjamin's own
view of the relation between history and redemption. This fact
explains the historico-philosophical basis for his fascination with
epochs of historical decline, from which the utterly negative relation in which history stands vis-à-vis salvation can be most
clearly perceived. In the "Theologico-Political Fragment" he further specifies the nature of this relationship: "To the spiritual
restitutio in integrum, which introduces immortality, corresponds
a wordly restitution that leads to the eternity of downfall, and the
rhythm of this eternally transient wordly existence, transient in
its totality, in its spatial but also in its temporal totality, the rhythm
of Messianic nature, is happiness. For nature is Messianic by reason
of its eternal and total passing away."[85]

For Benjamin the idea of history is understood as *natural history*, as a condition bent on a course of eternal decline and decay. Its essence is to perish, and there is no aspect of natural life that stands as an exception to this rule. In his later work the influence of this historico-philosophical perspective can be most clearly perceived in his discussion of Paul Klee's painting *Angelus Novus* in the ninth of his "Theses on the Philosophy of History." Here, Benjamin develops his conception of historical life as a vast heap of ruins that grows incessantly higher with the passage of time. Yet, at one end of the catastrophe-laden continuum of history, there seems to lie the light of redemption; though it is to be found apparently only in the *opposite* direction from the course of historical progress. This passage, nearly identical in content to the "Theologico-Political Fragment" of twenty years earlier, like its predecessor, is capable of illustrating the relation in question only by way of metaphorical means. In it, Benjamin proceeds by envisioning the angel in Klee's painting as the "angel of history":

His face is turned toward the past. Where we perceive a chain of events, he sees one single catastrophe which keeps piling ruin upon ruin and hurls it in front of his feet. The angel would like to stay, awaken the dead, and make whole what has been smashed. But a storm is blowing from Paradise; it has got caught in his wings with such violence that the angel can no longer close them. The storm irresistibly propels him into the future to which his back is turned, while the pile of debris before him grows skyward. This storm is what we call progress.[86]

It is worthy of note that in terms of the imagery developed by Benjamin, the storm of progress is viewed as blowing *from* Paradise. Thus, there appears to exist a mysterious relation between the pile of debris that represents progress (the storm) and Paradise, though they seem to lie at opposite ends of the continuum of history. The further the angel is blown helplessly along the path of progress, the higher the pile of ruins that accumulates, and the further it seems to travel from the "source" of the storm, from Paradise.

The imagery of "ruin upon ruin" in terms of which Benjamin perceives the course of history in this passage is strikingly reminiscent of the Kabbalistic description of the "end of history," which precedes the advent of the Messianic era. Faced with the seemingly inexplicable series of horrors and catastrophes of Jewish history (above all, the expulsion from Spain in 1492), the Kabbalists proceeded to attach an inverse, mystical significance to these events, which were assumed to represent signs of the impending Messianic age—its "birth pangs." As Scholem explains:

> The dread and peril of the End form an element of shock and the shocking which induces extravagance. The terrors of the real historical experiences of the Jewish people are joined with images drawn from the heritage of myth and mythical fancy. . . . This catastrophic character of redemption, which is essential to the apocalyptical conception, is pictured in all these texts and traditions in glaring images: in world wars and revolutions, in epidemics, famine, and economic catastrophe; but to an equal degree in apostasy and the desecration of God's name, in the forgetting of the Torah and the upsetting of all moral order to the point of dissolving the laws of nature.[87]

Consequently, on the basis of the foregoing historico-philosophical motifs, Benjamin discovered the ideal object of investigation for his critical method in the genre of *Trauerspiel* and the technique of allegory. These Counter-Reformation dramas, whose heyday coincided with the traumas of the Thirty Years War, stand fully convinced of the vanity and worthlessness of all mortal life, bound as it is to an inevitable decline and decay; and thus they point all the more vehemently to the hope embodied in the *next* world as the only possible source of salvation. This "negative" system of references is ensured by the technique of allegory, through which the morbid imagery of the plays' manifest, profane material content becomes valueless in and of itself and ultimately acquires significance only by way of pointing to an external, transcendent referent. The didactic, repeatedly emphasized allegorical content of *Trauerspiel* is the theme of *redemption through death*. For in the context of an utterly hopeless and profane earthbound existence, the inevitability of death was perceived as nothing less than the guarantee of release. Proceeding from these eschatological premises the inspired Protestant playwrights of *Trauerspiel*, Gryphius, Opitz, and Lohenstein, openly reveled in the piles of corpses which cluttered the stage, the exaggerated death-agonies of their martyr-heroes, and the mortality of everything earthly. For only in this fashion could they convey the passion of their religious conviction concerning the valuelessness of everything mortal in contrast to the blessed sublimity of immortal life. In his exemplary extolment of the cardinal virtues of *Trauerspiel* (here, "tragedy"), Opitz makes the following claim: "Tragedy is equal in majesty to heroic poetry . . . because it deals only with the commands of kings, killings, despair, infanticide and patricide, conflagrations, incest, war and commotion, lamentation, weeping, sighing and such-like."[88] Such was the path to redemption pursued by *Trauerspiel*.

Allegory

In a *curriculum vitae* discovered in Benjamin's estate, he describes the mission of his major study on *Trauerspiel* as follows: "This book undertook to provide a new view of German drama of the seventeenth century. It sets itself the task of contrasting its form—*Trauerspiel*—to tragedy and attempts to indicate the affinity that exists between the literary form of *Trauerspiel* and the art form of allegory."[89] And in an earlier *curriculum vitae*, Benjamin remarks that the *Trauerspiel* book "was dedicated to the philosophical content of a forgotten and misunderstood art form, allegory."[90] It is only through an examination of the decisive relationship between *Trauerspiel* and allegory that the essential unity and meaning of this chief work of his early years can be determined. For according to Benjamin's conception of the methodology of literary criticism, allegory represents the "truth content" of *Trauerspiel*, in the programmatic sense of the term as defined in the introductory exposition on the philosophy of criticism in the *Elective Affinities* essay. There, Benjamin declared that criticism must begin with the task of "commentary," with an analysis of the "material content" of works of art. For it is only first through the mediation of the transitory, historically variable material content that access to the enduring truth content of the work can be attained. He proceeded to show how once the "mythic" material content of Goethe's novel was stripped away or "mortified," its truth content, the hope for everlasting life *beyond* the spell of mythical fate that governs this-worldly existence, stood revealed. Once the philosophical plane of truth content is reached, the investigation passes from its initial phase, commentary, to its ultimate goal, criticism proper, in which the *redemptive significance* of the work becomes manifest. It is according to this methodological perspective that the relation of Parts I and II of the *Trauerspiel* book, which deal respectively with *Trauerspiel* as a genre and the art form of allegory, must be understood. For Part I is almost entirely *descriptive*. It consists of an unadulterated presentation of the most salient extravagances and affectations of the dramas themselves. Whereas with the examination of the underlying allegorical structure of the plays in Part II, the rightful domain of criticism, the plane of truth content, has been reached. In no uncertain terms, Part I undertakes an investigation of the material content of *Trauerspiel* and Part II, "Allegory and Trauerspiel," consists of an analysis of its truth content.

For Benjamin, all beauty is implicated in illusion (*Schein*). It is inherently transient, fated to fade. Beauty is the external appearance or illusion projected by classical works of art, whose underlying structure is in essence *symbolic*. Unproblematical, classical works of art entail a claim to totality, to an unmediated communion with the absolute in and of themselves. This is what they "symbolize." As such, it becomes the task of the critic to mortify the veil of beautiful illusion in which classical works of art are enshrouded in order thereby to permit the expressionless (*Ausdruckslose*), to appear.[91] But the expressionless can "appear" only in a paradoxical sense, insofar as it is defined as being devoid of appearance per se. For the expressionless is nothing less than the truth content of the work of art—that which emerges once the material content of beautiful illusion has been immolated in the flame of criticism. Commentary remains fixated at the external level of beautiful appearance, at the level of the work's material content. It is incapable of penetrating the kernel of truth content that lies embedded in the work's core. In this sense, criticism which remains confined to the stage of commentary is predestined to failure. Benjamin explains the relation between the two through the use of the following bold analogy:

> If, to use a metaphor, one views the growing work as a funeral pyre, its commentator can be likened to a chemist, its critic to an alchemist. While the former is left with the wood and ashes as the sole object of his analysis, for the latter, only the flame itself contains an enigma: the enigma of that which remains living [*des Lebendigen*]. Thus the critic inquires after the truth content whose living flame continues to burn over the heavy logs of the past and the light ashes of life gone by.[92]

Through the mortification of the material content (represented in the preceding metaphor by the funeral pyre) the critic allows the "expressionless," the truth content of the work, to step forth. As such, criticism must appear destructive of the beauty inherent to symbolic works of art. It is inimical to all appearance. In the case of Goethe's *Elective Affinities* the relationship between Ottilie and Eduard is, according to Benjamin, doomed to failure since it is based on the ephemeral attraction characteristic of beauty. Genuine love needs something deeper than the transitory, superficial passion sparked by a beautiful countenance if it is to survive. Seventeenth-century *Trauerspiel* thus provided Benjamin with an ideal object for his conception of criticism inasmuch as these plays are already *ruins*; that is, *Trauerspiel*, by virtue of its allegorical substructure, accomplishes in and of itself the destruction of the beautiful illusion, the pretension to totality characteristic of symbolic works of art.

Like its successors, romanticism and expressionism, the allegorical drama of the baroque period "was concerned not so much with providing a corrective to classicism, as to art itself. And it cannot be denied that the baroque, that contrasting prelude to classicism, offers a more concrete, more authoritative, and more permanent version of this correction."[93] By setting in relief the allegorical procedure of *Trauerspiel* Benjamin seeks to counteract the romantic prejudice in favor of the symbol as the sole appropriate vehicle for the sensuous representation of the nonsensuous (the expressionless); and the widespread misapprehension, promoted largely by neo-Aristotelian criticism, of *Trauerspiel* as merely a bastardized version of classical tragedy. To be sure, in

Trauerspiel nowhere was the golden mean of classicism to be found. But those who sought it there overlooked entirely its historico-philosophical specificity, which forms the crux of Benjamin's analysis. For the allegorical form in which *Trauerspiel* finds expression is *the* form adequate from a historico-philosophical standpoint to those ages in which man's relation to the absolute has become problematical—i.e., in which that relation has ceased to be immanent to life. Consequently, allegory devalues everything tainted by this-worldliness—the material content of its personages, emblems, and situations—turning them instead into lifeless signposts of an enigmatic path to the absolute. In ages of decline the immediate, symbolic claim to totality promoted by classical works of art would only be chimerical. They become the province of unreflective epigones. For these reasons, allegory and symbol have antithetical attitudes to the problem of time. Whereas for the symbol the ideal of time is found in the fulfilled mystical instant (*Nu*), for allegory it is represented by the idea of an unfulfilled infinite progression. For the one, the relation to redemption is immediate; for the other it is infinitely removed:

Whereas in the symbol destruction is idealized and the transfigured face of nature is fleetingly revealed in the light of redemption, in allegory the observer is confronted with the *facies hippocratica* of history as a petrified, primordial landscape. Everything about history that, from the very beginning, has been untimely, sorrowful, unsuccessful, is expressed in a face—or rather in a death's head. And although such a thing lacks all "symbolic" freedom of expression, all classical proportion, all humanity, nevertheless, this is the form in which man's subjection to nature is most obvious. . . . This is the heart of the allegorical way of seeing, of the baroque, secular explanation of history as the Passion of the world; its importance resides solely in the stations of the world's decline. The greater the significance, the greater the subjection to death, because death digs most deeply the jagged line of demarcation between physical nature and significance.[94]

The symbol aspires to an immediate unity with that which it intends. It overlaps with the universal and thus carries the moment of transcendence within itself. At the same time, insofar as the symbol signifies an *aesthetic* category and not an *ontic* one (i.e., not a category of reality), it always remains in part implicated in the world of *Schein*. It can never *actually* embody the union of universal and particular, but only *represents* this unity for the imagination. Rather than being a detriment, this fact actually serves to underline the *utopian* horizon with which the symbol always converges. For by virtue of its "imaginary" status the symbol becomes a category of the realm of objective possibility, indicative of a relation to a "not-yet-being" (Bloch) whose reality can nevertheless be dimly perceived on the horizon of the future.[95] Greek art was symbolic. The rivers, hills, and skies of its mythical panorama were portrayed as the actual dwelling places of the gods. Human life was, as it were, never more than an arm's length away from the gods. In allegory, too, nature takes on an important signifying function. As Benjamin remarks, "The epic poem is in fact a history of signifying nature in its classical form, just as allegory is its baroque form."[96] Yet, for the stylized dramas of the baroque, nature is no longer symbolically represented by serene Olympian deities, but allegorically by a "death's head": as the eminently profane soil on which the pageant of eternal mortality and decomposition that constitutes "creaturely" history, historical life after the fall, takes place. At the same time, as allegorical emblems, neither the death's head nor the skeleton embodies *in itself* the idea of the condition of putrefaction toward which natural history irreversibly inclines, but each merely *stands for* this idea. In contrast to the symbol, neither exists in a self-sufficient relation to the idea it seeks to represent, but remains in need of completion from an outside source—the allegorist. The meanings of allegorical images are by no means self-evident, for according to the historico-philosophical dynamic of the allegorical world view, *all* meaning has ceased to be self-evident. In this chaotic cosmos of desultory, miscellaneous fragments, the allegorist alone is sovereign. He is responsible for bestowing meaning in an inverted world in which any "person, any object, any relationship can mean absolutely anything else. With this possibility a destructive, but just verdict is passed on the profane world: it is characterized as a world in which the detail is of no great importance."[97] Although the profane world is totally devalued—that is, all objects cease to be beings-for-self and now exist only as beings-for-other (i.e., for the allegorist)—nevertheless, insofar as it is in turn read as an allegorical cryptogram of redeemed life, its status is simultaneously elevated. Benjamin refers to this unique dual status of profane life as the "antinomy of allegory."[98]

In the domain of allegory the allegorist rules "like a stern sultan in the harem of objects . . . by no means avoiding that arbitrariness which is the most drastic manifestation of the power of knowledge."[99] The problem of the *arbitrariness* of knowledge has, in the post-paradisiacal state of the world, become *the* problem of knowledge. This fact is attributable to the profane origin of knowledge which coincides with man's expulsion from the Garden of Eden. Before the fall there existed no division between name and thing. Man spoke in the divine language of names, which stood in an immediate relation to the creative word of God. As such, there was as yet no need for an external knowledge to bridge the gap between thinking and being. The pure *Ursprache* preceded the breach between subject and object which all subsequent knowledge has attempted to remedy. In this sense the utter sinfulness of the creaturely world described in the allegories of the baroque epitomizes a confused, godless condition in which name and thing have become separated, in which objects and their proper meanings no longer coincide. That the problematical relation in which the creaturely world stands to the absolute has become formidable and pervasive legitimates the unrestricted license conferred on the allegorist in his extravagant forays into the world of objects and meanings. Moreover, it accounts for the melancholic temperament that characterizes the allegorical world view:

If the object becomes allegorical under the gaze of melancholy, if melancholy causes life to flow out of it and it remains behind dead, but eternally secure, then it is exposed to the allegorist, it is unconditionally in his power. That is to say it is now quite incapable of emanating any significance or meaning of its own; such significance as it has, it acquires from the allegorist. He places meaning within it, and stands behind it; not in a psychological but in an ontological sense. In his hands the object becomes something different; through it he speaks of something different and for him it becomes a key to the realm of hidden knowledge; and he reveres it as the emblem of this.[100]

The flagrant rejection of the classical ideal of beauty reflected in the ruins which constitute the material content of *Trauerspiel* has its counterpart, on the level of truth content, in the baroque's distinct preference for the allegorical over the symbolic mode of representation. For the profane world of *Trauerspiel* there could be no other solution, which underlines the extreme misinterpretation it suffered at the hands of its neo-Aristotelian detractors. For *Trauerspiel*'s rejection of the ideal of beauty was purely voluntary. In the forsaken, creaturely world in which its dramas were staged, any symbolic pretension to totality in the here and now would have been sheer ideology. All art, whether it chooses to acknowledge it or not, is concerned with the representation of man's relation to the absolute. Allegory signifies the necessarily fragmentary nature of that relation in a world that has itself been reduced to fragments or ruins. In this sense, Benjamin's profound concern with the *historico-philosophical* significance of genres reveals a marked indebtedness to the early aesthetics of Georg Lukács: to his understanding of the historical uniqueness of tragedy in *Soul and Form* and his analogous demonstration of the historical specificity of the modern novel in *The Theory of the Novel*. Benjamin's emphasis on a historico-philosophical approach points to the obsolescence of judging art by way of the dogmatic application of the so-called timeless standards of classical aesthetics and the necessity of comprehending works of art in terms of the material circumstances in which they originate. The ruins of *Trauerspiel* are in no way a frustrated emulation of the classical ideal, but instead "the finest material in baroque creation."[101] Through the technique of allegory the writers of the baroque period were able to conjure a relation to meaning in an age that seemed infinitely distanced from all meaning.

The leitmotif of redemption represents the truth content of *Trauerspiel*; yet not a disembodied truth that would be separable in some way from the material content in which it is cloaked, but one which is thoroughly mediated by that material content and only attainable by way of such mediation. For Benjamin there is no doubt as to the direction in which the ultimate significance of these dramas of lamentation point. The solution to the riddle of

Trauerspiel is to be found in the fact that not in spite of but *because of* the utter squalor and despair of its material content, it is ultimately transformed into a theological drama of salvation. Unquestionably, the extravagance and bombast of its material content must have appeared to later critics as its most remarkable feature, so far was it removed from the serenity and proportion of classical standards. Naturally, this extreme deviation from the golden mean was usually the basis for its summary dismissal. Yet, such a verdict fails to take into account the *dynamic* character of *Trauerspiel's* allegorical structure—in contrast to symbolic art, its relation to the universal is not immediately present. Benjamin asks, "Above all: what is the significance of those scenes of cruelty and anguish in which the baroque drama revels?"[102]: the protracted death-agonies of its martyrs, the ignominious ruin that repeatedly awaits its monarchs, the intrigue and scheming of the corrupt courtier, the opulence of its language, and decadence of its imagery. It is only if these dramatic celebrations of the transience and mortality of everything earthly are understood as allegories of salvation that they are prevented from tumbling headlong into a vertiginous eddy of sheer catastrophe and despair. "For a critical understanding of the *Trauerspiel*, in its extreme allegorical form, is possible only from the higher domain of theology; so long as the approach is an aesthetic one, paradox must have the last word."[103] When the light of salvation shines forth, the paradox embodied in the valuelessness of earthly life is resolved. For it is only from the point of view of the higher medium of redeemed life that the folly of human existence first becomes intelligible. According to Benjamin, the structure of allegory is dialectical. It proceeds by way of antitheses. In theological terms, it provides the key to a negative theology whereby fragments of profane life are transformed into emblems of salvation.

The allegories of *Trauerspiel* are at home in the world of the fall, the profane world of "knowledge," where the original, divine relation between things and their proper meanings—their *names*—has been sundered. Yet, by virtue of the peculiar process of inversion which distinguishes allegory, the universal mortification of fallen life paves the way for entrance into the realm of salvation. For the secret of the allegorical content of *Trauerspiel* lies in the imagery of death and decline in which it revels, which immediately calls forth a vision of redemption. The "dialectic" of allegory causes all manifest content to be transformed into its opposite: *the death's head becomes an angel's countenance*. Basing itself on the theological conception of the diametrically opposite relation in which profane life stands to the life of salvation, it goes all out in its attempt to dramatize the *wretched* nature of earthly life in order thereby to set in contrast all the more emphatically the *blissfulness* of the life beyond. *Trauerspiel* proceeds according to the religious conviction that the more frank its avowal of its own baseness, the more readily it will qualify for admittance into the sphere of eternal life. Between history and salvation, the breach was absolute. By proceeding through an antithetical system of references the allegories of *Trauerspiel* sought to pile ruin upon ruin, thereby illustrating not only the sheer hopelessness and futility of earthly existence, but more importantly, the sovereign hope for mankind that rests with the Almighty as redeemer. For the two contrasting visions are merely the complementary poles of the drama of sin and atonement in which creaturely life finds its ultimate meaning. Once the profane material content of *Trauerspiel* is consumed in the fire of critical examination, their truth content as *allegories of redemption* is revealed.

"[An] appreciation of the transcience of things, and the concern to redeem them for eternity, is one of the strongest impulses in allegory," remarks Benjamin. The baroque preoccupation with the finitude and transience of earthly life has an immediate historical reason and an underlying theological reason. The former lies in the monumental social upheavals of this period, in the profound instability of all institutions, secular and religious, of an era marred by the Thirty Years War and the fleeting alliances and counteralliances of Counter-Reformation political intrigue. The latter finds its explanation in the network of guilt which envelops creaturely life, a guilt which derives from the original sinfulness of the human condition and which prevents things from uniting with their proper significances, the prerequisite for their salvation. It is the guilt of mere life and the concomitant separation of this-worldly existence from the possibility of salvation that accounts for the *Trauer* ("mourning" or "lament") of *Trauerspiel* and for the acedia of the allegorist. Consequently, the allegorist's task is to provide a *restoration* of meaning through the "miraculous" transfiguration of the hideous and profane material content of *Trauerspiel* into a parable of redeemed life. He struggles essentially for the restoration of a state in which things would once more be called by their proper names. The arduousness of his mission and the hermeticism of his approach result from a condition in which the immanence of meaning, and thereby the objective possibility of salvation, seems to have flown from the world. Hence, the allegorist is never interested in the thing itself, but only in its allegorical meaning—i.e., its significance in relation to the theological concept of salvation. The peculiar paradox involved in his quest for absolute knowledge, that which is ideally the most "objective," is that he is compelled to resort to an extreme subjectivism in his fervent endeavors to bestow meaning on things once he has stripped them of their intrinsic meanings. His approach is an insatiable "will to meaning."

Nevertheless, an important element of consolation is to be found in the extreme subjectivism of the allegorical procedure. For ultimately, this subjectivism testifies to the *chimerical* character of the state of perpetual ruination to which natural life seems condemned in *Trauerspiel*. In relation to the divine scheme of things, this life is a mere shadowplay, appearance. The nullity of mere knowledge, from a theological standpoint, points to the veritable insubstantiality of its representations. If knowledge can never by itself yield the absolute, the ultimate significance of the sorrowful material content of *Trauerspiel* must be other than what it appears to be. The primordial deficiency of knowledge thus leads—allegorically—to an unusual process of self-cancellation. Every claim it makes, every statement it utters, immediately entails its own negation. The profane network of references and signs reverses itself. The idea it conveys inexorably is that appearance and essence do not coincide, but are related to each other only *inversely*. Herein lies the device behind the ultimate redemption enjoyed by *Trauerspiel*. It is in this sense that the following explanation by Benjamin must be understood:

Allegory goes away empty-handed. Evil as such, which it cherished as enduring profundity, exists only in allegory, is nothing other than allegory and means something different from what it is. It means precisely the nonexistence of what it presents. The absolute vices, as exemplified by tyrants and intriguers, are allegories. They are not real, and that which they represent, they possess only in the subjective view of melancholy. . . . By its allegorical form, evil as such reveals itself to be a subjective phenomenon.[104]

By virtue of its inauthentic origin in the subjective contemplation of the allegorist, the evil of *Trauerspiel* ultimately proves illusory. In itself the world is God's creation: "And God saw everything that he had made, and, behold, it was very good" (Genesis 1:31). Only *for man*—that is, subjectively—does evil exist. Only after his fall from the original state of grace does evil enter the world, and also that knowledge which corresponds to the distinction between good and evil. Evil is merely an illusory object with which man enters into relation during the period of separation from the original divine stream of life into which he is cast after the fall. This is the origin of the illusion in which knowledge is always implicated so long as it remains removed from the original purity and goodness of the world as created by God:

Knowledge of good and evil, then, is the opposite of all essential [*sachlichen*] knowledge. Related as it is to the depths of the subjective, it is basically the knowledge of evil. It is "nonsense" [*Geschwätz*] in the profound sense in which Kierkegaard conceived the word. This knowledge, the triumph of subjectivity and the onset of an arbitrary rule over things, is the origin of all allegorical contemplation. . . . For good and evil are unnameable, they are nameless entities, outside the language of names, in which man, in paradise, named things, and which he forsakes in the abyss of that problem.[105]

Consequently, because of the objective inadequacy of the representations of mere knowledge, the profane material content of *Trauerspiel* is rendered null and void in itself and is miraculously transfigured into an allegorical image of redemption. By virtue of the universal inversion of meanings which characterizes allegorical emblematics, the more graphically mere knowledge portrays the hollowness of natural life, the more emphatically it calls to mind its allegorical referent, the sphere of redeemed life. The sphere of knowledge which corresponds to the guilt-laden context of creaturely existence voluntarily sets its own baseness in relief in order thereby to indicate the theological sphere in which the light of salvation resides in fact. The highest function that objects and personages in the realm of the profane can perform is to serve as allegorical references to the superior realm of redeemed life. For in a world in which all immanent hope for fulfillment seemed to be brutally denied, the playwrights of *Trauerspiel* perceived the frank acknowledgment of the depravity of the human condition as the only hope for establishing a relation to the absolute. Only according to this peculiar theological outlook can the all-important relation between the profane material content and the sacred truth content of *Trauerspiel* be adequately appreciated:

For it is to misunderstand the allegorical entirely if we make a distinction between the store of images, into which this about-turn into salvation and redemption takes place, and that grim store which signifies death and damnation. For it is precisely visions of the frenzy of destruction, in which all earthly things collapse in a heap of ruins, which reveal the limit set upon allegorical contemplation, rather than its ideal quality. The bleak confusion of Golgotha, which can be recognized as the schema underlying the allegorical figures of hundreds of the engravings and descriptions of this period, is not just a symbol of the desolation of human existence. In it transitoriness is not signified or allegorically represented, so much as, in its own significance, displayed as allegory. As the allegory of resurrection. Ultimately, in the death-signs of the baroque the direction of allegorical reflection is reversed; on the second part of its wide arc it returns, to redeem. . . . Allegory, of course, thereby loses everything that was most peculiar to it: the secret, privileged knowledge, the arbitrary rule in the realm of dead objects, the supposed infinity of a world without hope. All this vanishes with this *one* turn-about, in which the immersion of allegory has to clear away the final phantasmagoria of the objective and, left entirely to its own devices, re-discovers itself, not playfully in the earthly world of things, but seriously under the eyes of heaven. And this is the essence of melancholy immersion: that its ultimate objects, in which it believes it can most fully secure for itself that which is vile, turn into allegories, and that these allegories fill out and deny the void in which they are represented, just as, ultimately, the intention does not faithfully rest in the contemplation of bones, but faithlessly leaps forward to the idea of resurrection.[106]

The allegorical truth content of *Trauerspiel* follows the archetypal model of Christian eschatology: the sacrificial death of Christ. Resurrection is the link between the finitude of this life, represented by death, and the eternal life of the realm of redemption. One must take care, however, not to ascribe directly to Benjamin the Counter-Reformation world view of the *Trauerspiel* poets (whose leading representatives were in fact all Protestants). The theological impulses behind his fascination with this art form remain much more indebted to Kabbalistic historico-philosophical motifs, a fact born out by the paramount role played by his two earlier, most Kabbalistically influenced studies in his understanding of *Trauerspiel*: "On Language as Such and the Language of Man" and the "Theological-Political Fragment."

It is no accident that Benjamin rediscovered the significance of allegory in the intellectual climate of the early 1920s. For the extreme subjectivism of the allegorical method immediately calls to mind the proliferation of like-tempered artistic movements that came into existence at this historical juncture as a self-conscious reaction to the mechanization of social life that had proceeded unchecked since the time of the industrial revolution. One thinks of the appeal to the powers of *Verinnerlichung* enunciated in Kandinsky's expressionist manifesto, "Über das Geistige in der Kunst" (1911); the *Blaue Reiter* Almanac, edited by Kandinsky and Franz Marc, and its rehabilitation of folk art, children's art, and other forgotten genres; André Breton's exaltation of the sovereign power of the imagination in his "Manifesto of Surrealism" (1924); and the related surrealist adoption of the technique of automatic writing. In addition to these examples from the artistic avant garde, one might also list the unprecedented subjectivization of narrative structure in the novels of Proust and Joyce. In sum, these tendencies are united in a rejection of "realism," a renunciation of a mimetic approach to the artistic representation of reality, and a concomitant turn to more spiritualized, subjectivist modes of expression. With the rapid expansion of photography and journalism in the latter half of the nineteenth century, the arts increasingly began to distance themselves from the task of the *description* of external reality and moved toward the *expression* of man's "inner self."[107] To be sure, the extreme devaluation of the empirical world and the accompanying subjective derivation of meaning characteristic of allegory would find itself at home in this spiritual environment. In fact, the genesis of allegory in the baroque is attributable to an analogous dialectic. Its Counter-Reformation world view was polemically directed against the self-confident this-worldly orientation of the Renaissance, whose reintroduction of pagan (Greek) figures and humanist themes was perceived as a direct threat to authentic Christian values. The popularity of allegory in medieval art proceeds from a similar impulse: the desire to divert men's minds from the temptations of profane life, symbolized by the pagan values of the Greco-Roman world, and to turn them instead toward the contemplation of other-worldly beliefs. All three periods—medieval, baroque, and expressionist—seek salvation through a subjectivized conception of experience once it is clear that their hopes for fulfillment are only repulsed in empirical reality.

Benjamin's guiding impulse in this study is as much aesthetic as it is theological, though the truths of both spheres differ only in form and not in substance. His rehabilitation of *Trauerspiel* is an exercise in *rettende Kritik*. He is concerned with "redeeming" the genre of *Trauerspiel* as a "now-time" threatened with historical oblivion, and with establishing the validity of fragmentary or problematical art as the form of expression historico-philosophically appropriate to ages of decline. The allegorical structure of *Trauerspiel* presents a bold image of redemption *despite* the thoroughly profane era in which it is situated, an effort which Benjamin considers exemplary, yet does not view as an absolute, timeless model. By first proceeding through an examination of the dense, alienating material content of baroque drama, he ultimately encounters a revelation: the compelling vision of redemption presented by the playwrights of *Trauerspiel*. *Trauerspiel* is not an inconsummate rendition of classical tragedy, but an expression of aesthetic truth valid in its own right. Its interpretation not only frees the idea of aesthetics from a mass of neoclassicist prejudices as to what art ideally "should be," but also offers invaluable insight into the fecundity of a spiritual age that had been hitherto either neglected or abused. "In the ruins of great buildings the idea of the plan speaks more impressively than in lesser buildings, however well preserved they are; and for this reason the German *Trauerspiel* merits interpretation. In the spirit of allegory, it is conceived from the outset as a ruin, a fragment. Others may shine resplendently as on the first day; this form preserves the image of beauty to the very last."[108]

Chapter Three

IDEAS AND THEORY
OF KNOWLEDGE

Anti-Historicism

THE "Erkenntniskritische Vorrede" or "Epistemo-Critical Prologue" of the *Trauerspiel* study represents the only independent statement by Benjamin concerning theory of knowledge and epistemology outside of two earlier essays which were dealt with in the previous chapter, "Über das Programm der kommenden Philosophie" and "On Language as Such and on the Language of Man." The latter essays remained unpublished during Benjamin's lifetime, and there is evidence to suggest that he was particularly selective about precisely who would be allowed to view them. This attitude was consistent with his lifelong hesitancy to furnish outright the metatheoretical rudiments of his thinking, for it was his firm conviction that "method" was not something that existed in a state of isolation from the process of research, but instead should itself be determined immanently, through the inherent dictates and necessities of the *object* of research itself. The Prologue to the *Trauerspiel* book consummates many of the insights relevant to the theory of knowledge first developed in the two aforementioned essays and at the same time elevates these ideas to an entirely new, systematic plane. It is without doubt one of the more terse and recondite pieces of philosophical prose to have been written in this century, a living testament to Benjamin's belief that a "continual pausing for breath" is the rhythm most appropriate to the process of philosophical contemplation.[1] That Benjamin conceived of the Prologue as being intimately related to the 1916 essay

79

"On Language" is indicated by a remark in a letter to Scholem of June 1924 from the Italian island of Capri, where Benjamin had retreated to write his ill-fated *Habilitationsschrift*: "You will find in it [the Prologue] for the first time since the work 'On Language as Such and on the Language of Man' an essay on the theory of knowledge."[2] And in a letter of January 1925, as his work on the *Trauerspiel* study was in its final stages, Benjamin characterizes the Prologue as "an immeasurable chutzpah—nothing more or less than a prolegomena to the theory of knowledge; thus a second—I know not whether better—stage of the early work on language, which, as you know, appears as a theory of ideas."[3]

Its status in relation to the material part of the *Trauerspiel* study is equivocal. Benjamin appears to have omitted most of it from the version of the study which was presented to the faculty at the University of Frankfurt,[4] in what would prove to be a vain attempt to forestall a negative reception. Franz Schultz, who had originally agreed to represent Benjamin's work before the faculty, withheld his support at the eleventh hour and suggested that Benjamin submit it to the department of Aesthetics instead of that of German Literary History as had been planned originally. Ultimately, Benjamin, faced with the threat of having his work rejected, succumbed to the pressure of Hans Cornelius and Rudolf Kautzsch (of the faculty of Aesthetics) and withdrew the *Trauerspiel* study voluntarily. Many years later, Scholem offered the following pertinent reflections concerning Benjamin's mistreatment at the hands of the academy:

Even at that time he had lost contact with the university and its scientific operations, and the foundering of the effort [to habilitate], to which he felt obligated, caused him—as much as its circumstances must have embittered him—at the same time to breathe an audible sigh of relief which was detectable in his letters. He knew only too well how things worked in academic philosophy departments and academic literary history. Through the withdrawal of the work he had facilitated the possibility of prefacing the published edition with a forward . . . which would eternalize the disgrace of the university which renounced it. For one might indeed say that this work . . . was one of the most significant and pathbreaking habilitation studies ever presented to a philosophy faculty. Its rejection, which ultimately sent Benjamin along the path of the free-lance writer—or better still, of the "homme de lettres"—who is forced to earn his living with a pen, was a symbol of the state of literary science and the spiritual make-up of the scholars in the now much-praised Weimar era. Even when it was all over and done with, long after World War II, a highly cultivated representative of this scientific discipline could actually bring himself to write concerning the foundering of this academic effort the malicious and shameless statement: "one can't habilitate spirit." [Geist kann man nicht habilitieren.][5]

Later both Schultz and Cornelius would claim they understood not a word of Benjamin's text. Though the Prologue itself did appear intact in the original edition of the *Trauerspiel* book published by Rowohlt in 1928, it was the object of much critical ridicule and misunderstanding (as one critic would write in a letter to Scholem, "Pseudoplatonism—that is the signature under which Benjamin's book appears to me to be characterized"),[6] largely owing to the critics' erroneous presupposition that it had been intended as an introduction to the *Trauerspiel* study per se; whereas in fact only the last of its three "movements" (beginning with the section entitled "Neglect and Misinterpretation of Baroque Tragedy") contains remarks which have a direct bearing on the main text itself; and although the theory of knowledge elaborated in the Prologue is by no means irrelevant from a methodological standpoint to the text which follows, it would be undoubtedly more appropriate to view it primarily as an independent formulation of epistemological insights. Support for this point of view is provided by Max Rychner, who reports that upon complaining of enormous difficulties in comprehending the "Vorrede," Benjamin responded by claiming that it would be incorrect to *begin* reading the book with this section, and that instead it should only be read at the end (and that only someone familiar with Kabbalah would be able to understand it in any event).[7]

Insofar as his methodology explicitly attacked the historicism and relativism of the approach to criticism which had more or less dominated German university circles since Schleiermacher, it is likely that the failure of Benjamin's efforts to habilitate came as no great surprise to him. For example, he criticized Johannes Vokelt's influential study *Ästhetik des Tragischen* for indiscriminately categorizing all examples of tragic art under the same rubric and then proceeding to deduce the concept of tragedy itself from the "average" traits of these examples. Whereas in truth not only does such an approach err seriously in lumping together the tragedies of Aeschylus and Euripides with those of the *Trauerspiel* poets (and Benjamin's study goes to great lengths to demonstrate that *Trauerspiel* has virtually nothing in common with Greek tragedy); Vokelt's procedure also annihilates the specificity of dramatic types, insofar as the *essence* of each is not to be found in their "average" characteristics, but rather in the *extremes*. It is therefore the vulgar classificatory, empathizing, relativist tendencies of the historicist approach to understanding literary history which Benjamin confronts head on in his methodological remarks in the Prologue; and in this way he seeks to win back the serious intentions of criticism; the dimension of criticism that is concerned less with the sweeping historical classification of works of art according to a technique that might be labeled "genre-fetishism"—i.e., the enumeration of certain "average" features of a genre and the presumptive condemnation or approbation of individual works according to whether or not they satisfy such arbitrarily determined, extrinsic criteria—than with the desire to determine in immanent terms the *truth content* of a work of art, an aspect which had been, since the German romantics, wholly neglected in German critical and aesthetic discourse. Benjamin reflects on this situation in a letter of December 1923 to Florens Christian Rang (whose sudden death early in 1925 had caused the *Trauerspiel* book to lose, as Benjamin once phrased it, "its only authentic reader"),[8] which is of inestimable value insofar as it consists of a preliminary adumbration of the epistemological framework of the entire Prologue. In these considerations Benjamin addresses a problem which had long concerned him: how something enduring and ineffable—truth itself—can emerge from something sensuous and time-bound, a work of art. Literary historians had customarily focused on the latter aspect of literature to the exclusion of the former. Therefore, in the following passage, Benjamin attempts both to explain why literary works originate at a determinate point of time, and have a "history," and to preserve what is enduring in them (their truth content) from the caprice and contingency of the historicist outlook that enjoyed academic favor during this era:

What concerns me is the idea of how works of art are related to historical life. What is certain to me is that there is no such thing as art history. Whereas in human life, for example, the concatenation of temporal events do not proceed solely in a causal, intrinsic, and essential way—rather without this concatenation in development, maturity, death, etc., human life essentially could not exist—things are entirely different in the case of works of art. The attempt to situate the work of art in historical development does not open perspectives which lead to its intrinsic being. . . . Current investigations in the history of art lead only to the history of form or content, for which works of art appear only as examples or models, as it were; a history of the works of art themselves never comes into question. There is nothing which links them both extensively and intensively. . . . The essential connection between works of art remains intensive. In this respect works of art appear similar to philosophical systems, in that the so-called "history" of philosophy is either the history of uninteresting dogmas or philosophers, or a history of problems, in which case the interest in temporal extension is in danger of being lost and passing over into a-temporal, intensive *interpretation*. The specific historicity of works of art is in any event one which is never revealed in "art history," but only in interpretation. In interpretation mutual relations between works of art emerge which are a-temporal, though not without importance from a historical point of view. Namely, the same powers which in the world of revelation (which is history) become temporal in an explosive and extensive way, appear intensively in the world of reticence [*Verschlossenheit*] (which is the world of nature and works of art).[9]

And this power which through interpretation appears *intensively* in works of art is the power of the idea. "Criticism is in relation to these considerations (where it is identical with interpretation and in opposition to all current methods of understanding art) the presentation of an idea."[10] Benjamin is in opposition to literary history's search for the average traits of a given genre, as a result of which the works of art, which should *themselves* be the object of critical investigation—i.e., in terms of their *intrinsic* makeup or "natural history"—are degraded to the status of mere examples or illustrations of the genre. Therefore he focuses his attention in the *Trauerspiel* study on the *extreme characteristics* of baroque drama (i.e., the "material content" which becomes the focal point of Part

I), in order that *Trauerspiel* might be revealed not as an example, but as *exemplary*—as an Idea in the metaphysical sense. It becomes therefore Benjamin's sworn methodological intention to permit *Trauerspiel* to emerge as an idea through an entirely immanent juxtaposition of its extreme features in a philosophically informed configuration. He describes this procedure as follows:

Philosophical history, the science of origin, is the form which, in the remotest extremes, in the apparent excesses of development, allows the configuration of the idea to emerge from the totality produced by the juxtaposition of such opposites. The representation of an idea can under no circumstances be successful unless the whole range of possible extremes it contains has virtually been explored.[11]

The Essay as Mediation Between Art and Philosophical Truth

In his *Studien zur Philosophie Walter Benjamins*, the most extensive treatment of Benjamin's theory of knowledge to date, Rolf Tiedemann makes the following claim:

Objectively, Benjamin's epistemology resumes that polemic which in European philosophy dates back to Plato and Aristotle. An answer to the perpetual question whether ideas attain being as objects of philosophical research, whether they should be interpreted realistically, or whether they are products of consciousness in an idealistic sense, merely "brought along" by consciousness, to use Goethe's expression; whether philosophy must proceed from matter or form, from nature or from spirit as its Πρῶτον [proton]; whether induction, the way from below—from the manifold nature of the phenomenally given—represents the royal road of philosophy, or deduction, the way from above, beginning from the realm of ideas as a noumenally revealed realm—an answer to such questions is sought in the *Trauerspiel* book, if partisanship is declared for neither one nor the other way of proceeding.[12]

In the Prologue to the *Trauerspiel* study Benjamin is concerned as much with the problem of philosophical representation—i.e., with the "how" of truth, with its *mode* of presentation—as with its explicit content. The question of discovering an appropriate philosophical method becomes irrelevant unless at the same time the problem of representation is explicitly addressed. In this sense, not only the Prologue itself, but also Benjamin's lifelong preference for the essay form as a vehicle of philosophical expression, betrays a marked indebtedness to the lead article of Lukács's *Soul and Form*, "On the Nature and Form of the Essay." For both Lukács and Benjamin emphasize the historico-philosophical appropriateness of the essay form in a godforsaken world in which man's relation to the absolute has become decidedly problematic. For both men, the *fragmentary nature* of the essay reflects accurately the immanent loss of meaning in the world. As such, their mutual emphasis on the virtues of the essay (or "treatise" as Benjamin terms it in the Prologue) represents a rejection of the traditional ideal of Western philosophy—the ideal of the all-encompassing system—at a stage in history in which empirical life has itself become *refractory* to meaning and thus shuns all attempts at an independent, comprehensive, conceptual totalization. This insight has found consummate expression in the following passage of Adorno's work:

In relation to scientific procedure and its philosophical foundation as method, the essay, according to its idea, draws the full consequence from the critique of the system. . . . Doubt concerning the unconditional validity [of method] was, in the procedure of thinking itself, realized almost exclusively by the essay. It does justice to the consciousness of non-identity, without thereby merely expressing the latter—radical in its non-radicalism, in abstinence before all reduction to a principle, in accentuating the partial over against the total, in the fragmentary. . . . The essay refuses obedience to the principle of reflection of organized science and theory that, according to Spinoza's saying, the order of things is the same as the order of ideas. Because the seamless arrangement of concepts is not one with that which exists, the essay does not aim at a closed, deductive or inductive edifice. It revolts especially against the doctrine, which has taken root since Plato, that the changing and ephemeral would be unworthy of philosophy; against that old injustice to the transient, as a result of which it is anathematized once more in the concept.[13]

Benjamin's own reflections on the inadequacies of systematic philosophy are of a remarkably kindred nature:

Inasmuch as it is determined by this concept of system, philosophy is in danger of accommodating itself to a syncretism which weaves a spider's web between separate kinds of knowledge in an attempt to ensnare truth as if it were something which came flying in from outside. . . . If philosophy is to remain true to the law of its own form, as the representation of truth and not as a guide to the acquisition of knowledge, then the exercise of this form—rather than its anticipation in the system—must be accorded due importance.[14]

The essay presents itself as a *problematical form* of writing: as the young Lukács knew well, its conceptual character disqualified it as a *form-creating* vehicle, such as poetry or literature, and yet its limited scope compels it to stop short of the totalizing claims of systematic philosophy. As Lukács recognizes: "When something has become problematic . . . then salvation can only come from accentuating the problems to a maximum degree, from going radically to its root. The modern essay has thus lost the backdrop of life which gave Plato and the mystics their strength."[15] The virtue of the essay as a form of mediation between pure literature and philosophy per se lies in its capability to grasp truths which lie dormant in the void between symbolic and conceptual modes of representation. "Science affects us by its content, art by its forms," observes Lukács. "Science offers us facts and relationships between facts; art offers us souls and destinies."[16] As a vehicle of philosophical representation, the essay provides the mediation between form and life, planes of existence which in and of themselves are prevented from experiencing immediate contact with one another. Life (or soul) views the ordering principles of form as a restriction, and form, for its part, views life as inherently unordered or chaotic. The essay succeeds simultaneously in providing form with life—without which it remains an empty shell—and life with form—without which it remains mere inarticulate immediacy.

Both Lukács and Benjamin conceive of criticism as the proper métier of the essay insofar as it is ideally suited to achieve the desired synthesis between the two poles of philosophical abstraction and aesthetic concreteness.[17] Thus, it is not by chance that Benjamin begins the Prologue with the following citation from

Goethe:

Neither in knowledge nor in reflection can anything whole be put together, since in the former the internal is missing and in the latter the
external; and so we must necessarily think of science as art if we expect
to derive any kind of wholeness from it. Nor should we look for this
in the general, the excessive, but, since art is always wholly represented
in every individual work of art, so science ought to reveal itself completely in every object treated.[18]

Knowledge (*Wissen*) grasps objects externally at the expense of the
moment of subjectivity or reflection; reflection falls victim to the
obverse dilemma insofar as its retreat to pure inwardness lacks the
moment of sensuousness or concreteness truth needs for fulfillment. Hence, Goethe's recommendation that we regard "science
as art" in our search for wholeness aims at remedying the shortcomings of each position when taken in isolation by comple-
menting the *abstractness* of knowledge with the *sensuousness* of art.
For knowledge proceeds to the universal directly, straight away;
it is therefore unconcerned with the being of truth as embodied
particularity—i.e., with the problem of the representation of truth
as something concrete and individual. On the other hand, in and
of itself art represents the moment of unmediated sensuousness
or sheer particularity—i.e., truth in its merely inchoate form, as
yet separated from the redemptive embrace of the universal. Yet,
what would it mean actually to regard science as art? Goethe's
own solution, the poeticized science of the *Farbenlehre*, the fanciful
quest for the origins of natural life in terms of the mysterious
Urphänomen, is manifestly unsuitable. It is Benjamin's proposal
to seek the mediation of the two extremes in terms of the idea of
the criticism of individual works of art, in order thereby to permit
the universal to unfold *from within the boundaries of the particular
itself*—the work of art. Criticism seeks out the truth content of
works of art—the moment of universality—as it exists immersed
in the material content of the work; it thus attempts to redeem
the latter from its immediate condition of speechless particularity
by translating the nonconceptual language of art into the conceptual language of philosophical truth. As a form for the presentation
of truth, criticism shows itself superior to philosophy per se, insofar as, by taking the work of art as its point of departure, it can

take into account the sensuous dimension of truth—the problem of *representation*—which the inherently abstract nature of the philosophical concept cannot help but suppress.

The young Lukács also readily acknowledged the necessary relationship between the endeavor of criticism and the realm of ideas. "The idea is there before any of its expressions, it is a soul-value, a world-moving and life-forming source in itself: and that is why criticism will always speak of life where it is most alive," observes Lukács, in the same Neo-Platonic spirit which would find distinct resonance some fifteen years later in Benjamin's Prologue. "The idea is the measure of everything that exists, and that is why the critic whose thinking is 'occasioned by something' already created, and who reveals its idea, is the only one who will write the truest and most profound criticism," he continues.[19] However, Lukács definitely failed to share Benjamin's view of the essay as an independent end in itself. Instead, the orientation of the critic ultimately derives from "the great value-definer of aesthetics, the one who is always about to arrive, the one who is never yet there, the only one who has been called to judge." For Lukács, the critic remains merely the precursor of the "great aesthetic" of the future, and "it seems highly questionable whether, if left entirely to himself—i.e., independent from the fate of that other of whom he is the herald—he could lay claim to any value or validity." For whereas the essay can "proudly and calmly set its fragmentariness against the petty completeness of scientific exactitude or impressionistic freshness . . . its purest fulfillment, its most vigorous accomplishment becomes powerless once the great aesthetic comes."[20] In this way the great aesthetic symbolizes for Lukács the prospect that the world might be made whole once more, that form and life, value and existence, might ultimately be reconciled. Benjamin, on the other hand, holds fewer illusions about the intrinsic capacities of a philosophical aesthetic to restore the lost totality of fulfilled life, in keeping with the fundamentally "negative theological" impulses of his eschatological horizon. Lukács's relentless quest for a *positive* image of totality eventually led him to champion the forced reconciliation (*erpresste Versöhnung*)[21] of the Soviet camp.

Because of its profound insight into the essential nature of the relationship between truth and beauty Benjamin confers canonical status upon Plato's *Symposium*. For the chief merit of Plato's dialogue is that it "presents truth—the realm of ideas—as beautiful. It declares truth to be beautiful."[22] In taking into considerations the sensuous side of truth, Plato thus confirms one of the fundamental ideas of Hegel's *Science of Logic*, the notion that "essence must appear." Benjamin claims that Plato's understanding of the relationship between truth and beauty must not only become constitutive for every study relevant to the philosophy of art, but that it is also "indispensable to the definition of truth itself."[23] For it indicates the necessity of confronting the question of the *representation* of truth, it recognizes that the "representational impulse in truth is the refuge of beauty as such."[24] In its investigation of the truth content of art, criticism is obligated to respect the latter impulse, which goes hand in hand with its incarnation in the beautiful. Hence, criticism tempers the philosophical desire to proceed to the universal aspect of beauty directly; and thus the act of determining the truth content of art "is not an unveiling which destroys the mystery, but a revelation which does it justice."[25] The truth content of beauty, "does not appear in the unveiling; rather, it is revealed in a process which might be described metaphorically as the immolation of the veil as it enters into the realm of ideas, as the cremation of the work in which its form reaches its most brilliant degree of illumination."[26]

The Prologue of the *Trauerspiel* book attempts therefore to codify insights concerning the relationship between art and truth which were originally formulated by Benjamin in his 1919 dissertation on the German romantics. Its specification of the relationship between these two spheres is wholly consistent with the attempt on the part of the earlier study to annihilate criticism as an *evaluative* discipline which takes its bearings from arbitrarily determined external standards and to reestablish it as an *immanent, work-centered* undertaking, in line with the conception originally elaborated by Friedrich Schlegel. As Benjamin explains in the dissertation: "Criticism should do nothing else than uncover the secret predispositions of the work itself, complete its hidden intentions. According to the meaning of the work itself, i.e., as its reflexion, it should proceed beyond the work and thereby make it absolute. This much is clear: for the romantics criticism is much less the evaluation of a work than the method of its completion."[27] In this way, Schlegel sought to free art from all heteronomous, rationalist aesthetic prejudices by turning the internal construction of the work of art itself into the standard of aesthetic judgment as a "medium of reflexion." By dispensing with all universal concepts such as "harmony" and "organization," Schlegel thereby "secured on behalf of the object or work-side that autonomy in the realm of art which Kant had conferred on the faculty of judgment in its critique."[28] Benjamin's radical dissatisfaction with all subjectivist philosophical doctrines thus extends to Kant's attempt in the Third *Critique* to ground aesthetics in the standpoint of the observer or recipient rather than in terms of the work of art itself.

Elsewhere Benjamin presents the following parable to describe the kindred relation between the work of art and philosophy:

Simile: one learns to know a young person who is handsome and attractive, yet, who appears to conceal a secret within. It would be indelicate and objectionable to use force to pry it from him. However, it is permissible to inquire whether he has brothers or sisters and whether their character and nature could to some extent explain to us the mysterious nature of the stranger. It is precisely in this way that the true critic inquires after the brothers and sisters of the work of art. And every work of art has its sibling (brother or sister?) in a philosophical domain.[29]

Constellation, Origin, Monad

Adorno once described the theory of knowledge elaborated in the Prologue to the *Trauerspiel* study as a "metaphysical salvation of nominalism."[30] In this albeit extremely terse characterization, he nevertheless has identified the fundamental paradox of Benjamin's epistemological strivings: the attempt to reestablish the discipline of metaphysics, and thereby secure access to the noumenal world, through an approach which not only undertakes a far-reaching critique of the identitarian biases of rationalism—

a critique of the belief that the being of the object would of necessity correspond a priori to the structure of the concept—but which also gives full due to the Kantian admonition concerning the need for philosophy to remain within the bounds of phenomenal experience. Thus, his relentless philosophical will to transcendence is at the same time linked to a "thinking that is so bound up with its material that it, paradoxically, draws near empirical methods, to 'experience.'"[31] For Benjamin, "truth content can only be grasped through the most precise immersion in the details of a material content."[32]

Nowhere is Benjamin's undying concern with the idea of redemption more evident than in the Prologue. The concept of experience he strives to present seeks to approximate the fullness of theological experience, and thus the suspicion of dogmatism can never be entirely scotched. However, it is never a *positive* image of redemption that one finds reproduced in his writings; rather, by viewing the world from the standpoint of a hypothetical intelligible realm, it is his intention to set its degraded condition in relief all the more vividly. The "as if" character of Benjamin's philosophical perspective is therefore thoroughly radical in its intransigent refusal to brook compromise with any theoretical outlook that would rest content to maintain a this-worldly point of view. Even if it in fact fails to possess the absolute, it falls due to philosophy to criticize that which exists just as relentlessly as if it really did speak from the vantage point of the unconditioned. Once again, it was Adorno—whose conception of "negative dialectics" represents the most consequential, albeit "secularized," appropriation of Benjamin's philosophical legacy—who recognized better than anyone else the virtue and necessity of this methodological practice when he observed:

The only philosophy which can be responsibly practiced in face of despair is to contemplate all things as they would present themselves from the standpoint of redemption. Knowledge has no light but that shed on the world by redemption: all else is reconstruction, mere technique. Perspectives must be fashioned that displace and estrange the world, reveal it to be, with its rifts and crevices, as it will appear one day in the messianic light. To gain such perspectives without velleity or violence, entirely from felt contact with its objects—this alone is the task of thought. It is the simplest of all things, because the situation calls imperatively for such knowledge, indeed because consummate negativity, once squarely faced, delineates the mirror-image of its opposite. But it is also the utterly impossible thing, because it presupposes a standpoint removed, even by a hair's breadth, from the scope of existence, whereas we well know that any possible knowledge must not only be first wrested from what is, if it shall hold good, but is also marked, for this very reason, by the same distortion and indigence it seeks to escape.[33]

It is therefore the *redemption* of the phenomena under investigation that Benjamin's theory of knowledge desires: if not their *actual* redemption, their *symbolic* redemption. The method he employs to achieve this end he describes as thinking in "constellations." By regrouping the material elements of phenomena in a philosophically informed constellation, an idea will emerge and the phenomena will thereby stand redeemed. In this way Benjamin seeks to transpose the technique of redemptive critique from the domain of criticism to that of epistemology. "Ideas are timeless constellations, and by virtue of the elements' being seen as points in such constellations, phenomena are subdivided and at the same time redeemed," he observes.[34] Ideas thus acquire a paradoxical status insofar as they are said to emerge from the empirical world, and yet at the same time they are deemed full-fledged members of the intelligible world. In this dual status of ideas rests the fundamental contradictory striving of Benjamin's theory of knowledge: to force the phenomenal sphere itself to yield noumenal truth. For on the one hand, the idea is declared to be "preexistent": it "belongs to a fundamentally different world from that which it apprehends."[35] On the other hand, ideas are denied an existence independent of phenomenal reality: "For ideas are not represented in themselves, but solely and exclusively in an arrangement of concrete elements in the concept: as the configuration of these elements."[36] The precise nature of the relationship between phenomena and ideas is suggested by Benjamin's claim that the ideas serve the end of "a representation of phenomena," they are "the objective interpretation of phenomena." As such, he seeks to illustrate their relationship through the following bold analogy: "Ideas are to objects as constellations are to stars."[37] And as the "representation" or "objective interpretation" of phenomena, ideas do not thereby acquire "knowledge" of the latter: rather, they effectuate their *redemption*.

The distinction between knowledge as a profane operation of mind and the noncognitive apprehension of phenomena characteristic of Messianic insight, a distinction which played so large a role in the 1916 essay "On Language," also becomes constitutive for the theory of knowledge of the *Trauerspiel* book. Benjamin is adamant that an idea in no way contributes to *knowledge* of phenomena: "The question of whether it comprehends what it apprehends, in the way in which the concept genus includes the species, cannot be regarded as a criterion of its existence."[38] Ideas therefore are less concerned with comprehending phenomena in the conventional sense than they are with the task of "representing" or "interpreting" phenomena as if they were being viewed from the standpoint of redeemed life. Benjamin identifies "knowledge" with the misplaced philosophical preoccupation with method, which dates from the time of Descartes. The goal of knowledge is the *possession* of objects and not their emancipation. Knowledge, in this sense identical with the Nietzschean "will to power," will stop at nothing to reach this end, and its preferred technique, from the Cartesian cogito to the transcendental ego of Kant and Husserl, has been the imperious assertion of the primacy of the knowing subject over the object to be known; a practice which falls victim to the logical fallacy of assuming what is eminently mediated—consciousness—is authentic immediacy.[39] The desire to avoid this fallacy accounts for the persistent and unyielding anti-subjectivism of Benjamin's philosophical standpoint, which is evident in his castigation of all attempts to turn the being of ideas into an object of "intuition" (*Anschauung*), either in the Kantian sense or according to the Husserlian program of an "intuition of essence" (*Wesenerschauung*). For Benjamin, truth is not something which can be grasped by the intentionality of the knowing subject; on the contrary, it "is an intentionless state of being. The proper approach to it is not therefore one of intention and knowledge, but rather a total immersion and absorption in it. Truth is the death of intention."[40]

Knowledge is the medium of the concept, whereas the medium of the idea is truth. Although they embody qualitatively opposed forms of cognition, there is nevertheless a point of contact between them: it falls due to the concepts of knowledge to achieve the rearrangement of phenomenal elements in the constellation, and in this way it participates in a subordinate manner, in the process whereby ideas become manifest. It is through this function alone, when subordinated to the imperatives of the higher "realm of ideas," that the concepts of knowledge prove capable of divesting themselves of their profane, merely analytic character: "Conceptual distinctions are above all suspicion of destructive sophistry only when their purpose is the salvation of phenomena in ideas."[41] For conceptual knowledge proceeds by way of division and dispersal; in and of itself it remains incapable of providing the moment of "collection" which Plato, in his description of the art of dialectic in the *Sophist*, deemed equally important, the moment which alone can account for the *unity* that remains essential to the idea of truth. Nevertheless, the analytical activity of concepts possesses an important role in Benjamin's schema insofar as: "Phenomena do not . . . enter into the realm of ideas whole, in their crude empirical state, adulterated by appearances, but only in their basic elements, redeemed."[42] Hence, concepts are charged with the indispensable propaedeutic task of dissolving phenomena into their individual elements, a task which serves as a necessary prerequisite for their ultimate admittance into the world of ideas, the homeland of truth. As Benjamin remarks at one point: "It is the function of concepts to group phenomena together, and the division which is brought about within them thanks to the differentiating power of the understanding is all the more significant in that it brings about two things at a single stroke: the redemption of phenomena and the representation of ideas."[43]

The concepts of the understanding in this way function as the *emissaries* of the noumenal realm in the subaltern world of phenomenal being. The mediating function of conceptual knowledge is crucial in the philosophical construction of constellations, insofar as truth, which remains something *ideal*, is precisely on that account forbidden from entering into immediate contact with the unredeemed world of appearances. It is only upon being dissolved into their constituent elements that phenomena are first rendered fit for the ultimate philosophical reordering in the redemptive embrace of the constellation, for the latter consists of nothing more than the simple rearrangement of these elements themselves. In this respect it resembles the Jewish descriptions of the Messianic realm, according to which everything would be the same and only different in a trifle.[44] The production of constellations from which an idea will emerge relies on the sheer, immediate power of representation alone and is thus devoid of all subjective intentionality and mediation. As Benjamin observes: "The structure of truth, then, demands a mode of being which in its lack of intentionality resembles the simple existence of things, but which is superior in its permanence. Truth itself is not an intent which realizes itself in empirical reality; it is the power which determines the essence of this reality."[45]

For Benjamin, then, the authentic task of philosophy consists of a hypothetical description of the world of ideas. This has been the objective of all great philosophical systems, which, even once they become anachronistic in terms of the specific terminology and material content of their respective conceptual edifices, remain relevant insofar as they are understood not as depictions of the empirical world but of the a-temporal world of ideas.

To be sure, the Neo-Platonic tenor of the theory of knowledge set forth in the *Trauerspiel* book risks above all heralding a reconciliation of existence and essence, of phenomenon and truth, which would be premature and illusory. Only by virtue of a consummate theoretical balancing act can Benjamin avoid an outright contravention of the theological *Bilderverbot* and prevent his theory of knowledge from succumbing to the same false reconciliation to which idealist doctrines have fallen victim in the past.[46] It is a fate he escapes in part, because his is really more of a *negative* theory of knowledge than a positive one: it is a program whose realization in truth would first fall due to a resurrected humanity and therefore remains in its essentials unfulfillable in the here and now. For this reason it assumes more the character of an "infinite task" or a "regulative ideal" in the Kantian sense than that of a concrete program demanding immediate completion. On the one hand, Benjamin remains acutely sensitive to the identitarian prejudices of rationalism, to the philosophical willingness, from Parmenides to Hegel, to grant precedence to the universal over the particular, the one over the many, the hypostatized general concept over the individual in the fullness of its concrete positivity; and it is as a result of this awareness that he insists on the necessity of allowing the idea to emerge in a purely immanent fashion—i.e., from a concrete constellation of philosophically reconstituted material elements. On the other hand, he nevertheless situates his theory of knowledge squarely within the legacy of Western metaphysics, drawing especially from the Platonic doctrine of anamnesis and the Leibnizian theory of monadology.

His theoretical reliance on the metaphysical tradition becomes especially apparent in his employment of the categories of "origin" and "monad" to illustrate the being of ideas. Through the concept of origin, Benjamin attempts both to ensure the actuality of ideas in empirical reality and to account for their relation to history. Origin, Benjamin claims, is a historical category, yet it has nothing to do with the idea of genesis, i.e., with the idea of the emergence of a given phenomenon at a determinate moment in time. Instead origin refers to a history of a different type: not empirical history, in which the inessential being of the phenomenon persists in its mere facticity, unredeemed, but a type of *essential history*, in which the phenomenon stands revealed as it will one day in the light of Messianic fulfillment. The "origins" of this concept for Benjamin are twofold. It derives, firstly, from Kabbalistic lore, according to which origin inherently contains a teleological dimension. It represents an original condition of harmony and perfection (paradise), which is subsequently squandered (the fall), yet ultimately recaptured (with the advent of the Messianic era), though not in the static sense of a simple return, but in a return which simultaneously unleashes and actualizes a superior potential latent in origin to begin with. In this sense origin constitutes a return which is simultaneously a qualitative leap beyond the original condition of perfection, its realization on a higher plane. Thus, Benjamin remarks at one point, "On the one hand [origin] needs to be recognized as a process of restoration and re-establishment, but, on the other hand, and precisely because of this, as something imperfect and incomplete."[47] Secondly, it derives from Goethe's discussion of the "*Urphänomen*" in the *Farbenlehre*, a notion Benjamin claims to have transferred from the pagan domain of nature to the Jewish-theological domain of history. As he explains:

While studying Simmel's presentation of Goethe's concept of truth, especially in view of his excellent commentary on the *Urphänomen*, it became irrefutably clear to me that my concept of origin in the *Trauerspiel* book is a rigorous and compelling transposition of this fundamental Goethean concept from the realm of nature to that of history. "Origin": that is the concept of *Urphänomen* as something theologically and historically different, theologically and historically living, transposed to the Jewish historical context from the pagan natural context. "Origin": that is the *Urphänomen* in the theological sense. Only in this way can it satisfy the concept of authenticity.[48]

And thus in an earlier draft of the "Prologue," in which its underlying theological impulses are far less muted, Benjamin makes the following claim for the concept of origin. "Everything original appears only as a determinate being in a twofold sense: everything original is an uncompleted restoration of revelation. . . . Were it not to rediscover itself in revelation, then no sign of its original character [*Ursprünglichkeit*] would be present."[49]

Benjamin refers to the criterion of "authenticity" as "the central feature of the idea of origin," as "the hallmark of origin in phenomena."[50] By this designation he wishes to emphasize that every original phenomenon possesses a uniqueness which differentiates it from the majority of empirical phenomena we encounter in history; although at the same time, he stresses the fact that as opposed to certain idealist doctrines, the element of historical becoming represents an inalienable feature of origin: "There takes place in every original phenomenon a determination of the form in which an idea will constantly confront the historical world, until it is revealed fulfilled, in the totality of its history."[51] The concept of origin therefore *subsumes* history, as opposed to "unoriginal" phenomena which remain at the mercy of history, and thus unredeemed. In this way the category of origin signifies an important anticipation of the category of now-time in the 1940 "Theses on the Philosophy of History," which is also endowed with the capacity to transcend the unfulfilled continuum of historical life.

Though the discussion of the relationship between origin, authenticity, and history transpires on a discursive plane which remains incrediby terse and abstract, it nevertheless possesses an extremely precise and determinate relevance for the methodological construction of the *Trauerspiel* book as whole. Specifically, in his reinterpretation of Goethe's concept of *Urphänomen*, Benjamin substitutes *works of art* for *plants*; and thus instead of searching for the foundations of natural history in terms of individual *Urpflanze* as Goethe does, he seeks to identify those few precious and unique works of art which both serve as the ultimate models for other works of a given genre and offer privileged access to the supra-historical world of ideas. As we have already indicated, in its conventional forms literary history employs the concept of genre merely to deduce the *average* representative and its traits; as opposed to this method, Benjamin, in his quest for works of art which are at the same time *exemplary, standard-bearers,* and thus *origins*, looks not at the average type but toward the *extremes*: toward "the most singular and eccentric of phenomena, . . . the weakest and clumsiest experiments and the overripe fruits of a period of decadence."[52] Only a standpoint which remains willing to acknowledge the extremes would be capable of grasping the uniqueness and unconventional majesty of a genre such as *Trauerspiel*. The work of art as origin: herein lies the *telos* of Benjamin's conception of criticism. For if it is "authentic," it will contain, foreshortened, the entire past and subsequent history of an art form within itself, collected magically into a totality, a focal point, as it were. It will thereby serve as living proof of the thesis that the universal must be deduced from *within* the boundaries of the particular. It is in this sense that the following essential insight must be understood: "It is . . . precisely the more significant works, inasmuch as they are not the first and, so to speak, ideal embodiments of the genre, which fall outside the limits of the genre. A major work will either establish the genre or abolish it; and the perfect work will do both."[53] The relationship of *Trauerspiel* to classical tragedy must be perceived from this point of view.

The category of "monad" serves as an additional illustration of the being and specificity of the idea. Like origin, the monad knows history not in terms of its extensive empirical being, but as something *integral* and *essential*: "Its history is inward in character and is not to be understood as something boundless, but as something related to essential being, and it can therefore be described as the past and subsequent history of this being. The past and subsequent history of such essences is, as a sign of their redemption or collection in the preserve of the world of ideas, not pure history, but natural history."[54] "Once this redeemed state of the being of the idea is established, then the presence of the inauthentic—that is to say natural historical—past and subsequent history is virtual. It is no longer pragmatically real, but, as natural history, is to be inferred from the state of completion and rest, from the essence."[55] The concept of monad thus redefines the mission of philosophy in the traditional sense: "to establish the becoming of phenomena in their being."[56] In this way the concept of monad prefigures Benjamin's later materialist theory of Dialectical Images (also known as Dialectic at a Standstill), in which the course of history—now, no longer "essential" history, but *real* history—is frozen into an image in order thereby to demystify it in its natural giveness and thus make it serviceable for concrete revolutionary ends.

The relationship to historical becoming characteristic of origin and monad is therefore identical. Both dissolve history as something transient and immediate; by virtue of the recrystallization of its elements in the constellation of the idea it is elevated to the level of the universal, so to speak. The end result of this process is the *redemption* of individual historical phenomena. As Benjamin remarks at one point: "There is no analogy between the relationship of the individual to the idea, and its [the individual's] relationship to the concept; in the latter case it falls under the aegis of the concept and remains what it was: an individuality; in the former it stands in the idea, and becomes something different: a totality. That is Platonic 'redemption.'"[57] The discussion of monad, however, does add one important new dimension to the understanding of ideas, a dimension suggested by the term's Leibnizian basis: the monad contains "an indistinct abbreviation of the rest of the world of ideas, just as, according to Leibniz's *Discourse on Metaphysics* (1686), every single monad contains, in an indistinct way, all the others."[58] Or as Benjamin observes in the same context: "The idea is a monad—that means briefly: every idea contains the image of the world. The purpose of the representation of the idea is nothing less than an abbreviated outline of this image of the world."[59] The concept of monad therefore attempts to stress the irreducible individuality of the ideas as opposed to their traditional hierarchical ordering within the philosophical system:

Ideas subscribe to the law which states: all essences exist in complete and immaculate independence, not only from phenomena, but, especially from each other. Just as the harmony of the spheres depends on the orbits of the stars which do not come into contact with each another, so the existence of the *mundus intelligibilus* depends on the unbridgeable distance between pure essences. Every idea is a sun and is related to other ideas just as suns are related to each other.[60]

By characterizing the idea as an "image," Benjamin seeks to emphasize the importance of a sensuous-intuitive view of the whole, a view which attempts to facilitate the representation of the nonidentical, the nonconceptual, the moment which traditional metaphysics has suppressed owing to the inordinate value it has placed on an access to truth which is exclusively *categorical*. A concern with the *image-character* of truth would become a permanent feature of Benjamin's philosophical discourse in all its phases; for in this way he sought to confer equal rank to the *spatial* aspect of truth and thereby do justice to the moment of representation which is obscured once truth is viewed solely as a logical phenomenon. His persistent terminological asceticism, his withdrawal before the so-called "great concepts" of philosophy, would thus lead in his writings to an extremely fruitful contrasting emphasis on the metaphorical side of language; and also, as Adorno has observed, to an emphasis on "those things which were not embraced by [the historical dynamic of victory and defeat], which fell by the wayside—what might be called the waste products and blind spots which have escaped the dialectic. . . . Benjamin's writings are an attempt in ever new ways to make philosophically fruitful what has not yet been foreclosed by great intentions."[61]

The disquieting aspect of the theory of ideas, however, is that in both the origin and the monad real historical life evaporates into the chimerical realm of an "essential history." This approach would be remedied only in Benjamin's later theory of the Dialectical Image, in which determinate aspects of social life themselves form the material content of the ideational constellations, and the redemption of these phenomena or material elements is no longer guaranteed in advance either by Platonic anamnesis or a Leibnizian prestabilized harmony ("The idea is a monad—the prestabilized representation of phenomena resides within it").[62] Instead, the prospect of redemption is transposed to the realm of historical praxis, where the historical character of phenomena is no longer idealistically remystified and where a priori guarantees of reconciliation are nonexistent. Yet, for Benjamin, to surrender historical being entirely to the capricious interplay of secular forces would be tantamount to a total capitulation before contingency. Thus, he was never able in his theoretical work to break completely with the Messianic philosophy of history of his early period, which remains forever latent in his thinking as a hedge against despair.

Benjamin's theory of knowledge can circumvent the charge of providing an illusory—i.e., merely conceptual—reconciliation with a still antagonistic empirical world by virtue of the *symbolic* status he attributes to the redemptive ideas of the Prologue. As symbols the ideas assume a crucial ideological-critical function: by virtue of their "superior" character, they relentlessly unmask and excoriate the deficient state of the world as mere—i.e., unredeemed—being; and they also thereby take on an equally significant *anticipatory* role: by virtue of their noncoercive, intentionless relation to phenomena, they prefigure a world in which the heteronomous reign of necessity would be dissolved and the realm of freedom would truly come into its own; a state in which potentiality and actuality, existence and essence, the real and the rational, would for the first time coincide. He would therefore be the first to concede—though on the basis of theological conviction—that the attainment of reconciliation falls outside the province of the philosopher, who deals with phenomena externally, through the technique and cunning of conceptual logic, in order, as it were, to entrap the "in itself" of things. In fact, not only can the separation between meaning and thing not be eliminated by merely conceptual means, insofar as the word, the concept, is merely receptive and not productive, but the deficiency of conceptual knowledge in this regard is itself a primary symptom of the original breach between name and thing, and thus fully powerless to address it. For this reason Benjamin's theory of knowledge might be termed a *negative* theory of knowledge, insofar as it remains acutely illusion-free concerning the inadequacies of mere knowledge vis-à-vis the lacerated condition of the empirical world as such. Thus, it does not desire as much to provide concrete images of fulfillment in the here and now, as it, in full respect for the *Bilderverbot*, seeks unremittingly to expose and unfold the distorted nature of reality such as it is, in order thereby to accentuate the desperate need for its imminent transformation.

In this respect those who have, like Hannah Arendt, sought to link Benjamin to the Heideggerian tradition err greatly: it is less sheer being in its ontological immediacy that he seeks to exalt than a being which has never yet been. And while both thinkers show a deep concern with the linguistic being of truth, Benjamin would no doubt have found the existentialist's drastic attempt to revamp the traditional language of philosophy as abhorrent. "In philosophy . . . it is a dubious undertaking to introduce new terminologies," he once observed. "Such terminologies—abortive denominative processes in which intention plays a greater part than language—lack that objectivity which history has endowed the principal formulations of philosophical reflections."[63] Moreover, those theorists of a materialist persuasion who would scoff presumptively at Benjamin's naïve employment of idealist phraseology would do well instead to contemplate the manner in which the prohibition against interpreting the world has historically degenerated into a *prohibition against reflection in general*, as diamat Marxism turns into a "science of legitimation" (O. Negt) in the lands of "really existing socialism." What is overlooked all too readily by the apostles of scientific socialism—whose Messianic historical terminus is guaranteed in advance by the apocalyptic momentum of productive forces alone—is that what Marx originally intended was not the vulgar *elimination* of idealist philosophy, but rather the authentic transposition of its ideals to reality—i.e., the *realization of philosophy*—and thus its *dialectical Aufhebung*. The effort to fan the waning fire of those ideals in an era in which the ideology of technocracy has become the credo of bureaucratic socialism and state-managed capitalism alike thus becomes, paradoxically, a genuinely radical practice.

Ultimately, it is the theological philosophy of language as originally formulated by Benjamin in 1916 which serves as the underlying basis for the theory of knowledge of the *Trauerspiel* book; nor would it be unfair to suggest that it was this philosophy of language which provided the metatheoretical underpinnings for the entirety of his early work. It is, then, the "intentionless being" of the divine name which Benjamin seeks to approximate in his theory of ideas: a condition of pure restfulness, harmony, and unity in which there is no need of analytic conceptual insight to contrive a forced reconciliation between word and thing. As something which lies beyond all intention, truth is the power which determines the essence of empirical reality; and the "state of being, beyond all phenomenality, to which alone this power belongs, is that of the name. This determines the manner in which ideas are given. But they are not so much given in a primordial language as in a primordial form of perception, in which words possess their own nobility as names, unimpaired by cognitive meaning."[64] As something beyond all merely cognitive insight, the name exists beyond all relations of domination, in which words have been degraded to the level of a means of communication, a tool of commerce. To conceive of words as names is a polemical act directed against a bourgeois society predicated on the principles of calculation and utility—i.e., the idea of universal being-for-other—and the name, by virtue of its sheer lack of intention, thereby prefigures a condition of universal being-for-self, where things will be united once more with their proper meanings—and thus redeemed. It is for this reason that Benjamin, in a provocative twist, deems Adam, not Plato, the "father of philosophy":

In philosophical contemplation the idea is released from the heart of reality, reclaiming its name-giving right. Ultimately, however, this is not the attitude of Plato, but the attitude of Adam, the father of the human race and the father of philosophy. Adam's action of naming things is so far removed from play or caprice that it actually confirms the state of paradise as a state in which there is no need to struggle with the communicative significance of words. Ideas are displayed, without intention, in the act of naming, and they have to be renewed in philosophical contemplation. In this renewal the primordial mode of apprehending words is restored.[65]

Like Platonic ideas, which were in effect little more than deified words or verbal concepts, "The idea is something linguistic, indeed, it is that moment in the essence of the word in which it is a symbol."[66] As a symbol, the unity between word and thing which the idea purports to present cannot be an actual or empirical unity, but merely an *anticipatory unity*, and it falls due to philosophical reflection to attempt to approximate this unity in its strivings. The symbolic aspect of the word always lies concealed beneath its profane, cognitive meaning—the meaning it assumes in its everyday practical employment where it is implicated in a network of heteronomous functional relationships; and it becomes the mission of philosophy to resuscitate this lost and occluded symbolic dimension of language, which provides a foretaste of the realm of redemption. In this way it is the intentionless, expressive, representational side of linguistic being that Benjamin seeks to recapture, that side of language which has been repressed by virtue of the contemporary hegemony of the denotive, communicative, functional utilization of language. He expresses this insight as follows:

In empirical perception, in which words have become fragmented, they possess, in addition to their more or less hidden, symbolic aspect, an obvious profane meaning. It is the task of the philosopher to restore, by representation, the primacy of the symbolic character of the word, in which the idea is given self-consciousness, and that is the opposite of all outwardly-directed communication. Since philosophy may not presume to speak in the tones of revelation, this can only be achieved by recalling in memory the primordial form of perception.[67]

Thus as Tiedemann has noted, "If all science is concerned exclusively with the intention to communicate the meaning of the real, for Benjamin the task of science is to cast off the 'oppressive and alien meaning' with which things have been burdened and which alienates them. . . . in the symbol historically repressed and forgotten nature should be assisted to a condition of permanence."[68]

As symbolic entities, in their essential anticipatory structure, the ideas of the Prologue bear an important resemblance to the symbolic utopian images of Bloch's philosophy. Both Bloch and Benjamin view traditional metaphysics as a vast, heretofore un-tapped wealth of utopian semantic potentials, and thus for both thinkers it is the task of reflection to attempt to redeem the latter by making them relevant for the present. In their reliance on the legacy of metaphysics, in their mutual willingness to cede to the realm of ideas an existence independent of phenomenal reality, they have not so much relapsed into a pre-Marxian, idealist po-sition, as they have attempted to accentuate the historical non-identity between subject and object, between the real and the ideal—a fact which differentiates their speculative thinking markedly from idealism in its classical Hegelian form. For Benjamin as well as Bloch, the symbolic character of ideas is representative of a *Messianic* relation to reality: it seeks both to reveal reality in its indigence and to assist it—though only symbolically—to an im-manent condition of perfection or fulfillment. In this connection, Hans Heinz Holz has attempted, with reference to Marx's "Theses on Feuerbach," to show in an extremely fruitful way how Ben-jamin's theory of ideas might be made serviceable for an enlight-ened materialist understanding of history. As is well known, in the "Theses" the chief object of Marx's attack was Feuerbach's static, inert, *contemplative* materialism; and it is, in contrast, *idealism* he credits above all with having developed the *"active* side" of the dialectic.[69] Holz's reflections proceed from an analogous conviction:

The more theory and practice approximate one another, in order finally to combine in a unity, to pass over into each other, the more the idea loses its idealist tinge and becomes an integral moment in the great equivalence of consciousness and being, man and nature, which is at-tained in the humanization of nature and the naturalization of man. However, because the being-thus of the idea as *Ordo* already anticipates this solution, i.e., it contains within itself archetypically, as it were, utopian existence and thus refers to the latter allegorically, one should interpret ideas (as the wish-architecture and wish-landscape of spirit) again and again in terms of their wish-content, their utopian kernel. The idea establishes itself at the border where the real transforms itself into the possible. That this possible contrasts itself to the real as not-being [*Nichtsein*] (and in no way as nothing [*Nichts*]) constitutes the ideal character of the idea. Yet, because possible being is the latent *being* of a nonexisting thing, the idea is capable of being the objective interpretation of the world: namely, the interpretation of its objective possibilities.[70]

It is precisely in these terms that the relevance of Benjamin's theory of knowledge—as well as that of speculative thought in general—should be sought today.

Chapter Four

FROM MESSIANISM
TO MATERIALISM

DESPITE ITS pronounced esotericism, Benjamin's early literary criticism is consistent, at times single-minded, in the pursuit of its program. At issue is the "fallen" character of human history, which takes on the appearance of *"natural history,"* a history that is consigned to an inexorable fate of decay and decline. The subjective corollary of this fate is inescapable network of guilt which originates with man's expulsion from Paradise and which serves as a ceaseless testimony to the seemingly infinite distance that separates historical man from the state of grace represented by the Messianic era. Benjamin takes his stand, initially, in the midst of profane life. And from his lowly station in the fallen historical world, he sifts through the ruins of bygone ages for traces of redeemed life in the hope that if these traces can be renewed for the present, the link between the Messianic era, the key to which is mysteriously inscribed in man's past, and the present era, however godforsaken it may appear, can be, if not guaranteed, at least prevented from fading into oblivion. The paradox, the magic, the labor of Sisyphus of Benjamin's early aesthetics consisted in his effort to conjure images of "Messianic time" in the midst of an iniquitous historical era that could only seem emphatically removed from all hope of salvation.

In contrast, the aesthetic concerns of the later Benjamin are hardly so univocal in character. They traverse a spectrum ranging from a rather narrow historical materialist approach to understanding cultural phenomena ("Paris of the Second Empire in Baudelaire" and "Eduard Fuchs: Historian and Collector") and an urgent appeal for the necessity of a direct surrender of art to the imperatives of political-pedagogic aims ("The Work of Art in the Age of Mechanical Reproduction" and "The Author as Producer"), to a rather nostalgic chronicle of and lament over the disappearance of historically outmoded, community-rooted forms of artistic communication, such as the epic, story-telling, and lyric poetry ("The Storyteller: Reflections on the Work of Nikolai Leskov" and "On Some Motifs in Baudelaire") to, finally, the reemergence of theological motifs identical to those of his early period ("On the Mimetic Faculty," "Kafka," and the seminal "Theses on the Philosophy of History").[1] The multiplicity of concerns, the plurality of methodological approaches that characterize the thought of the later Benjamin account for the differing portraits of him that have emerged with the recent availability of his *Gesammelte Schriften* in nearly its entirety and the often acrimonious debate over which is the *authentic* Benjamin, the "materialist" or "theological."[2] The lack of consensus accurately reflects the dilemmas posed by the conflicting political choices which forced themselves on Benjamin. Indeed, given the turbulence of the political era through which he lived—from the economic and political tumult of Weimar, to the rise of National Socialism, to the consolidation of the Hitler–Stalin pact—politics intruded on Benjamin's life from without. That Benjamin, who was apparently so maladept at practical matters—as is shown from his failed *Habilitationsschrift* to his unfortunate death on the Franco-Spanish frontier in 1940[3]—was thrust into the political arena, albeit as a man of letters, accounts for the "experimental" approach of many of his later projects (in many ways, he always considered his flirtation with Marxist principles over the last fifteen years of his life as a kind of experiment), the loss of unity as compared with his earlier work, and—it must be said—in certain instances, a correspondent diminution in quality.

Radical Communism

The ultimate motives behind Benjamin's sudden fascination with the materialist conception of history can in a certain measure be reconstructed hypothetically, but perhaps will never be known with certainty. Until an eventful encounter with Ernst Bloch and Asja Lacis during a sojourn on Capri in the spring and summer of 1924, and an intensive study of Lukács's *History and Class Consciousness* ("an extraordinary collection of Lukács's political writings")[4] in the following year, Benjamin led a life that was remarkably apolitical. As we have noted previously, his early participation in the German Youth Movement was morally rather than politically motivated;[5] and it appears that the failure of this experience only further reinforced his innate distrust of organized political involvement. Benjamin was a bitter opponent of World War I; but Scholem has cautioned against viewing him as a pacifist on this account: it was *this war* in particular to which Benjamin objected, and not violence in general[6]—a fact which is supported by his provocative early study "Critique of Violence" (1921), which shows a profound indebtedness to the teachings of Georges Sorel.[7] His distaste for the war led him to sympathize with the position of the leaders of the Social Democratic left, Karl Liebknecht and Rosa Luxemburg, who, unlike the rest of the party, had voted against the war credits act of August 1914; but he never appears to have seriously entertained the idea of translating these sentiments into a determinate form of political commitment. He was largely oblivious to the monumental political convulsions that shook Germany and Europe following World War I: the Hungarian Soviet Republic, which he considered a "childish error," interested him only insofar as it was rumored to have endangered the life of one of Bloch's friends, Georg Lukács; and his attitude toward the Bavarian Soviet Republic was also marked by indifference.[8] A telling indication of the level of Benjamin's political development at this time is Scholem's report that he had come more and more to view a recently published volume of Dostoyevsky's political writings as the most significant political document of the modern age.[9]

In addition to the fundamental question of the reason for Benjamin's turn toward historical materialism, a more specific question presents itself: why is it that Benjamin escaped politicization at the seemingly most logical moment, i.e., at the time of the great shock-wave of workers' republics (in Hungary, Bavaria, and Russia) that swept Europe following the war (the time when

Lukács underwent his great conversion), and arrived at a materialist perspective only some seven years later, when the revolutionary swell had all but evaporated? It is almost inconceivable that he would wholly decline to take a stand at this critical historical juncture when, as Sandor Radnoti remarks, "Germany, his homeland, either in theory or in practice, plays out virtually all its historical possibilities, from social democratic collapse in 1914, through the short-lived alternative of Soviet government in 1918, the tragic experiment of the small revolutionary avant-garde, Spartacus, and the Bavarian soviet republic to the liberal solution of the social-democratic bourgeois compromise."[10]

A partial answer to this question is that at this point in his development, Benjamin's allegiance to Germany as a political entity was less important than his identification with the cultural tradition with which Germany was associated. For Benjamin thought of himself, above all, as an intellectual and a man of letters—and a Jewish one at that—which goes far toward explaining his refusal to embrace the various political options which presented themselves in the years immediately following the war. Forced to the margins of society as a Jewish intellectual, Benjamin felt its disintegration no less acutely. Yet, as an outsider,[11] his response to the crisis necessarily took on a more esoteric character: the theologically oriented method of "redemptive criticism" that characterizes his work through the *Trauerspiel* study; a method whose philosophy of history condemned history *in toto* as categorically *incapable of fulfillment*, and instead directed its hopes to the purifying powers of the suprahistorical Messianic age. This was the solution Benjamin discovered in his personal search for wholeness, his philosophical response to the lacerated condition of war-ravaged Europe. The dilemma of his position as a Jewish intellectual is perhaps best expressed in these revealing observations of 1923: "In the most horrible moments of a people's history, only those who belong to it are called upon to speak, and no one else: only those who belong to it in the most eminent sense, those in a position to say not only *mea res agitur*, but also *propriam rem ago*. Certainly, the Jew must not speak."[12]

As a Jewish intellectual, Benjamin understandably felt alienated from the destiny of the German nation, and thus his spiritual energies sought an outlet that was nonpolitical, one more in conformity with his literary inclinations. Yet, before long the constraints of his own situation compelled him to view matters differently. In the early twenties, after experiencing a serious break with his parents, and with the onset of the catastrophic inflation of 1923, he found himself at the mercy of the general economic upheavals of the times. The withdrawal of monetary support on the part of his parents came as a special blow. For once Benjamin had decided to pursue a university career, he would have still been dependent upon them financially, since Jews were rarely granted professorships and thus could only hope to accede to the unpaid position of *Extraordinarius*.[13] Evidence suggests that rather early on Benjamin looked upon the entire effort to habilitate himself somewhat skeptically, insofar as at times he seems to have considered himself temperamentally unsuited to university life.[14] Thus, he was already contemplating other possibilities such as journalism or Jewish studies. The ultimate rejection of his *Habilitationsschrift* on *Trauerspiel* in the summer of 1925 was only the crowning blow, one which Benjamin had anticipated for some time. Therefore, he increasingly came to view himself as a member of Weimar's growing army of dispossessed intellectuals. In addition, the failure of his efforts to secure a teaching position had a very significant effect on the nature of his future literary output, not to mention its political slant. Now forced to lead a hand-to-mouth existence as a man of letters, Benjamin's major source of income was his activity as a *Publizist*, as a literary commentator for the major liberal publications of the Weimar period, among them the *Frankfurter Zeitung* and *Literarische Welt*, in which most of his work from 1925 to 1933 (when they were both shut down by Nazis) appeared.[15] Consequently, the majority of his work during this period took on the form of short book reviews and literary notes;[16] and his desire to produce great literary essays, after the model of his 1922 masterpiece on Goethe's *Elective Affinities*, was of necessity deferred.

The first significant indications of a serious turn to leftist politics on Benjamin's part appear in a letter to Scholem from Capri in July 1924, where he was engaged in writing the *Trauerspiel* book. Benjamin mentions that events have transpired that could be properly communicated only in the course of a face to face meeting with his friend; events which work, "not to the advantage of my dangerously interrupted work, nor to that of the bourgeois rhythm of life so indispensable for every such work, but absolutely to the advantage of an essential release and an intensive insight into the relevance of radical communism. I have made the acquaintance of a Russian revolutionary from Riga, one of the most remarkable women I have ever met."[17] The woman to whom he referred was the Latvian Bolshevik and assistant to Brecht, Asja Lacis, with whom Benjamin, now separated from his wife, had undoubtedly fallen in love.[18] It was in the course of conversations with her and Bloch, who was also residing in Capri at this time, that Benjamin's attraction toward "radical communism" was first catalyzed. It was Bloch who first recommended Lukács's monumental work, *History and Class Consciousness*, to Benjamin; and the book was to have a dramatic impact on him both politically and intellectually. In September of that year, he describes his initial reaction to Lukács's study in a letter to Scholem:

What struck me was the fact that Lukács, proceeding from political considerations to a theory of knowledge, at least in part—though perhaps not as extensively as I first assumed—arrives at principles which are very familiar to me and endorsed by me. In the realm of communism the problem of theory and praxis is posed in such a way that in spite of their real disparities, any definitive insight into theory is bound up with praxis. And I find it important that in Lukács this claim is in no way a bourgeois-democratic platitude but possesses a solid philosophical kernal. . . . As soon as possible I plan to study Lukács' book, and I must not deceive myself if in the debate with Hegelian concepts and the claims of the dialectic the fundament of my nihilism vis-à-vis communism (not as a theoretical problem but, above all, *as an obligatory mode of conduct*) appears to me in a different light than before.[19]

That Lukács's book exerted such an influence on Benjamin, not to mention so many other left-wing intellectuals of his generation during the mid-twenties, is not surprising. To begin with, the fundamental problems of Marxist thought were reconstructed in terms of the author's masterful grasp of their conceptual prehistory—i.e., in terms of the rich philosophical legacy of Kant and Hegel. The appeal of such an approach to philosophically trained intellectuals such as Benjamin, who could find few points of spiritual rapprochement with the economistic orientation of the reigning orthodox Marxism, was immediately apparent. Furthermore, in his analysis of the "Antinomies of Bourgeois Thought"—the central section of the brilliant chapter on "Reification and the Consciousness of the Proletariat"—Lukács delivered an overwhelming critique of the moribund and myopic bourgeois contemplative consciousness, whose *"post festum"* character doomed it to remain transfixed at the immediate, apparent level of capitalist social relations. His passionate indictment of the bourgeois philosophical world view surely forced many a young thinker to pause and seriously probe the contradiction between his habitual convictions and the realities of his life situation, which the former helped to disguise. In Benjamin's case, the confrontation with *History and Class Consciousness* undoubtedly caused him to call into question the esoteric basis of his early method of redemptive criticism and also to investigate the possibility of an epistemological guarantee of wholeness that was other than theological in origin.

Let us for a moment return to examine in some detail the contents of the September 1924 letter from Benjamin to Scholem just cited. Despite the brevity of his remarks, Benjamin betrays some highly revealing aspects of his attitude toward the issue of communism. First, he mentions that Lukács, "proceeding from political considerations to the theory of knowledge," arrives at principles which Benjamin himself had come upon, though presumably from another direction. That other direction can be none other than theology. In *History and Class Consciousness* Lukács begins from a determinate political situation—the "immediate," reified condition of the proletariat in a capitalist world whose governing principle is the reduction of living relations between men to dead relations between things—and proceeds, by way of a thorough confrontation with Kantian and Hegelian *Erkenntnistheorie*, to the resolution of that situation: historical materialism as the heir of classical German philosophy, the proletariat as the identical subject-object of history. The antinomies of bourgeois existence, of thought and being, ought and is, that are brought to consummate expression in the thought of Kant, and *aufgehoben* merely contemplatively in Hegel, for the first time can be *actually* overcome through the *praxis* of the proletariat. If the bourgeois world in its immediacy seems in itself unknowable from the point of view of the theory of knowledge (the perspective of bourgeois philosophy), the standpoint of the proletariat, the level of "essence," defetishizes that seemingly impenetrably immediacy to reveal itself as the absolute locus whereby that world is comprehensible as a *totality*.[20]

It is not mere coincidence that Benjamin reached analogous conclusions—though again, from a theological standpoint—in the course of his early essay on Kant.[21] There Benjamin protested against the hollow concept of experience presented by Kant—and by way of analogy, against the bourgeois world to which that concept of experience corresponded—and sought a "superior" concept of experience that would be capable of providing a unified perspective from which the antinomy-ridden Kantian world of experience would be knowable as a whole. Thus, his search for wholeness vis-à-vis the fragmented empirical world clearly parallels Lukács's quest for totality in *History and Class Consciousness*. Benjamin, to be sure, arrives at a very different conclusion: only a concept of experience that recognizes *religion* as its basis would be capable of surmounting the Kantian mechanical (i.e., natural scientific) view of the world. Yet, in the last analysis perhaps the perspectives of Benjamin and Lukács are not as utterly divergent as may at first appear, in light of the manifestly eschatological role with which Lukács entrusts the proletariat, history's chosen "identical subject-object." In face of the objective fragmentation of empirical reality both Lukács and Benjamin eventually arrive at a *metaphysical* point of reference through which reality would once again be comprehensible as a whole.[22]

However, what is especially noteworthy about the letter is the characteristically idiosyncratic attitude with which Benjamin approaches the idea of communism. Surprisingly, he admits that "in the debate with Hegelian concepts and claims of the dialectic" he fully expects the "fundament of [his] nihilism" concerning communism to surface. The pronounced skepticism displayed here is unquestionably a holdover from the basic distrust of *all* organized political movements dating back to the anarchist orientation of his early years. Yet, if Benjamin in this way prejudices his initial encounter with communist ideas, then what is the reason for the great enthusiasm which at the same time pervades the tone of this letter (as well as others of the same period)? The answer is to be found a few lines later, where he reveals that even if his old nihilism were to resurface, this would not change the fact that his attitude toward the "political praxis of communism" now "stands in a different [i.e., more positive] light than before." If even at this point, after his intensive discussions with Bloch and Lacis, Benjamin's appraisal of the actual *goals* of communism remains as cynical as ever, it is not, however, this aspect of the communist ideal that attracts him. Instead it is, above all, communism "as an obligatory mode of conduct" that seizes his imagination, the idea of communist praxis as the *historically appropriate embodiment of the categorical imperative*. In his article on Benjamin's political development, Radnoti expresses a similar insight: "Politics, which appears for the first time in Benjamin's thinking in 1924, is important not as politics, but as the adequate form of morally and philosophically decisive action."[23] In this sense, Benjamin's incipient attitude toward the communist movement parallels his relation to the German Youth Movement some ten years earlier. In both instances, political involvement mattered less as a means to a determinate end than as an autonomous, *moral* end in itself. Consequently, in Benjamin's diffidence vis-à-vis the concrete goals of communist politics, one detects strong vestiges of the same unyielding Kantian ethical standpoint which characterized his dealings with Wyneken's "Free School Community" in his early years.

Additional light is shed on the motivations behind Benjamin's adoption of communist principles as a compulsory ethical stance in an important letter to Scholem of May 29, 1926. Benjamin, currently engaged in the composition of *Einbahnstrasse*, begins by discussing the necessity he feels "to take leave of the purely theoretical sphere." There are only two ways, he continues, to go about this:

through religious or political conduct. Essentially, I would not admit to a difference between these two types of conduct. But neither is there an overlap [*Vermittlung*] between them. I am speaking of an identity which paradoxically, manifests itself in transformations of one into the other (in both directions); and the essential consideration is that every instance of action proceed ruthlessly, and, in its own self-understanding, radically. Therefore, the task is plainly not to decide once and for all, but rather at every moment. But what is essential is *to decide*. . . . If I one day were to join the Communist Party (which again would be dependent on a final push from chance), my own conviction would be to proceed radically, never consistently, in the most important matters. The possibility of my remaining a member is therefore to be determined experimentally; of interest and in question is not so much the yes or no, but how long? As far as certain irrefutable principles are concerned (e.g., the inadequate materialist metaphysic, or, in my view, also the insufficient materialist conception of history), in a serious case such brazen weapons can be used just as much for communism as against it. If, as you write, I have fallen "behind certain principles" . . . then "behind" means above all: whoever amongst our generation seriously feels and understands the present historical moment as a struggle cannot reject the study and praxis of that mechanism whereby things (and relations) and masses affect one another. It may be then that such a struggle, viewed from the standpoint of Judaism, proceeds altogether differently, disparately (but never hostilely). That cannot be helped: "justified," radical politics will always be serviceable for Judaism, and, what is infinitely more important, will find Judaism serviceable for itself. . . . therefore, you will be forced, if I am not mistaken, to infer quite a bit from this brief explanation: chiefly, why I do not contemplate "abjuring" my present stand; why I am not ashamed of my "earlier" anarchism; why I consider anarchist methods unserviceable and Communist goals meaningless and non-existent. *Which does not detract from the value of Communist action one iota, because it is the corrective of Communist goals**—and because meaningful *political* goals are non-existent. [24]

Benjamin endorses "Communist action" as a mandatory *moral* standpoint in an age of "struggle" in which the "mechanism whereby things and masses affect one another" (that is, the point of view of class struggle) has attained such historically irrefragable relevance. Yet, he goes to some lengths to reassure his friend that he has not chosen "once and for all," but only for the moment; that he views the possibility of joining the Party as a type of temporary experiment; that in the last analysis he views "Com-

* Emphasis added.

munist goals"—like all merely "political goals"—as meaningless. Indeed it can be inferred that, for Benjamin, the only *ultimately* worthwhile goals are still the Messianic ends that were the focal point of his earlier days, in comparison with which all merely *temporal* goals must necessarily ring hollow. Nevertheless, historical man remains separated from these higher ends by an unbridgeable abyss. He is condemned to dwell in the profane, godless continuum of history. Thus historical man can never act immediately on these ultimate ends. For the Messianic and historical eras run in opposite directions: "Only the Messiah himself consummates all history, in the sense that he alone redeems, completes, creates its relation to the Messianic. For this reason nothing historical can relate itself on its own account to anything Messianic. Therefore, the Kingdom of God is not the *telos* of the historical dynamic; it cannot be set as goal. From the standpoint of history it is not the goal, but the end."[25] But, Benjamin affirms, even for historical man, "what is essential is to decide." The interrelation between the historical and Messianic kingdoms is always mysterious and oblique. Though one can never be certain in profane life if one is acting in a manner that will hasten the advent of the Messianic era, nevertheless, it is essential to act; to act "ruthlessly" and "radically," and never "consistently"—for to act consistently would be tantamount to an avowal of belief in the meaningfulness of profane ends, a compromise that is fatal from a Messianic point of view. Whereas if one acts radically, from one's own innermost convictions, there is still the distant, infinitesimal hope that one is somehow hastening the advent of the Messianic age.

For these reasons, and in full accord with his earlier theological perspective, Benjamin disparages the value of Communist (as well as all political) *goals* and speaks of communist *action* for its own sake as a "corrective" to those goals (To be sure, portions of his argument might have been inserted in order to mollify Scholem, who was 2,000 miles away in Jerusalem at the time and obviously distressed over his friend's recent political leanings. But I believe that, for the most part, Benjamin's account here is genuine.) This also explains the highly paradoxical statement at the beginning of the quotation that although there is no "overlap" between the domains of political and religious conduct, they are essentially identical. For as an "obligatory mode of conduct," Benjamin views communist praxis as complementary to and, as it were, subsumed by his earlier theological outlook; for even though all conduct in the historical world is profane, one must nevertheless act; one must *choose*. It remains temporal man's *ethical* responsibility to take a stand, despite the often contradictory and confused manner in which the choices present themselves in the prosaic context of empirical life. In view of Germany's recent economic collapse, the corruption and duplicity of political life in Weimar, and the heroic struggle of the Russian masses to overthrow feudal tyranny and build a new society, it is hardly surprising that communist praxis recommended itself to Benjamin at this time. What Benjamin tries to clarify for his concerned friend is his belief that in the overall scheme of things these two paths, religious and political, are not incompatible: "'justified' radical politics will always be serviceable for Judaism, and, what is infinitely more important, will find Judaism serviceable for itself."

Scholem was extremely skeptical about his friend's scheme to mediate between the two discordant spheres, and not without good reason.

One-Way Street and Dialectical Images

The effects of Benjamin's newly adopted materialist views on his literary production are well documented in two important studies from the late twenties: *One-Way Street* (1928), a collection of aphorisms, and the monograph "Surrealism" (1929).[26] Both are transitional works, which mark Benjamin's passage (his "one-way street") from the metaphysically oriented essays of his early period to the more militant perspective his writing would assume in the early thirties, when his association with Brecht was the dominant intellectual force in his life. In these works it is not uncommon to discover insights of purely metaphysical origin standing side by side with those of Marxist vintage. In addition to the shift in theoretical direction that becomes apparent at this time, there also occurs a noticeable change in Benjamin's thinking about the type of texts which merit critical scrutiny. Whereas his earlier studies had been tinged by a certain antiquarian focus (e.g., his studies on Goethe's *Elective Affinities*, the German romantics, and *Trauerspiel*), his later criticism concentrates either on contemporary authors (Kraus, Kafka, Brecht, Proust, Breton) or significant nineteenth-century writers (Baudelaire and Nikolai Leskov). This tendency is consistent with a conscious attempt to modify the esoteric criticism of his early years in the direction of a reception-oriented criticism. For Benjamin this new emphasis meant the rejection of a purely aesthetic, contemplative attitude toward great works of literature and an active concern with the relevance (*Akualität*) of art. As he affirms in *One-Way Street*, "The critic has nothing to do with the interpreter of past artistic eras." Instead, "The critic is a strategist in the literary struggle."[27]

The acedia that dominates the mood of Benjamin's early writings is carried over, if for different reasons, to the later period. It was out of theological conviction that he identified so profoundly with the saturnine world view of the baroque poets. Their allegorical dramas portrayed the natural history of creaturely life, whose separation from the eternal light of redemption was deemed irrevocable. "All the wisdom of the melancholic is subject to the nether world; it is secured by immersion in the life of creaturely things, and it hears nothing of the voice of relevation."[28] Subsequently, however, Benjamin found occasion for melancholy in the situation of the art of letters in the modern world and in the dilemma of the intellectual, traditionally entrusted with the task of safeguarding this art. As he remarks in *One-Way Street*: "Writing, which had found an asylum in the printed book, where it led an autonomous existence, is unavoidably cast out onto the streets by advertising and subjected to the brutal heteronomies of economic chaos."[29] Under these circumstances, the intellectual can no longer in good conscience remain faithful to the position he originally assumed in the late eighteenth century (the period of the emergence of the bourgeois public sphere)[30]—that of proponent and upholder of the allegedly "universal" values of the bourgeoisie—once the particularistic character of its class rule became apparent with the suppression of the revolutions of 1848.

He too is "cast out onto the streets" if he should dare to question his emasculated, postrevolutionary status as a simple purveyor of cultural commodities. No small cause for lament is the affirmative-apologetic position culture comes to occupy with the advent of nineteenth-century *l'art pour l'art*—i.e., art as the sublimated sphere where the values denied in material life can be harmlessly realized and enjoyed.[31] In addition to this pointedly asocial "high" art, the nineteenth-century witnesses an unprecedented proliferation of entertainment literature—e.g., the *feuilletons* of the Paris dailies.[32]

In essence, once bourgeois society in its counterrevolutionary phase demands an art that is uncontroversial, innocuous, and untroublesome to its conscience, the entirety of traditional culture is also placed in a problematical light, insofar as it, too, is subjected to the bourgeois *veneration and worship of culture*, an act of sanctification intended to defuse its potentially damning powers of social criticism. For Benjamin, whose whole life until now had been passionately immersed in the world of letters, the realization that even this sphere had become implicated in the all-encompassing network of exchange relationships was a source of profound disillusionment. It was in pointed opposition to the complacent bourgeois attitude toward culture that Benjamin set forth the following claim: "The products of art and science owe their existence not merely to the effort of the great geniuses that created them, but also to the unnamed drudgery of their contemporaries. There is no document of culture which is not at the same time a document of barbarism."[33] Because of this situation it falls due to the critic to abandon his former attitude of naïve appreciation toward great works of art and assume the role of strategist in the literary struggle.

As Ernst Bloch astutely noted in his 1929 review, in *One-Way Street* Benjamin strives to make philosophy surrealistic.[34] The book is a patchwork of images, thought-collages, and miscellaneous reflections, which often take some seemingly trivial aspect of everyday life as their point of departure and end by offering a more general comment on the current trajectory of social life.

It is, above all, in works like *One-Way Street* that Benjamin's celebrated capacity for "micrological thinking"—his method of compressing the particular until the universal seemingly bursts forth from within—is evidenced. In his reminiscences of his friendship with Benjamin, Bloch offers the following pertinent observations concerning the characteristic inclinations of his friend's thinking:

Benjamin had what Lukács so enormously lacked: he had a unique sense for the significant detail, for the near at hand, for the fresh elements which burst forth in thinking and in the world, for singularities which are unsuitable for practical use and thus deserving of an entirely unique consideration. Benjamin possessed a peerless micrological-philosophical sense for such details, such significant signs of the off the beaten track.[35]

In terms of its content, *One-Way Street* (dedicated to Lacis) represents a frontal assault on the hypocrisy and decadence of the bourgeois class, its catastrophic mismanagement of economic life, its ruthless sacrifice of all personal, affective considerations to the self-serving ideology of maximizing one's profits, its savage devastation of nature, to the detriment of that precarious symbiotic relation between man and nature which is so essential to the quality of species life. Benjamin presents the following reflections on the last-named motif:

The earliest customs of peoples seem to send us a warning that in accepting what we receive so abundantly from nature we should guard against a gesture of avarice. For we are able to make Mother Earth no gift of our own. It is therefore fitting to show respect in taking, by returning a part of all we receive before laying hands on our share. This respect is expressed in the ancient custom of libation. Indeed, it is perhaps this immemorial practice that has survived, transformed, in the prohibition on gathering fallen ears of corn or forgotten grapes, these reverting to the soil or to the ancestral dispensers of blessings. An Athenian custom forbade the picking up of crumbs at the table, since they belonged to the heroes. If society has so degenerated through necessity and greed that it can now receive the gifts of nature only rapaciously, that it snatches the fruit unripe from the trees in order to sell it more profitably, and is compelled to empty each dish in its determination to have enough, the earth will be impoverished and the land yield bad harvests.[36]

Benjamin renews the theme of the supreme importance of the species' relation to nature in the magnificent concluding aphorism, "To the Planetarium." He begins by nostalgically comparing the relationship of ancient man to the cosmos to that of modern man: "Nothing distinguishes the ancient from the modern man so much as the former's absorption in a cosmic experience scarcely known in later periods." Whereas for the ancients intercourse with the heavens was characterized by the "ecstatic trance," an infinite wonder in the contemplation of what is both "nearest to us and what is remotest to us—and never of one without the other," for the moderns, beginning with the great astronomers of the sixteenth century, Copernicus, Brahe, and Kepler, exclusive emphasis was placed on "the optical connection to the universe," a portent of the narrow-minded rational-purposive relation to the firmament that would in the future gradually take precedence. More and more, Benjamin continues, the idea of an ecstatic relation to the cosmos is relegated "to the individual as the poetic rapture of starry nights," and the idea of a *communal* relation to the cosmos, so essential for the preservation of a harmonius relation of the species to nature, falls into oblivion. During World War I, mankind witnessed "an attempt at a new unprecedented commingling with cosmic powers":

Human multitudes, gases, electrical forces were hurled into the open country, high frequency currents coursed through the landscape, new constellations rose in the sky, aerial space and ocean depths thundered with propellers, and everywhere sacrificial shafts were dug in Mother Earth. This immense wooing of the cosmos was enacted for the first time on a planetary scale, that is, in the spirit of technology. But because the lust for profit of the ruling class sought satisfaction through it, technology betrayed man and turned the bridal bed into a blood bath. The mastery of nature, so the imperialists teach us, is the purpose of all technology. . . . In the nights of annihilation of the last war the frame of mankind was shaken by a feeling that resembled the bliss of an epileptic. And the revolts that followed it were the first attempt of mankind to bring the new body under its control. The power of the proletariat is the measure of its convalescence. If it is not gripped to the very marrow by the discipline of this power, no pacifist polemics will save it. Living substance conquers the frenzy of destruction only in the ecstasy of procreation.

In speaking of the ecstatic "frenzy of destruction" of the war, Benjamin touches on the insidious enthusiasm for the carnage displayed by so many, a Freudian death wish that is the perverse counterpart to the will to emancipation.[37] Furthermore, the ultimate victory of the proletariat remains for him a *conditional* proposition, in keeping with the "nihilism" of his former days. There are no preordained economic mechanisms, as in the evolutionary Marxism of Social Democracy, which lead infallibly to the triumph of the working class and the advent of the realm of freedom. To be sure, social conditions have become too grave for any naïve trust in the Enlightenment myth of cumulative historical progress. In view of the atrocities and horrors of the war to come, Benjamin's provocative depiction of the world historical consequences of the employment of technology for purposes of mass annihilation can hardly seem an overdramatization. In *One-Way Street*, as in many other instances, when Benjamin invokes the cause of the proletariat it is almost as a last resort. For him, capitalism is a social formation objectively set on a collision course with disaster. The timetable is already established and the only question is whether or not the proletariat can at the last moment grab the helm to avert total catastrophe. It is the old question of "socialism or barbarism":

For whether the bourgeosie wins or loses the fight, it remains doomed by the inner contradictions that in the course of development will become deadly. The only question is whether its downfall will come through itself or at the hands of the proletariat. The continuance or the end of three thousand years of cultural development will be decided by the answer. . . . And if the abolition of the bourgeoisie is not completed by an almost calculable moment in economic and technical development (a moment signaled by inflation and poison-gas warfare), all is lost. Before the spark reaches the dynamite the lighted fuse must be cut.[38]

The proximity of Benjamin's view of the "contingent" nature of the revolutionary transition to Lukács's position in *History and Class Consciousness* is quite striking—if at the same time the latter's appraisal of the possibility of a successful revolution was, in 1923, decidedly more optimistic. For Lukács, too, the collapse of the capitalist system is preordained, yet the successful transition to the realm of freedom is nevertheless dependent on whether the proletariat, at the moment of crisis, has become aware of its historical mission and thus can seize control of its own destiny; on whether or not it has attained *class consciousness*, i.e., has become *for itself* what it has hitherto been only *in itself*.[39] In the above citation Benjamin's nondeterministic conception of the relationship between the crisis of capitalism and the subsequent transition to socialism is undoubtedly taken over from Lukács's seminal treatment of the problem.[40] In both instances the adversary is the fatalistic view of revolution advocated by social democratic theorists, who perceived the advent of socialism as a progressive, evolutionary result of the developmental laws of the capitalist system itself, rather than as a definitive *break* with those laws. As Benjamin would remark at a later point, "Nothing has corrupted the German working class so much as the notion it was moving with the current."[41]

Yet, the significance of *One-Way Street* far transcends its status as a political document. In it Benjamin consummates stylistic tendencies which would remain a distinctive feature of his discourse in all his subsequent work. We have already mentioned his desire to render philosophy surrealistic. Through this intention he sought to reduce the discrepancy between philosophical thought and everyday life by incorporating elements of the latter directly—at times, almost positivistically—into the field of philosophical reflection itself. As the most cursory glimpse at surrealist poetry and painting of the period will bear out, this tactic was a cardinal weapon in the surrealist arsenal. To produce the desired result, Benjamin felt obliged to obliterate every trace of subjective interference, so that the object, the thing itself, could shine forth in all its splendor. The overall effect of this procedure on the reader was intended to be one of *shock*: by wrenching elements of everyday life from their original contexts and rearranging them in a new constellation, Benjamin hoped to divest them of their familiarity and thereby stir the reader from a state of passivity into an active and critical posture. Benjamin referred to this method as his theory of "Dialectical Images" (also known as "Dialectic at a Standstill"). Its objective was, by virtue of its affinities with the concrete, to rescue traditional philosophy from a fate of excessive abstraction. As Adorno remarks in his 1955 review of *One-Way Street*:

The fragments of *"Einbahnstrasse"* . . . are picture puzzles, attempts to conjure through parables that which cannot be expressed in words. They aim not as much to give check to conceptual thinking as to shock by way of their enigmatic form and thereby to set thinking in motion; for in its traditional conceptual form, thinking grows obdurate, appears conventional and antiquated.[42]

Benjamin outlines the philosophical rudiments of the theory of Dialectical Images in the following passage:

Again and again, in Shakespeare, in Calderon, battles fill the last act, and kings, princes, attendants and followers, "enter, fleeing." The moment in which they become visible to spectators *brings them to a standstill.* The flight of the *dramatis personae* is arrested by the stage. Their entry into the visual field of non-participating and truly impartial persons allows the harassed to draw breath, bathes them in new air. The appearance on stage of those who enter "fleeing" takes from this its hidden meaning. Our reading of this formula is imbued with the expectation of a place, a light, a footlight glare, in which our flight through life may be likewise sheltered in the presence of onlooking strangers.[43]

When the stream of life's movement is brought to an abrupt halt, "sheltered in the presence of onlooking strangers," the customary and familiar are viewed in a radically new light. The method of "Dialectic at a Standstill" has an *estrangement* or *shock-effect* on objects: it temporarily freezes them as slides under the microscope of the critic, lifts them momentarily from their natural environment in order to make them relevant for the present. It is a game of philosophical freeze-tag in which objects, places, events are stripped of their immediacy, in order that they might be released from the sterile continuum of the always-the-same. The principle of estrangement is carried over from the surrealist technique of montage. As a result of the new "shocking" juxtaposition of everyday objects in the Dialectical Image, these objects demand a unique, critical consideration and thus cease to be serviceable for the ends of the ruling powers.

The employment of the theory of Dialectical Images in *One-Way Street* and other works of this period represents an attempt on Benjamin's part to transpose the theory of "ideas" or "monads" of the *Trauerspiel* study from an idealist to a materialist framework. However, both versions of the theory prove authentically materialistic, insofar as each displays, above all, a healthy philosophical respect for the concrete specificity of the phenomena under investigation. The major difference between the two renditions of the theory is that the later form abjures reference to the tradition of Western metaphysics and instead draws its inspiration from concrete aspects of contemporary social life. Nevertheless, the fundamental intention of both "idealist" and "materialist" versions of theory is identical: both attempt to deduce an image of transcendence while remaining wholly *within* the boundaries of the empirical world of experience. The ultimate concern of both approaches is the *redemption* of phenomena from the profane continuum of historical existence and their transformation into images of fulfillment or *now-time*. As Benjamin remarks in the late thirties: "The dialectical image is a flashing image. Thus, the image of the past . . . is to be held fast as an image that flashes in the Now of recognition. Redemption, which is accomplished in this way and only in this way, can always be attained only as that which in perception irredeemably loses itself."[44]

Surrealism

Benjamin composed his "Surrealism" essay in 1928, the year *One-Way Street* was published. His interest in surrealism dates back to 1925, the year Breton's first "Manifesto of Surrealism" appeared. In a letter to Rilke of that year, Benjamin writes: "In particular what struck me about surrealism . . . was the captivating, authoritative, and definitive way in which language passes over into the world of dreams."[45] The surrealist fascination with dream life was fully endorsed by Benjamin, and in his 1935 outline of the Arcades Project, he would raise this obsession with the emancipatory potential embodied in dreams to the level of a methodological canon.[46] In his "Manifesto," Breton presented the following reflections on the value of dream experience:

Freud very rightly brought his critical faculties to bear upon the dream. It is, in fact, inadmissible that this considerable portion of psychic activity (since, at least from man's birth until his death, thought offers no solution of continuity, the sum of the moments of dreams, from the point of view of time, and taking into consideration only the time of pure dreaming, that is the dreams of sleep, is not inferior to the sum of the moments of reality or, to be more precisely limiting, the moments of waking) has still today been so grossly neglected. I have always been amazed at the way an ordinary observer lends so much more credence and attaches so much more importance to waking events than those occurring in dreams.[47]

One-Way Street, not to mention his autobiographical writings of this period such as *Berliner Kindheit um Neunzehnhundert*, abounds with references to dreams and dream images. Yet, against Freud, and like the surrealists, it is not the latent or unconscious meanings of dreams that attracts Benjamin, but the manifest content of the dream images themselves. The dream, for Benjamin, becomes an autonomous source of experience and knowledge, a hidden key to the secrets and mysteries of waking life. Dreams become the *repositories of the utopian visions of mankind*; they serve as the refuge of the aspirations and desires that are denied to humanity in the sphere of material life. Adorno touches on this point when he observes that for Benjamin, "the dream becomes a medium of unregimented experience, a source of knowledge opposed to the stale superficiality of thinking."[48] The fact that dreams reorganize the images of waking life in a strange and unfamiliar context suggests marked affinities with Benjamin's concept of Dialectical Images. In dreams, "The absurd is presented as if it were self-evident, in order to strip the self-evident of its power."[49] As such, the dream represents the realm of the possible, the nonidentical, it serves to contest the pretension to "Being-in-Itself" of the dominant reality principle.[50]

From a theoretical standpoint, both *One-Way Street* and the "Surrealism" essay stand in very close relation to one another. However, the latter study is more openly concerned with "strategic" questions, insofar as it explicitly reflects on the dilemmas and issues confronting radical intellectuals in the late twenties. Specifically, it attempts to cast light, if often in rather Aesopian language, on a debate which had begun to rage in surrealist circles at that time over whether surrealism should place itself directly "in the service of the Revolution" (*Surréalisme au Service de la Révolution* became the title of the movement's main literary organ in 1930) or should instead work toward preserving the autonomy of spirit in defiance of the party line on matters concerning art and literature, while nevertheless remaining aligned with the party on political matters.[51] This is the key political problem with which Benjamin grapples in the essay, though the question is viewed through the surrealist movement as a prism, as it were, rather than in terms of particulars of the surrealist controversy itself. Because Benjamin had such an urgent personal stake in the resolution of this question, his discussion of the way the problem of "commitment" manifested itself in the surrealist milieu can be read as largely autobiographical. In addition, the "Surrealism" essay respresents a significant turn away from the field of *Germanistik* and toward the horizons of French culture. As he remarks in a letter to Hugo von Hofmannsthal in July 1927: "whereas in Germany I feel, in terms of my interests, entirely isolated among the men of my generation, there are isolated presences in France— e.g., the writer Giraudoux, and especially Aragon, and also the surrealist movement—in which I see at work things that concern me."[52] And in a letter to Scholem of January 30, 1928, he mentions in passing that the *Trauerspiel* book represented the conclusion of that phase of his work concerned with the domain of German studies.[53]

Moreover, it was Benjamin's interest in surrealism which first led him to formulate the preliminary outlines of his "Pariser Passagen" or Arcades Project. Originally conceived of as a study of approximately 50 pages, the project soon grew to monumental proportions, and he would work on it on and off until the end of his life. The ultimate stimulus behind his decision to undertake the study was provided by Louis Aragon's 1926 novel *Paysan de Paris*. Benjamin would say of it at a later date: "at night in bed I could never read more than two or three pages at a time, for my heartbeat became so strong that I was forced to lay the book down."[54] It is not surprising that of Aragon's work, this book in particular elicited Benjamin's enthusiasm: the first half of *Paysan de Paris* takes place in an arcade, the Passage de l'Opera. "Where humans engage in their most suspicious pursuits," remarks

Aragon,

the inanimate will sometimes reflect their most secret motives: our cities are populated with unrecognized sphinxes who will not stop the passing dreamer to ask him life and death questions unless he directs his distracted meditations toward them. But if this sage knows how to find and interrogate these faceless monsters, it is his own abysses that he will discover there. . . . these covered arcades, which radiate in large numbers from the great boulevards, are called, for some strange reason, *passages*. . . . these human aquaria, already stripped of their original life, merit consideration as repositories of several modern myths.[55]

The Aragon passage itself affords valuable insight concerning the methodological intent of the Arcades Project. For Benjamin's aim was to shed light on the nature of the modern age by way of an allegorical reading of the physiognomy of urban life. The most seemingly trivial social phenomena would be used, once reassembled in the Dialectical Image, to deduce the most profound aspects, the innermost truths, of bourgeois society. Taking the Parisian arcades of the nineteenth century as his point of departure, Benjamin's object was to demonstrate the manner in which the always-the-same of prehistory manifests itself in the modern, insofar as the modern manifests itself as the always-the-same.[56] The purpose of this intention was not to attempt to discover rudiments of archaic life in the modern per se, but rather, to unmask the idea of the modern itself—i.e., the idea of an endless stream of consumer goods or "fashion"—as that of eternal recurrence or the always-the-same. By characterizing the modern as eternal recurrence, one could therefore show how it coalesces with the idea of mythical repetition, which dominates life in prehistory. Thus, prehistory returns to dominate the modern era under the mythical guise of commodity exchange, in which the self-identical perpetually presents itself as the new. The "Surrealism" article constitutes Benjamin's first significant attempt to delineate this theoretical problematic; it stands, in his own words, as "an opaque paravent in front of the Arcades study."[57] Like *One-Way Street*, it represents an effort "to determine the most concrete qualities of an epoch as they present themselves here and there in children's games, a building or in one of life's random situations."[58] For as

Benjamin asserts in one of his most provocative and self-revealing aphorisms: "The eternal would be the ruffles on a dress rather than an idea."[59] To be sure, nothing could be more faithful to the philosophy of surrealism than the elevation of the ephemeral and mundane to a position of preeminence.

Benjamin's fascination with the ruins of the bourgeois world—i.e., its *commodities*—parallels his preoccupation with the emblematic fragments of the baroque era in the *Trauerspiel* study: "The emblems of the baroque return as commodities."[60] He indicates a further similarity between the two works in a letter to Scholem: "just as the *Trauerspiel* book unfurls the seventeenth century from the standpoint of Germany, [the Arcades Project] will unfurl the nineteenth century from the standpoint of France."[61] The technique of allegory is also central to both works, and it is, above all, in the lyric poetry of Baudelaire that Benjamin perceives the allegorization of capitalist society. Unlike those of the baroque period, however, the allegorical images of the thoroughly *profane* world of bourgeois society are deprived of a transcendent referent: "In opposition to the baroque, the allegory of Baudelaire bears traces of the wrath necessary to smash in this world, to lay its harmonious images in ruins."[62] The allegories of bourgeois culture do not find their truth content in an image of redeemed life, but, conversely, in an image of *catastrophe*. "Progress as catastrophe," therefore, is the sign under which the ruins of bourgeois civilization present themselves for decipherment to the splenic gaze of the allegorist: "The idea of progress must be based on the idea of catastrophe. That things have gone this far *is* the catastrophe. Catastrophe is not what threatens to occur at any given moment but what is given at any given moment. Strindberg's conception: Hell is nothing that stands ahead of us—rather, *this life in the present*."[63] The possibility of reconciliation has diminished correspondingly. Under such conditions, "Redemption preserves itself in a small crack in the continuum of catastrophe."[64]

The "Surrealism" essay, then, must be viewed as a type of "prolegomena to the Arcades Project."[65] Through incorporating elements of the everyday into their projects the surrealists have not only narrowed the gap between art and life, they have transformed the very concept of art itself: for "the writings of this circle are not literature."[66] Surrealism, therefore, is not to be understood as merely another fashionable artistic movement. From the beginning, "Breton declared his intention of breaking with a praxis that presents the public with the literary precipitate of a certain form of existence while withholding that existence itself."[67] Not only did the surrealists desire to extend the boundaries of art by way of compelling it to assimilate miscellaneous fragments of everyday life, but they also sought to revolutionize everyday life itself by subjecting it to the intoxicating powers of poetic imagination and dream experience. Everything which came into contact with their enchanted outlook seemed magically transformed, no matter how apparently trivial or unelevated. Since his 1918 essay on Kant, Benjamin had sought to formulate an anti-positivistic, "superior" concept of experience. Not only did he believe he had discovered such a concept in the case of surrealism, but the surrealist concept of experience had the further advantage of assuming a profane, *exoteric* form, which provided an encouraging counterbalance to Benjamin's own earlier forbiddingly hermetic criticism. His enthusiasm for the movement is often rhapsodic, in expression of solidarity with the dithyrambic quality of surrealist discourse itself:

The surrealists were the first to perceive the revolutionary energies that appear in the "outmoded," that appear in the first iron constructions, the first factory buildings, the earliest photos, the objects that have begun to ebb from them. The relations of these things to revolution—no one can have a more exact concept of it than these authors. No one before these visionaries and augurs perceived how destitution—not only social, but architectonic, the poverty of interiors, enslaved and enslaving objects—can be suddenly transformed into revolutionary nihilism. Leaving aside Aragon's *Passage de l'Opéra*, Breton and Nadja are the lovers who convert everything we have experienced on mournful railway journeys (railways are beginning to age), on God-forsaken Sunday afternoons in the proletarian quarters of great cities, in the first glance through the rain-blurred window of a new apartment, into revolutionary experience, if not action. They bring the immense forces of "atmosphere" concealed in these things to the point of explosion.[68]

In sum: "To win the energies of intoxication for the revolution—this is the project about which surrealism circles in all its books and enterprises."[69] The redemptive relation of surrealism vis-à-vis insignificant objects, the detritus of social life, represented for Benjamin a model of poetic praxis, the posture that the arts must assume if they are to cease from becoming a matter of indifference. It was the decided lack of literary commitment in Germany that led Benjamin to despair over the state of the arts in his native land and to look not only toward France, but also toward the revolutionary experiments in the fields of journalism and film-making which were occurring in Soviet Union in the late twenties.[70]

Benjamin spoke of the surrealist road to the redemption of everyday reality as the method of *profane illumination* and identified profoundly with this conception. In an analogous manner, he would attempt to set free the secular forces of inspiration embedded in important literary works, and in his more sociologically oriented undertakings, such as the Baudelaire book, he would strive to elevate allegorically the ruins of commodity society through the use of surrealistic dream-images. Profane illumination represents the "creative overcoming of religious illumination," which founders in the illusory regions of otherworldliness; it is, in contrast to the latter, "a materialistic, anthropological inspiration, to which hashish, opium or whatever else can give an introductory lesson"—if a dangerous one.[71] Like religious illumination, profane illumination captures the powers of spiritual intoxication in order to produce a "revelation," a vision or insight which transcends the prosaic state of empirical reality; yet it produces this vision in an *immanent* manner, while remaining within the bounds of possible experience, and without recourse to otherworldly dogmas. Benjamin clearly has in mind the intoxicating, trancelike effect induced by surrealist "romances" such as Breton's *Nadja* and Aragon's *Le Paysan de Paris*, in which the streets of Paris, the most seemingly commonplace locations and objects, are transformed into a phantasmagorical wonderland of chance encounters and surprise, where the monotony of convention is burst asunder by the powers of *l'hasard objectif*. After traversing these enchanted landscapes, could life ever again be experienced with the same complacency and indolence as before?

At the same time, like every other movement or idea that captured his imagination, Benjamin never simply adopted the techniques of surrealism wholesale; he employed them selectively within the basic framework of his own critical ideals. As Scholem astutely notes, "Benjamin was no ecstatic, yet the ecstasies of revolutionary utopia and of the surrealist plunge into the unconscious were for him, as it were, a key to the opening of his own world, for which he sought entirely different, rigorous and disciplined forms of expression."[72] Given his growing concern with the politics of "radical communism," Benjamin views the surrealist movement with distinct reservations; and his skepticism regarding its romantic and mystical proclivities can legitimately be read as a denigration of his own esoteric side. Initially conceived of as a resolutely apolitical movement, the scorn and ridicule of bourgeois society increasingly drove surrealism toward the left. To be sure, in terms of its capacity to set in motion heretofore untapped *critical* and *negative* energies—the powers of "revolutionary nihilism"—surrealism is without equal: "Since Bakunin, Europe has lacked a radical concept of freedom. The surrealists have one. They are the first to liquidate the sclerotic liberal-moral-humanistic ideal of freedom."[73] Yet, according to Benjamin, it remains to be seen whether ultimately the surrealists can cast off "a number of pernicious romantic prejudices" and accommodate themselves to "the constructive, dictatorial side of revolution. In short, have they bound revolt to revolution?"[74] For to place exclusive emphasis on the negative, anarchistic dimension of the revolutionary process

would be to subordinate the methodical and disciplinary preparation for revolution entirely to a praxis oscillating between fitness exercises and celebration in advance. . . . For histrionic or fanatical stress on the mysterious side of the mysterious takes us no further; we penetrate the mystery only to the degree that we recognize it in the everyday world, by virtue of a dialectical optic that perceives the everyday as impenetrable, and the impenetrable as the everyday.[75]

Benjamin's remarks represent an exercise in self-criticism as much as a reproach against surrealism. They also reveal the first manifestation of tendencies in his thinking concerning the relationship between art and politics which subsequently led to his endorsement of some extremely tenuous and dogmatic points of view. For Benjamin the surrealist praxis of "profane illumination" is laudable as an artistic mode of conduct; its practice of harnessing the energies of revolutionary nihilism signifies a crucial element of the so-called negative and critical phase of the revolutionary process. However, if that process were to fail to progress beyond this phase—the phase of mere *revolt*—and neglect to transform itself ultimately into a methodical and disciplined *political* movement, even this salutary nihilistic stage would eventually degenerate into a privatized and meaningless form of intellectual recreation; it would become a matter of indifference, indistinguishable from all the other intellectual fashions that had preceded it. Benjamin accurately identifies the contradictions of the notion of a "poetic politics" ("Anything rather than that!" he mockingly interjects), which deludes itself into believing a mobilization of aesthetic powers alone would be capable of changing the world. Nevertheless, as history has demonstrated only too brutally in recent times, the political instrumentalization of the aesthetic faculty has deprived many "successful" revolutions of a vital source of self-knowledge whose existence might have somewhat mitigated their Thermidorian proclivity to devour their own children. The distance between art and life must be preserved. In truth, the conclusion Benjamin stops just short of drawing must be reversed: it is, above all, once art and politics become fused that art threatens to become a matter of indifference.

"I believe in the future resolution of these two states," declares André Breton, "dream and reality, which are so seemingly contradictory, into a kind of absolute reality, a *surreality*, if one may so speak. It is in quest of this surreality that I am going."[76] It is Benjamin's fear that if the very real creative energies of surrealism are diverted for the sake of providing cheerful images of reconciled life in the here and now—a likelihood implicit in the concept of a *surreality*—then the movement will have essentially retreated into a private dream-world, in fatal disregard of social concerns which were becoming more and more pressing each day. Benjamin refuses to sanction the outright political instrumentalization of the surrealist movement. Instead, he merely seeks to call attention to the real danger he perceives of its backsliding to the complacent level of aesthetic consolation. Not optimism but pessimism is the order of the day: "Surrealism has come ever closer to the Communist answer. And that means pessimism all along the line. Absolutely. Mistrust in the fate of literature, mistrust in the fate of freedom, mistrust in the fate of humanity, but three times mistrust in all reconciliation: between classes, between nations, between individuals. And unlimited trust only in I. G. Farben and the peaceful perfection of the *Luftwaffe*."[77]

The real task of surrealism, therefore—and, by extension, the task of radical intellectuals in general—consists in "the organization of pessimism" and the discovery in politics of "a sphere reserved one hundred percent for images."[78] The object is not the unrealistic goal of transforming the left-wing writer of bourgeois lineage into a proletarian writer (such writers would emerge only from a successful revolution) but instead, "of deploying him, even at the expense of his artistic activity, at important points in the sphere of imagery."[79] His role is that of shattering the affirmative semblance of universal harmony and well-being promoted by the bourgeois "image-sphere" and simultaneously assisting in the production of a radically new image-sphere in which the contours of the realm of freedom are prefigured. Yet, this necessitates a break with the "metaphysical materialism" of surrealist aesthetics and the transition to a more thoroughly profane "anthropological materialism," which aims not at the creation of an otherworldly, transcendental reality, but the practical transformation of reality in the here and now. The intellectual or the artist, according to Benjamin, must not deceive himself into believing he can, in this role, exert an immediate influence on the proletarian masses. His activity will always in a certain measure remain class-bound. Instead, his role is limited to that of a "strategist in the literary struggle." He attempts to enlighten other left-thinking bourgeois intellectuals concerning their complicity with the established social order and their responsibilities as intellectuals in the impending social struggle. As such, Benjamin perceives the radical intellectual in bourgeois society as a member of a fifth column charged with the *destructive* task of undermining the established order from within; of compelling other members of the bourgeois intelligentsia to abandon their unwitting function as hired apologists for the status quo.[80] The terrain on which this struggle is waged is that of the so-called literary "image sphere." It therefore falls due to the method of profane illumination to facilitate the wholesale reorganization of the image sphere of the fragmented bourgeois world, that is, to introduce *a completely new sphere of radical, revolutionary images.* "The collective is a body, too. And the *physis* that is being organized for it in technology can, through all its political and factual reality, only be produced in that image sphere to which profane illumination initiates us."[81] In this way, surrealism accomplishes the transition from the nebulous and mystical perspective of *metaphysical materialism* (among whose representatives Benjamin includes Rimbaud, Nietzsche, and Georg Büchner) to the politically effective perspective of *anthropological materialism.*

In his provocative study *Theorie der Avantgarde,* Peter Bürger analyzes the twentieth-century avant garde in terms of its desire to achieve the integration of art and life praxis.[82] In his investigation, he makes explicit reference to two concepts of Benjaminian derivation in support of his claim, the concepts of allegory and montage. Both concepts point to something of invaluable significance for understanding the phenomenon of aesthetic modernism: that the traditional point of reference for aesthetic judgement— the integral, self-contained work of art—has entered into a state of irreversible decompositon. Bürger correctly views this trend as a self-conscious and concerted assault on the part of aesthetic consciousness against the bourgeois "institution of art"[83] as it emerged in the late eighteenth century—namely, the conception of art as an independent realm of human endeavor which finds its raison d'être in the fact that it exists as something wholly *separate* from the purposive ends of bourgeosie society. As such, this conception found its classical justification in Kant's idea of "disinterested pleasure" (*interesseloses Wohlgefallen*).[84]

The attempts by dadaism and surrealism to mock openly the sacral attitude of bourgeois aestheticism stand at the heart of Bürger's interpretation. However, in the case of surrealism, he errs distinctly in his estimation of the degree to which a break was made with the values of aestheticism.[85] Instead of representing a definitive departure from the bourgeois ethic of aesthetic autonomy, surrealism in truth embodied the continuation of that ethic, albeit according to a different set of presuppositions concerning the nature of artistic praxis. In the last analysis, it proved incap-able—especially in the case of its more intransigent representatives such as Breton—of relinquishing the modern ideal of art as an absolute value. For all its scorn of the bourgeois notion of the inviolability of the aesthetic realm, the surrealist movement ul-timately made its stand *this side* of the sphere of aesthetic auton-omy. In this sense, its affinities and links with the symbolist move-ment of the late nineteenth century prove far more decisive that its ties with dada, its immediate historical precursor. It was pre-cisely the pronounced residues of this aestheticist heritage in sur-realism that aroused Benjamin's suspicions. As we have already indicated, the surrealist technique of profane illumination exerted a lasting influence on the plans for his major theoretical under-taking of the thirties, the Arcades Project, not to mention his self-understanding of what it meant to be a theorist in an age of gas warfare, commodity production, and class conflict. However, his quest for an authentic form of artistic commitment remained un-satisfied until an eventful encounter soon after with Bertolt Brecht and the notion of epic theater.

Chapter Five

BENJAMIN AND BRECHT

"Crude Thinking"

IN HER essay on Benjamin, Hannah Arendt observes that with the encounter between Brecht and Benjamin "the greatest living poet met the most important critic of the time, a fact both were fully aware of."[1] Nevertheless, the intellectual alliance between the two cannot help but strike one as peculiar, for never were two modes of thought so diametrically at odds: on the one hand there was Brecht, with his glorification of "crude thinking" (*plumpes Denken*), who, as Benjamin reports, had painted the words "the truth is concrete" on a beam supporting the ceiling of his study, and who kept a small wooden donkey nearby with a sign around its neck saying, "Even I must understand it;"[2] on the other hand there was Benjamin, whose thinking seemed to incline naturally toward involution, depth, and essence, who, despite all his efforts, was never able to abandon the very "purely literary" interests which in his Brechtian writings had become an object of unrelenting scorn.

There are indications which suggest that the friendship may not always have proceeded on an even-handed basis. It is clear that in terms of a mutual interest in what might be referred to as functional or committed literature, Benjamin stood to learn much from Brecht whereas the reverse proposition would not necessarily hold. Brecht's reputation as a playwright had been firmly established with the Berlin production of *Threepenny Opera* by the time of their friendship in the early 1930s, whereas Benjamin's notoriety was largely posthumous—although those who were in the know concerning literary matters during the Weimar years were without doubt well acquainted with Benjamin's unique talents as a writer and critic.[3] Rolf Tiedemann has gone so far as to suggest that theirs was a relationship of dependency, with Benjamin the weaker party, and that therefore their association "must *also* be explained biographically-psychologically."[4]

Precisely how fruitful it would be to view their relationship in predominantly psychological terms, given the sincerity of Benjamin's commitment to the idea of a politically aware literature, remains to be seen. However, Benjamin's diary record of "Conversations with Brecht" (he enjoyed several lengthy stays at the latter's exile residence in Skovbostrand, Denmark from 1934 to 1938) are noteworthy for the faithful, well-nigh reverent tone with which the master's each and every word was recorded, even on occasions where Brecht, for whom the bourgeois virtue of tactfulness was apparently unknown, seemingly sought to stretch Benjamin's patience and good will to the limits of tolerance. On one occasion, for example, Brecht, in the course of a discussion of Kafka (whose work occupied Benjamin's attention intensively during these years) accused Benjamin's essay on the Prague writer of being guilty of promoting "Jewish Fascism."[5] In another talk, Brecht would dismiss Dostoyevsky, whom Benjamin was known to esteem, as a "little sausage" (*Würstchen*), reportedly Brecht's favorite term of derision during this period. Moreover, he suggested that Benjamin's recent illness was undoubtedly attributable to the unwholesome effects produced by Benjamin's current reading matter, *Crime and Punishment*.[6]

To those familiar with Brecht's naturally abrasive demeanor, such anecdotes would come as little surprise.[7] However, given Benjamin's incredible sensitivity in dealings with others, which has been so well-documented by Scholem's book,[8] the fact that he appears to have not only acquiesced without protest but to have actively sought to maintain the friendship seems indeed remarkable. If the attempt to view their relationship in psychological terms merits any validity, then Benjamin's devotion to Brecht would seem to signify in no uncertain terms a death wish, vis-à-vis his earlier esoteric criticism and love of literature as an autonomous medium of spiritual expression. For no one's work was more staunchly opposed to such conventional bourgeois literary values than was Brecht's.

There is, however, unquestionably more truth than untruth in Tiedemann's claim that "The interpretations which [Benjamin] devoted to individual works by Brecht sound as if their author strove for the position of authorized exegete."[9] This extremely literal fidelity to the intentions of an author stands in sharp contrast to Benjamin's *usual* method of criticism, in which literary works served both as self-contained monads as well as springboards for the imaginative-creative capacities of the critic himself. Nevertheless, Benjamin's admiration for Brecht's work appears to have gone unreciprocated. The few references to Benjamin that appear in Brecht's *Arbeitsjournal* are consistently uncomplimentary. Let us take the example of Brecht's reaction to Benjamin's notion of the "aura," which forms the conceptual basis of one of his most "materialist" essays, "The Work of Art in the Age of Mechanical Reproduction"[10]—an essay which he told Adorno he wrote "in order to outdo Brecht, whom he feared, in radicalism."[11] If this were in fact the case, then Benjamin would appear to have fallen far short of his purported aim, as Brecht's comments indicate:

[Benjamin] proceeds from something he calls *aura,* which relates to dreams (to day-dreams). he says: if you feel a gaze directed at you, even behind your back, you return the gaze (!). the expectation that what one looks at looks at one in return, produces the aura. the latter has recently been in decline, along with the cultic. benjamin has discovered this through an analysis of film, where the aura disintegrates through the reproduction of the works of art. all mysticism, under the guise of anti-mysticism. this is the form in which the materialist conception of history is adapted! it is fairly dreadful.[12]

If any further proof of Brecht's disdain for "The Work of Art" essay is needed, one might also mention that it was rejected for publication by a journal coedited by Brecht, the German emigré publication *Das Wort,* and published in 1936 by the organ of the Institute for Social Research, the *Zeitschrift für Sozialforschung.*

There is little doubt that the partnership with Brecht represented the decisive intellectual influence on Benjamin in the 1930s.

Though his writings directly concerned with Brechtian dramaturgy are relatively scant in number, Brecht's influence remains
prominent, at least indirectly, in virtually all Benjamin's explicitly
materialist writings during this period. Brecht provided the decisive impetus for Benjamin's serious investigations concerning
a historically adequate Marxist theory of culture, as Scholem cor-
roborates: "The manifestation of stronger Marxist accents from
1929 on is clearly related to the influence of Asja Lacis and
Brecht. . . . with Brecht an entirely new element—an elementary
force in the truest sense of the word—enters into his life."[13]

An initial meeting between the two was arranged by Lacis,
who had previously worked as a production assistant to Brecht
for *Eduard II*. Benjamin's initial impressions of Brecht were quite
favorable, as can be seen by the following remarks from a letter
to Scholem of June 1929: "It will interest you to know that friendly
relations have developed between Bert Brecht and myself, less for
reasons of his work (I know only 'Threepenny Opera' and the
ballads) than for the fundamental interest his present plans have
aroused."[14]

The oblique allusion to Brecht's "present plans" is undoubtedly
a reference to the development of the theory of epic theater, which
was then in its crucial formative stages. For Benjamin, whose
interest in "radical communism" as an obligatory form of moral
conduct had left him searching for an authentic vehicle for the
realization of the still vaguely defined ideal of an "effective" literary praxis, the encounter with Brecht must have seemed a god-
send. Yet, this search for a nonaffirmative, politically relevant
form of literary engagement must be set within the more general
context of the "crisis of criticism" which manifested itself increasingly as what little stability Weimar had possessed in the mid-
twenties collapsed with the onset of the Great Depression of
1929—a situation which was further aggravated by the growing
threat, at the polls and in the streets, posed by the fascist right.
In light of these events confidence in the ability of the liberal-
democratic literary public sphere to meet the threat posed by the
budding alliance between the forces of fascism and big industry—
which had been curiously prophesied by the composite gangster-
businessmen types of Brecht plays such as *Threepenny Opera*—

had been completely eroded; and it was specifically as a polemical counterbalance to the seeming nonchalance and unresponsiveness of traditional literary forms vis-à-vis the impending social crisis that Brecht's attempt to formulate a "non-Aristotelian" theory of drama had originated. Benjamin commented on the failure of nerve on the part of Weimar's left-wing intelligentsia in his article "Linke Melancholie," a review of a recently published collection of poems by Erich Kästner:

The left-radical publicists of the stamp of Kästner, Mehring or Tucholsky are the proletarian mimicry of a decaying bourgeois class. Their function is, from a political point of view, to produce cliques rather than parties, from a literary point of view, to produce fashions rather than schools, from an economic point of view, to produce agents rather than producers. Indeed, for fifteen years this left intelligentsia has continuously been the agent of all intellectual market trends, from Activism, to Expressionism, to the New Objectivity. . . . In brief, this left radicalism is precisely that attitude which in general no longer corresponds to any political action.[15]

However, at the same time there were independent developments of a technological nature which underlined the contradiction between a medium like print, which, according to the classical definition of the bourgeois public sphere, was supposed to be inherently democratic, and the particularistic employment to which it unavoidably fell victim in practice. Bernd Witte has dealt with this problem in the following terms:

The reason why the crisis [of criticism] first became fully conscious as such to the literati in the 1920s can only be surmised if one . . . takes into account matters relevant to the theory of communication. Namely, only with the origin of the mass media did the paradox fully develop that information like literary criticism, that is disseminated in a medium that could and should reach virtually everyone, was actually destined only for a small, highly specialized intellectual circle of readers. The technical and social possibilities of the medium unavoidably recall to mind the original claim to universality of the literary public sphere, a recollection facilitated by historical reflection.[16]

Until his meeting with Brecht, Benjamin's search for a genuine critical and committed form of artistic discourse had led him to encounters both with French surrealism and with innovative developments on the Russian literary scene. But in his native Germany encouraging signs were few. The situation in the Soviet Union was considered more advanced than in France, where the bourgeoisie remained firmly in power. Hence, whereas the surrealists were compelled to resort to "shock tactics" in an effort to stir the bourgeois consciousness from its state of enforced passivity, literary production in Russia was already based on urgent practical and organizational questions. The full extent of Benjamin's commitment can be gauged from his 1927 article "Die politische Gruppierung der russischen Schriftsteller," where he extols the fact that in the Soviet Union it is no longer *aesthetic* but *political* interests that determine the formation of literary groups.[17]

In the Soviet Union the autonomous status of literature has been, in Benjamin's eyes, authentically *aufgehoben*: literature has ceased to be the privileged plaything of bourgeois elites and is transformed into a tool for the political education of the masses. For the Russian writers, "the chief task is to approach the masses. This public will only recoil from refinements in psychology, word choice, and formulation. What it needs are not formulations but information, not variations but repetitions, not works of virtuosity but stirring reports."[18] Once it assumes this pedagogical function, literature can reclaim its role as a constitutive component of a truly democratic public sphere, a function it forfeited as the bourgeoisie assumed an increasingly reactionary and defensive posture after the short-lived revolutions of 1848. Benjamin, so it seemed, wished to have nothing further to do with affirmative bourgeois culture. In 1926, he took a trip to Moscow, although he spoke no Russian and had to rely on Lacis, who had arranged his two month visit, for his information. Apparently, the voyage left him convinced that the future of literature lay in its role as an auxiliary tool in the construction of socialism—though he was hardly naïve enough to believe that Russian developments could be transposed as such to the very different social situation in the rest of Europe. He concludes "Die politische Gruppierung der russischen Schriftsteller" with the following provocative metaphor: "The best Russian literature, if it is to fulfill its potential, can therefore only be the colorful image in the primer from which the farmers, in the shadow of Lenin, learn to read."[19]

Consequently, whereas conditions in Germany were hardly as favorable for the emergence of a politically oriented literary praxis as in the Soviet Union—where, after all, the means of production had already been "socialized"—at the same time, it did appear that conditions there were more favorable than in France. In keeping with a good Marxist analysis, the German economic situation was deteriorating at a more rapid rate. Thus, Benjamin came to view Brecht's theater as a form of literary praxis halfway between the more autonomous surrealist approach and the manifestly political literature of the Soviet Union—the form most suitable to the German situation, which was rife with political tension, but far from revolutionary.[20]

At the same time, Benjamin's attraction toward surrealism, Soviet pedagogical writing (at this stage, it had not yet reached the full-blown didacticism of the Zhdanov period), and his immediately enthusiastic reception of Brecht's epic theater were, at least in one important respect, consistent with his earlier aesthetic investigations; they point to his persistent and abiding concern with *the anti-aesthetic forces within art*—a concern which received its consummate treatment in the *Trauerspiel* study and has become the defining feature of all twentieth-century modernism.[21] As such, Benjamin's various quests in the late twenties and early thirties for suitable forms of nonaffirmative art coincides with the theory of allegory in the *Trauerspiel* book insofar as they, too, sought the sublation of traditional, rounded, symbolic works of art in favor of a form of aesthetic expression that was fragmentary and profane, devoid of the grandeur and sublimity associated with the so-called great works of art. At this point, however, Benjamin would insist that the promise of transcendence traditionally ensconced in autonomous works of art must be redeemed *exoterically*—for the public sphere in general—rather than *esoterically*—for a small coterie of initiates.

In this connection, it was only natural that he would be strongly attracted by the dramaturgical breakthroughs of Brecht's approach. For Brecht represents a genuinely unique figure in the annals of modern aesthetics insofar as his conception of epic theater managed to bring to fruition an artistic technique which combined in equal measure the more advanced tendencies of the twentieth-century avant garde and a pronounced concern for political content usually associated with the name of *l'art engagé*. In many respects, Brecht consummates an anti-aesthetic trend in modern art which commenced with the dadaist movement of World War I and was renewed by surrealism: a trend which rejected the traditional self-enclosed, autonomous self-definition of high art—i.e., the "work-character" of art—and instead sought to bridge the gap separating art from life. As Brecht announces in 1930: "The publication of the 'Versuche' occurs at a point in time where certain works of art are no longer as much individual experiences (have a work-character), but are instead directed toward the utilization (trans-formation) of determinate institutes and institutions."[22] Thus, in his rejection of the nineteenth-century theatrical standard, the "pièce bien faite,"[23] Brecht expresses his solidarity with the sur-realist attack on the bourgeois ideal of *l'art pour l'art* (though bi-ographically speaking, his early plays derive their inspiration from expressionist sources such as the work of Frank Wedekind). "I refuse to utilize [*verwerten*] my talent 'freely,' I utilize [*verwerte*] it as an educator, politician, organizer. There is no reproach against my literary persona—plagiarist, disturber of the peace, saboteur—which I would not claim as a compliment for my unliterary, anonymous, yet systematic procedure," observes Brecht.[24]

It is not by chance that in his *Versuche* he often refers to his drama as an "experiment" or "laboratory." For in this respect, too, his work, like that of Joyce and Kafka, parallels the avant garde renunciation of the aestheticist ideal of the isolated, self-contained, perfect work and presents itself instead as a "work-in-progress." As Adorno has noted, prototypical for modern works of art is the phenomenon of fireworks: "the only form of art that would not want to endure, but rather to radiate for a moment and then disappear in smoke." He continues: "If all art is the secular-ization of transcendence, then every work participates in the di-alectic of enlightenment. Art has given itself over to this dialectic with the conception of anti-art; no conception of art is conceivable without this moment. That means nothing less than the fact that art must pass beyond its own concept in order to remain faithful to it."[25]

That Brecht conceives of his theater as a laboratory indicates that he was as concerned with the enlightenment the performers themselves would gain in the very process of acting out their roles as he was with the "effect" his dramas would have on the public at large. In his more reflexive moments he had few illusions about the immediate political consequences that might accrue from the production of his plays—he was well aware that it was largely Berliners of a middle class stamp out for an evening of entertainment who constituted the audience for his "successful" plays such as *Threepenny Opera*. It was this fact, plus the rising tide of fascism, which pushed him toward the less reflexive direction of the *Lehrstücke* (didactic plays) in 1929. Yet, his original conception of epic theater centered around the ideal of enlightenment in the positive sense. What he desired was for art to become part of a large-scale process of social demystification, portraying social relations as the soulless and rigid second nature which they have become in fact, so as to hasten the advent of their transformation. The subjective corollary of this conviction was a fundamentalist faith in man as an infinitely malleable and indomitable creature, a point of view conveyed most unflinchingly in his portrayal of Galy Gay in *Man is Man,* but also evident in the later "Stories from Herr Keuner." To be sure, his plays of the late 1920s are populated largely by criminals and ruffians of various sorts. "However, one would err if one were to assume these characters interested the author only as negative (*abschreckende*] examples," observes Benjamin astutely. "They are for him indeed egoistic and anti-social types. However, it is Brecht's constant effort to portray these hooligans and anti-social types as potential revolutionaries." Benjamin continues:

If Marx posed to himself the problem of how the revolution would proceed from its sheer opposite, from capitalism, without making any ethical claims, Brecht transposes this problem into the human sphere: he wants to make the revolutionary emerge from the base, selfish type, entirely on his own and without ethical compunction. Just as Wagner wants to develop Homunculus in the alembic from a magical mixture, Brecht wants to develop the revolutionary in the alembic of baseness and vulgarity.[26]

Epic Theater

Thus, Brecht's theory of epic theater went far toward ful-filling Benjamin's desire for a de-aestheticized, effective successor to bourgeois autonomous art. As opposed to surrealism, which had never been able to abandon completely the ideal of aesthetic autonomy,[27] epic theater, while incorporating many of surreal-ism's techniques, proved itself unquestionably on the other side of the debate over commitment by virtue of the preeminence it granted to problems of aesthetic reception. Brecht's conception of epic theater was itself formulated in conscious opposition to the affirmative character of traditional theater, to the culinary notion of theater as a harmless evening of cultural diversion. From the beginning, he fought against the idea of art as "consolation" in all its forms and, from the standpoint of reception aesthetics, against the notion of *l'art pour l'art* (the notion that the work of art represents a fully autonomous entity whose status must remain entirely independent of all external conditions—to the point where it becomes a matter of indifference whether the work is "received" or not). In this connection the extreme reversal in Benjamin's own earlier attitude toward art necessitated by his endorsement of epic theater can be best illustrated by a citation from his 1923 essay "The Task of the Translator," where he begins by observing that:

In the appreciation of a work of art or an art form, consideration of a receiver never proves fruitful. Not only is any reference to a certain public or its representatives misleading, but even the concept of an "ideal" receiver is detrimental in the theoretical consideration of art, since all it posits is the nature and existence of man as such. Art, in the same way, posits man's physical and spiritual existence, but in none of its works is it concerned with his response. No poem is intended for the reader, no picture for the beholder, no symphony for the listener.[28]

Whereas in stark contrast to all such aestheticist ideals concerning the innate purity of the work of art, the Brechtian alternative was to place the emphasis in his work squarely on the moment of its *effect* on the recipient. Through this mechanism he sought to stir the viewer into assuming an active and critical attitude vis-à-vis the work of art, in opposition to the traditional work which pro-

motes passivity by tending to absorb the viewer within its parameters. He referred to his technique as a process of *alienation* (*Ver-
fremdung*), which he counterposed to the *identification* of the viewer
with the work (and its characters) in traditional theater. By alienating the viewer Brecht sought to forestall an illusory, merely
aesthetic resolution of the conflicts that have arisen in the drama
and spur the viewer to rational, independent judgment—not just
judgment about art, but judgment about crucial facets of life itself
which serve as the drama's content. In epic theater, reason was
meant to triumph over emotion. Because it opposed all catharsis,
the false purging of emotional tension with the conclusion of the
play, Brecht at times referred to his dramaturgy as a theory of
non-Aristotelian drama. Thus, the "effect" Brecht sought to pro-
mote was one of critical, rational distance rather than immediate
identification in relation to the events on the stage. In this sense
however, it is important to distinguish between Brecht's early
"anarchistic" plays and his transition to the *Lehrstücke,* beginning
with *Der Flug der Lindberghs* and his adaptation of Gorky's *Die
Mutter* in 1929. For whereas the effect intended by the earlier plays
was one which merely emphasized provocation or a heightening
of social awareness on the part of the audience, in the *Lehrstücke*
the social content of the drama became much more explicit—if
not didactic.

Benjamin had originally intended to write a comprehensive appraisal of the poet's work, but this intention, like so many others,
never came to fruition. Nonetheless, his commentaries on Brecht's
work are characterized throughout by an attitude of unqualified
approbation. To him, the theory of epic theater represented the
only vital alternative to the congealed state of the bourgeois arts;
moreover, Brecht's work had, more generally, assimilated the
most advanced techniques of contemporary art forms such as radio
and film, and placed them for the first time within the framework
of a truly radical aesthetic program. As such, Benjamin viewed
it as his mission as critic to facilitate the reception of epic theater
among the public in general—and among left-wing intellectuals
in particular—along the lines which had already been sketched on
various occasions by the playwright himself. Hence, the predominantly restrained, exegetical quality of his essays on Brecht, in

marked contrast to the distinctly imaginative flair that had been the hallmark of his other writings. It was the publication of the *Versuche* in 1930 which had stimulated Benjamin's profound interest in Brecht's work, and he describes his reaction to them as follows: "These writings are the first—that is, among poetic and literary writings—which I can back as a critic without any (manifest) reservations. . . . more clearly than other attempts, they provide insight into the spiritual conditions under which the work of people like me takes place in this country."[29]

In "What is Epic Theatre?" Benjamin sought to describe the devices by virtue of which Brecht attempted to divest theater of all illusionary pretense and thereby prevent the traditional empathetic relation of the observer to the work of art. As such, Brecht's dramas constantly seek to point to their own artificiality, to the fact they are distinct from reality, something merely constructed. In Benjamin's words:

The naturalistic stage is in no sense a public platform; it is entirely illusionistic. Its own awareness that it is theatre cannot fertilize it; like every theatre of unfolding action, it must repress this awareness so as to pursue undistracted its aim of protraying the real. Epic theatre, by contrast, incessantly derives a lively and productive consciousness from the fact that it is theater. This consciousness enables it to treat elements of reality as though it were setting up an experiment, with "conditions" at the end of the experiment not at the beginning. Thus they are not brought closer to the spectator but distanced from him. When he recognizes them as real conditions it is not, as in naturalistic theatre, with complacency, but with astonishment. . . . Epic theatre, then does not reproduce conditions but, rather, reveals them.[30]

By self-consciously seeking to differentiate itself from the illusionism of traditional drama, epic theater compels the viewer to assume a measure of critical distance versus the dramatic events unfolding before him. One of the predominant mechanisms employed by Brecht to achieve this measure of distance (the *Verfremdungseffekt*) is the method of interruption: "This uncovering of conditions," Benjamin continues, "is brought about through processes being interrupted."[31] Brecht's employment of songs to break up the dramatic action periodically is one example of this technique. Another such instance is his concept of the "literarization"—the addition of titles or short commentaries which serve to punctuate and complement the action. "The literarization of theatre," Benjamin explains, "by means of verbal formulas, posters, captions, is intended to, and will, 'make what is shown on the stage unsensational.'"[32] In this way the process of literarization strives to destroy the aura of aesthetic illusion, to divert the attention of the viewer, and thus undermine the theater's capacity to absorb his concentration totally within the boundaries of the artificial reality it has created. The captions moreover serve as directives intended to spur the viewer to critical reflection on the course of the dramatic action. They work against the recipient's passive consumption of the drama as entertainment. As Brecht comments, "once illusion is sacrificed to free discussion, and once the spectator, instead of being enabled to have an experience, is forced as it were to cast his vote; then a change has been launched which goes far beyond formal matters and begins for the first time to affect the theatre's social function."[33] The technique of literarization thus seeks to abolish all traditional, culinary employment of theater and turn the spectator into an informed, critical judge. As Brecht remarks, "By these means one would soon have a theatre full of experts, just as one has sporting arenas full of experts."[34]

Benjamin compares the use of interruption in epic theater to the function of quotations in written texts, a practice at which he personally excelled: "Quotations in my works are like robbers by the roadside who make an armed attack and relieve an idler of his convictions," he once observed.[35] Interruption, he notes with reference to epic theater, is "to mention just one of its aspects, the origin of the quotation. Quoting a text implies interrupting its context."[36] Like the well-timed "gesture" in epic theater, a well-placed citation serves to interrupt the flow of a text and, at the appropriate juncture, concentrate the attention of the reader at a focal point. In this respect Brecht's desire in epic theater to "make gestures ["*Gestus*," meaning both "gist" and "gesture"] quotable" coincides with Benjamin's own methodological procedure of this period, which centered around the theory of Dialectical Images. Both techniques sought not merely to represent reality, but to uncover it. Both attempted, by virtue of a process of alienation,

to make seemingly ordinary events "strange," and thereby pro-
voke the astonishment of the recipient in the hope that he would
cease to regard them as natural and acceptable. Epic theater and
the Dialectical Image—the former by way of the "quotable gesture," the latter by way of the pithy citation—both sought to
freeze the normal flow of events in life in order to subject them
to an intensive process of critical scrutiny. The strategy of interruption common to both procedures thus aimed overall at dis-
seminating an effect of *distraction,* an effect diametrically opposed
to the *immersion* of the recipient in traditional aesthetic or—to use
the terminology developed by Benjamin later in "The Work of
Art" essay—auratic works of art.

In this way, for Benjamin epic theater seemed to employ to
maximum advantage the artistic technique which had been a favorite of the surrealists, which had influenced decisively his own
theory of Dialectical Images, and whose origins ultimately derived
from the medium of film: the technique of *montage.*[37] The essential
characteristic of montage-construction is the autonomy of the individual parts versus the work of art as a whole. In this respect
it is a procedure which proves fundamentally inimical to the aforementioned "work-character" of art; and it also proves antithetical
to one of the mandatory prerequisites of drama as defined by
Aristotle's *Poetics:* the unity of time and place. Brecht defines the
montage-character of epic theater, in contrast to the *unitary* effect
sought by traditional drama, in the following passage:

The bourgeois novel in the last century developed much that was "dramatic," by which was meant the strong centralization of the story, a
momentum that drew the separate parts into a common relationship. . . .
The epic writer [Alfred] Döblin provided an excellent criterion when he
said that with an epic work, as opposed to a dramatic, one can as it were
take a pair of scissors and cut it into individual pieces, which remain
fully capable of life.[38]

Brecht himself was the first to acknowledge that it was above
all *technical advances,* most of which were associated with the field
of film, which had paved the way for the transformation of theater
according to epic rather than dramatic criteria: "The possibility

of projections, the greater adaptability of the stage due to mechanization, the film, all completed the theatre's equipment, and did so at a point where the most important transactions between people could no longer be shown simply by personifying the motive forces or subjecting the characters to invisible metaphysical powers."[39] Hence, these technical innovations enabled the epic playwright to demonstrate that people's actions were less a product of their own autonomous needs and desires than of an objective network of social relations in whose all-emcompassing web their lives had become entangled. It was precisely this *objective, social* dimension of human behavior which Brecht sought constantly to highlight in his drama in a collected and rational way, as opposed to the more emotionally disposed, character-centered orientation of traditional theater. It was his seminal reflections on the intimate relation between cinematic technique and epic theater in *Versuche* 3 (1931) which sparked Benjamin's own fascination with the emancipatory potential embodied in the new medium. As Brecht remarks at one point, "This apparatus [film] can be used better than almost anything else to supersede the old kind of untechnical, anti-technical 'glowing' art, with its religious links. The socialization of these means is vital for art."[40] This passage, from Brecht's "Threepenny Trial," undoubtedly had an enormous impact on Benjamin's later development of the antithesis between "auratic" and "mechanically reproduced" art in "The Work of Art" essay (to be discussed at length in the ensuing chapter). In "What is Epic Theatre?" Benjamin pinpoints the precise nature of the link between epic theater and film when he observes:

Epic theatre proceeds by fits and starts, in a manner comparable to the images on a film strip. Its basic form is that of the forceful impact on one another of separate sharply distinct situations of the play. The songs, the captions, the gestural conventions, differentiate the scenes. As a result intervals tend to occur which destroy illusion. These intervals paralyse the audience's capacity for empathy.[41]

In this sense, epic theater seeks to impart to the audience an experience which was not only the hallmark of cinematic technique, but which, according to Benjamin, had become the distinguishing feature of modern life in all its aspects: the experience of *shocks*.[42]

The Author as Producer

In addition to the various commentaries explicitly devoted to the theme of epic theater, the Benjamin essay from this period in which Brechtian motifs are displayed most prominently is "The Author as Producer." This essay represents Benjamin's furthest advance into the realm of "committed" literature and, not paradoxically, is the work which shows his position at its most vulnerable. That the work was conceived of by Benjamin as standing in the closest proximity to the 1931 version of "What is Epic Theatre?" can be seen from a letter to Adorno of April 1934 in which he remarks, "If you were here, the lecture I spoke of would provide, I believe, much material for debate. It is called 'The Author as Producer,' will be presented at the 'Institute for the Study of Fascism' before a very small but qualified audience, and represents an attempt to accomplish for literature what I sought to achieve for the stage in the work on 'Epic Theater.'"[43] One month later he wrote to Brecht: "Under the title 'The Author as Producer,' I have attempted to produce a pendant, in subject-matter and scope, to my earlier work on epic theater."[44] Nevertheless, it is of interest to note that even while Benjamin was engaged in writing "The Author as Producer," he was at the same time involved in a serious correspondence with Scholem concerning the status of Franz Kafka in the history of Jewish letters and a suitable metaphysical basis for the interpretation of his work—an exchange of ideas that came to fruition in Benjamin's Kafka essay of that same year, a work as far removed as could be imagined from his Marxist interests; in fact a work which represented an undisguised return to the Messianic concerns that had dominated his early writings.[45]

Benjamin begins his address by rehashing the (by his own admission) all-too-familiar and sterile controversy in left-wing circles as to whether the correct political tendency or the artistic quality is of foremost importance in literature. It had been frequently asserted either that adherence to the correct political line absolves a work of art from having to measure up to any "bourgeois" standards of quality or, on the other hand, that for a work of art to surmount the level of mere propaganda, some consideration of the moment of quality would be essential. Benjamin identifies with the latter school of thought. However, he insists, the relationship between tendency and quality cannot be merely posited in the abstract. Rather, there exists a necessary interrelation between these two moments, and Benjamin takes it upon himself to demonstrate this interrelation with certainty. His intention is to prove that in fact the correct political tendency of a work *includes* the moment of literary quality, for the relation between the two is ensured by a third term: its "literary tendency." For in his view, "this literary tendency, which is implicitly or explicitly included in every *correct* political tendency, this and nothing else constitutes the quality of a work. The correct political tendency of a work includes its literary quality *because* it includes its literary tendency."[46] That is, the union of political tendency and literary quality of a work are guaranteed as long as the artist follows the correct *literary tendency*.

As in "The Work of Art" essay, in "The Author as Producer" Benjamin's argument hinges upon his reliance on the category of *technique*. "Social relations are," Benjamin notes, "as we know, determined by relations of production."[47] Up until now, though, materialist criticism has not treated this dictum in a sufficiently systematic fashion. For in Benjamin's eyes, it is literary technique that determines whether or not an artist is following the correct literary tendency; and thus it is the issue of technique that in the last analysis ensures the ultimate concordance between political tendency and literary quality. Literary technique "directly concerns the function the work has within the literary relations of production of its time."[48] Therefore, and in no uncertain terms, if a writer follows the most advanced technique given the general level of development of the literary forces and relations of production, this will be a sufficient criterion to guarantee not only the correctness of the work's political tendency, but also its quality. Thus, it follows logically from this extremely literal reading of Karl Marx's specification of the cause and effect relationship between "base" and "superstructure" in the Preface to the *Contribution to the Critique of Political Economy* that the "forces of literary production"—technique—prove determinant in relation to political tendency and literary quality—which in this way are degraded to the status of mere epiphenomena of technique. On this point Benjamin is adamant:

> By mentioning technique I have named the concept which makes literary products accessible to immediate social, and therefore materialist, analysis. At the same time, the concept of technique represents the dialectical starting point from which the sterile dichotomy of form and content can be surmounted. . . . If, then, we were entitled earlier on to say that the correct political tendency of a work includes its literary quality because it includes its literary tendency, we can now affirm more precisely that this literary tendency may consist in a progressive development of literary technique, or in a regressive one.[49]

The work of art will be progressive if it follows the most advanced artistic techniques—epic theater, film, Soviet journalism—and regressive if it follows traditional, outmoded artistic practices—regressive, that is, in terms of both its political tendency and quality. Benjamin's attempt to establish the idea of materialist criticism on the basis of the concept of technique relies inordinately on supra-individual "forces of artistic production," a mechanism the individual artist can elect whether or not to conform to, but which otherwise seems to operate entirely independent of his will. As in the 1936 "Work of Art" essay, Benjamin's analysis is vitiated by the vulgar materialist presupposition that the use of technologically advanced means will have unilaterally positive results for art.

It is not, however, as if the advanced technological apparatus can be taken over wholesale and unaltered from the bourgeoisie. Rather, Benjamin recognizes that it is the responsibility of left-wing artists to transform the apparatus in order to make them serviceable for progressive political goals, just as it will fall due to the revolution to convert bourgeois into socialist relations of production. In this respect his position echoes Marx's verdict on the Paris Commune of 1871, which collapsed because of the naïve belief that it could take over the state apparatus of the bourgeoisie unchanged. However, Benjamin's immediate inspiration for this line of argumentation was undoubtedly the conclusions drawn by Brecht in the "Threepenny Trial," his account of the 1930 lawsuit against the producers of the film version of *Threepenny Opera*, who had reneged on their promise to allow Brecht some measure of control over the final product. This legal battle played a significant role in Brecht's own awareness that in the domain of art, as well as economics, the bourgeois technical infrastructure must be "refunctioned" (*"umfunktioniert"*). As he remarks at one point: "Innovations remain regressive as long as they merely serve the renewal of outmoded institutions."[50] In "The Author as Producer" Benjamin sought to generalize the lessons of Brecht's experience in the Threepenny trial. As Benjamin notes: "He was the first to address to the intellectuals the far-reaching demand that they should not supply the production apparatus without, at the same time, within the limits of the possible, changing that apparatus in the direction of socialism."[51]

Benjamin invokes the work of the Soviet writer and journalist Sergey Tretyakov as a model example of the practice of *Umfunktionierung*. His approach to journalism does not seek merely to report facts or inform the reader; rather, Tretyakov is an "operative writer" who actively seeks to intervene in and thus alter his medium. "Tretyakov distinguishes between the operative and informative writer. The operative writer's mission is not to report but to fight; not to assume the spectator's role but to intervene actively."[52] For Benjamin this is all part of a process of the world-historical transformation of literary genres along de-aestheticized, functional lines: "Novels did not always exist in the past, nor must they necessarily always exist in the future; nor always tragedies; nor great epics. . . . we are in the midst of a mighty recasting of literary forms, a melting-down in which many of the oppositions in which we have been accustomed to think may lose their relevance."[53]

In Tretyakov's transformation of the medium of print, for example, the traditional bourgeois distinction between writer and reader is broken down. Contributions are solicited from the readers themselves, who thus cast off their earlier role as passive receivers of information. As his concerns are thematized and voiced from his own point of view in Soviet newspapers, the worker is encouraged to take on a more active role in public life. The readers themselves are turned into writers, into "experts"—the effect upon the theatergoer that was desired by Brecht. The domain of literature is no longer the province of specialists in the academy; everyone has become a specialist and the conditions of daily life are thus literarized. All this while the conditions of the bourgeois press become more and more debased. The salvation of the press can only lie in its being refunctioned through the dissolution of the traditional distinction between author and writer and the adoption of the viewpoint of the working individual.

For Benjamin, it is essential that artists refrain from taking possession of their media *tel quel,* and instead exercise an *organizing function* vis-à-vis those media, thereby making them serviceable for progressive political ends: "the bourgeois apparatus of production and publication is capable of assimilating, indeed propagating, an astonishing amount of revolutionary themes without ever seriously putting into question its own continued existence or that of the class which owns it."[54] Adoption of the correct political line is never a sufficient condition for a work of art. Only by pursuing the most advanced artistic technique can the link between tendency and quality be guaranteed. "The more completely [the artist] can orient his activity toward this task [*Umfunktionierung*], the more correct will be the political tendency, and, necessarily, the higher will be the technical quality of his work."[55]

It is for these reasons that the work of Brecht appeared so exemplary to Benjamin. By turning the technique of interruption or montage into an integral element of his theater, Brecht had totally recast the shape of contemporary drama. The example of epic theater would serve as the model for all the other arts to emulate. The methods of mechanical reproduction—such as montage—were thus uncritically identified with the great heretofore untapped potentials of art that were to be transformed along revolutionary lines. By studiously adhering to these new techniques, the artist's work was assured of simultaneously advancing the correct political tendency and of possessing aesthetic quality as well—since, according to Benjamin's extremely undialectical reading of Marxism, the pursuit of the most technologically advanced means sufficed to ensure the most progressive political and artistic results. The incorporation of techniques such as montage, literarization, alienation, etc., within the context of traditional bourgeois art forms would explode the latter from within, so to speak. The arts of literature, film, and theater would thereby cease to be serviceable for the passive absorption of the recipient within the languid and indifferent world of bourgeois aesthetic illusion and stimulate him to take an active and critical role versus his environment and fate.

The relationship between art and society today is very different from the period in which Benjamin and Brecht wrote. To take their prescriptions at face value in changed historical circumstances would be the surest way to eviscerate them, to reify their positions by turning them into lifeless historical relics. The work of both men has already suffered noticeably from an ignominious posthumous fate of this type. The politically motivated desire to glorify precisely those didactic features of Brechtian drama which represent its most problematical aspects are counterbalanced by an equally reprehensible attempt on the part of contemporary partisans of affirmative culture to save Brecht the artist from Brecht the politician. Benjamin, too, has been either enthroned as the patron saint of a new functional art or condemned to scholastic irrelevance as an arch-defender of the realm of pure spirit. Originally, both men, in sharp contrast to their more dogmatic contemporary supporters, were fundamentally less concerned with the naïve belief that art possessed an independent capacity to change the world than they were inspired by the possibility of transforming art itself from within, and thus preventing it from degenerating to the level of mere consolation. Both men were sufficiently self-conscious concerning their training in high culture to realize the inherent foolhardiness of attempting to reach the masses directly; instead, they sought to influence other left-leaning intellectuals of similar background. It was specifically on the basis of this mutual objective that Benjamin and Brecht sought to co-edit a journal, *Krisis und Kritik,* in the early 1930s. The methods of criticism were intended to render explicit the pedagogical function which works of art convey in a language that is nonconceptual. Benjamin, however, ultimately withdrew from the project when it appeared to be on the verge of taking a more "committed" turn.[56]

Brecht, on the other hand, from the beginning had remained

attached to a more narrowly rationalist, edifying conception of the function of art, and with the groveling obeisances to the idea of Party unity characteristic of works such as *The Measures Taken*, pedagogics degenerated into the out and out propaganda which it latently was to begin with. "The wild roar of *The Measures Taken* drowns out the noise of the disaster that has overtaken the cause, which Brecht convulsively tries to proclaim as salvation," Adorno once remarked. "When Brecht became a panegyrist of [socialist] harmony, his lyric voice had to swallow chalk, and it started to grate."[57] When Benjamin himself, in "From the Brecht Commentary," announces that "The purpose of the commentary . . . is to advance the pedagogical effect as much as possible and to retard the poetic one,"[58] he was already flirting with the calamity that would be realized four years hence in "The Author as Producer."

Above all, what has been abolished in the decades since the concept of epic theater was developed is precisely that independent public sphere which had been originally conceived of as its necessary prerequisite. That is, the same autonomous bourgeois individuals whom Brecht had counted upon as his ideal addressees— as his potential "experts"—have themselves been eradicated as a result of the final stages of the dialectic of enlightenment, when under the purportedly benevolent auspices of the New Deal alliance between government and industry, mass culture turns into ideological terror. As a result of the historical suppression of the nineteenth-century ideal of autonomous individuality—the necessary precondition for any claim to authentic collectivity that would be other than a mere sham—the call for the urgent renewal of this ideal under contemporary social conditions becomes a genuinely *radical* demand. In light of these developments, the following remarks by Tiedemann concerning the historical afterlife of the association between Benjamin and Brecht assume added significance:

If Brecht today, according to the often denied yet still unrefuted saying of [Max] Frisch, has been reduced to the supreme impotence [*Wirkungslosigkeit*] of a classical author, then the recently completed installation of Benjamin in the market place of scholarship and culture, not to mention the authority his commentaries on Brecht have commanded, presents only the other side of the general lack of acknowledgement and dissipation which distinguished the commentaries during the lifetime of their author. . . . Justice would be done to the claim of the Benjamin-Brecht commentaries only by he who would decipher their literal meaning in its historical presuppositions; to whom their apparent simplicity would show itself as the complex into which the nearly one-half century of changed experiences since the time of their composition has retransformed them.[59]

With the Nazi seizure of power in 1933 the immediate hope shared by both Benjamin and Brecht for the triumph of a politically effective mass art was quashed. For both writers the possibility of their work having any widespread meaningful influence was virtually eliminated when they were forced into exile. Brecht continued to write poems and plays in Denmark, but was essentially without an audience. For Benjamin, forced emigration from Germany brought his career as a *Publizist* to a terminus, although for a while he continued to publish in Germany under a pseudonym. Yet, this turn of events had the unforeseen advantage of allowing him to devote more time to the *Passagenarbeit* and other more involved studies. Thus, the diminished possibilities for struggle on the literary front also brought the theoretical inclinations of his thought to the fore once again. Under the impact of the Moscow trials and the manifest stultification of the Revolution under Stalin's rule, Benjamin's disenchantment with the communist movement grew steadily—if nevertheless his allegiances to the materialist conception of history remained firm for the time being. As Brecht would confide to Benjamin in 1938, "There can't be any doubt about it any longer: the struggle against ideology has become a new ideology."[60] A regular salary from the Institute for Social Research beginning in 1935 helped somewhat to alleviate Benjamin's extremely precarious financial situation over these years. The definitive break with the politics of communism would only come with the Stalin-Hitler pact of 1939, which threw into total doubt the strategy Benjamin had pursued in the previous years of placing the powers of criticism in the service of the revolution.

Upon learning of Benjamin's death in 1940, Brecht is reported to have said it was the first real loss Hitler had inflicted on German literature.[61]

Chapter Six

THE ADORNO–
BENJAMIN DISPUTE

THE ADORNO-BENJAMIN dispute of the 1930s represents without question one of the most significant aesthetic controversies of our century—not only because of the intellectual stature of the participants but, more importantly, owing to the gravity and import of its content. In addition, the debate affords invaluable insight into the meta-theoretical presuppositions that stand behind Benjamin's various material investigations in his later years—most notably in the case of the Arcades Project. For in the majority of his writings Benjamin scrupulously eschewed explicit thematization of the methodological premises underlying his work. In this respect his thought coincides with Hegel's polemic against Kant in the "Introduction" to the *Phenomenology of Spirit*. Like Hegel, Benjamin seeks unselfishly to surrender the movement of thought to the inner logic of the object under investigation, in order thereby to permit its essence to emerge unscarred by the prejudices of method. Unlike Hegel, however, whose dialectic advances through the subjective category of mediation, Benjamin's conception of truth seeks to approximate the idea of "theological immediacy" whereby things are called by their proper names and thus redeemed. As we shall see in the third stage of the debate, Benjamin went so far as to attempt to apply this theological conception of truth to one of his most thoroughly profane and "materialist" of works, "The Paris of the Second Empire in Baudelaire."[1]

In the debate with Adorno, he was roundly criticized for his inattention to the theoretical category of mediation, an oversight

163

which at times resulted in what might be referred to as a distinctly positivistic streak in his thought. Moreover, his serious attempt in the thirties to assimilate the method of historical materialism amidst the older theological residues of his thinking led to an accentuation of this positivistic bias which had some extremely problematical consequences for his later work as a whole. It was precisely this often confused and unwholesome blend of materialist and theological elements which Adorno attempted to redress in their philosophical correspondence of this period. In Adorno's view, in consequence of his wholesale and uncritical conversion to the world view of historical materialism, Benjamin did violence not merely to his original theological mode of conceptualization, but to the materialist point of view as well. Adorno objected less to Benjamin's adherence to a materialist perspective than to his undialectical, ritualistic employment of it. As Benjamin himself later realized, his methodological procedure in the *Trauerspiel* book—allowing the universal to step forth from a philosophically informed constellation of material elements, a configuration of fragments or ruins—was not in itself entirely incompatible with the principles of historical materialism. As he observes in a letter of March 7, 1931:

My book, *The Origin of German Trauerspiel,* testifies to what extent a rigorous consideration of genuine academic methods of research departs from the present attitude of bourgeois-idealist science, insofar as it has been deemed worthy of review by no German academics. Now this book was certainly not materialistic, if at the same time [it was] already dialectical. However, something which I was unaware of at the time of its composition became soon after more and more clear to me: that proceeding from the standpoint of my very unique philosophy of language, there exist points of contact [*Vermittlung*]—however strained and problematic—with the methods of dialectical materialism. However, with the saturation of bourgeois science, [there are] none at all.[2]

Yet, when treated as type of *prima philosophia,* and not solely as a heuristic, yet binding methodological guideline for sound historico-philosophical investigation, the materialist world view unquestionably remained opposed to the innermost tendencies of Benjamin's thinking. It was a method with which he never seemed entirely comfortable; often, materialist observations seem awkwardly grafted on to metaphysical insights—with the zeal characteristic of a new convert. This practice is most blatant in his "Karl Kraus" essay,[3] but is detectable in his work throughout this period. Try as he might, Benjamin was never able to sever totally his relation to the tradition of speculative thought toward which his thinking naturally inclined; and in his philosophical last will and testament, the "Theses on the Philosophy of History," this tradition would gain the upper hand for a final time. In the debate, then, Adorno confronts the "Marxist" Benjamin from the standpoint of the "metaphysical" Benjamin of the *Trauerspiel* book period in an effort to bring his friend's theoretical outlook in line once more with its genuine impulses, as it were. "God knows there is only one truth," remarks Adorno in a November 1938 letter criticizing Benjamin's first Baudelaire study,

and if your intelligence lays hold of this one truth in categories which on the basis of your materialism seem apocryphal to you, you will capture more of this one truth than if you use intellectual tools whose movements your hand resists at every turn. After all, there is more of this truth in Nietzsche's *Genealogy of Morals* than in Bukharin's *ABC's of Communism*. . . . Your study of Goethe's *Elective Affinities* and your Baroque book are better Marxism that the wine duty and the deduction of phantasmagoria from the behaviour of the feuilletonists."[4]

At the same time, the intensity of the controversy can be explained as much by the profound nature of the intellectual commitment between the two protagonists as by the growing theoretical breach between them.[5]

The Philosophical Rapprochement Between Benjamin and Adorno in the Early 1930s

What has come to be known as the Adorno-Benjamin dispute consists of Adorno's detailed epistolary responses to three of Benjamin's writings of the 1930s: "Paris, Capital of the Nineteenth Century" (also known as the Arcades Exposé); "The Work of Art in the Era of Mechanical Reproduction"; and "The Paris of the

Second Empire in Baudelaire." Having first met in 1923, Adorno and Benjamin consolidated their intellectual bond in 1929 during a series of "unforgettable conversations in Königstein,"[6] where Benjamin first revealed to Adorno his plans for the Arcades Project.[7] In Königstein they presumably discussed the possibility of developing a common philosophical program, a supposition that is substantiated by the distinctly Benjaminian tenor of Adorno's writing in the early thirties. Adorno, Benjamin's junior by eleven years, was most obviously influenced by the latter's *Trauerspiel* book; and it is known that in 1931, his first year as Professor at the University of Frankfurt, Adorno taught a seminar on Benjamin's failed *Habilitationsschrift*.

Adorno's theoretical indebtedness to Benjamin is most transparent in two seminal addresses of the early 1930s, "Die Idee der Naturgeschichte" and "The Actuality of Philosophy." In retrospect, both pieces can be viewed as preliminary expositions of a philosophy of history and theory of knowledge which would receive their consummate expression in Adorno's philosophical magnum opus, *Negative Dialectics* (1966)—indicating a remarkable continuity to an *oeuvre* that spans some 40 years.[8] "Die Idee der Naturgeschichte" was originally presented in July 1932 as a lecture to a gathering of the *Kantgesellschaft* in Frankfurt. The very title of the address already betrays a telling affinity with Benjamin's work: for it was his interpretation of history as *"Naturgeschichte,"* a history condemned to a fate of transience and decline, that served as the central historico-philosophical theme of the *Trauerspiel* study. It is precisely this motif that Adorno seizes upon in his 1932 address, for it was his avowed intention "to transcend [*aufzuheben*] the customary antithesis of nature and history . . . to push these concepts to a point where their pure opposition is transcended."[9] According to Adorno, this act of transcendence can be accomplished, given the present constellation of socio-historic forces, only if each side of the antithesis can be perceived as passing over into its opposite. That is, in order for the true nature of the customary dualism between nature and history to manifest itself, the *natural* side of history and the *historical* side of nature must be allowed to step forth. By referring to the "natural side of history" Adorno intends the same meaning which the term "Naturgeschichte" had for Benjamin in the *Trauerspiel* book: history as an inescapable, mythical and rigid continuum of fate, as it presents itself (and here, Adorno's historicization of Benjamin's original use of the term becomes apparent) to mankind under the iron laws of commodity society. Consequently, according to Adorno the concept of "nature" can best be translated in philosophical parlance by the concept of "myth." Myth signifies "what is eternally present, what human history endures as a pre-given 'being' that is structured by fate."[10]

Conversely, the historical dimension of nature must also be recognized: nature itself undergoes a vast, far-reaching process of transformation when subjected to the formidable powers of human labor and industry. The upshot of the dialectic of nature and history, then, in Adorno's view, is that nature has been *historicized* while history has been *naturalized*. In this way the traditional rigid opposition between the two concepts is dissolved; for over the course of history, they pass over into each other. Hence, a satisfactory answer to the question of the relation between nature and history can only be given if *"historical being, in its most extreme historical determinancy, where it is most historical, is grasped as a natural being"* and *"nature, where it apparently hardens itself most thoroughly into nature, is grasped as an historical being."*[11]

In *The Theory of the Novel* Lukács, through his employment of the Hegelian category of "second nature," succeeded in representing the moribund and ossified condition of spirit in the modern world. However, according to Adorno, Lukács understood the all-important possibility of a *"re-awakening of spirit"* under the grip of natural history only in mystical, a-historical, theological terms: namely, in terms of a recapturing of the lost totality of the Golden Age of classical antiquity through a miraculous and apocalyptical process of spiritual renewal, as prefigured in the novels of Dostoyevsky. "Lukács can only think this Golgotha [of spirit] in terms of the category of a theological awakening, in terms of an eschatological horizon,"[12] remarks Adorno. On the other hand, he argues, it is Benjamin, in the *Origin of German Trauerspiel,* who "has raised the problem of the re-awakening of second nature from infinite distance to infinite nearness and has made [it] into an object of philosophical contemplation."[13]

Through a hermeneutical confrontation of the subject matter of German baroque drama with the category of allegory, Benjamin is able to gain a more precise, i.e., more historical, determination of the scope and meaning of natural history: for in the dramas of the baroque period nature and physis come to serve precisely as an *allegorical representation of history*; and conversely, history itself is interpreted as merely "natural," i.e., as consigned to a fate of inevitable decline and putrefaction. Consequently, in the ideational constellations constructed by Benjamin, which gain their filling, so to speak, from the determinate, historical, material elements— *the ruins*—of this era, the idea of natural history acquires definitive presentation. The "re-awakening" of the ruins of past and present must be accomplished in an *immanent* manner, that is, by way of assembling the fragments of social life into a historical constellation, and not through immediate recourse to extrinsic, suprahistorical, eschatological motifs. Only in this way, through the method of immanent criticism, do the objects which confront the theorist as historically isolated and unfulfilled stand a chance of being redeemed. At the same time, although as a result of this method the objects may be redeemed for the theorist—*for us*— they remain as yet unredeemed in themselves. Such are the intrinsic, subjective limits to the powers of theoretical redemption.

Yet, even at this early stage, one perceives a discrepancy between the actual intentions of the early Benjamin and the value assigned to them in Adorno's address. For it is Adorno's desire to assimilate Benjamin's aims to his own methodological intentions, intentions that center around the Marxist notion of ideology critique. Whereas for Benjamin the truth content of German *Trauerspiel* was only esoterically redeemable, for Adorno, this truth content could only be redeemed *exoterically*: the truth of history as "natural history" cannot simply remain the "possession" of the individual theorist, but must be recognized by humanity in general: only in a reconciled world would the claim to universality of that truth be "safe." Hence, its relevance for us in the present is not, according to Adorno, to be found in any *immediate* claim to redemption, but rather must be explained in terms of its ideology-critical function. Consequently, the truth content of the idea of history as natural history does not lie in the allegorical transformation of the ruin into a vision of redemption (the "death's head" into an "angel's countenance"), as it did for the poets of the baroque, but instead serves as a *critical concept* through which the semblance of reconciliation in this life is demystified and unmasked as the illusion and deception it is in fact—as an ideological veil which serves merely to conceal the suffering and injustice that lie at history's core.

For the early Benjamin the ideology-critical moments of categories such as "allegory" and "natural history" were unquestionably subordinated to their *redemptive significance*; however, in Adorno's reinterpretation of them, just the opposite is true. Speculation concerning a *positive* image of reconciled life can under no circumstances be produced independently by the theorist, but only by humanity collectively, i.e., through social praxis. The theorist who elects to flirt with such images always runs the risk of providing ersatz consolation for real historical suffering. The utopia of the critic can only be a *negative* one. His task is the informed theoretical articulation of the various retrograde aspects of social life at present which militate against the establishment of a free society—the articulation of those aspects in the full range of their contradictoriness and negativity. Only when these are set right in reality can talk of utopia have any real, concrete referent. In this way, Adorno demonstrates respect for the theological "taboo against graven images" and its Enlightenment counterpart, the Kantian proscription against venturing into the intelligible realm. Of course, this purely *negative* idea of the function of theory was far removed from the early Benjamin's conception of redemptive criticism.[14]

"The Actuality of Philosophy," Adorno's 1931 inaugural lecture to the philosophy faculty at the University of Frankfurt, is in truth little more than a gloss on the methodological insights of the "Prologue" to Benjamin's *Trauerspiel* study supplemented by a brief critique of recent philosophical attempts to resuscitate the tradition of ontology, to re-pose the "question of Being" (Husserl, Scheler, Heidegger). The claims of rationalism and idealism to be able to comprehend reality in its totality within the framework of the philosophical system must be grasped as fictive and ideological. In accordance with the fragmentary condition of reality, it falls due to philosophy to forsake the "great questions" which have served as the traditional object of metaphysical inquiry—of all the failed attempts to achieve an enduring *prima philosophia*—and to seek legitimation through an investigation of the reality-fragments themselves: "No justifying reason could rediscover itself in a reality whose order and form suppresses every claim to reason; only polemically does reason present itself to the Knower as total reality, while only in traces and ruins is it prepared to hope that it will come across correct and just reality. Philosophy which presents reality as such today only veils reality and eternalizes its present condition."[15]

For Adorno, the original sin of all traditional philosophy is that it attempts to grasp the nonconceptual through conceptual means; moreover, in the case of idealism, it attempts to resolve *actual* contradictions through merely *conceptual* solutions (shades of Marx's critique of Hegel). The resolution of this dilemma is to be found in the Benjaminian practice of thinking in historical constellations. Philosophy thereby divests itself of the identitarian prejudice of rationalism—the conviction that the totality of the real is ultimately identical with or can be subsumed by thought—in order to yield a more intimate and faithful knowledge of reality. By recrystallizing the diffuse and discrete elements of reality in a new historical constellation, those elements combine to form an idea. In Benjamin's view, this process possesses the salutory capacity to effectuate the *redemption* of those phenomena or elements. For Adorno, it has the ideology-critical function of demystifying the pseudo-reconciliation of the antagonistic, fragmentary elements of reality performed by idealism; and consequently, the idealist (i.e., purely conceptual) manner in which the problem is posed dissolves, and the problem is thus transposed to that plane on which it can alone be resolved in fact—the plane of reality. Adorno has in mind the reinterpretation of Benjamin's theory of constellations or monads in the *Trauerspiel* book along the lines of a *materialist* theory of knowledge—the elimination of the overt theological residues of that theory such that it becomes compatible with materialist principles:

Interpretation of the unintentional through a juxtaposition of the analytically isolated elements and illumination of the real by the power of such interpretation is the program of every authentically materialist theory of knowledge. . . . the function which the traditional philosophical inquiry expected from meta-historical, symbolically meaningful ideas is accomplished by inner-historically constituted, non-symbolic ones. . . . history would no longer be the place from which ideas arise, stand out independently and disappear again. On the contrary, the historical images would at the same time be themselves the ideas, the configuration of which constituted the unintentional truth.

The interpretation of given reality and its abolition are connected to each other, not, of course, in the sense that reality is negated in the concept, but that out of the construction of a configuration of reality the demand for its [reality's] real change always follows promptly. The change causing gesture of the riddle process—not its mere resolution as such—provides the image of resolutions to which materialist praxis alone has access. Materialism has named this process with a name that is philosophically certified: dialectic. Only dialectically, it seems to me, is philosophical interpretation possible. When Marx reproached the philosophers, saying that they had only variously interpreted the world, and contraposed to them that the point is to change it, then the sentence receives its legitimacy not only out of political praxis, but also out of philosophical theory. Only in the annihilation of the question is the authenticity of philosophical interpretation first successfully proven, and mere thought by itself cannot accomplish this [authenticity]: therefore the annihilation of the question compels praxis.[16]

The correct posing of the philosophical riddle—e.g., the enigma of the "thing in itself" or the "fetishism of commodities"—the re-articulation of its elements in an illuminating historical constellation, leads not to the solution of that riddle but to the point where it dissolves as a philosophical question *per se* and passes over into the sphere of "materialist praxis." This procedure represents the dialectical *Aufhebung* of idealist contemplation, through a process whereby idealism's contradictions are permitted to unfold themselves to the point where it becomes apparent that their resolution on a purely philosophical plane would be merely illusory and that their actual resolution could only be accomplished in the sphere of material life itself.

This program of an immanent, materialist liquidation of bourgeois philosophy as outlined in the 1931 inaugural lecture was subsequently brought to fruition in Adorno's superb Kierkegaard study of 1934. There, he sought to demonstrate that the retreat to the sphere of "pure inwardness" proposed by Kierkegaard as a solution to the problem of the progressive disenchantment and rationalization of life, the problem of the positivistic indifference to spiritual values characteristic of the rational-purposive bourgeois consciousness, was merely a pseudo-solution; that the Kierkegaardian subject was in reality incapable of sustaining itself in its state of self-imposed isolation, and thus of necessity sought refuge in a flight into the irrational—in the humility and devaluation of the self in face of the omnipotence of an infinitely distant godhead; a solution which in the last analysis provided a tacit justification for the irrationality of the course of the world, a course whose incomprehensibility was only logical and plausible from the standpoint of the lowly human consciousness.[17] The truth content of the existential dilemma expressed in Kierkegaard's writings, his portrayal of the degradation and inauthenticity of the modern world, his sympathetic depiction of the loneliness and *Angst* which grip the isolated bourgeois consciousness under such conditions, is only increasingly mystified when it is provided with a solution that is merely philosophical, doctrinal, or religious. The authentic resolution of this dilemma could only be accomplished once its origins were sought in terms of the material conditions of life which are themselves responsible for this state of universal alienation, i.e., once it is no longer conceived of as a purely philosophical problem. The ideology-critical examination of the traditional problems of bourgeois thought thus redeems their truth content—that moment in them which pertains to the *antagonistic structure of reality itself* (and not merely to the structure of *thought*)—and annihilates the ideological veil of reconciliation which afflicts all merely conceptual solutions. Such are the lines along which Adorno—unquestionably the better Marxist of the two—sought to recast Benjamin's theory of thinking in "Dialectical Images" or "monads." These images or constellations no longer, in line with Benjamin's conception, remain empowered with the capacity *to redeem phenomena theoretically,* esoterically, as it were, but instead play a crucial role in the immanent, *philosophical liquidation of idealism.* In this way Adorno supplants their redemptive function with an ideology-critical function. This already existing misunderstanding, which had remained unthematized in the previous contact between the two, emerged in full force only during the first leg of the debate itself.

The Arcades Exposé

In 1935 Adorno was of the opinion that he and Benjamin were in the process of developing a common philosophical program whose methodological basis had been outlined in the "Prologue" to the *Trauerspiel* book. Whereas in the years 1929–32 their intellectual partnership had been consolidated through a series of intense philosophical discussions (Benjamin refers to these discussions as "historical" in their import),[18] personal contact between them during the exile years was sporadic, with Adorno residing in Oxford and Benjamin alternating between Paris and Brecht's estate in Skovbostrand, Denmark. As a result, their correspondence in these years assumed added significance. In Adorno's absence, however, the association with Brecht increasingly became the dominant intellectual force in Benjamin's life—an eventuality of which Adorno had been aware and feared. Benjamin attempted to mollify these misgivings: "I know that it is the language of most genuine friendship . . . which moves you to the conviction that you would consider it a true misfortune if Brecht should gain influence on this work [the Arcades project]."[19] Yet, he nevertheless goes on to refer to his acquaintance with Brecht as a "decisive encounter" for his thinking concerning the development of the Arcades study. Still, Adorno had little idea of precisely how the Brechtian influences would make themselves felt until he received a copy of the 1935 Arcades Exposé. Considering his stake in the intellectual partnership with Benjamin— and the programmatic addresses of the 1930s discussed above testify emphatically to such a partnership—the sense of desertion felt by Adorno must have been keen, as his rejoinder of August 2, 1935, would seem to indicate.

Adorno's main criticism of the draft pertained to the generous infusion of surrealist and Brechtian themes which in his opinion made for a pseudo-dialectical approach and served to vitiate an authentic, materialist analysis of the phenomena under investigation—the "phantasmagoria of the nineteeth century." Furthermore, the copy of the Exposé received by Adorno constituted a betrayal, he felt, of the original intentions of the project as outlined by Benjamin in their earlier discussions and letters. The original intention as Adorno understood it, and as Benjamin himself had avowed on frequent occasions, was to adopt a methodological standpoint very close to the plan for the baroque book: to present a consideration of the nineteenth century analogous to the *Trauerspiel* study's treatment of the seventeenth century. The theoretical focal point of the study would be the concept of the "prehistory of the nineteenth century" (*"Urgeschichte des 19ten Jahrhunderts"*) or a "prehistory of the modern." For just as the *Trauerspiel* book had probed behind the ruins of the baroque age to reveal the underlying conception of history as "natural history," in the Arcades Project Benjamin intended in a similar vein to exhume rudiments of prehistory—such as myth, fate, and the always-the-same—beneath the apparent phantasmagoria of *nouveauté*, the fantastic array of commodities and innovations that swept the nineteenth century under the banner of "the modern." His intention was therefore less to demonstrate how manifestations of prehistory themselves recurred in the modern, than to show how the modern itself regressed to the level of prehistory. Or, more precisely, he sought to demonstrate how the phantasmagorical proliferation of new commodities which distinguished urban life under conditions of nineteenth-century capitalism in reality constituted a regression to the notion of "eternal recurrence" or "mythical repetition"; i.e., it represented a return to the notion of *cyclical time* dominant in prehistoric life, insofar as the novelties themselves were thoroughly interchangeable. When viewed from the vantage point of consumption, full-scale commodity production signified the reversion to a Great Myth: the reproduction of the always-the-same under the semblance of the production of the perpetually new.

In Adorno's view, however, Benjamin's actual outline of the project differed vastly from the original conception. Above all, the motif of prehistory appeared not under the hellish sign of "eternal recurrence," but surprisingly, as a *Golden Age,* the return to which was deemed the *telos* of a free humanity. Benjamin elaborates this new conception of the Arcades Study, which is fundamentally predicated on a substantially revised conception of his earlier theory of Dialectical Images, in the following crucial passage of his "Paris, Capital of the Nineteenth Century" (the Arcades Exposé). After quoting Michelet's *"Chaque époque rêve la suivante,"* he continues:

To the form of every new means of production, which to begin with is still dominated by the old (Marx), there correspond images in the collective consciousness in which the new and the old are intermingled. These images are wish-images, and in them the collective seeks not only to transfigure, but also to transcend, the immaturity of the social product and the deficiencies of the social order of production. In these wish-images there also emerges a vigorous aspiration to break with what is outdated—which means, however, with the most recent past. These tendencies turn the image-fantasy, which gains its initial stimulus from the new, back upon the primal past. In the dream in which every epoch sees in images the epoch that is to succeed it, the latter appears coupled with elements of pre-history—that is to say, of a classless society. The experiences of this society, which have their storeplace in the collective unconscious, interact with the new to give birth to the utopias which leave their traces in a thousand configurations of life, from permanent buildings to ephemeral fashions.[20]

The significance of this passage for understanding Benjamin's revised conception of the object of the Arcades Project would be difficult to overestimate. For it explains his new interpretation of the study as a prehistory of the modern, his fascination with the ruins of the nineteenth century (paralleling his preoccupation with those of the seventeenth century in the *Trauerspiel* study), and his understanding of Baudelaire as an allegorist (once again following his conception of the dominant formal principal of the German baroque era). The revised version of the theory of Dialectical Images proceeds from the following conviction. From the ruins of modernity—visible "in a thousand configurations of life, from permanent buildings to ephemeral fashions"—there arise in the "collective consciousness" wish-images which are harbingers of a new order; yet these image-fantasies, which derive initially from the new, ultimately hark back to elements of the primal past which over the course of centuries have been deposited in the collective unconscious. These collective visions prove to be nothing less than *images of a classless society,* which are released from their state of dormancy in the process whereby old and new interact. (Yet, according to Benjamin's complex schema, old and new are ultimately interchangeable; for the "old," classless society of prehistory will ultimately become the "new" or utopia; and the "new," the ruins of modernity, will at this point turn into the "old"— i.e., "prehistory" in the Marxian sense.) Consequently, the ruins of modernity, eminently displayed in the poetry of Baudelaire— who indeed turns these ruins into lyrical subjects or idylls—suggested to Benjamin a network of correspondences with prehistory—correspondences which he viewed as the ultimate stimulus to utopia or a classless society. For with capitalism's tremendous unleashing of productive forces, utopia has become a real possibility; yet, the leap into the realm of freedom remains at the same time impeded by the retrograde state of the relations of production under capitalism. Hence, for the first time man's dream of utopia has ceased to be merely a dream; its concrete traces abound in the modern age and are, as it were, just waiting to be resurrected in the rational form of a socialist society.

This is the reason, according to Benjamin, why it is specifically through the intermingling of old and new in the *modern* era that such utopian correspondences or wish-fantasies originally embedded in the collective unconscious tend to be released. For it is only with the onset of industrial capitalism that utopia has ceased to be a mere fantasy and become potentially realizeable in fact. Baudelaire's unique role was to have latently sensed the specifically modern character of the relation between decadence and emancipation. According to this conception, the tendency for the modern to have recourse to elements of prehistory is no longer perceived simply as a regression, but rather, as a *prefigurement of utopia*: as the awakening in the collective unconscious of the memory of a "pre-historic classless society."

The brunt of Adorno's criticisms is directed against Benjamin's new specification of the Dialectical Image as a dream, a vision of utopia. For Adorno, this shift of emphasis results in a crucial "de-dialecticization" of the original conception of the relationship between the modern and prehistory, in which the former reverted to the latter as the image of Hell. The negative image of history as natural history had been in this way abandoned by Benjamin in the Arcades Exposé—an image which remained crucial in Adorno's own writing. In Benjamin's eyes, the tremendous productive capacities of capitalism could not help but call to mind the deficient state of the *relations of production* in which those capacities remained shackled, relations which led to a growing polarization of wealth and the deplorable immiseration of the masses. From this increasingly undeniable contradiction between the potential for a society of abundance and the inequitable, privative control of social wealth under capitalism originated the social longing for utopia—and Benjamin, not fortuitously, makes frequent reference to the writings of Saint-Simon and Fourier in this connection.[21]

Benjamin, Adorno believed, had seemingly relinquished his earlier conception and now in the Dialectical Image saw only the positive, utopian moment in the relationship between the modern and prehistory. As a result, not only were there serious distortions of fact, but formidable methodological problems were also raised. Benjamin had been guilty not only of idealizing the potentially utopian side of commodity production, but also of a fatal romanticization of prehistory as a Golden Age. For Adorno, it would be more accurate to describe both periods through the *category of Hell* (which apparently played an important role in an unpublished earlier version of the Exposé) than through the category of *utopia,* as did Benjamin. Adorno's reproach runs as follows:

> you construe the relationship between the oldest and the newest, which was already central to your first draft, as one of a Utopian reference to a "classless society." Thus the archaic becomes a complementary addition to the new, instead of being the "newest" itself; it is de-dialecticized. However at the same time, and equally undialectically, the image of classlessness is put back into mythology instead of becoming truly transparent as a phantasmagoria of Hell. Therefore the category into which the archaic coalesces with the modern is far less a Golden Age than a catastrophe.[22]

By mythologizing the relationship between the "oldest and newest" as "utopia" or a "classless society," Benjamin glosses over the real negativity of the new as the actual perpetuation of the (prehistoric) spell of the always-the-same. Its alleged novelties represent in fact merely a new type of mythical spell, and this aspect, and not a return to a lost utopian age—if indeed the latter ever existed as such—signifies its real affinity with prehistory. It is in this sense that Adorno claims that the "new" has become the "archaic"—merely the perpetuation of traditional relations of domination under the illusory guise of unending novelty—a state of affairs that at best tends to divert the consumer's attention from the true nature of those relations. Benjamin's analysis is de-dialecticized insofar as he fails to take into consideration *both* moments of the phenomenon under investigation: its *regressive* as well as its *emancipatory* side. Adorno's disparagement of Benjamin's capacities as a "dialectical thinker" was a charge that would also resurface at a crucial juncture in the second stage of the debate. In attempting to represent the relationship between the modern and prehistory as a catastrophe rather than utopia, Adorno strove desperately to bring Benjamin back to the conception of history of the *Trauerspiel* book, i.e., the idea of history as a continuum of disaster, the conception Adorno had made his own in "Die Idee der Naturgeschichte." Yet, at this point in his intellectual development, Benjamin felt that the retention of the *equally undialectical* pessimistic philosophy of history of his theological phase would be incompatible with a genuinely materialistic perspective—which emphasized the progressive emancipation of mankind through the mechanism of class struggle. In Benjamin's acquiesence to the Marxian point of view, Adorno rightly detected the behind-the-scenes influence of Brecht.

At the same time, the theory of Dialectical Images presented in the Arcades Exposé raised methodological difficulties which Adorno correctly criticized as being prejudicial to an authentic materialist analysis of culture. He was especially critical of Benjamin's interpretation of the Dialectical Image as a dream, a holdover from the earlier essay on surrealism. According to Adorno, by seeking to assimilate a concrete historical analysis of nineteenth-century social life to the surrealist glorification of dream-images, Benjamin risked the dissipation of the real content of the study in irrational, idealist categories. As he explains, "If you transpose the dialectical image into consciousness as a dream . . . you also deprive it of that objective liberating power which could legitimate it in materialistic terms. The fetish character of the commodity is not a fact of consciousness; rather, it is dialectical, in the eminent sense that it produces consciousness."[23] If the manifestation of commodity fetishism in dream-images were to serve as the focal point of Benjamin's investigation, the real origins of commodity fetishism in material relations of production would remain occluded. Moreover, the transformation of fetishistic dream-images into utopian dream-images would accomplish nothing toward the end of eradicating commodity fetishism in reality. For Benjamin's study to gain the objective weight needed to authenticate it as a rigorous materialist analysis, it was the *social* origins of commodity fetishism that would have warranted investigation and not its status a dream-image. When social phenomena are understood merely as "facts of consciousness" or dreams, they are grasped only superficially or ideally. An analysis of the phenomenon of commodity fetishism as it makes itself felt on the plane of consciousness—i.e., as the *reification of consciousness*—which desires to solve this problem by an interpretation which remains *immanent to the sphere of consciousness* overlooks the crucial fact that the actual cause of reification lies outside of that sphere. By reducing the phenomenon of reification to a fact of consciousness, theory divests it of the full range of its power and significance; it disguises its nature as a concrete, material force and creates the illusion that the precondition for its abolition would somehow be merely a change in one's "patterns of thought." What especially irks Adorno about Benjamin's presentation is that he has not only sacrificed the earlier metaphysical version of the theory of Dialectical Images, but that he has also replaced it with a reputedly immanent, materialist conception of the theory in which the social content for whose sake the metaphysical approach was eliminated fails to materialize nevertheless. This content merely evaporates in the dream.

A related aspect of the theory which Adorno, understandably, finds highly objectionable is Benjamin's marked reliance on the concept of the "collective unconscious," a term he takes over from the reactionary doctrines of Jung and Klages. Benjamin employs this term, it would seem, in order to transcend the standpoint of the *individual subject* of surrealist dream theory. In that Dialectical Images are thus envisioned by a *collective subject,* they become all the more suitable for political ends. Yet, Adorno attempts to show that as a result of his utilization of this questionable category, Benjamin runs the risk of lapsing into the same bad mythologization of historical life to which Jung and Klages fall victim. In point of fact the phantasmagoria of commodities—commodity fetishism—manifests itself not in some pristine, mythical collective ego, but in *"alienated bourgeois individuals"*—"a mass ego exists only in earthquakes and catastrophes, while otherwise objective surplus value prevails precisely through individual subjects and against them."[24] By using this category Benjamin runs the risk of hypostatizing a mythical collective subject, which can only serve to mask the real divisions and fragmentation which militate against the possibility of a legitimate collective subject coming into its own. To be sure, the notion of collective unconscious, as it appears in the writings of Jung, has precisely the retrograde ideological function of veiling real historical suffering by appealing to an illusory, unattainable vision of solidarity cloaked in archaic images. As Adorno points out, "The notion of collective consciousness was invented only to divert attention from true objectivity. . . . It should be a clear and sufficient warning that in a dreaming collective no differences remain between classes."[25]

Similar mythologizing tendencies govern Benjamin's reliance on the notion of an *ur*historical classless society, a prehistoric Golden Age, the return to which is posited as the goal of emancipation. His idealization of the past in this case is reminiscent of the neoromantic theories of Klages. In essence, Benjamin's draft aims not at the dialectical *Aufhebung* of commodity society but at an irrationalist regression to a mythical, pristine stage of civilization which has yet to be tainted by the capitalist division of labor and the fatal separation between the "use value" and "exchange value" of goods. In his criticisms, Adorno stops short of calling Benjamin's theory reactionary, though he does suggest that it is in places indistinguishable from the thinking of Jung and Klages. However, it is not merely the influence of the latter two fascist sympathizers which Adorno discovers lurking in the background of Benjamin's formulations. It is equally the influence of

Brecht which disturbs him: "Perhaps you will see from these reflections, whose substance concerns precisely those categories in your draft which may conform to those of Brecht, that my opposition to them is not an insular attempt to rescue autonomous art, but addresses itself to those motifs of our philosophical friendship which I regard as basic."[26] Brecht's "'collective' and . . . unmediated concept of function have always been suspect to me," Adorno continues, "as themselves a regression." What Benjamin borrowed from Brecht, according to Adorno, was a tendency to hypostatize such notions as "collectivity" or "proletariat," investing them with immediately positive attributes, without bothering to reflect on the real historical forces at work—Taylorism, reification, etc.—which account for their actual *fragmented* condition. It was an analogous blind confidence in the innate revolutionary potential of the laboring masses which led the German Communist Party to underestimate fascism's potential to acquire support on a mass basis. Similarly, Brecht's unflagging trust in the concept of "function" implied an extremely naïve faith in the intrinsic, ontological capacity of a technical apparatus—be it film, theater, or radio—to deliver revolutionary results. Moreover, in the Exposé Benjamin displays an irrational faith in the notion of a "prehistoric classless society," a mythical community in which "use-value" reigns supreme, and presents this society as a model. In fact, commodity society must be "*aufgehoben*" dialectically, i.e., immanently. Not only would it be impossible for society to return somehow to this putative Golden Age, but the alleged idyllic character of this era has in any event undoubtedly been exaggerated beyond all relation to historical fact. In order to delineate in truth the theoretical prerequisites for the abolition of bourgeois society, "The *specific* commodity character of the nineteenth century, in other words the industrial production of commodities, would have to be worked out much more clearly and materially."[27] What is needed is not a return to an earlier stage of civilization governed by use-value—an era subjected to the whims of untamed nature and problems of scarcity—but a transcendence of capitalism that is *immanent,* one whose content can be determined only by an understanding of the real socio-historic forces at work in a given epoch.

The conception of Dialectical Images advanced by Benjamin in the Arcades Exposé falls victim to a distinctly Brechtian falsifying positivity, and it is to this tendency that Adorno objects primarily in his stern rejoinder. The utopian "intermingling of old and new" is something merely posited by the theory itself and, as Adorno attempts to demonstrate, it is refuted by an examination of the objective situation. For theory to undertake to effect the redemption of an essentially fragmented reality only further confuses the matter. As Rolf Tiedemann has observed in this connection: "The dialectic, as a method, cannot find a crack and extend beyond the immanent context of society in which it originates; it cannot transcend the standstill of society. It must instead, as the authentic intentions of the Arcades study do, critically reflect on its own position [verbleiben] in a coercively organized society."[28] The role of theory is a limited, critical one. Therefore, Adorno attempts to remind Benjamin of the dangers which lie in the tendency to collapse theory and life: "as models, dialectical images are not social products, but constellations in which 'the social' situation represents itself. Consequently, no ideological or social 'accomplishment' can ever be expected of a dialectical image."[29]

Behind this disagreement, however, stands the more fundamental misunderstanding between the two concerning the true historical mission of theory discussed earlier in the chapter. For Benjamin theory possesses an inalienable constructive or redemptive function; for Adorno its task is to aid in the ideology-critical unveiling of socially engendered false consciousness—if it should attempt to do anything more than this, it runs the risk of providing illusory consolation for real historical suffering. Adorno, however, fails to recognize that Benjamin's "positive" conception of the role of theory is not merely attributable to the nefarious influences of Brecht's unreflexive Marxism, but rather has its roots in the notion of redemptive criticism originally formulated by Benjamin in the Trauerspiel study—i.e., the idea of theory as redeeming forgotten and misunderstood literary texts. However, whereas it lies within the province of theory to accomplish this feat for works of literature, it is quite another matter entirely when it addresses itself to the sphere of social life itself. Thus, Adorno believes the problem at hand would clear up if only Benjamin would cast off his materialist world view and return to his earlier theological perspective: "If I were to close the circle of my critique with one bold grip, it would be bound to grasp the extremes. A restoration of theology, or better yet, a radicalization of the dialectic into the glowing center of theology, would at the same time have to mean the utmost intensification of the social-dialectical, indeed economic, motifs."[30] In fact, however, the theoretical longing for redemption displayed in the Dialectical Images of the Arcades Exposé was perfectly consistent with Benjamin's earlier theological approach.

Art and Mechanical Reproduction

The second phase of the Adorno-Benjamin debate concerns Benjamin's celebrated essay "The Work of Art in the Age of Mechanical Reproduction." It was the most explicitly Marxist and most Brechtian of his published writings. In fact, because of its provocative employment of Marxist phraseology, the Institute for Social Research agreed to publish it only after substantive changes were made. For example, in the printed version of the essay references to "communism" were replaced by the euphemism "the constructive forces of humanity," and references to "fascism" were substituted for by the phrase "the totalitarian state." Moreover, a controversial first paragraph in which Benjamin's left-wing political convictions were set forth in stark and unambiguous terms was stricken altogether. The essay itself was originally published in French translation in the 1936 (volume 5, no. 1) issue of the *Zeitschrift für Sozialforschung,* since both Benjamin and Horkheimer agreed that the impact of its "propaganda value" (*sic*) would be felt much more keenly on the French cultural scene, in view of the fact that autonomous culture in Germany had been virtually obliterated Goebbels and company. For this reason, the *Zeitschrift* had recently incorporated a special French language section and had commissioned Raymond Aron to supervise its production. What circulates today as "The Work of Art" essay (the German version first printed in the 1955 two-volume edition of Benjamin's *Schriften* edited by Adorno and his wife, which then served as the basis for the English translation in *Illuminations*) is actually a *second* German version Benjamin composed shortly after the French version appeared, which he hoped to have published in the Moscow-based German émigré publication *Das Wort,* which was edited by, among others, Bertolt Brecht.

"The Work of Art" essay must be understood both within the framework of Benjamin's program of a materialist *Aufhebung* of affirmative bourgeois culture and within the context of the European political situation in 1935. It contains his most consistent and forceful argument for the functional transformation of culture along Marxist lines. Benjamin's conception stands in the closest proximity to Brecht's aesthetic theory—the adoption of which only becomes fully intelligible when viewed in light of facism's crass but powerful aestheticization of political violence—in face of which bourgeois autonomous art seemed truly "epiphenomenal." Benjamin's counterproposal was to meet force with force: "Mankind which in Homer's time was an object of contemplation for the Olympic gods, now is one for itself. Its self-alienation has reached such a degree that it can experience its own destruction as an aesthetic pleasure of the first order. This is the situation of politics which Fascism is rendering aesthetic. Communism responds by politicizing art."[31]

Benjamin interprets fascism's aesthetics of violence—indeed, with all its regalia and spectacles, Nazism proved itself to be perhaps the most aesthetically self-conscious regime in history—as the culmination of *l'art pour l'art*. It raised the sublimation of desire in aesthetic contemplation to new heights, insofar as the self-destruction of mankind had been turned by fascism into a gradiose and grotesque aesthetic pageant. Benjamin's response to this situation was to mobilize the so-called forces of aesthetic production for political ends. Whereas fascism had aestheticized politics, communism would reply by politicizing aesthetics.

However, Benjamin failed to recognize that in practice an aestheticized politics and a politicized art are, at least formally speaking, equivalents. His crucial oversight subsequently became the focal point for Adorno's critique. However, in 1935 as the

Nazis began building up their war machine, whether or not autonomous art could be salvaged seemed to Benjamin an entirely otiose, scholastic question. All prevalent tendencies pointed, in his view, to such art's imminent demise and the incorporation of its dying vestiges into the fascist program of self-glorification. In face of the threat to civilization posed by fascism, bourgeois talk about the preservation of culture seemed reprehensibly self-indulgent. As far as culture was concerned, the only practice that seemed to make sense at the time was to render art serviceable for progressive political ends, for ends that were staunchly opposed to those of fascism: the ends of communism. As Benjamin remarks in the opening pages of "The Work of Art" essay: "The concepts which are introduced into the theory of art in what follows differ from the more familiar terms in that they are completely useless for the purposes of Fascism. They are, on the other hand, useful for the formation of revolutionary demands in the politics of art."[32]

Insight into the methodological presuppositions of "The Work of Art" essay is provided in a letter to Horkheimer of October 1935. Benjamin states that now that the "historical image" of the Arcades Project has been provisionally established (in the Exposé written that year), that image had been set aside in favor of "considerations" which "will determine the total image of the work." The "considerations" to which he refers in this context are the preliminary outlines of "The Work of Art" essay. He continues:

As provisional now as these constructive considerations for their part may be in the form in which I have established them, I may however say that they make an advance in the direction of a materialist theory of art, which for its part leads far beyond the sketch with which you are acquainted [the Arcades Exposé]. This time it is a question of specifying the precise place in the present which my historical construction will take as its point of departure. If the theme of the book [the Arcades Project] is the fate of art in the nineteenth century, then this fate therefore has something to tell us because it is contained in the ticking of a clockwork whose knell has first pierced *our* ears. The hour of fate of art has, I would thus like to say, sounded for us, and I have set forth its signature in a series of preliminary reflections which carry the title, "The Work of Art in the Age of Mechanical Reproduction." These reflections make an attempt to give questions about the theory of art a truly contemporary form: and indeed, through avoidance of all *immediate* relation to politics.[33]

It would seem reasonable to conjecture that given the exigencies of the political situation at hand, Benjamin felt compelled to break off work temporarily on his major study of this period, the Arcades Project, and focus his attention on more contemporary issues. To be sure, if the specific historical focus of the two works were quite different, they remained closely interrelated at the methodological level. As Benjamin comments in a letter to Scholem: "These reflections [in "The Work of Art" essay] anchor the history of art in the nineteenth century in an understanding of the situation of art as it is experienced by us in the present"[34]—implying that the art of the nineteenth century, the subject of the Arcades Project, could itself only be fully comprehended on the basis of an understanding of the fate of art in contemporary life. An even more precise specification of the nature of the relation between the two works appears in a letter to Werner Kraft on December 27, 1935:

In conclusion I would like to remark that I have finished a programmatic work on the theory of art. It is called "The Work of Art in the Age of Mechanical Reproduction." Materially speaking, it stands in no relation to the large book [the Arcades Project] whose outline I have mentioned; however *methodologically* [it stands] in the closest relation, since every historical work, if it is to be relevant for historical materialism, must be preceded by a precise determination of the present situation as far as the things whose history is to be written are concerned: . . . the fate of art in the nineteenth century.[35]

Here, Benjamin reaffirms the view expressed in the letter to Scholem that the key to the comprehension of *past* (nineteenth-century) art lies in an understanding of the *present* situation of art—a statement reminiscent of Marx's dictum that the key to understanding the anatomy of the ape is human anatomy. Through this statement Marx meant to suggest that all precapitalist economic formations could finally be understood only in light of the capitalist economy. Benjamin's perspective is slightly less teleological, if it attempts nonetheless to express an analogous sentiment: there is a process whose rudiments are detectable in nineteenth-century art—a process of *de-aestheticization*—which could be fully comprehended only if its mature form in the present age of "mechanical reproduction" were projected back on to it, as it were. This is the reason why Benjamin believed that the fundamental insights of "The Work of Art" essay would prove so crucial for the Arcades Project. Moreover, he had in mind this understanding of the relation between "past" and "present" when he mentioned to Horkheimer, in the letter of October 1935, that the fate of nineteenth-century art is contained in the "ticking of a clockwork whose knell has first pierced *our* ears." To render Benjamin's metaphor more specific: the "ticking of the clockwork" represents the impending demise of auratic art whose death knell sounds only in the present era—though the outlines of its ultimate fate were already perceptible in nineteenth-century art, most notably in the work of Baudelaire. Consequently, Benjamin conceived of "The Work of Art" essay as a study that was of far-reaching significance for the Arcades Project insofar as it would illuminate the ultimate consequences of a process of "de-aestheticization," in terms of which alone the incipient influences of industrialization on the art of the nineteenth century first became comprehensible.

The central category employed by Benjamin in "The Work of Art" essay to analyze the social history of art is the "aura." The aura refers to the customary historical role played by works of art in the cultural legitimation of traditional social formations: e.g., the death mask of the magician (magic), Homer's *Iliad* (myth), and medieval Christian painting (religion). Benjamin describes this aspect as the ritual or *cultic function* of the work of art. It refers to the fact that throughout the history of culture works of art have had a dependent status—that is, they have owed their existence primarily to their implication in processes of social integration: "It is significant that the work of art with reference to its aura is never entirely separated from its ritual function."[36] As an object of religious veneration and worship, the work of art acquires a sense of uniqueness, an authenticity, a *hallowed character.* Thus, Benjamin defines the aura as "the unique phenomenon of a distance, however close [an object] may be."[37] The aura testifies to the *authority* of art in its cultic form, its condition of inimitable uniqueness, a singularity in time and space which is the hallmark of its authenticity. "The uniqueness of a work of art," Benjamin observes, "is inseparable from its being embedded in the fabric of tradition."[38]

With the advent of Renaissance painting the *ritualistic* basis of artistic production is challenged and a *secular* cult of beauty comes into its own. At this point, art begins a long and hard-fought struggle for autonomy, which is vigorously renewed by romanticism, and which culminates in the pinnacle of aestheticism, *l'art pour l'art*, which Benjamin refers to as the "theology of art." *L'art pour l'art* seeks *a restoration of the aura though within* the frame-work of aesthetic autonomy. It originates as a reaction against the rampant commodification of art (and spirit in general) which oc-curs under developed, nineteenth-century capitalism. At the same time, Benjamin seeks to link its emergence to the sense of im-pending crisis experienced by art with the advent of photography. *L'art pour l'art* protests against the reintegration of art into the mundane sphere of utilitarian interests by attempting to supress all traces of its relation to social life.

For Benjamin, the most significant aspect of the production and reception of works of art in the twentieth century is the increased intervention of *technical means* in these processes. The result of this intervention is the "decline of the aura." By substi-tuting a plurality of copies for a unique original, mechanically reproduced art has according to Benjamin destroyed the very basis for the production of auratic works of art—that singularity in time and space on which they depend for their claim to authority and authenticity. When produced en masse, the originality or individuality of a work of art becomes a matter of indifference, insofar as every work is now replaceable. "From a photographic negative, for example, one can make any number of prints," Ben-jamin observes; "to ask for the 'authentic' print makes no sense."[39] In consequence, the work of art becomes incapable of command-ing respect as a ritual or cult object as was formerly the case. It ceases to be an object of religious veneration, forfeits its "cult value," and instead takes on a new function, an *"exhibition value"*: the locus of attention shifts from the work of art itself as a priv-ileged entity to the *point of intersection between work and onlooker.*

This fact, according to Benjamin, opens up enormous, hitherto untapped potentials for the political employment of art. Above all, mechanically reproduced art enables "the original to meet the beholder half-way, be it in the form of a photograph or a phonograph record. The cathedral leaves its locale to be received in the studio of a lover of art; the choral production, performed in an auditorium or the open air, resounds in the drawing room."[40] The disintegration of the aura has its social origins, Benjamin continues, in

The desire of the contemporary masses to bring things "closer" spatially and humanly. . . . Every day the urge grows stronger to get hold of an object at very close range by way of its likeness, its reproduction. . . . To pry an object from its shell, to destroy its aura, is the mark of a perception whose "sense of the universal equality of things" has increased to such a degree that it extracts it even from a unique object by means of reproduction.[41]

Benjamin claims that these changes in the technical conditions for the production and reception of art constitute a world-historical break with tradition that effectively abolishes the previous ritual or cultic basis of art and paves the way for the predominance of the *political function* of art. This process represents a qualitative change in the intrinsic definition of art itself such that its status as an object of aesthetic enjoyment or satisfaction assumes a role subordinate to its function as an instrument of communication. "Cult value" turns into "exhibition value;" quantity is transformed into quality; the institution of art, it would seem, has reached a historical point of no return.

The individual medium to which Benjamin assigns a preeminent role in the world-historical "decline of the aura" is that of film. Film, he argues, represents the ultimate realization of the surrealist technique of montage, since a film in its entirety is actually nothing more than the final compilation of a series of individually shot sequences and scenes. Moreover, when considered from the all-important *collective* standpoint of its production and reception, film represents a concerted assault on the predominantly *private* and *solitary* conditions for the production and reception of bourgeois autonomous art (e.g., the novel and painting), making it ideally suited for the propagation of political content. Its superiority in "capturing" objective reality precipitates a crisis in the visual arts and the novel form, which are forced to seek out other, more subjectivistic modes of expression. Moreover, through its use of the principle of montage, film conveys a *shock-effect* which makes it incompatible with the predominantly passive, contemplative conditions of reception characteristic of bourgeois auratic art. If the viewer of traditional bourgeois art was passively absorbed in the work, film, by virtue of its shock-character, produces an effect of alienation or distraction, compelling the viewer to assume an active and critical role. In this way Benjamin attempts to transpose the virtues of Brecht's "*Verfremdungseffekt*" from the medium of theater to that of film. One might also draw a parallel between the titles and slogans employed by epic theater—as part of the process of "literarization"—and the manner in which the viewer of a silent film is urged to reflection by the use of captions.

Regardless of its shortcomings (which we shall take up shortly) Benjamin's "The Work of Art" essay remains a pathbreaking study in the field of modern aesthetics. Its fundamental insight is that, in consequence of revolutionary new techniques in the production and reception of works of art, the entire domain of art is shaken to its innermost core, to the point where it seemingly negates its entire prehistory (i.e., its former auratic or cultic guise). That insight stands as a prerequisite for any informed analysis of art in its present (de-aestheticized) form.[42] The current idea of the "crisis of the arts," in particular the crisis of the uniquely bourgeois forms of painting and the novel, bespeaks of a situation in which the aesthetic representation of the external world by traditional bourgeois forms has been *objectively surpassed* by photographic means. Certainly, the remarkable paucity of significant painters and novelists today would seem to be symptomatic of this development—whereas the same can by no means be said in the case of film.

Moreover, in his study Benjamin correctly points out that all works of art, no matter how exalted or sublime, are always simultaneously *faits sociaux*. Their form is always in part conditioned by the level of advancement of the "forces of aesthetic production," which are in turn indebted to the level of development of society's technical forces of production. By taking the social or material preconditions for artistic production as his point of departure, Benjamin is able to show the transient, historically determinate nature of all art forms and genres, a fact which undermines the neoclassicist attempt to define art in terms of eternally valid aesthetic categories such as "beauty," "genius," "creativity," etc.—categories which are patently inapplicable to the entirety of "modernism." In its rejection of the traditional concepts of aesthetic valuation, "The Work of Art" essay converges unexpectedly with the intention of the *Trauerspiel* study, despite the manifest differences in historical focus which separate the two works. In sum, Benjamin has convincingly demonstrated that, for better or for worse, technical forces have entered into the very heart of the process of aesthetic production in our age and, what is equally important, into the process of "aesthetic distribution." This situation has resulted in historically unprecedented changes in the very concept of art, such that it is gradually stripped of its traditional aesthetic qualities (auratic uniqueness and authenticity) and becomes instead a vehicle of (political) communication.

"Indeed I feel that our theoretical disagreement is not really a discord between us but rather, that it is my task to hold your arm steady until the sun of Brecht has once more sunk into exotic waters."[43] The preceding citation is from Adorno's March 18, 1936, letter to Benjamin which takes up the question of Benjamin's "The Work of Art" essay. Once again, Adorno would accuse Benjamin of proceeding undialectically. He criticizes Benjamin's unqualified and uncritical acceptance of technically reproduced art as well as the essay's complementary rejection of *all* autonomous art as being inherently "counterrevolutionary." The gist of his critique is contained in the following statement:

Dialectical though your essay may be, it is not so in the case of the autonomous work of art itself; it disregards an elementary experience which becomes more evident to me every day in my own musical experience—that precisely the uttermost consistency in the pursuit of the technical laws of autonomous art changes this art and instead of rendering it a taboo or a fetish, brings it close to the state of freedom, of something that can be consciously produced and made.[44]

That is, Benjamin fails to consider the fact that there occurs a "dialectic of rationalization" on the side of *l'art pour l'art* (or autonomous art) which *parallels* the "dialectic of technique" on the side of mechanically reproduced art, in consequence of which autonomous art *proceeds to divest itself of the aura* and its undesirable affirmative attributes. When viewed in terms of the more dubious twentieth-century representatives of autonomous art, such as Vlaminck and Rilke (both of whom Benjamin cites disparagingly in his study), autonomous art cannot help but appear retrograde and complacent. If, however, its more radical and advanced exponents are considered—e.g., Schoenberg or Kafka—it is clear that in such cases the affirmative semblance of reconciliation projected by the aura has been thoroughly rejected in favor of a fragmentary and dissonant formal aesthetic structure which possesses an inalienable socially critical function. For Adorno, therefore, the hallmark of *authentic* autonomous art is the radical disavowal of the illusionism and aestheticism of nineteenth-century *l'art pour l'art*—i.e., the renunciation of the notion of the closed, organic work of art and its replacement by the fragmentary, open-ended, "work-in-progress." By repudiating the ideas of closedness and totality, works of art stand as living testaments to the present state of *non-identity*, to the fact that "reason" and "reality" do not yet coincide. Consequently, Adorno recommends that, as a dialectical counterbalance to the argument of "The Work of Art" essay, Benjamin undertake a study of the poetry of Mallarmé, a study which would show the way in which the dialectic of technique or rationalization is itself operative on the plane of autonomous (as well as mechanically reproduced) art.[45]

As much as Benjamin is guilty of underestimating the contemporary significance of autonomous art,[46] he is, in Adorno's eyes, equally guilty of overestimating the progressive consequences to accrue from the institutionalization of mechanically reproduced art. More specifically, the revolutionary qualities he ascribes to the medium of film and the potential for class consciousness he attributes to film audiences are contradicted by empirical conditions. On the one hand, the culture industry was already engaged in an effort to restore a counterfeit aura to film, by virtue of the "cult of stars," the highly artificial and falsifying ideal of reality it sought to convey (thereby undermining the "natural objectivity" of the medium), and by pandering to the culinary and cathartic side of the medium, i.e., the idea of film as entertainment or cultural diversion. In this respect Benjamin exhibited a Brechtian uncritical and immediate fetishization of the powers of "technique," with fatal disregard for the manipulative social employment of that technique in reality. On the other hand, Benjamin displayed an equally Brechtian blind faith in the intrinsic revolutionary inclinations of the masses, an immediate appeal to "the actual consciousness of actual workers who have absolutely no advantage over the bourgeois except their interest in the revolution, but otherwise bear all the marks of mutilation of the typical bourgeois character."[47] Moreover, Adorno questions whether or not the medium's conditions of reception are in fact so suitable for the fostering of an active and critical consciousness (Brecht's "experts"). Would not the rapid flitting by of the images on the screen actually leave the spectator more passive and with less of an opportunity to respond critically? Do not the illusionistic pretensions of film—the deceptively convincing fabrication of reality it promotes—especially lend themselves to seductive and manipulative employment on the part of the established powers, both fascist and capitalist?

"Accordingly," remarks Adorno in conclusion, "what I would postulate is *more* dialectics."[48] It is not as though Adorno totally rejects Benjamin's account of the decline of the aura, whether on the side of autonomous art or on the side of technically reproduced art. On the contrary, Adorno is substantially in agreement with Benjamin's account of the world-historical, tradition-shattering effects that the phenomenon of rationalization has wrought in the domain of artistic production. However, in several crucial respects, Adorno finds Benjamin's argument perilously one-sided. To "dialecticize" the argument would mean in two important instances to furnish the absent moments. In the case of de-auraticized, mechanically reproduced art, it is the moment of "negativity" that is wanting: the fact that such art all too easily lends itself to manipulative rather than emancipatory ends, to the ideological co-optation and integration of the masses within the framework of existing social relations, rather than their political enlightenment. In the instance of autonomous art, it is the "positive" moment that has been omitted: radically articulated autonomous art undergoes a process of *self*-rationalization, such that it divests itself of the aura and its accompanying retrograde attributes. Yet, Adorno failed to recognize at the time that for Benjamin, the "philosopher of redemption," it was precisely those concrete, positive aspects of aesthetic rationalization that demanded emphasis, insofar as they exhibited, however, faintly, traces of the path to "salvation"—salvation from exile, salvation from the Nazis, salvation from nightmares that had yet to be invented. Whereas for Adorno, the dialectician, the critic of ideologies, the flaws in Benjamin's argumentation were all too visible, and it was the *negative* side of this phenomenon that stood out as most deserving of theoretical scrutiny. Mistakenly, however, Adorno assumed that the disagreement concerned merely a material issue, a question of emphasis. He failed to recognize the more fundamental methodological incommensurabilities that were responsible for the increasing divergence in their respective philosophical outlooks.

Adorno was prompted by the exchange with Benjamin to formulate a more concrete and detailed articulation of his own position. The result was the 1938 essay "On the Fetish Character of Music and the Regression of Listening," a landmark study in the sociology of art in its own right. Perhaps the study's most notable achievement was its systematic application of Lukács's concept of reification for the purpose of developing a comprehensive materialist theory of mass culture.[49] As such, the essay attempted to supply the moment of negativity which had been suppressed in Benjamin's enthusiastic consideration of the same phenomenon: the encroachment of the forces of technology upon the hitherto sacrosanct realm of art. However, in his study Adorno would confine himself for the most part to the sphere of music, though the results of his analysis proved readily generalizable to other domains of artistic endeavor.[50]

In his effort to offset Benjamin's premature optimism, Adorno focused on two significant aspects of the situation of music as well as the arts in general under advanced capitalism: their rampant commodification and the effective abolition of the traditional subject of aesthetic experience. By "commodification" Adorno means the organized process whereby the arts are alienated from their primary and traditional status as a *use-value,* an object of aesthetic experience, and become an *exchange value,* an object whose character is determined first and foremost by its relation to the market. In the case of music, examples of commodification abound. For example, there are the insidious hit tunes, all written according to formula and devoid of any intrinsic musical quality. They are composed for easy listening and do not attempt to place demands on the listener (thus, the "regression of listening"). For the sake of the largest possible sales, they attempt to appeal to as wide a spectrum of listeners as possible. This also means keeping all substance to a minimum, while perhaps allowing for the inclusion of a catchy phrase here or there, so that the consumer will remember *this* song when he or she goes to the marketplace.

In addition, there is the growing cult of musical "stars," the beneficiaries of a totally artificial and contrived buildup on the part of the industry. The result is that the specific quality of this or that individual song ceases to matter (not that it exists anyway), and it is purchased merely for the sake of the *name* of the artist. Art thereby regresses to *cult* in the full-fledged totemic sense of the word. It becomes nothing more than a *fetish,* part of the logic of commodification or the "fetishism of commodities" in Marx's sense. It is purchased for its *cult value*—the value it acquires by virtue of its commercial status or popularity, and no longer for its intrinsic merits as an aesthetic object.

A new genre of *Gebrauchsmusik* in the service of capitalism also emerges: commercial jingles and background music for films and radio shows. The staggering extent to which all music is sacrificed to the demands of the commodity form is further dramatized by the fact that even so-called "serious music" has been incorporated into the all-embracing clutches of industry: "Whoever still delights in the beautiful passages of a Schubert quartet or even in the provocatively healthy fare of a Handel concerto grosso ranks as a would-be guardian of culture among butterfly collectors,"[51] remarks Adorno. "The consumer is really worshipping the money he himself has paid for the ticket to the Toscanini concert."[52] The differences between "light" music and "serious" music—"domesticated under the barbarous name of classicism"—disappears as the latter, too, finds its ready-made niche in the world of administered culture. Only music which totally shuns all commercial requirements, such as that of the Schoenberg school, maintains the right to be taken seriously.

Thus, Adorno shows how at present the field of music is governed completely by the commodity form. All rudiments of pre-capitalist musical life have been extirpated. Whereas popular or folk art was once an authentic vehicle of expression for those who had been deprived of an education in the refinements of higher culture, today this has ceased to be true insofar as popular culture, too, has fallen under the hegemony of dominant interests. The result of these developments is the *reification of culture*. Its intrinsic substance and qualities have been hollowed out and only the shell, lifeless and inert, remains. With its obverse side, the liquidation of the individual, the reification of culture takes a totalitarian turn. The inmost capacities of the subject to perceive and think in other than the most programmed, standardized, and alienated patterns have become the stakes in a process of massive cultural indoctrination. This process, as Adorno explains, is intimately related to the employment of technological means for manipulative ends. The signature of the eclipse of the individual in the field of music is the phenomenon of "regressive listening": "Regressive listening appears as soon as advertising turns into terror, as soon as nothing is left for consciousness but to capitulate before the superior power of the advertised stuff and purchase spiritual peace by making the imposed goods literally its own thing."[53] In direct refutation of Benjamin's thesis in "The Work of Art Essay," he concludes:

Whether a technique can be considered progressive and "rational" depends on the meaning of its context and/or its place in the whole of society as well as in the organization of the particular work. Technical development as such can serve crude reaction as soon as it has established itself as a fetish and by its perfection represents the neglected social tasks as already accomplished.[54]

In his March 18, 1936, letter to Benjamin, Adorno observed that "Both positions are the torn halves of an integral freedom, to which however they do not add up."[55] His statement implies that whereas Benjamin's standpoint preserves the moment of the political effectiveness of art at the expense of its critical function, his own perspective retains the latter while forfeiting all claims to generalizability. The debate at this point seems to take on the character of an *antinomy*,[56] with no imminent prospects for resolution. Both positions have their drawbacks. Benjamin's willingness to sacrifice the principle of aesthetic autonomy for the sake of mechanically reproduced, generalizable art—an art suited to the ends of political communication—runs the risk of prematurely surrendering art to the domain of utilitarian interests. And as we have shown, these interests can be equally progressive or reactionary. On the other hand, Adorno's steadfast defense of de-auraticized autonomous art relinquishes all potential for communication on other than the most privatized, esoteric basis—to the point where such art is accessible (as, for example, in the case of Schoenberg) only to the "expert." In his dispute with Benjamin, Adorno is compelled paradoxically to invoke arguments originally set forth by the Benjamin of the *Trauerspiel* book period, in order to convince his friend of the continued validity of the autonomous art. For no one had shown more convincingly than the early Benjamin how a given artistic genre could, while in pursuit of its own formal laws, render itself fully *de-auraticized* and *profane*. In his "Surrealism" essay and his studies on Baudelaire, Benjamin concerned himself with an analogous phenomenon: the process whereby under determinate social conditions the aura of reconciliation proves insupportable to works of art, so that they come to assume a de-aestheticized, fragmentary form. In his letter of criticism, then, Adorno would claim to be doing nothing more than attempting to bring his friend's thinking in line once again with its innermost tendencies. It is likely that he was not truly aware of the full extent of the theoretical gap that separated them until the final episode of the dispute.

Methodological Asceticism, Magic and Positivism

The third stage of the Adorno-Benjamin debate concerns Benjamin's three-part study "The Paris of the Second Empire in Baudelaire," which represents the most extensive portion of the *Passagenarbeit* published to date. It was the enthusiastic reaction of Horkheimer and Friedrich Pollock to the Arcades Exposé ("Paris—the Capital of the Nineteenth Century") back in 1935 which had won Benjamin a position with the Institute for Social Research. The Baudelaire study was then commissioned by the Institute in 1937. It was originally conceived of as only one part of the entire Arcades study (Part 5 according to the plan of the Exposé), but soon grew to such proportions that it became a separate book. Benjamin himself had not planned on writing the Baudelaire section of the Arcades Project first, but changed his mind owing to a request by the Institute. As Horkheimer wrote in a letter of March 28, 1937: "A materialist article on Baudelaire has long been needed. If you could write this part of your study first, I would be extremely grateful."[57]

Benjamin acceded to Horkheimer's entreaty. However, he repeatedly emphasized that he needed first to work out a preliminary methodological draft, whose focal point would be a critique of the concept of "archaic images" as it appeared in the work of Jung and Klages from the standpoint of his own theory of Dialectical Images. As he writes to Adorno in May of the same year: "Today I want only to assure you of what is already self-evident: that the explanation of the Dialectical Images in terms of the archaic image, now as before, defines one of the most decisive philosophical tasks of the '*Passagen*.'"[58] Moreover, he questions how meaningful the Baudelaire work would be for the Arcades Project as a whole if the discussion of archaic images were omitted. The reason he considered this methodological excursus so essential is clear. For if the dominant motif of the study was the relation between the *ur*historical and the modern, a relation that came to expression in the *correspondances* of Baudelaire's poetry,[59] then a refutation of the rival theory of archaic images in Jung and Klages would lead to an indispensable clarification of Benjamin's own methodological intentions.

In any event, his proposal for the Jung-Klages critique was rejected by Adorno and the Institute. It is likely that they felt his treatment would not have been critical enough, insofar as his elaboration of the theory of Dialectical Images in the Arcades Exposé had been, in Adorno's eyes, one of its more problematical aspects. Similar problems could be kept to a minimum, they hoped, if Benjamin would concern himself exclusively with Baudelaire. Upon learning of this verdict, Benjamin spoke of it as a "shadow" that had fallen across his work.[60]

Benjamin wrote the three parts of the Baudelaire study ("The Bohème," "The Flaneur," and "Modernism") in the summer and fall of 1938. Ultimately, the Institute's refusal of the Klages-Jung critique was to play an important part in the story of the work's reception. Benjamin had warned Horkheimer in advance of the problems that had arisen because he had been required to compose the work's *material portion* first. For what survives today as "Paris of the Second Empire in Baudelaire" is itself only the middle section of a projected three-part book on Baudelaire. According to Benjamin, the first part, "Baudelaire as Allegorist," represented the statement of the problem. The third part, "The Commodity as a Poetic Object," embodied the "solution," for which the second part, "The Paris of the Second Empire in Baudelaire" (the only part ever completed), would provide the material data. As Benjamin explained to Horkheimer in a letter of September 28, 1938:

The function of the second part is, generally speaking, that of an antithesis. It turns its back decisively on the methodological questions concerning the theory of art raised in the first part and undertakes the socially critical interpretation of the poet. This interpretation is a prerequisite for the Marxist interpretation of the poet, however, it does not fulfill this aim on its own. This task is reserved for the third part. . . . The second part stands as the antithesis to the first; in it critique in a more narrow sense, namely the critique of Baudelaire, has its place. The boundaries of execution must be set forth clearly in this part; the interpretation is only undertaken in the third part. The latter will have an independent range of concerns. The basic theme of the old Arcades

Project, the new and the always-the-same, will first come under consideration there.[61]

Above all, Benjamin stresses the following point: "It is by all means important to emphasize that the philosophical foundations of the book *as a whole* can not be comprehended, nor should they be, from the second part."[62] His message is clear. The section of the Baudelaire book commissioned by the Institute, that section dealing *exclusively* with Baudelaire, remains in a crucial sense unintelligible without the accompanying two methodological sections, the first of which (Part I) poses the theoretical problem: "Why do allegorical elements enter into Baudelaire's creative activity?"; the second of which (Part III) presents the resolution in terms of the "metaphysical subtleties and theological niceties" (Marx) of the commodity form. Thus, Part II, merely supplies the *"material content"* of the study. At the same time, Benjamin remained convinced that the piece could stand on its own as a kind of "philological study." His efforts to forestall a negative reception from the Institute through explanations of this nature proved to be in vain.

The Baudelaire study had been anticipated by the inner circle of the Institute in New York as a literary event of the first order, for it represented the first installment of a project with which Benjamin had occupied himself now for approximately ten years. The disillusioned tone of Adorno's response reflects inversely the original expectations which the work had evoked. It had become undeniably clear to Adorno that mere "differences in perspective" no longer sufficed to account for the theoretical divergences that separated them. There was virtually no trace in this study of the brilliant, theologically derived insights which had lent Benjamin's earlier work its unique powers of illumination. "Motifs are assembled but not elaborated," Adorno charges. "Panorama and 'traces,' *flaneur* and arcades, modernism and the unchanging, *without* a theoretical interpretation—is this a 'material' which can patiently await interpretation without being consumed by its own aura?"[63] There was no longer any question as to which side of Benjamin's self-avowed "Janus-Face" had, at least temporarily, won out. The influences of Brecht were omnipresent. Yet, it was not Benjamin's espousal of the materialist perspective that provoked Adorno's damning verdict. Rather, it was his employment of an unmediated and undialectical brand of materialism which in the end led him into a type of correspondence-mongering between cultural traits and their economic correlates:

I see a close connection between the points at which your essay falls behind its own a priori and its relationship to dialectical materialism. . . . Unless I am very much mistaken your dialectic lacks one thing: mediation. Throughout your text there is a tendency to relate the pragmatic contents of Baudelaire's work directly to adjacent features in the social history of his time, preferable economic features.[64]

In Adorno's view cultural phenomena were not merely economically determined, but first became comprehensible in terms of their mediation by the *total social process*. Rather than, for example, explaining Baudelaire's poem "The Ragpicker's Wine" through a new tax on wine (as Benjamin does in the study), Adorno suggests what is of greater significance in the poem from a materialist standpoint is that it shows how under industrial capitalism even *rubbish* takes on an *exchange value*. Benjamin's approach to Baudelaire would be more successful, he argues, if the socially relevant aspects of his poetry were analyzed under the sign of commodity fetishism or reification, rather than being given an immediate economic significance. As the re-write of the Baudelaire study ("Some Motifs in Baudelaire") demonstrates, Benjamin would take this recommendation to heart.

Moreover, Adorno continues, Benjamin's "ascetic" practice of refusing to supply directly the meta-theoretical presuppositions on which the material content of his writing was based gave his work the character of a "magical positivism," which ended up remystifying what it originally sought to demystify. As Adorno observes:

To express it another way; the theological motif of calling things by their names tends to turn into a wide-eyed presentation of mere facts. If one wished to put it very drastically, one could say that your study is located at the crossroads of magic and positivism. That spot is bewitched. Only theory could break the spell—your own resolute, salutorily speculative theory. It is the claim of this theory alone that I am bringing against you.[65]

The essence of his critique is then summarized in the following statement:

The impression which your entire study conveys. . . . is that you have done violence to yourself. Your solidarity with the Institute, which pleases no one more than myself, has induced you to pay tributes to Marxism which are not really suited either to Marxism or yourself. They are not suited to Marxism because the mediation through the total social process is missing, and you superstitiously attribute to material enumeration a power of illumination which is never valid for a pragmatic reference but only for a theoretical construction. They do not suit your own individual nature because you have denied yourself your boldest and most fruitful ideas in a kind of precensorship according to materialist categories (which by no means coincide with Marxist categories).[66]

The attitude of Adorno and the Institute as a whole vis-à-vis the Baudelaire study might be considered unjust, insofar as the monograph actually represented the material portion of a larger work whose methodological prelude they had already rejected. Nevertheless, Benjamin had submitted the work in the belief that it could stand as an independent whole. As the most cursory perusal of the essay will show, Adorno's criticisms were neither exaggerated nor out of place. Without some prior knowledge as to Benjamin's underlying methodological intentions—and these are nowhere to be found in the essay itself—the work borders on incomprehensibility. The thoroughness of Adorno's critique would seem to have paid off, since the re-write, "Some Motifs in Baudelaire," proved to be one of Benjamin's finest studies of the 1930s, an important contribution to a materialist theory of culture.[67]

In his response to the November 10, 1938, Adorno letter, however, Benjamin shows himself to be unrepentant. He reiterated the contention expressed in his original covering letter to Horkheimer that the absence of theoretical mediation is attributable to the fact that the section in question represents merely the philological part of the study. At the same time, the study transcends the level of mere philology, he asserts, insofar as the individual philological observations are integrated within the guiding context of a historical construction. It is precisely because of this subordination of philological materials within a governing historical framework that the essay transcends the level of a desultory compilation of facts and takes on a contemporary relevance which restores these facts to life: "The appearance of a closed facticity which attaches to a philological investigation and places the investigator under its spell, fades to the extent that the object is construed in an historical perspective. Thus, the object constitutes itself as a monad. In the monad everything that used to lie in mythical rigidity as a textual reference comes alive."[68]

The reference to the redemptive powers of the "monad" in this context makes it clear that what Benjamin had in mind was a program to recast the theory of Dialectical Images (originally, the theory of "ideas" in the *Trauerspiel* book) along immanent, materialist lines. It is the "historical perspective" of the monad which releases "facts" from the "mythical rigidity" they have in the scholastic investigations of the philologist and makes them relevant from the standpoint of materialist concerns. Materialist philology thereby redeems facts in accordance with the interests of social emancipation. It is in this context that Benjamin's alleged suppression of his earlier metaphysico-theological perspective must be understood. For he has expressly renounced a metaphysical point of view so that the phenomena are now open to being redeemed *exoterically* rather than *esoterically*. *To begin* from the standpoint of speculative theory or theology would vitiate the investigation, insofar as the analysis would thus be guided by a non-immanent, extrinsic point of reference.

What Adorno failed to realize in his critique was that this was precisely the aspect of his earlier philosophy that Benjamin was trying to hold in check: the unwarranted, unverifiable, speculative aspects which are incompatible with the principles of materialist research. It is for this reason that Benjamin emphasizes in his letter the necessity for the "ideas" of his study to emerge autonomously from the "construction" alone—i.e., from the historical arrangement of material elements, without the prior illegitimate admixture of esoteric speculative insights. It is precisely by virtue of this technique that Benjamin believed himself to have transcended the speculative theory of ideas of his early theological period in the direction of an exoteric, materialist theory of Dialectical Images; and he perceived this accomplishment as the salutory achievement of his materialist phase:

> If I refused in San Remo, in the name of my own productive interests, to adopt an esoteric intellectual development for myself and, disregarding the interests of dialectical materialism, . . . to get down to business, this involved, in the final analysis, not . . . merely loyalty to dialectical materialism, but solidarity with the experiences which all of us have shared for the last fifteen years. Here too, then, it is a matter of very personal productive interests of mine; I cannot deny that they occasionally do violence to my original interests. Between them lies an antagonism of which I could not even in my dreams wish to be relieved. The overcoming of this antagonism constitutes the problem of my study, and the problem is one of construction. *I believe that speculation can start its necessarily bold flight with some prospect of success only if, instead of putting on the waxen wings of the esoteric, it seeks its source of strength in construction alone.* It is because of the needs of construction that the second part of my book consists primarily of philological material. What is involved here is less an "ascetic discipline" than a methodological precaution.[69]

Fifteen years earlier, 1923, was the year of Germany's devastating inflation. Benjamin emphasizes that his adoption of the outlook of historical materialism has not been a question of arbitrarily selecting this or that theoretical perspective, but a decision to which he has been driven by the weight of historical circumstances. In accordance with the principles of materialism as he conceived of them, it would be inadmissible to allow for speculative insights to shape a priori the materials of his investigation; rather, such insights are only legitimate insofar as they emerge a posteriori, from the construction of materials itself. In the *Trauerspiel* book theory of "ideas" or "monads," the ideas emerge from a determinate constellation of material elements ("Ideas are to objects as constellations are to stars") to reveal a vision of redemption. In the "monads" or "Dialectical Images" of the Arcades Project, the material elements are situated in a historical configuration and thereby redeemed for the forces of social emancipation. The former theory derives its thrust from an esoteric, metaphysical outlook, the latter from the standpoint of a secular, inner-worldly concept of reconciliation.

In his essay "Bewusstmachende oder rettende Kritik—die Aktualität Walter Benjamins," Habermas states that Adorno's critique of Benjamin is of interest "as much for what it misunderstands as for what it understands."[70] He thus suggests that Adorno failed to take into account that Benjamin proceeded according to the demands of "redemptive critique"—a process of rescuing endangered semantic potentials—rather than that of "ideology critique"—a process of demystifying socially engendered false consciousness. However, there seems in addition to be something more at stake in the disagreement. Adorno not only neglects the redemptive component in Benjamin's criticism, but also fails to recognize the reasons why Benjamin, in his later theory of Dialectical Images, has attempted systematically to bridle the speculative origins of his thinking. This practice is not explicable simply in terms of ad hoc obeisances to dialectical materialism, but represents the culmination of a line of development in his thinking which began with his "Surrealism" essay and was then accentuated decisively by Brecht. In the end, Benjamin's redemptive criticism had become thoroughly profane. It ceased to concern itself with presenting an image of otherworldly truth. Instead, its task became one of emancipating cultural products from the debilitating grip of ideological falsification and thereby rendering their truths serviceable for the impending revolutionary transformation of society. As Benjamin remarks, "Only that historian will have the gift of fanning the spark of hope in the past who is firmly convinced that *even the dead* will not be safe from the enemy if he wins. To be sure, only a redeemed mankind receives the fullness of its past— which is to say that only for a redeemed mankind has its past became citable in all its moments."[71] For once these endangered semantic potentials are permanently lost to us, be it through repression (in the psychoanalytic sense) or oppression, the capacity for happiness and fulfillment in this-worldly life will have been irretrievably diminished.

That Adorno was incapable in these years of recognizing the full extent of the growing methodological differences which separated them—and by no means was he totally blind to these—is not solely attributable to his own myopia. The "Janus-faced" Benjamin of the thirties,[72] at times fully torn between mutually exclusive theoretical perspectives, made a habit of shielding from his most intimate friends ideas and theories which were likely to be offensive. Contrary to the usual practice, Scholem never received a copy of "The Author as Producer." After the experience with the Kafka essay, it is highly unlikely that Benjamin consulted Brecht concerning his draft of "On the Mimetic Faculty." Benjamin wrote enough important essays during this period—those on Kraus, Proust, Leskov, and Kafka to mention only a few—which had in varying degrees achieved an effective fusion between his Messianic and materialist interests. As a result, both Scholem and Adorno, on the one hand, and Brecht, on the other, were kept in perpetual doubt as to which moment of his thinking would ultimately triumph. His own theoretical vacillation in the 1930s was at the same time exacerbated by a sort of intellectual tug of war between each faction over which direction of his thought would eventually gain predominance. No matter which course Benjamin attempted to pursue, he was bound to lose on one side; and (which must have appeared to him as the ultimate in frustration) his efforts to please a given contingent seemed only to bring increased reprisals. We discussed in the previous chapter Brecht's disparaging verdict concerning the Kafka essay—Brecht accused it of promoting "Jewish fascism." According to Scholem, however, the Kafka essay was not *theological enough*.[73] When Benjamin, down and out in Paris, and often literally wondering about the source of his next meal, received Adorno's extremely frank letter of censure informing him that his "The Paris of the Second Empire in Baudelaire" had been roundly rejected by the Institute's editorial board, one cannot help but sympathize with him, regardless of the theoretical issues involved, when he responds by saying that the letter "makes me feel as if the ground were giving way under my feet."[74]

Ultimately, the theological current in his thought would triumph for a last time in the "Theses on the Philosophy of History," which were Benjamin's response to the Stalin-Hitler pact.[75] Like so many others, Benjamin could only feel duped and betrayed for having so readily placed his trust in the secular forces of history. The "Theses" therefore represent an unmitigated return to the Messianic philosophy of history of his early period. The relation between history and redeemed life remains forever indirect and enigmatic. For while, on the one hand, the "angel of history" correctly perceives progress as "one single catastrophe which keeps piling ruin upon ruin and hurls it in front of his feet," on the other hand, "every second of time is the strait gate through which the Messiah might enter."[76]

Beyond the Dispute

It is clear that when one inquires into the *Aktualität* or contemporary significance of the Adorno-Benjamin dispute it is the second stage of the debate, in which the relationship between art and technology in the modern age is thematized, that assumes preeminence. It was suggested earlier that the respective positions defended by Benjamin and Adorno in this context take on the form of an "antinomy"—in philosophical parlance, two mutually exclusive, yet equally valid propositions concerning an object or state of affairs. I would like now to focus on a remark by Adorno cited above, which represents a fitting epilogue to the debate: his observation that, "Both positions are torn halves of an integral freedom, to which however they do not add up." This claim indicates the fundamental insufficiency of each position when taken individually and points out that only under radically transformed social conditions could the unsatisfactory one-sidedness of each perspective be truly overcome. For, to restate in brief the underlying antagonism at issue: Benjamin, by emphasizing the importance of mechanically reproduced art as a vehicle of mass political communication, forfeits the measure of distance art needs vis-à-vis society in order to fulfill its inalienable critical function. His position thereby risks heralding the *false* overcoming of autonomous art, one in which art is prematurely integrated within the functional context of social life, without the prior *authentic* transposition of the utopian *promesse de bonheur* contained in the aura of autonomous bourgeois art to society itself.

Adorno, on the other hand, staunchly preserves the moment of negativity embodied in the works of the twentieth-century avant garde, though at the expense of all hope of making their content accessible on other than the most narrow and private basis. The deficiencies of this position are readily discernible. The more pervasive the grip of the totally administered world becomes, the more the artistic avant garde is forced, for the sake of its own self-preservation, to distance itself from that world. It renders itself necessarily more and more esoteric in order to escape the reifying network of commodity production and thereby maintain its powers of negation and refusal. Ultimately, however, as in the cases of Joyce and Schoenberg, modern art turns into such a thoroughly specialized endeavor that it proves accessible only to a coterie of specialists—professional critics and other artists. In the last analysis, then, it preserves its radicality only at the expense of its universality.

When viewed in a slightly different light the Adorno-Benjamin debate appears as the renewal of a longstanding theoretical conflict concerning the opposition between "high culture" and "mass culture." As Leo Lowenthal has shown, this conflict originally found expression in the writings of Montaigne and Pascal, who (though they were not contemporaries) disagreed over the relative merits of art as "diversion." Montaigne (1533–1592), writing at a time when the claim to universality of the feudal-Christian world view had been shattered by the break with tradition precipatated by the radical new values of Renaissance and Reformation—believed that in an unstable world, it was the function of art to serve as a *release* (or "diversion") from the pressures of day-to-day existence, and thereby facilitate the adaptation of man to society. Whereas in his *Pensées* Pascal fears that to accede to the notion of art as entertainment or diversion would represent an ill-advised capitulation before man's ignoble faculties and inclinations, in fatal neglect of his higher spiritual needs, such as the salvation of his soul.[77]

As Lowenthal implies, at this early stage in the debate, the issue at stake was less the more modern antagonism between high culture and low culture than that between "art" and "popular culture." Only with the emergence of the romantic era toward the end of the eighteenth and beginning of the nineteenth century, does the modern dichotomy between so-called high and low art become thematically codified in aesthetic discourse. Only at this point, with the final demise of courtly patronage, do artists acquire the necessary freedom to turn artistic production into a fully autonomous, self-referential endeavor. At the same time, there arise the first signs of a new breed of art—the work of art as commodity—which drives this incipient rivalry between high and low art to new and unequaled heights.

Nevertheless, art's newly won freedom from all traditional social obligations simultaneously engenders an unprecedented crisis in aesthetic consciousness. For precisely insofar as it is emancipated, art has burned all bridges to traditional nonautonomous art; it thereby also severs all ties with those proven, time-honored standards which could provide objective guidelines as to how it might proceed henceforth. This dilemma between the new need for radical independence and self-definition on the one hand, and an intrinsic need for minimal objective standards on the other, proves constitutive for the entirety of modernism. Adorno has expressed this quandary as follows: "It has become self-evident that that which concerns art is no longer self-evident, neither in relation to itself, nor in relation to the whole—nor even in relation to its right to exist."[78]

Despite the importance of the "prehistory" of the controversy between high and low culture, in the Adorno-Benjamin dispute this conflict receives an especially radical and unique articulation. For with the advent of techniques of mechanical reproduction in contemporary times, the debate over mass culture has been transformed qualitatively. No longer can the issue of mass culture be brushed aside as an episodic phenomenon; in its modern administered, electronic variants mass culture has become perhaps *the* salient feature of social life at present.[79] In this sense, culture ceases to be merely another subsystem of society in general—as it was, for example, in the form of nineteenth-century autonomous art. As a massive, quasi-autonomous apparatus of ideological cohesion, it comes to subsume society itself. It was the salutory achievement of both Benjamin and Adorno in the 1930s to have been among the first to give theoretical expression to this tendency—which Benjamin observed in the case of the Nazi propaganda machine and Adorno attributed to the culture industry of the West.

The "torn halves of an integral freedom" of which Adorno speaks cannot be made whole in a social totality which itself remains lacerated. Hence, the antinomical form of the debate corresponds to an objective social predicament, rather than pointing to a logical deficiency of the dispute itself. For either position, if taken in isolation, ultimately proves self-defeating. Each requires the other as its necessary complement. Politically committed art and avant garde art need not preclude each other. Both play an indispensable role, though in contrasting ways, in the critique of the existing social order. Mechanically structured media such as film possess an unprecedented capacity to convey socially relevant themes to vast numbers of people. This potential can neither be dismissed outright, as Adorno tends to do, nor can it be, following Benjamin, hypostatized as "intrinsically revolutionary." Above all, the overly simplistic didactic tendencies of committed art must be curbed if it is to distinguish itself from mere propaganda, be it of a Soviet or culture industry slant. Any form of aesthetic communication that seeks to program its recipients to think in a certain manner immediately forfeits its claim to an emancipatory potential. The task of political art can never be anything more than to initiate a process of critical self-reflection and debate—a fact of which Brecht took cognizance in theory, whereas in his practice it was honored more in the breach than the observance. The mission of art can never be one of dispensing readymade ideological slogans and then marketing them as revolutionary truths. Adorno's position serves as an important corrective to such tendencies.

At the same time, autonomous avant garde art, by refusing to become involved immediately in society, retains a capacity for critique that is all the more radical. For it is precisely through this moment of refusal, its unwillingness to play the game, so to speak, that modern art convicts the unreason of society of its own absurdity. By remaining useless for social purposes, modernism stands as the living indictment of a society based on the bourgeois principle of utility. Moreover, the esoteric guise assumed by modernism points to the fact that truth is not always necessarily immediately generalizable. An intellectual or artistic avant garde must often play a crucial role in initiating a process of social criticism among a relatively small contingent of persons under objective conditions where critique remains incapable of being realized on a mass basis. As Adorno has remarked, "Art respects the masses by presenting itself to them as that which they might become, instead of adapting itself to them in their degraded state."[80] In his view, committed art inherently suffers from the tendency to identify uncritically with the immediate, empirical consciousness of the masses, instead of trying to mediate the latter and thereby upgrade it.

In a similar spirit, Sandor Radnoti has in a recent essay taken note, on the one hand, of the unsatisfactoriness of a situation in which art (as opposed to mass culture) exists in a state of detachment and isolation from the rest of society, a situation which in effect concedes the vast and important realm of mass culture to the culture industry. Thus, he expresses a sincere desire for the "pacification of the universal concept [of art], the conclusion of the *war* of emancipation of art"[81] which society has witnessed for the past two centuries, and recognizes how essential it would be for serious attention to be directed once more to the sphere of "low art," which plays such an important role in the lives of the majority of men and women. At the same time, he correctly acknowledges that today the dichotomy between high culture and low culture presents itself in essence as a *fait accompli*. The entrenched hiatus between the two spheres can in a certain measure be tempered, but it can never be healed completely; it has become a constitutive aspect of modern culture. In Radnoti's words:

This reconstruction of culture, this widening of the concept of truth [to include low culture], this reduction of universality, cannot however mean the restoration of the organic character of art, that is, the preference for an art growing continuously out of traditions, nor can it mean the production of a radically new culture which would start a new tradition on the basis of wholesale discontinuity. . . . [The] revocation of the alienation [of high art from society in general] is not only impossible in dynamic societies, it is not even desirable. It is not desirable because the exclusive character of the demand of recognizing and merely belonging to the world would annihilate the criticism exercised by the work over the world.[82]

Mechanically reproduced arts such as film and autonomous avant garde art ultimately find themselves in solidarity with one another insofar as both embody an anti-aesthetic impulse within art. Each in its own way aims at the destruction of the illusions of affirmative bourgeois culture, which reached its apogee with the *l'art pour l'art* movement of the nineteenth century. Each attempts to destroy the myth of culture as an independent preserve in which the values denied to us in everyday life can be lived. This process of destruction is precisely what Benjamin captured in his account of the "decline of the aura." For both types of art, traditional aesthetic values appear as an unconscionable luxury in a society in which human misery has grown to such proportions. Avant garde art undermines affirmative culture from within, whereas mechanically reproduced art seeks to undermine it from without. In this way, each proves the necessary corrective of the other. Ultimately, however, the meaningfulness and relevance of a given work of art cannot be determined by whether or not it belongs to a given aesthetic category, but only by considering it as an individual entity. The latter task is the mission of art criticism. Both Benjamin and Adorno were well aware of this fact. In spite and because of their disagreements, their attempts to formulate a materialist theory of culture remains of great contemporary relevance. For the work of each manages to avoid the dogmas of both non-Marxist and Marxist theories of culture: the former pretend to know nothing of the work of art's social origins, and the latter know the work only insofar as it is reducible to those origins.

Chapter Seven

BENJAMIN'S
MATERIALIST THEORY
OF EXPERIENCE

In his early aesthetics Benjamin had pursued the problem of the disintegration of experience—i.e., the decline of man's capacity to live a meaningful and fulfilled existence—from a decidedly theological perspective. Life in the profane continuum of history was considered incapable of fulfillment a priori insofar as it was deemed the diametrical antithesis of the Messianic age, the sphere of redeemed life. So extreme was the opposition between these two domains that neither could have any direct and immediate bearing on the other. They existed in a state of pure antithesis. Hence, for the early Benjamin, as soon as one begins surveying the unreconciled domain of historical life, one finds the continuum of experience in a state of perpetual disintegration. However, exceptions are to be found in the realm of *aesthetic experience,* where the artist momentarily breaks through the mythical realm of historical life, the realm of eternal repetition or the always-the-same (*das Immergleiche*), to produce a fragile image of transcendence. It becomes the task of the critic to redeem these images from the fate of historical oblivion that incessantly threatens to overwhelm them, to breathe new life into them and thereby make them relevant for the present.

In Benjamin's later aesthetics the transcendent point of reference—the category of redemption—temporarily recedes from view, although it never disappears entirely from the horizon of his thought. It recedes for strategic reasons. Once Benjamin took up the profane cause of the class struggle (to be sure, in his own highly stylized fashion), his theological impulses ran the risk of being seriously misconstrued. Thus, in the thirties he resumed his investigation of the problem of the disintegration of the capacity for qualitative experience from a quasi-sociological, materialist perspective. As we have noted in earlier chapters, he made a concerted effort—not always prudent nor always successful—to abandon his earlier "bourgeois" reverence for cultural goods and to assist in the annihilation of traditional, prejudicial aesthetic categories such as genius, creativity, beauty, etc.,[1] in favor of an approach which took the material conditions of the production and reception of works of art as its point of departure:

The concept of culture, as the substantive concept of creations which are considered independent, if not from the production process in which they originate, then from the production process in which they continue to survive, carries a fetishistic trait. Culture appears in a reified form. Its history would be nothing but the sediment formed by the curiosities which have been stirred up in the consciousness of human beings without any genuine, i.e., political experience.[2]

Nevertheless, Benjamin's self-understanding as a historical materialist bore a distinct resemblance to the metaphysically oriented method of redemptive criticism of his early period. In both cases the theoretical adversary was a static, empathetic, historicist relation to the work of art which tries to present the latter "the way it really was" (Ranke), as a dead, lifeless object, sedimented in the historical past, devoid of all contemporary relevance or now-time. The methods of "cultural history" turn tradition into a dead weight from which humanity must be emancipated: "Cultural history, to be sure, enlarges the weight of the treasure that accumulates on the back of humanity. Yet cultural history does not provide the strength to shake off this burden in order to be able to take control of it."[3]

For Benjamin, the primary consideration in approaching past works of art must be the demand of *relevance*. How a work of art was experienced by its contemporaries is at best a scholastic question. Benjamin's mission therefore was simultaneously the "destructive" task of negating the false semblance of autonomy and self-sufficiency the realm of spirit assumes from the perspective of cultural history—an approach which reifies works of art as beautiful but irrelevant cultural commodities—and the complementary "constructive" goal of resuscitating those elements of tradition that can once more be made serviceable for humanity in its contemporary hour of need:

Historicism presents the eternal image of the past; historical materialism presents a given experience with the past, an experience which stands unique. The replacement of the epic element by the constructive element proves to be the condition for this experience. The immense forces which remain captive in historicism's "once upon a time" are freed in this experience. To bring about the consolidation of experience with history, which is original [*ursprünglich*] for every present, is the task of historical materialism. It is directed towards a consciousness of the present which explodes the continuum of history.

The historical materialist explodes the epoch out of its reified "historical continuity," and thereby lifts life out of this epoch, and the work out of this life work.[4]

To be sure, the conception of historical materialism set forth in the above citations bears little resemblance to any of the conventional versions of that doctrine. The notion of materialist methodology advanced here demonstrates that one can discern in the work of the later Benjamin a strong tendency which competes with the more reductionist, Brechtian understanding of Marxist theory evinced in his essays on Brecht and related works. One might describe this so-called counter-tendency in terms of an effective fusion of his early metaphysical and later materialist concerns. The attempt to merge these two modes of thought approximated the perspective of "anthropological materialism" praised by Benjamin in the closing pages of his "Surrealism" essay. However, this attempt, which I have dubbed Benjamin's "materialist theory of experience," must be differentiated from the *unmediated* admixture of Marxist and theological motifs in, e.g., "Paris of the Second Empire in Baudelaire." In the latter work Benjamin's materialist and theological impulses converged in his preoccupation with capturing the significant detail in the absolute immediacy of its material presence. It was on this account that Adorno criticized him for his "wide-eyed presentation of facticity,"[5] without the faintest trace of the supporting theoretical focus which alone could link the various materials assembled and unfold their real meaning. But the aforementioned competing tendency in his later writing—evidenced above all in works such as "The Storyteller," "The Image of Proust," "Some Motifs in Baudelaire," and "On the Mimetic Faculty"—permitted the full scope of that salutory capacity for speculative insight, which had proved the distinctive feature of his early literary studies, to come to the fore once again, though this time within the framework of a materialist approach. Moreover, this tendency was also characterized by the abandonment of the desire to correlate facets of cultural life immediately with corresponding features of the economic "base"—a practice notable in his first version of the Baudelaire study. Instead, in the essays enumerated above, works of art receive their full due as phenomena which are at once socially mediated and autonomous sources of knowledge in their own right. As such, they not only mirror ongoing social processes, but they also reorganize diffuse features of social life into intelligible wholes, and thereby present at the same time an independent perspective polemically directed back at the same matrix of social relations from which they originated. It was undoubtedly this particular mode of assimilating the materialist philosophy of history which resulted in the greatest theoretical achievements of Benjamin's later years.

The modern-day science of hermeneutics originated with Schleiermacher in the early nineteenth century. It was born out of an awareness that as moderns our relation to tradition (in Schleiermacher's case, our relation to classical antiquity) has ceased to be self-evident, that our way of life has become separated from that of our ancestors by a chasm of misunderstanding, that to understand the past through the eyes of the present is to commit a grave injustice to it, (i.e., to "the way it really was"), and that, consequently, there arises the need for a special type of knowledge charged with the responsibility of revealing these misunderstandings and thereby creating more solid ground for a bridge between past and present.[6]

Benjamin's investigation of the demise of the *traditional* or *communal* basis of experience proceeds from a similar impetus (though, to be sure, minus the historicist implications of Schleiermacher's approach). He is disturbed that the abyss separating the modern world from past historical life has expanded to the point where an entire array of tradition-bound meanings have become unrecognizable, if not patently unserviceable, to us in the present. Not only does he fear the loss of past experience, but also the serious impairment of the present-day capacity to assimilate experience in general. The implacable advance of the forces of production in the modern age, which rapidly renders all remnants of tradition obsolete, eventually comes to penetrate *all* aspects of existence, so that ultimately even the human faculty of perception itself is diminished. Consequently, not only has the quality of experience deteriorated in modern life to an unprecedented degree, but the subjective capacity to detect this development, and thus possibly redress it, has likewise been seriously eroded.

The problem of the rationalization of social life and the concomitant diminution of the capacity for qualitative experience became a paramount concern in the work of the later Benjamin. He recognized the decline of traditional life forms which this process of rationalization entailed as an irreparable *loss*: for the meaning potentials objectified in the cultural products of traditional societies contain a promise of transcendence; they are the objects in which past ages have deposited their collective dreams and longings, their aspirations for a better life, aspirations which adverse historical conditions have heretofore frustrated; and it falls due to future generations to preserve such hopes for a better life, if not to redeem them outright. As Benjamin observes: "The past carries with it a temporal index by which it is referred to redemption. There is a secret agreement between past generations and the present one. Our coming was expected on earth. Like every generation that preceded us, we have been endowed with a *weak* Messianic power to which the past has a claim. This claim cannot be settled cheaply. Historical materialists are aware of that."[7] This citation illustrates unequivocally the degree to which the theological motifs of Benjamin's earlier "redemptive criticism" have been preserved in his later writing. The foremost danger of modernity is that its radical disrespect for tradition runs the grave risk of totally eradicating our links with the past, thus squandering that invaluable "temporal index of redemption" which tradition contains. An *authentic* sublation of past would necessarily *preserve* the promise of redemption that has been sedimented in the artifacts and ruins of traditional life.

The Disintegration of Community: Novel Versus Story

In his 1936 essay "The Storyteller: Reflections on the Work of Nikolai Leskov," Benjamin attempted to show, by contrasting the "epic" element of the story to the fortuitous character of events in the novel, just how far experience itself, and our capacity to convey experiences, has diminished in modern life. The inability of men and women to exchange experiences in the contemporary world is merely the obverse side of the fact that the very structure of experience itself has undergone significant and far-reaching transformations. Today, Benjamin observes, it has become obvious that "experience has fallen in value. And it looks as if it is continuing to fall into bottomlessness. Every glance at a newspaper demonstrates that it has reached a new low, that our picture, not only of the external world but of the moral world as well, overnight has undergone changes which were never thought possible."[8] In keeping with the Marxist principle of understanding cultural phenomena as they originate within determinate material conditions of life, Benjamin offers the following persuasive depiction of the multifarious and sudden transformations in the traditional structure of experience around the time of World War I, transformations so swift and extensive that it would seem almost humanly impossible for one to adapt to them:

For never has experience been contradicted more thoroughly than strategic experience by tactical warfare, economic experience by inflation, bodily experience by mechanical warfare, moral experience by those in power. A generation that had gone to school on a horse-drawn streetcar now stood under the open sky in a countryside in which nothing remained unchanged but the clouds, and beneath these clouds, in a field of force of destructive torrents and explosions, was the tiny, fragile human body.[9]

The art of storytelling is a genre which falls midway between the epic of antiquity and the novel of the modern era. Yet, its clear affinities with the "epic side of truth" betray the fact that it stands incomparably closer to the earlier genre. It is an art form in which meaning is unquestionably immanent to and transparent in life. It flourished in the context of what the young Lukács referred to as "integrated civilizations."[10] Its traditional representatives were the "resident tiller of the soil" and the "trading seaman." In the latter case, the tale was stamped with an aura of authority because it had come from afar; in the former, it acquired this aura by virtue of the experience and wisdom of its teller—his ancestors had dwelled in the same region for countless generations, so that he was steeped in the lore of *tradition,* which was all-important. The journeymen of the Middle Ages, who represented a sort of fusion of the two basic historical types of the storyteller, brought about a significant expansion in the art of storytelling. As Benjamin notes, "If peasants and seamen were past masters of storytelling, the artisan class was its university. In it was combined the lore of faraway places, such as a much-traveled man brings home, with lore of the past, as it best reveals itself to the natives of a place."[11]

That meaning is immanent to life in the world of the story is apparent from the fact that the story always contains something *useful*—practical advice, a kernal of wisdom, or a conventional moral. That such knowledge acquires an immediate self-evidence bespeaks of a situation in which there exists a *continuity and flow* to the continuum of experience, where time has the character of a meaningfully ordered, organic sequence of events, and where even the phenomenon of death fits meaningfully within this sequence. Under such conditions advice and counsel are readily communicable and seemingly step forth from life itself of their own accord. Benjamin contrasts this situation to the very different structure of experience in modern life, where events take on a desultory and isolated, overwhelmingly *private* character; where "experiences" are at best meaningful for the individual, but have forfeited the attribute of *universality* from which the element of wisdom, the moral of the story, traditionally derived. "In every case the storyteller is a man who has counsel for his readers. But if today 'having counsel' is beginning to have an old-fashioned ring, this is because the communicability of experience is decreasing. In consequence we have no counsel either for ourselves or for others."[12] Benjamin insists that this development is not merely another symptom of decaying values or the crisis of modernity. Rather, it has a determinate social origin as a "concomitant symptom of the secular productive forces of history."[13] It is a tendency which becomes especially apparent upon examination of the social history of literary genres. Such an analysis shows that there is far more at stake than the historical obsolescence of this or that art form: the demise of storytelling signals a corresponding loss of meaning in life itself. The fabric of experience has ceased to be structured in an intelligible and coherent fashion, such that one could readily extract wisdom or meaning from its individual episodes; it has instead become fragmented and discontinuous, thus rendering the very concept of "wisdom" problematical: "Counsel woven into the fabric of real life is wisdom. The art of storytelling is reaching its end because the 'epic side of truth,' wisdom, is dying out."[14]

The obverse side of the decline of storytelling is the rise of the novel. According to Benjamin, "What differentiates the novel from all other forms of prose literature—the fairy tale, the legend, even the novella—is that it neither comes from oral tradition nor goes into it."[15] Insofar as stories are handed down orally from generation to generation, they become, as it were, the property of the community. They represent the primary means of recording experience in those societies where *handicraft* was the dominant mode of production. Indeed, the distinct imprint of craftsmanship inheres in the very process of storytelling itself: "traces of the storyteller cling to the story the way handprints of the potter cling to the clay vessel."[16] In the case of the novel, however, the communal aspect of the artistic process—both in terms of the conditions of its production and of its reception—has disappeared: "The novelist has isolated himself. The birth place of the novel is the solitary individual, who is no longer able to express himself by giving examples of his most important concerns, is himself uncounseled, and cannot counsel others. . . . In the midst of life's fullness, and through the representation of this fullness, the novel gives evidence of the profound perplexity of the living."[17] The novel is produced by solitary individuals and read by solitary individuals. The individual's "profound perplexity" results from his having been sundered from traditional conditions of life in a capitalist society which has become a *bellum omnium contra omnes,* where the credo of self-serving individualism has become the dominant principle of conduct. Try as he might to integrate his private experiences within a more universal, meaningful framework, the hero of the novel, from Don Quixote to "K," is predestined to confusion and ruin. As Benjamin notes, "Even the first great book of the genre, *Don Quixote,* teaches how spiritual greatness, the boldness, the helpfulness of one of the noblest men, Don Quixote, are completely devoid of counsel and do not contain the slightest scintilla of wisdom."[18]

In modern life the wisdom of the story has been supplanted by the proliferation of *information.* Concomitant with the advent of the division of labor and the universal predominance of the bureaucratic form of administration, the vast social stockpiling of information indicates the degree to which the parameters of society have been quantitatively extended at the expense of its former integral unity. Thus, we know more about everything, yet this knowledge is poorer in quality: it has ceased to be related to those so-called ultimate questions which are directly concerned with the meaning of life. The increase in quantity remains forever incapable of compensating for the decrease in quality. The emergence of information as the dominant form in which experience is stored is thus a primary symptom of the crisis of experience, of our inability to communicate experiences in other than the most shallow and truncated fashion. As Benjamin notes, "Every morning brings us the news of the globe and yet we are poor in noteworthy stories."[19] For Benjamin, journalism represents the deliberate sabotage of experience, its reduction to a minimum number of superficial facts and statistics, a process of distortion which aims at destroying the public's capacity for independent judgment. The press attempts to manufacture an artificial consensus, "public opinion," by appending insipid psychological explanations to each story in order to suggest how the average man on the street should interpret events. He notes that "by now almost nothing that happens benefits storytelling; almost everything benefits information."[20] Thus, the fragmentary character of contemporary social life meets the desultory journalistic processing of experience half way. The story, in contrast, was devoid of all such psychological intentions, permitting the material richness of life to step forth unprocessed, in all its fullness. In this way each story retained a meaning (or moral) for the community of listeners which was inexhaustible and lasting. On the other hand: "The value of information does not survive the moment in which it was new. It lives only in that moment; it has to surrender to it completely and explain itself to it without losing any time."[21] In the form of information, experience no longer has anything lasting to teach us; it has simply become another fungible aspect of modern life, an item of momentary interest which will soon cease to be topical and then be promptly discarded.

The lack of manifest psychological motifs in the story further differentiates it from the novel. The striking absence of a self-evident meaning to life in the novel results in the novelist's concerted attempt *to procure meaning synthetically*. "The 'meaning of life' is really the center about which the novel moves,"[22] observes Benjamin. It is because of the lack of a readily apparent meaning of life that the novel so often assumes the form of a search for meaning; whereas in the world of story, where something as fundamental as the "meaning of life" is never openly thrown into doubt, the *problem* of meaning never needs to become explicitly thematized.

In the background of Benjamin's discussion of the novel stands Lukács's pre-Marxist study *The Theory of the Novel*, a work which Benjamin held in very high esteem.[23] In his attempt to produce a typology of the novel form, Lukács counterposes the "integrated civilization" of the Homeric epic—paralleling Benjamin's use of storytelling—to the bourgeois world of "transcendental homelessness" as portrayed in the modern novel. For Lukács, "The novel is the epic in an age in which the extensive totality of life is no longer directly given, in which the immanence of meaning to life has become a problem, yet which still thinks in terms of totality."[24] It is the art form appropriate to the bourgeois age of "absolute sinfulness" (Fichte), where life is governed by "a second nature, and, like [first] nature, it is determinable only as the embodiment of recognized but senseless necessities and therefore it is incomprehensible, unknowable in its real substance."[25]

Benjamin cites the following important observation from *The Theory of the Novel*: "Only in the novel are meaning and life, and thus the essential and the temporal, separated. . . . Only in the novel . . . does there occur a creative memory which transfixes the object and transforms it."[26] Here, Lukács suggests that it becomes the task of the novelist *to make over experience subjectively*; for if he were merely to transmit it to the reader as he found it, in its mere facticity, he would be simply presenting a congeries of meaningless, discrete facts. The conscious recasting of experience, an integral part of the creative process for the novelist, is something very different from the activity of the storyteller, a type of secularized medieval chronicler, who merely takes it upon himself to describe events as they happen (or as they have been said to happen), convinced that their significance will shine through on its own, independent of any subjective interference.

The profound longing of the novel to rejuvenate the mundane character of experience peaks with Proust's masterpiece, *A La Recherche du Temps Perdu,* the threshold of the modern novel of consciousness. In Proust's work, the novel reaches the point of no return, so to speak, insofar as it is no longer the *objective nature* of the events themselves that is of foremost importance, but the haphazard manner in which they materialize now and again in the *mémoire involuntaire* of the novelist. In Proust, the power of remembrance invests the events of life with the aura of significance they lacked as they occurred in *mere* life, life in its inchoate immediacy: "For an experienced event is finite—at any rate, confined to one sphere of experience; a remembered event is infinite, because it is only a key to everything that happened before and after it."[27] The loneliness of the reader of the novel corresponds to the loneliness of a world of experience which remains opaque and unintelligible to the subject, which will not readily lend itself to being shared. In the language of the young Lukács, the novel provides us with a *substitute totality,* in compensation for the absence of totality in life itself. The capacity of the novel to restore a semblance of coherence and unity to an existence which is otherwise notably lacking in such qualities accounts, on the psychological level, for the tremendous popularity of this genre over the last two centuries. It stands out as a wealth of vicarious satisfaction. As Benjamin remarks: "The novel is significant, therefore, not because it presents someone else's fate to us, perhaps didactically, but because this stranger's fate by virtue of the flame which consumes it yields us the warmth we never draw from our own fate. What draws the reader to the novel is the hope of warming his shivering life with a death he reads about."[28]

Benjamin wrote the Leskov article in the summer of 1936, shortly after he had completed his essay on "The Work of Art in the Age of Mechanical Reproduction." That the two works were closely related in his mind can be seen from his remarks to Adorno in a letter of July 1936, where he speaks of the Leskov piece as a work "which, though it cannot in the least lay claim to the scope of the essay on the theory of art ["The Work of Art" essay], indicates several parallels with the 'destruction of the aura,' from the fact that the aura perishes with the art of storytelling."[29] Yet, the Leskov study reveals at the same time a sudden and dramatic change of heart on Benjamin's part concerning the issue of modern technological methods versus traditional forms of life. The exuberant acceptance of the process whereby traditional aesthetic genres are sacrificed to the all-encompassing onslaught of rationalization, characteristic of "The Work of Art" essay, a process credited with opening up tremendous, heretofore untapped possibilities for the political employment of art, is a sentiment totally absent from "The Storyteller." In the Leskov essay, Benjamin has come round to a diametrically opposite assessment of this trend: he now recognizes that rather than leading automatically to the progressive transformation of artistic forms (as the naïve materialist view would have it), the contemporary rationalization of aesthetic experience signifies the irreparable destruction of a vital part of our cultural heritage, the loss of unrenewable structures of meaning and experience whose claims to reconciliation and happiness would necessarily fall due to any and every future emancipatory movement worthy of our trust. The auratic or affirmative aspect of traditional art, which Benjamin, rather undialectically, condemns in "The Work of Art" essay as "counter-revolutionary," contains an indispensable *utopian* moment, an as yet unfulfilled *promesse de bonheur,* which, if abstractly negated, forces art to degenerate to the level of merely one more thing among things in the utilitarian mill of social life. Unless the auratic *promesse de bonheur* has been actually realized in life itself—which was certainly not the case with the cinematic trends of 1936 which Benjamin lauds—the uncritical acceptance of de-auraticized, mechanically reproduced mass art itself runs the risk of heralding a reactionary and false *Aufhebung* of autonomous art. With these facts in mind, Benjamin re-evaluates his former position. And it is with no small measure of anguish that, in describing the demise of the art of storytelling in the Leskov essay, he observes resignedly, "It is as if something that seemed inalienable to us, the securest among our possessions, were taken from us: the ability to exchange experiences."[30]

Consequently, in "The Storyteller" (as well as his 1939 work, "On Some Motifs in Baudelaire") Benjamin rejects the position of "The Work of Art" essay insofar as he comes to realize that the application of technological advances to the sphere of art will not necessarily in and of itself result in the transformation of art along progressive and emancipatory lines; and that traditional auratic art, instead of being simply reactionary, serves as the repository of the hopes and aspirations of past ages, and as such functions as an important stimulus to change in the present—the loss of which could only have the gravest consequences.

By the same token, the methodology employed by Benjamin in the Leskov essay is by no means problem-free. Though he stops short of explicitly calling for a mobilization of the "healthy" forces of tradition against the decrepit conditions of modernity (with its obvious reactionary overtones), a solution of this nature seemingly lies in store beneath the surface of the essay. There is considerable nostalgia in his tone when he speaks wistfully of the decline of the integrated fabric of experience which was characteristic of communal social life; and redeeming aspects of modernity are nowhere to be found. Moreover, the sets of antitheses which form the methodological basis of the essay—story and novel, community and society, tradition and modernity—only reinforce the impression that the author seeks to establish an abstract opposition between past and present, compelling the reader to choose between one or the other—when in reality a choice so simple does not in fact exist. Fundamentally, then, the antinomy established by Benjamin between traditional and modern societies is overly rigid and potentially misleading. In truth, communal social organization was never so idyllic as modern romantics tend to imagine it. These were societies beset with problems of privation and scarcity, at the mercy of nature, where social rank was decided by birth, and in which formal legal channels to address injustice and grievances were highly underdeveloped. The gains made by advanced industrial societies in all these areas are by no means inconsequential and their loss would be tantamount to wholesale regression. In a similar vein, modern societies, by exploding the closed, tightly knit structure of traditional communities, have opened up a wealth of possibilities which admittedly remain largely distorted or unfulfilled under current social conditions, but which nevertheless would have remained inconceivable in past ages. The very fact that today they exist as "unfulfilled" serves as an important spur toward their future realization. The dichotomous nature of Benjamin's presentation neglected these important facts, the inclusion of which would have made the choice at issue decidedly more complex, and rightfully so.

Baudelaire, Modernity, and Shock Experience

In his 1939 essay "Some Motifs in Baudelaire" Benjamin pursues a similar theme: the fragmentation of the continuum of experience in modern times as it manifests itself in the realm of aesthetic experience. Yet, in this work the major methodological shortcoming of the Leskov essay stands corrected. No longer does Benjamin abstractly seek to counterpose an idyllic past to the decadent present. Instead, he attempts to work through the dilemmas of modern social life in a more immanent fashion. Baudelaire assumed such pride of place in the thought of the later Benjamin because he stood at the crossroads of traditional and modern societies. The fact that he consciously incorporated the often grotesque images of mid-nineteenth-century city life into his poetry qualifies him as the first "modernist," the first true poet of urbanism. Because he stood so to speak on the cusp between two historical eras, witnessing the extirpation by modern industrial capitalism of the last vestiges of traditional life, Baudelaire was ideally situated to chronicle this important process of transition. In this connection, Benjamin seeks to show how the philosophy of history penetrates the very heart of the purportedly autonomous activity of the artist.

A primary indication of the decline of the traditional fabric of experience is the emergence of "shocks" as an inalienable feature of modern urban life. Whereas experience was traditionally governed by the principles of continuity and repetition, making it, at least in theory, something that was always familiar and predictable, the shocks of city life disrupt these familiar patterns of experience. The predominance of the experience of shocks is intimately bound up with the emergence of the crowd. Being incessantly jostled by the mass of passers-by in the city streets was a new phenomenon in nineteenth-century life. "Fear, revolusion, and horror were the emotions which the big city crowd aroused in those who first observed it," remarks Benjamin.[31] "Moving through this traffic involves the individual in a series of shocks and collisions. At dangerous crossings nervous impulses flow through him in rapid succession, like the energy in a battery."[32] The teeming masses become a perpetual obstacle in trying to get from one point to another in the city. The din of the crowd proves inimical to the idea of having thoughts of one's own. While the crowd vastly increases the opportunity for chance encounters, it is also the breeding ground for a notorious callousness and indifference among men and women.[33] For sheer numbers and the struggle for survival that characterizes urban life make it nearly impossible—not to mention against one's "interests"—to deal with each individual in a humane and personal manner. Even if the theme of the city masses never becomes the explicit subject of Baudelaire's poetry (as it does for example in the novels of Victor Hugo), it serves as its ever-present background. As Benjamin comments, "The mass was the agitated veil; through it Baudelaire saw Paris."[34]

It is Benjamin's contention that with the advent of shock experience as an elemental force in everyday life in the mid-nineteenth century, the entire structure of human experience is transformed. In support of this claim he cites Freud's thesis from *Beyond the Pleasure Principle* that "becoming conscious and leaving behind a memory trace are processes incompatible with one another in one and the same system." Instead, memory traces are "often most powerful and most endurable when the incident which left them behind was one that never entered consciousness."[35] Here, Freud acknowledges that consciousness's role in the *protection against stimuli* (*Reizschutz*) has become infinitely more important than its *reception of stimuli*. For in modern life consciousness must make itself so highly protective against the proliferation of aversive stimuli or shocks that the majority of memory traces which previously registered as experience in a direct and natural way now fail to do so. As a result, our capacity to have experiences in the traditional sense is irreversibly diminished.

Today experience has been so thoroughly *reduced by* and *filtered through* consciousness that what remains is an experience reduced to its barest essentials, an experience necessary for the task of mere survival. In consequence, not only has the human apparatus of perception itself been significantly altered, but the very cornerstone of the traditional conception of experience, the idea of *Gedächtnis* or remembrance, has also been destroyed. The experiences deposited in remembrance could be passed on from generation to generation; and the wisdom of life was thereby preserved. But in modern life, *Gedächtnis* has been supplanted by *Erinnerung*: the matter-of-fact *preservation* of memory traces has given way to their *disintegration* in consciousness—in order for them to be assimilated by consciousness and thus stored. For otherwise the shock character of experience would *overwhelm* consciousness; and thus experience would simply prove unassimilable. Only by virtue of this mutilating process of censorship and pre-formation can experience register in consciousness and thus in the strict sense be said to have been "lived." As Benjamin explains:

The greater the character of the shock factor in particular impressions, the more consciously consciousness has to be alert as a screen against stimuli; the more efficiently it is so, the less do these impressions enter experience [*Erfahrung*], tending to remain in the sphere of a certain hour of one's life [*Erlebnis*]. Perhaps the special achievement of shock defense may be seen in its function of assigning to an incident a precise point in time in consciousness *at the cost of the integrity of its contents.*[36]

The loss of the "integrity of the contents" of experience be-comes thematic not only in the lyric poetry of Baudelaire, but plays an equally important function in the work of Proust. Proust's point of departure is the inferior character of *conscious* experience in modern life, as opposed to the pure, unbroken stream of ex-perience of the *mémoire involuntaire*. The work of Bergson also makes this problem its starting point. Yet, he errs in supposing that *temps vécu* can be recaptured in its pristine state by way of the fully conscious, *voluntary* activity of the *mémoire pure*. Whereas for Proust, voluntary memory—memory at the service of the intel-lect—whose primary function is to screen out potentially dis-turbing memory traces, always remains deficient; it is only ex-perience as it arises unconsciously in the *involuntary* memory that is fully capable of repossessing the wealth of those memory traces which has been occluded by conscious memory. And thus it is the narrator's adventitious encounter with the madeleines he once enjoyed as a boy which provokes the chain reaction of spontaneous reminiscences which serves as the point of departure for Proust's remarkable novel. As Benjamin notes, "*A La Recherche du Temps Perdu* may be regarded as an attempt to produce experience syn-thetically . . . under today's conditions, for there is less and less hope it will come into being naturally."[37] In this way Proust seeks to preserve the integral function memory—*Gedächtnis*—against its fragmentation in the modern age at the hands of *Erinnerung*. "Proust's eight-volume work conveys an idea of the efforts it took to restore the figure of the storyteller to the present generation."[38]

Benjamin detects a remarkable confirmation of Freud's theory concerning the shock-preventative function of consciousness in Baudelaire's characterization of poetic creation in "Le Soleil" as a type of "fantastique escrime" (fencing): that is, a process of parrying the shocks of modern life on the part of the poetic imagination.[39] Elsewhere, Baudelaire referred to the creative process as "a duel in which the artist, just before being beaten, screams out in fright."[40] In this way Benjamin seeks to show that it is not merely in terms of the *content* of Baudelaire's work that the experience of shocks proves central, but that this experience has also penetrated the formal side of the creative process. By voluntarily renouncing the aestheticist pretensions of *l'art pour l'art*, Baudelaire was able to give expression to a world-historical process of social transformation, a fact which distinguishes his work from that of many of his contemporaries. Thus, in a fragment from the *Passagenarbeit*, Benjamin describes him as a "secret agent" in the enemy camp, "an agent of the secret discontent of his class with its own rule."[41] The high level of consciousness in his poetry— illustrated by the aforementioned fencing metaphor—testifies to the fact that Baudelaire's "work cannot merely be categorized as historical, like anyone else's, but intended to be so and understood itself as such."[42] The inclusion of innumerable images of urban decay and putrefaction—set in a lyric context which causes them to stand out as all the more shocking—was by no means fortuitous; rather, it was Baudelaire's systematic intent. As he explains in the dedication to his collection of prose poems *Spleen de Paris*: "Which one of us, in moments of ambition has not dreamed of the miracle of a poetic prose, musical, without rhythm and without rhyme, supple enough and rugged enough to adapt itself to the lyrical impulses of the soul, the undulations of reverie, the jibes of consciousness? It was above all, out of my exploration of huge cities, out of the medley of their innumerable interrelations, that this haunting ideal was born."[43]

Benjamin views Baudelaire's work as being of great significance insofar as it represents the first concerted attempt to destroy from within the affirmative values of bourgeois aestheticism, the first selfconscious effort to incorporate the contingencies of everyday life into the hitherto sacred preserve of autonomous art—an approach which would henceforth become paradigmatic for the entirety of modernism. As such, *Les Fleurs du mal* appears as the first historical incarnation in the modern era of *de-aestheticized art*: a post-auratic art which seeks to divest itself of all illusionary, class-bound trappings and reintegrate itself with the concerns of material life. As Benjamin observes in an important letter to Horkheimer of April 16, 1938: "The unique significance of Baudelaire consists in the fact that he was the first to have unflinchingly apprehended the productive power of a self-alienated humanity in the double sense of the term—agnosticized [*agnosziert*] and intensified through reification."[44] And in a similar vein, he remarks in an as yet unpublished sketch for the Arcades Project that Baudelaire "armed a self-alienated humanity against the reified world."[45] In Benjamin's view, therefore, it was Baudelaire's practice to accentuate the growing tendency toward total reification to the point where it would pass over into its opposite: "into the reconciliation of man and thing, man and nature."[46] This intention was entirely consistent with his employment of allegory: for just as the commodity turns objects (and persons) into lifeless abstractions (into exchange values), so too does allegory devalue the intrinsic meanings of things for the sake of its own arbitrary meanings. As such, allegory, which proceeds by way of reification, embodies the perfect technique for the poetic representation of a capitalist society which, according to its innermost laws, operates by virtue of the principle of reification: the transformation of social relations between men into lifeless relations between things—commodities. "Allegories represent what the commodity makes out of the experiences which men of this century have," observes Benjamin. "The allegorical mode of intuition is always built on a devalued phenomenal world. The specific devaluation of the world of things, which occurs in the commodity, is the basis of the allegorical intention of Baudelaire."[47] Hence, Benjamin proceeded from the conviction that the allegorical poetics of Baudelaire constituted a privileged vantage point from which to view the plight of a "self-alienated humanity" in the era of industrial capitalism.

In Benjamin's account of the disintegration of the structure of experience in the nineteenth century, the life situations of two social types stand out as prototypical: the factory worker (not surprisingly) and the gambler. The notion of shock experience is employed as the universal metaphor through which the transition from traditional to modern societies is grasped. As Benjamin notes: "The shock experience which the passerby has in the crowd corresponds to what the worker 'experiences' at his machine."[48] In support of this contention he relies extensively on Marx's seminal account of the transition from techniques of handicraft production to the methods of manufacture and machine industry in chapters 14 and 15 of *Capital* I.[49] Benjamin's argument proceeds from the fact that the continuity of experience, so essential for handing down experiences in traditional societies, has been replaced in contemporary life by the wholesale fragmentation of experience. Yet, in the Baudelaire essay there is no question of nostalgia for what has been lost; instead, the past is used in an ideology-critical sense, in order to provide by way of contrast an index of the vast transformation of the quality of life which the modern era has wrought. Whereas under conditions of handicraft production there existed a determinate sequence which connected one act on the part of the craftsman to the next, under the conditions of modern factory labor this connection has been dissolved to the point where the worker's activity has been degraded to the status of a mere appendage of the machine. For this reason the possibility of the worker deriving any intrinsic satisfaction from his activity, e.g., the satisfaction which would accrue from his having produced the finished product in its entirety, is denied.

Instead, on the assembly line he repeatedly performs the same monotonous, partial function. He must force his actions to conform to the autonomous rhythm of the machine. His activity thus degenerates to that of a mindless automaton. It is *reified,* becomes thing-like. Therefore, the idea of experience, i.e., the notion that one can become through practice well-versed in the talents and skills necessary for the accomplishment of a given task, proves anachronistic—so totally specialized and one-sided has labor become. Moreover, with the advent of machine industry, labor comes to be prized precisely insofar as it has become unskilled; for the more unskilled the worker, the lower the wage. As Benjamin avers, "The unskilled worker is one of the most deeply degraded by the drill of machines. His work has been sealed off from experience; practice counts for nothing there."[50]

Ultimately, the process of rationalization effectuates a *universal leveling* of the conditions of experience. The onslaught of reification,[51] initially confined to the workplace, becomes absolute and all-inclusive in modern life; society in its entirety is dominated by the technical considerations of formal reason. The man on the street betrays the symptoms of this fate no less than the worker on the assembly line: the behavior of both has become strictly regimented, stripped of its individuality, and rendered homogenous. As Benjamin notes, Marx's description of the degradation of the factory worker to the status of an automaton, a mere appendage of the machine, sheds "a peculiar light on the absurd kind of uniformity with which Poe wants to saddle the crowd—uniformities of attire and behaviour, but also a uniformity of facial expression. Those smiles provide food for thought. They are probably the familiar kind, as expressed in the phrase 'keep smiling'; in that context they function as a mimetic shock absorber."[52] The pedestrians in Poe's text "act as if they had adapted themselves to the machines and could express themselves only automatically. Their behaviour is a reaction to shocks. 'If jostled, they bowed profusely to the jostlers.'"[53] In the arts, this process has reached its apogee in the case of film, where the experience of shock (rapid cutting, multiple camera angles, instantaneous shifts in time and space) has been elevated to a formal principle. "That which determines the rhythm of production on a conveyor belt is the basis of the rhythm of reception in a film,"[54] observes Benjamin.

For Benjamin the figure of the gambler becomes a parable for the disintegration of coherent experience in modern life. At first the employment of the gambler as an example appears somewhat contradictory: for are not the activities of the laborer and the gambler as antithetical as work and play? Yet, gambling can be said to resemble factory labor insofar as here, too, experience counts for nothing. Each action on the part of the gambler is independent from the one preceding it: the result of the previous game has no bearing on the game that follows it. Each spin of the roulette wheel is an action unto itself, and thus, one is constantly starting over again from scratch. Therefore, there can be no *ac-*

cumulation of knowledge or experience. As Benjamin remarks, "The manipulation of the worker at a machine has no connection with the preceding operation for the very reason that it is its exact repetition. Since each operation at the machine is just as screened off from the preceding operation as a *coup* in a game of chance is from one that preceded it, the drudgery of the labourer is, in its own way, a counterpart to the drudgery of the gambler. The work of both is equally devoid of substance."[55]

To be sure, the drudgery of wage labor has none of the adventure of gambling. But the quality of the experience in both cases is quite similar. Both gambling and the labor of the worker become all-consuming activities. Each ultimately comes to pervade the very psyche of the subject. The experience in both cases proves enervating rather than satisfying. The "futility, the emptiness, the inability to complete something," are characteristic failings of the activity of both the gambler and the factory workers. This is the prototypical experience of modern man who has been "cheated out of his experience"; it is the model of experience in hell where one is never allowed to complete what one has begun. Baudelaire immortalized the figure of the gambler in his poem "Le Jeu":

> Round the green tables sat lipless faces,
> Blood-drained lips, toothless gums,
> And fingers possessed by a hellish fever,
> Fumbling in pockets or blind passion.
>
> Thus the macabre dream I saw unfold
> Before my clairvoyant eyes one night;
> Myself I saw in a silent corner of the cave,
> Cold, mute, jealous—hunched in fright.[56]

As Habermas has noted, Benjamin was usually less concerned with bursting the ideological illusions of the cultural sphere than with redeeming those utopian moments of tradition which are incessantly endangered by the oblivion of forgetting. Whereas "Some Motifs in Baudelaire" in many respects comes closest to the method of ideology-critique valued by his friend Adorno, at the same time Benjamin's lifelong preoccupation with discovering possible traces of reconciled life occupies a prominent place in the concluding pages of the essay. In his view, all knowledge which fails to concern itself with the question of redemption remains partial and inferior.

Benjamin detected strong evidence of this concern in Baudelaire's theory of *correspondences*. It was by virtue of this theory that Baudelaire was able to invoke images of *collective experience*, the last rudiments of which were being rapidly extinguished before his very eyes. What the modern era lacked was a basis for continuity which would prevent experience from disintegrating into a desultory and meaningless series of events. For Benjamin—and the importance of this fact for his thought cannot be overemphasized—"Where there is experience in the strict sense of the word, certain contents of the individual past combine with materials of the collective past."[57] Only if this crucial relation is maintained can "the secret agreement between past generations and the present one"[58] be guaranteed. For it becomes the mission of the present generation to redeem the thwarted hopes, aspirations, and struggles of its ancestors, the disconsolate traces of which are inscribed in our cultural heritage. The ruthless expansion of rationalization renders this vital heritage more opaque and alien to us with each passing day. In contrast, it was the customary function of the great days of remembrance—the special days of festival, ceremony, and ritual which were consciously set off from the rest of the days of the calendar, as it were—to ensure the periodic intermingling of individual and collective pasts. These celebrations served to remind humanity of its "secret agreement" with the past. The *correspondances* of Baudelaire perform a similar function: "The *correspondances* are the data of remembrance—not historical data, but data of prehistory."[59] Like the festivals of old, what makes them "great and significant is the encounter with an earlier life."[60] The *correspondances* are the key to Baudelaire's use of allegory: from the ruins of modern life he is able miraculously to conjure forth the image of a collective past that has long since faded from memory. Such images are intended as an antidote or counter-image to the crisis-ridden state of modernity. "The murmur of the past may be heard in the correspondences, and the canonical experience of them has its place in a previous life,"[61]

Benjamin comments: "What Baudelaire meant by *correspondances* may be described as an experience which seeks to establish itself in crisis-proof form. This is possible only within the realm of ritual."[62] Baudelaire's poem "Correspondances" begins as follows:

> Nature is a temple whose living pillars
> Sometimes give forth a babel of words;
> Man wends his way through forests of symbols
> Which look at him with their familiar glances.
>
> As long-resounding echoes from afar
> Are mingling in a deep, dark unity,
> Vast as the night or as the orb of the day,
> Perfumes, colours, and sounds commingle.[63]

The *correspondances* do not merely evoke random images of past life. Rather, they are specifically concerned with re-creating an *animistic* relation to nature. Nature thereby ceases to be viewed as mere fodder for technical exploitation and is instead regarded as itself *ensouled*. The *correspondances* hark back to an *ur*historical state of reconciliation, a state prior to that point where the species had succeeded in individuating itself vis-à-vis primordial nature, in which man and nature existed in a condition of immediate, undifferentiated unity. The first stanza of 'Correspondances' personifies nature, it invests nature both with the capacity to speak and with the ability to return man's glance. Nature thereby appears as a partner instead of a hostile foe. In this way, the *correspondances* attempt to speak out against the unremitting technical mastery of the environing world and thus recapture a relation to nature whose last traces are being extirpated with the ruthless advance of rationalization. As Benjamin notes: "the *correspondances* record a concept of experience which includes ritual elements. Only by appropriating these elements was Baudelaire able to fathom the full meaning of a breakdown which he, a modern man, was witnessing."[64]

Yet, the theory of *correspondances* in no way recommends the wholesale regression of species-life to a prehistoric relation to nature where humanity would once more be at her mercy. The point is, rather, that in the process whereby mankind has succeeded in emancipating itself from its original condition of utter thralldom to nature, it has in its overzealousness simultaneously succeeded in destroying those crucial elements of reciprocity through which alone a condition of harmony between man and nature could be restored. Consequently, in accomplishing the subjugation of nature man has only succeeded in imitating her prehistoric harshness and rigidity, while repressing those elements of correspondence that would constitute a prerequisite for the authentic pacification of the struggle for existence. The moment that the history of domination has always tragically forgotten is that man, too, is part of nature and is therefore ultimately destined to fall victim to his own obsessive logic of coercion and control. The cardinal merit of Baudelaire's verse was to have recognized this tragic failing and attempted to remedy it by producing *correspondances* with past collective life.

That Baudelaire has bestowed upon nature the capacity to return man's gaze ("man wends his way through a forest of symbols/which look at him with their familiar glances") is indicative of the *auratic* character of nature. For in "Some Motifs in Baudelaire" Benjamin has altered the definition of the aura as it originally appeared in the 1936 "Work of Art" essay; moreover, in accordance with the Leskov essay, he has altered decisively his attitude toward the fact of its decline. Whereas in the 1936 work he embraced wholeheartedly the process whereby a unique, non-mechanically reproduced auratic art was sacrificed to the advance of rationalization, in the 1939 essay he has come round to realizing the irrevocable destruction of meaning potentials which results from this process in fact. In the later essay, his redefinition of the concept of the aura reads as follows: "Experience of the aura thus rests on the transposition of a response common to human relationships to the relationship between the inanimate or natural object and man. The person we look at, or who feels he is being looked at, looks at us in turn. To perceive the aura of an object means to invest it with the ability to look at us in return."[65]

In "Some Motifs in Baudelaire" Benjamin shows himself unwilling to relinquish the qualities of the aura without a struggle. To perceive the aura of an object means to endow it with humanized, animate traits usually reserved for relations between men. It means to conceive of inanimate objects *fraternally* rather than manipulatively, to grant them the capacity to project signals and attributes which transcend their simple quality of being-there. Nor is this merely an indulgence in mysticism on Benjamin's part. Rather it bespeaks of an earlier relation of man to nature which modern man has all but repressed from memory.

Benjamin further defines the aura as "the associations which, at home in the *mémoire involuntaire*, tend to cluster around the object of a perception."[66] It therefore refers to an indefinite series of correspondences and interrelations engendered by an object rather than a fixed image of the object per se. For this reason it is clear that photography proves destructive of the aura of objects, whereas painting, on the other hand, would preserve its traces most faithfully. For photography tends to *fix* the image of a thing at a given moment in time, it consciously freezes its associations. As Benjamin observes, "The perpetual readiness of volitional, discursive memory, encouraged by the technique of mechanical reproduction, reduces the scope for the play of imagination."[67] In this claim, the reversal of Benjamin's former, unilaterally positive valuation of the techniques of mechanical reproduction echoes clearly, insofar as photography is explicitly linked with the "volitional, discursive memory" which Benjamin, following Proust's emphasis on the liberating capacity of the *mémoire involuntaire*, disdained. The photograph is eminently non-auratic: it lacks the all-important capacity to return the gaze. Just the reverse is true of painting, though. Nonmechanically reproduced art— especially painting—qualifies as auratic because it is already *humanized*: that is, its contours have already been thoroughly shaped and fashioned by the human subject, and so, when viewed by the subject, it always stands ready to return what the subject has previously objectivated therein. Thus, in constrast to the photograph, "the painting we look at reflects back at us that of which our eyes will never have their fill. . . . [To] the eyes that will never have their fill of a painting, photography is rather like food for the hungry or drink for the thirsty."[68] Whereas the auratic object incessantly calls to mind an endless stream of associations, as if it were actually endowed with the autonomous capacity to speak to us by means of its own aesthetic language.

Nonsensuous Correspondences

The germ cell of the discussion of correspondences in "Some Motifs in Baudelaire" is the 1933 fragment "On the Mimetic Faculty," which was never published during Benjamin's lifetime. This draft and the accompanying sketches are of especial importance for understanding the theory of experience developed by Benjamin in the 1930s insofar as they demonstrate conclusively the extent to which he continued to rely on the metaphysical frame of reference developed in his early years. Above all, "On the Mimetic Faculty" indicates the degree to which Benjamin's early theological philosophy of language, originally elaborated in the 1916 essay "On Language as Such and on the Language of Man" (whose outlook informs virtually all his significant early writings, from his 1918 Kant critique, to "The Task of the Translator," to the "Prologue" to the *Trauerspiel* book), remained constitutive for much of his later thought.

"On the Mimetic Faculty" represents a second version of a work entitled "Lehre vom Ähnlichen" ("Doctrine of the Similar") which Benjamin had begun to work on in early 1933. To attempt to view the second version of the essay as the "final product," however, would be potentially misleading, since it constitutes in essence a truncated version of the earlier draft; in fact, it appears that by and large Benjamin composed "On the Mimetic Faculty" by merely copying out excerpts from the original fragment. At the same time, the difference in content between the two versions remains substantial and illustrative of the conflict between his innate attraction toward a theological mode of expression and his desire in these years to render that mode compatible with a materialist point of view. The editors of Benjamin's *Gesammelte Schriften* have observed that the essential difference between the two versions is the elimination of the many explicit allusions to occult and mystical motifs characteristic of the first draft.[69] Scholem has conjectured that this thematic difference might be explained by the fact that the two works were intended for different "addressees."[70] Yet, the latter supposition fails to explain then why Scholem himself received the later, less avowedly mystical version of the work ("On the Mimetic Faculty"). It would seem more plausible to suppose that given his continuing interest in materialist methods, Benjamin himself had ambivalent feelings concerning the strident theological tenor of the earlier draft and therefore felt more comfortable circulating the second "toned-down" version. Despite their manifest terminological differences, however, there is little doubt that the two fragments share a common theme (how the primitive capacity for perceiving correspondences has over the course of time found expression in the domain of language) and origin (the 1916 essay "On Language as Such and on the Language of Man)."

Benjamin concluded "On the Mimetic Faculty" in September 1933 on the island of Ibiza, where he had passed the summer after fleeing Hitler's Germany in the spring of that year. Two factors of a circumstantial nature combined to delay its completion. First, Benjamin decided in May 1933 that in order to achieve a truly rigorous reformulation of "Lehre vom Ähnlichen" it would be necessary for him to reexamine thoroughly the 1916 essay "On Language." The problem here was that his hurried departure from Germany left him without access to many of his books and papers, the majority of which—including "On Language"—remained in his Berlin apartment. Consequently, the only way for him to procure a copy was to have Scholem send the one in his possession resulting in a delay of approximately one month.[71] Second, toward the end of June Benjamin fell ill with malaria (which was not even properly diagnosed until his return to Paris that fall!). He remained stricken for several months and only finished the revision late that summer while still suffering severely from the effects of the disease.

That Benjamin was willing to postpone the rewriting until he received from Scholem a copy of the 1916 essay is a revealing indication of the important relation that existed between the two works in Benjamin's own mind. However, in *Die Geschichte einer Freundschaft* Scholem also provides some highly pertinent information concerning the relation between the two works:

Between the middle of June and the middle of August [1918, during Scholem's stay in Bern] we often spoke about . . . the world of myth and speculations concerning cosmology and the prehistoric world of man. . . . [Benjamin] read to me a long sketch about dreams and clairvoyance in which he also attempted to formulate the laws which dominated the pre-mythical world of spirits. He differentiated between two historical world ages of spirits and demons, which preceded the age of revelation—I proposed to call it the Messianic age. The actual content of myth was the enormous revolution which, in the polemic with the spirits, ended their era. Even at that time he was concerned with ideas about perception as a reading of the configurations of surfaces, in the way that primeval man regarded the world around him and especially the heavens. Herein lay the germ cell of the considerations which he employed many years later in his sketch "Lehre vom Ähnlichen." The genesis of constellations as configurations on the celestial surface, he claimed, was the beginning of reading, of the script which coincided with the development of the mythical age of the world. The constellations had been for the mythical world what revelation was to 'Holy Writ.'"[72]

Benjamin begins "On the Mimetic Faculty"—originally titled "Zur Sprachtheorie"—by suggesting that man's "gift of seeing resemblances is nothing other than a rudiment of the powerful compulsion in former times to become and behave like something else."[73] Such behavior was most common in primitive man who, lacking a rational understanding of nature, would attempt to influence and control nature by imitating her moods and movements. In the epoch before the species had begun to individuate itself rationally versus nature (the era of "spirits and demons" referred to by Benjamin in his 1918 conversations with Scholem), the law of similarity was all-dominant: "it ruled both microcosm and macrocosm."[74] In this way, the mimetic faculty manifested itself most vividly in the cult practices of primitive tribes, in their dance rituals and magical incantations. Benjamin's appreciation of the fecundity of the capacity for mimetic expression embodied in the concrete and sensuous language of primitive man was an insight that had been confirmed by the most advanced ethnographic research of the period. In his 1935 "Probleme der Sprachsoziologie," a review of contemporary scientific literature on theories of language, Benjamin quotes the French anthropologist Lucien Lévy-Bruhl in support of this conception: "Since here everything comes to expression in pictorial concepts, . . . the vocabulary of these "primitive" languages has access to a treasure of which our own language can provide us with only a very distant concept."[75]

Astrology represents a subsequent, more advanced stage in the development of the mimetic faculty than simple imitation. The constellations signify an animistic relation to the cosmos. Personified, the stars are invested with the classical quality of the aura: the capacity to return the gaze. As Benjamin speculates: "Do relations exist between the experiences of the aura and those of astrology [?]. Are there earthly creatures as well as things which look back from the stars? Which from the heavens actually return their gaze? Are the stars, with their gaze from afar, the prototype of the aura?"[76] In the constellations primitive man attempts "to read the language of nature," to elicit its hidden meaning. Thus the correspondences between celestial and earthly life expressed in astrology represent a more rationalized stage in the world-historical march of disenchantment: the stage which follows magic, the stage of *myth*.

At the same time, the ceaseless advance of civilization also entails the inexorable decay of the mimetic faculty: "clearly the observable world of modern man contains only minimal residues of the magical correspondences and analogies that were familiar to ancient peoples."[77] For all mimesis, even the most primitive, plays a part in the process of world-disenchantment: "Imitation may be a magical act; at the same time, one who imitates also disenchants [*entzaubert*] nature, in that he brings it closer to language."[78] Thus, even the most primordial instances of mimetic behavior constitute attempts by man to control his environment, to organize it in an, albeit rudimentary, rational and intelligible form. However, if man has through civilization succeeded in emancipating himself from the conditions of deprivation and adversity which prevailed during this primitive state of undifferentiated unity with nature, his rationalizing methods have at the same time rendered the prospect of an ultimate reconciliation with nature—this time on a higher plane—increasingly remote. Hence, in "On the Mimetic" Benjamin searches for a key accessible to contemporary man through which the lost traces of a mimetic relation to nature, as expressed in the prehistoric *sensuous* language of mimetic correspondences, might be recaptured, however damaged and unrecognizable they have become to us over the course of time.

He discovers this key in the faculty of language, the highest form of mimetic knowledge, the contemporary repository of *nonsensuous* correspondences. For language is *rationalized mimesis.* In language the element of correspondence or similarity is wrested away from its primordial state of undifferentiated immediacy (submersion in nature) and raised to the status of *expression.*[79]

The mimetic aspect of language reveals itself above all in the onomatopoetic theory of the origin of language. Insofar as language is clearly not an agreed system of signs, the idea of the onomatopoetic origin of individual words attains an especial plausibility. According to Benjamin, the relationship of language to the idea of nonsensuous similarity can be perceived even more clearly if one considers the written rather than the spoken word: "In brief, it is nonsensuous similarity that establishes the ties not only between the spoken and the signified, but also between the written and the signified, and equally between the spoken and the written."[80] If graphology, Benjamin continues, shows how the unconscious of the writer manifests itself in his handwriting, "It may be supposed that the mimetic process that expresses itself in this way in the activity of the writer was, in the very distant times in which script originated, of utmost importance for writing. Script has thus become an archive of nonsensuous similarities, of nonsensuous correspondences."[81] Just as the origin of the spoken word can be onomatopoetically traced to the sensuous character of the object it represents, so it may be conjectured that at the time of its genesis written language, too, incorporated the contours of the objects to which it refers in its letters or characters. Indeed, the mimetic aspect of writing can be seen clearly in the most primitive forms of script: in the hieroglyphics of ancient Egypt and in Chinese pictorial writing. As Hans Heinz Holz suggests, such writing in images would stand closest to a pure, metaphysical conception of language, insofar as the elements of structure and syntax which today have transformed language into a tool of commerce, a mere means of conveying something, are unknown to it.[82] In pictorial writing words are genuinely *emblems,* they *stand for* the objects they signify, the original, pristine correlation between word and thing remains intact. In it, a comprehensive network of mimetic correspondences is permitted to thrive.

For Benjamin, language represents the highest stage of disenchantment, insofar as it has exorcised all earlier deficient *mythical* images of nature and cosmos, while at the same time it has managed, unlike technical reason, to preserve traces of the essential mimetic relation to the environing world. All mythical world views remain ensnared in the web of unfulfilled life, the sphere of eternal repetition or the always-the-same. Today, when the mimetic faculty, the traditional guardian of a nonexploitive, *reciprocal* relation between man and nature, has all but disappeared, the correspondences of old have found a secure repository in language. Because of its abstract and mediated relation to the world it describes, Benjamin refers to the correspondences embodied in language as "nonsensuous." Purified of myth, language is the foremost domain of rationalized mimesis: "Line of development of language: the separation between the magical and profane function of speaking is liquidated to the advantage of the latter. The sacred lies nearer to the profane than to the magical."[83] The process whereby the *sensuous* similarities of earlier epochs are transformed over the course of time into the *nonsensuous* similarities of language represents a crucial stage in the conquest of myth, insofar as the mimetic relation of man to the environing world has thereby ceased to be physical and immediate and has become instead spiritualized and purified. "In this context a polarity is produced in the center of the mimetic faculty of man. It shifts itself from the eyes to the lips, thereby taking a detour around the entire body. This process would include the conquest of myth."[84] This is the imagery Benjamin employs to describe the passage from sensuous correspondences, where the faculty of *sight* remains predominant, to the sphere of nonsensuous correspondences, where the medium of *sound* is preeminent. Moreover, the nonsensuous correspondences of language are closer to reconciliation, to the sacred as Benjamin calls it, insofar as they come nearest to the divine origins of things in the creative language of God.

In "On the Mimetic Faculty" Benjamin summarizes the presentation of his mimetic theory of language as follows:

"To read what was never written." Such reading is the most ancient: reading before all languages, from the entrails, the stars or dances. Later the mediating link of a new kind of reading, of runes and hieroglyphs, came into use. It seems fair to suppose that these were the stages by which the mimetic gift, which was the foundation of occult practices, gained admittance to writing and language. In this way language may be seen as the highest level of mimetic behavior and the most complete archive of nonsensuous similarity: a medium into which the earlier powers of mimetic production and comprehension have passed, without residue, to the point where they have liquidated those of magic.[85]

If one considers Benjamin's writings on language on the whole—from the 1916 essay "On Language," to the "Prologue" to the *Trauerspiel* study, to the various notes and drafts for "Lehre vom Ähnlichen," and "On the Mimetic Faculty"—a common motif begins to emerge: a concern with the expressive, noninstrumental component of language; or, in the words of J. G. Hamann, an emphasis on "that aspect of language which is content-transcendent" (*"inhaltstranzendentale Inhalt der Sprache"*). The expressive dimension of language indicates its sensuous, phonic side, which transcends its status as a vehicle of communication in the pedestrian bourgeois sense. It is on the basis of this distinction that in "Lehre vom Ähnlichen" Benjamin contrasts the "magical" side of language—here, synonomous with its "mimetic" or "onomatopoetic" elements—to its "semiotic" or denotative function. At the same time, he recognizes that the "magical" mimetic aspect can only appear through "something alien, the semiotic or communicative component of language."[86] The semiotic component remains therefore the *vehicle* of the mimetic element in language: "the coherence of words or sentences is the bearer through which, like a flash, similarity appears."[87] The light metaphors employed by Benjamin to describe the emergence of the secret mimetic element of language (it is, he says, "limited to flashes" and "flits past") are strongly reminiscent of the type of insight which appears in the Dialectical Image ("a flashing image").

It was precisely the accentuation of the expressive dimension of language which Benjamin prized in Mallarmé's concept of "poésie pure"—a poetry which flowed in a language conceived of as a medium of autonomous being, divorced from considerations of communication or sense. Moreover, it was precisely over suspicions concerning the employment of language for instrumental ends which led Benjamin in 1916 to decline Martin Buber's invitation to work on the journal *Der Jude*:

> It is a widespread, indeed, omnipresently self-evident opinion that literature can influence the ethical world and the behavior of men, in that it provides motives for actions. In this sense language is only a means more or less for the suggestive *preparation* of motives, which determines the action in the depths of the soul. It is characteristic of this view that it fails to take into consideration an association between language and act in which the former would not be a means for the latter. This relation therefore pertains to an impotent conception of language degraded to a mere means and sees writing as an impoverished, weak act, whose source lies not in itself, but in whatever motives are named or expressed. . . . As far as effect is concerned, I can—as well as poetically, prophetically, and objectively—understand literature, however, only *magically*, that is, im-*mediate*-ly [un-*mittel*-bar]. Every effect of writing that is salutory and not intrinsically damaging touches its secret (of the word, of language). In however many forms language proves itself effective, it does not do so through the mediation of content, but through the purest disclosure of its dignity and essence. . . . I do not believe that the word stands any farther from the divine than "effective" action; thus it is also capable only of leading to the divine through itself and its own pureness. As a means it becomes usurious."[88]

These remarks concerning the divine nature of language clearly prefigure the themes elaborated by Benjamin later the same year in his essay "On Language." While that important essay precedes "On the Mimetic Faculty" by some seventeen years, both articles coincide in their rejection of an instrumentalist view of language and their emphasis on language as a privileged medium through which a "flashing image" of reconciliation between man and nature can be glimpsed. In "On Language" the guarantee of reconciliation was provided by the creative word of God, which established a theological basis for the correlation between words and things. In "On the Mimetic Faculty" it is the onomatopoetic theory of the origin of language which is credited with having established the same correlation, in keeping with Benjamin's later attempt to operate within the boundaries of a materialist, anthropological theory of knowledge. As such, the decisive theoretical link between the two essays on language is provided by "Lehre vom Ähnlichen," the original draft of "On the Mimetic Faculty," where Benjamin asserts the idea that the theory of language he has developed "is most intimately related to mystical or theological theories of language, without, however, thereby being alien to empirical philology."[89]

"There is no event or thing in either animate or inanimate nature that does not in some way partake in language, for it is in the nature of things to communicate their spiritual content. This use of the word 'language' is in no way metaphorical. For to think that we cannot imagine anything that does not communicate its spiritual essence in its expression is entirely meaningful."[90] This statement from the 1916 essay on language is to be sure the cornerstone of the theory of correspondences elaborated by Benjamin in the 1933 fragments on language and then in the 1939 Baudelaire essay. When we look upon nature positivistically, we view it as something to be mastered and manipulated for purposes of technical control. For precisely this reason, the prospect of a reconciliation with nature will forever elude the world view of scientism, the credo which the West has elevated to preeminence since Bacon's *Novum Organum*. In contrast, if we relate to nature *interpretatively*, and thus seek to allow her own intrinsic language to step forth, nature is thereby transformed into a partner in dialogue instead of a hostile foe to be conquered. This interpretative model must then ultimately be transposed to the intersubjective world of human social relations. As Hans Heinz Holz observes, "The world becomes language as soon as we relate to it hermeneutically rather than positivistically. It constitutes itself as *a context of meaning*. In this sense 'the language of man,' for Benjamin, is only a particular, articulated form of a universal 'language as such' which incorporates all essences."[91] According to Benjamin, the dignity of philosophy or metaphysics lies in the fact that it translates the mute language of nature into the audible language of man. Philosophy gives voice to the linguistic being of things which their nonverbal language prevents them from articulating of their own accord. Consequently, for the philosopher the world takes on the character of a subterranean context of meaning, an encoded text, to be deciphered. His lot is not to behave toward things imperiously, as their master, but to assist them to language, as their ally. For despite all scientific pretensions to the contrary, mankind is and always will be part of nature. The primordial unity between animate and inanimate nature, shattered by man, the rational animal, serves as the basis for the subsequent emergence of correspondences between the two spheres.

"[Benjamin] was manifestly torn between his sympathy for a mystical theory of language and the equally strong necessity to subdue it within the context of a Marxist view of the word," notes Scholem.[92] This contradiction between theological and materialist methodological frameworks is nowhere more apparent than in the purportedly anthropological theory of language in "On the Mimetic Faculty," which was so strongly indebted to the early essay "On Language as Such and on the Language of Man." In Benjamin's later years, neither moment of his thought proved able to triumph completely over the other. His "Janus-face" remained predominant. Yet, in a letter to Max Rychner of March 1931, at a time when his interest in historical materialism was at its peak, one discovers a surprisingly frank confession by Benjamin which goes far toward explaining his self-understanding as a thinker in general: "I have never been able to think and research otherwise than, if I may say so, in a theological sense—namely in accordance with the talmudic theory of 49 levels of meaning of each passage of the Torah."[93] Perhaps Holz best expresses the theoretical basis of Benjamin's ideological vacillation when he describes him as

a type of Marxist Rabbi; for him, the divine word had materialized itself in the world of things and their interrelations, so that a materialist dialectic had no need to take leave of a theological horizon in the interpretation of this-worldly reality, but merely needed to concretize that horizon. If the speculative view of the grounding of the detail in the totality was intended plainly as a theological outlook—and from a Jewish as well as a western-Christian point of view, the whole has been understood only in relation to the idea of God, or else positivistically, agnostically, or skeptically dissolved—then a materialist dialectic must also preserve within itself that methodological recourse to theological modes of establishing foundations [*Begrundungsweisen*]. For only through some kind of transcendence, through some kind of speculative a priori could the unity of the empirically fragmented world be guaranteed.[94]

For Benjamin, Marxism—especially given the failure of the European revolutions following World War I—in and of itself seemed incapable of guaranteeing some kind of whole vis-à-vis an empirically fragmented world. Indeed, as a social theory, Marxism itself has never sufficiently delineated, in materialist terms, the precise nature of the mediations by means of which the proletariat could elevate itself to its ascribed role as the universal subject of history, in face of the alienation and degradation of its immediate situation. Thus there arose a constant need on Benjamin's part to bolster his Marxism through recourse to the theological categories of his early period. For only theology—the idea of God—could provide a sure, untainted basis for the idea of totality, precisely insofar as its perspective is transcendent and external in relation to the fragmentation of this-worldly reality. As Benjamin affirms in an early letter: "That knowledge is metaphysical which attempts a priori to view science as a sphere in the absolute divine context of relations . . . whose content and cause is God, and which also considers the 'autonomy' of science as meaningful and possible only in this context."[95] For everything engendered by reality in the here and now remains of necessity contaminated by fragmentation and thus incapable of making itself whole again of its own accord. Thus, faced with the seemingly universal network of depravity and corruption in this-worldly life, Benjamin was impelled to seek a guarantee for the idea of totality in other-worldly existence. If such guarantees ultimately prove unserviceable for a genuinely materialist philosophy of history, they nevertheless anticipate the "other-worldly" character that a truly *radical* and *uncompromising* conception of emancipation must assume given the degenerate nature of orthodox Marxist discourse in the present historical epoch.

Chapter Eight

"A L'ÉCART DE TOUS LES COURANTS"

THE POSTHUMOUS fate of Benjamin's lifework confirms his own conviction that every product of culture experiences an autonomous post-history by virtue of which it transcends its determinate point of origin, his belief that, "The work is the death-mask of the conception."[1] Since the republication of his works began in the 1950s, concerted attempts have been launched from all sides to categorize his thinking according to a variety of rubrics—literary, theological, Marxist—all of which merit partial validity, but none of which captures the truth in its entirety. For Benjamin was all of these things and none of them. His *oeuvre* does not present itself as a harmonious synthesis of the afore-mentioned tendencies, nor does it remain consistent with any of these taken individually. Instead, it takes on the form of a series of contradictions, a network of discontinuous extremes—in no uncertain terms, it assumes the form of a *ruin*. The words Benjamin used to summarize his feelings toward Kafka in a letter to Scholem could just as well have been employed to describe his own work: "To do justice to the figure of Kafka in its purity and peculiar beauty, one must never lose sight of one thing: it is the purity and beauty of a failure."[2] Yet, to speak of the "failure" of Benjamin's work means the following: that it was precisely in terms of his incapacity to unite the extremes of his thought, in his unwillingness to subordinate the materialist side to the theological or vice versa, that the enigmatic character, the majesty (yes, ruins too can be majestic), the moment of his thought that remains living resides. Insofar as he refused to close prematurely the gap between these two dimensions, he escaped the fate of being merely one more in a long line of Marxist or theological thinkers. His theoretical strivings perpetually transcended the staleness of academic convention as well as all heteronomous methodological imperatives which seek to level the being-in-itself of things to standards which are posited abstractly by the knowing subject. In this way he sought to maintain a fundamental, almost precategorical allegiance to things themselves and their truth. It was, however, the insights of the philosopher to which Benjamin's own work in all its phases inexorably drew near. His concerns were not those of a philosopher in the traditional sense; rather, the question which ceaselessly animated his writings was what form philosophy must take in an age in which systematic philosophy has become impossible. Thus, he sought to latch on to those phenomena which had somehow miraculously escaped the all-enveloping web of social integration—childhood memories, drug experiences; above all, however, literary texts—and thereby emancipate the utopian potential that lay embedded therein. Like no philosopher before him, Benjamin elected to operate at a far remove from the so-called "great questions" of philosophy and to attempt nevertheless to force the most apparently ephemeral and insignificant phenomena to yield knowledge equivalent in stature to the most sublime metaphysical truth. As one critic has observed:

Philosophical experience of the world and its reality—that is how we can sum up the meaning of the term *metaphysics,* and that is certainly the sense in which it is used by Benjamin. He was a metaphysician; indeed, I would say a metaphysician pure and simple. But it was borne in on him that in his generation the genius of a pure metaphysician could express itself more readily in other spheres, any other sphere than in those traditionally assigned to metaphysics, and this was precisely one of the experiences that helped him to mold his distinctive individuality and originality. He was attracted more and more—in a fashion strangely reminiscent of Simmel, with whom otherwise he had little in common—by subjects which would seem to have little or no bearing on metaphysics. It is a special mark of his genius that under his gaze every one of these subjects discloses a dignity, a philosophic aura of its own which he sets out to describe.[3]

The significance of "extremes" for Benjamin's thinking cannot be overestimated, not only in the more blatant sense of the antinomy between materialism and theology which dominated his work after 1925, but also in his very choice of objects of philosophical investigation. *Trauerspiel* and surrealism, arcades and Kafka, are all rather unlikely topics of philosophical study which nevertheless occupied center stage in Benjamin's work. For Benjamin, who interpreted the continuum of history as being homogeneous and mythical, as a pageant in which the rulers incessantly asserted and reasserted their stranglehold over the oppressed—a sort of *List der Vernunft* stood on its head—the counterimages to "natural history" were to be sought in those figures and traces which history had subjected to scorn, derision, or the oblivion of forgetting. For Benjamin, the eternal, the significant, indeed resembled more closely the "ruffles of a dress than an idea."[4] It was the malcontents and maladapted of history—Baudelaire, Proust, Kafka—with whom he identified so profoundly and whose truths he struggled to immortalize in face of the transient nature of historical memory. From the excrescences and extremes of historical life, he sought to cull what was of lasting value for humanity; and thus in his own small way contribute to the process of resurrecting the dead and forgotten which would only be completed with the coming of the Messiah. Once the extremes have been gathered, wrenched from their original historical context—be it in the case of an individual lifework or a determinate historical epoch such as seventeenth-century Germany or nineteenth-century France—the goal was not to seek their average or common denominator, which would merely depotentiate them, but merely to set them in the liberating context of a philosophically informed configuration; and by virtue of the idea to which this configuration gave rise, the extremes would accede to their own inherent meaning (their "origin") and thereby stand *redeemed*.

In my concluding remarks I would like to focus more closely on Benjamin's philosophy of history, especially on its implications for the traditions of Marxism and critical theory. Both traditions have in various ways already staked claims to his theoretical legacy. At the same time, I wish to proceed with the clear understanding that whereas these two traditions present extremely fruitful avenues along which his work might be pursued in the future, the sheer breadth and imaginative force of his thought would preclude any attempt at wholesale assimilation within either of these theoretical currents.

As I have attempted to show, Benjamin's attitude towards the doctrines of historical materialism was neither consistent nor unequivocal. Altogether he displayed three different theoretical relations to Marxism. The first was embodied in the theory of Dialectical Images as articulated in the Arcades Exposé of 1935. There he sought to capture through the prism of Baudelaire's poetry the commingling of old and new forms of life in mid-nineteenth-century Paris in order to show how the "new" of the modern incessantly reverts to the always-the-same of myth:

Novelty is a quality which does not depend on the use-value of the commodity. It is the source of the illusion which belongs inalienably to the images which the collective unconsciousness engenders. It is the quintessence of false consciousness, of which fashion is the tireless agent. This illusion of novelty is reflected, like one mirror in another, in the illusion of infinite sameness.[5]

In his formulation of the concept of Dialectical Images, however, Benjamin attempted to envision a utopian dimension which compelled him to rely on the highly questionable Jungian conception of the "collective unconscious"; a reliance for which, as we have seen, Adorno sternly took him to task. Also, Benjamin's idea of Dialectical Images betrayed a strong indebtedness to the surrealist emphasis on the utopian value of dreams. As he contends at one important point in his argument, "The utilization of dream-elements in waking is a textbook example of dialectical thought."[6] It is not too difficult to see from this remark that Benjamin's understanding of dialectics differed significantly from not only the traditional idealist and materialist versions, but every other existing version as well. The conception of historical materialism that served as the basis for his *Passagenarbeit* remained characteristically nonconformist and fanciful. Whereas this conception paved the way for discoveries and insights which would have certainly remained imperceptible from a traditional Marxist standpoint, it nevertheless seems reasonable to conjecture that Benjamin, even when he believed himself to be dutifully following in the footsteps of the historical materialist legacy, was in fact engaged in something quite different and unique.

This judgment is reconfirmed in the case of the second phase of Benjamin's development as a Marxist critic, in which he operated most narrowly in accordance with Brechtian principles. Under Brecht's guidance he temporarily relinquished the theory of Dialectical Images (many of whose aspects, such as shock, montage, etc., he had rediscovered in Brecht's theory of epic theater), and began concentrating intensively on more immediate political concerns centering around questions of aesthetic reception. The fruits of these labors were essays such as "The Author as Producer" and "The Work of Art in the Age of Mechanical Reproduction," in which Benjamin argued for the definitive *Aufhebung* of autonomous culture and the necessity for the refunctioning of the bourgeois apparatus of cultural production along engaged, revolutionary lines. For the Benjamin of this period the power of "technique" in and of itself was deemed a sufficient indicator not only of "political tendency" but also of "aesthetic quality." Benjamin believed he could identify preliminary examples of the successful realization of this new aesthetics of commitment in Brecht's epic theater, Soviet journalism, and certain tendencies in the field of film, which, insofar as it was the most thoroughly technological of all the arts, was therefore considered the most "revolutionary." Yet, one must insist on the paradoxical fact that Benjamin's relevance for historical materialism is not to be discovered in those works where he considered himself to be operating most consistently according to Marxist convictions. The epistemological basis of both "The Author as Producer" and "The Work of Art" essay is a technological determinism, which is adopted from Marx's specification of the relationship between forces and relations of production in the Preface to the *Contribution to the Critique of Political Economy*. Benjamin sought to establish the absolute primacy of the forces of *aesthetic* production in the same way Marx attempted to do so for the forces of *economic* production. His efforts in this direction are thus vitiated by an extremely uncritical and reductionist reliance on orthodox Marxist dogmas. In this way he fell behind, in his rush to ensure immediate political relevance for his theory, the Western Marxism of Lukaćs and Korsch—not to mention that of critical theory—who had exposed those dogmas back in the early twenties. Hence, the Brechtian side of Benjamin's Janus-face demanded a sacrifice of theoretical integrity for the sake of political efficacy—a sacrifice from which no theory emerges unscathed. And despite all voluble, pseudo-radical clamor to the contrary, practice derives from theory, not vice versa.

Benjamin's earlier theory and certain aspects of his later materialist theory of experience serve as an important corrective to this tendency to elevate the political significance of art above all other moments. In his early work Benjamin attempted to show how genuine works of art displayed an autonomous post-history or afterlife, such that their truths refused to exhaust themselves in their own or successive epochs, and thus demanded critical interpretation anew with each passing generation. Works of art that possess an exclusively political significance, however, would prove devoid of that autonomy which differentiates them from mere life in general. By surrendering that element of autonomy, works of art would exhaust themselves in the here and now of the immediate present—in the language of reception aesthetics, the moment of their "effect"—and afterward become matters of indifference—as has proven the case with the great majority of so-called committed works of art to date. Adorno has commented on this state of affairs as follows:

The feigning of a true politics in the here and now, the freezing of historical relations which nowhere seem ready to melt, oblige the mind to go where it need not degrade itself. Today, every phenomenon of culture, even a model of integrity, is liable to be suffocated in the cultivation of kitsch. Yet paradoxically in the same epoch it is to works of art that has fallen the burden of wordlessly asserting what is barred to politics. . . . This is not a time for political art, but politics has migrated into autonomous art, and nowhere more so than where it appears to be politically dead.[7]

These remarks remain even more relevant today. For with the dissolution of the attempt by the twentieth-century avant garde to merge art and life practice—an attempt initially motivated by a salutory revulsion against the complacency of *l'art pour l'art* in a world which begged for change—there has emerged with the phenomenon of postmodernism a new variety of aesthetic complacency, in which the distance between art and material life has been dissipated in an art which retains the anti-aesthetic trappings of authentic modernism but none of the substance. That is, what has transpired in the transition from modernism to postmodernism has been the *recuperation of the radical intentions* of modernism in an art which, though it formally takes its bearings from the modernism of the pre-World War II period, remains fully compatible with the marketing prerequisites of the culture industry. Thus, the destruction of the hiatus between art and life—which for the avant garde was synonomous with transferring the radical aesthetic values of modern art to the domain of everyday life itself—has taken place but *in reverse:* rather than having been aesthetically transfigured, material life has actually *absorbed* the radical promise of modernism, which in the guise of postmodernism becomes indistinguishable from fashion. As one critic has recently observed: "When the containers of an autonomously developed cultural sphere are shattered, the contents get dispersed. Nothing remains from a desublimated meaning or a destructured form; an emancipatory effect does not follow."[8] Ultimately then, the "dispersion" of autonomous culture within the heteronomous world of administered culture means a regression behind *l'art pour l'art,* which still preserved, despite and because of its asocial posture, a potential for otherness and negation in the very act of formally distancing itself from the functional imperatives of commodity society in general. For this reason society today would have more to fear from a radically articulated, de-aestheticized autonomous art than it would from a thoroughly culinary and ornamental postmodernism or a committed art staged for a bourgeois public sphere which has in effect become imaginary and mythical.

At the same time, upon closer scrutiny, the "dialectic of technique" embraced by Benjamin was itself hardly immune from metaphysical rudiments—a fact noted by Brecht in his diaries and which led to his negative assessment of "The Work of Art" essay. For in truth the structure of that essay is governed by two contrasting impulses, one speculative, the other materialist, and there is virtually no attempt made to link the two sides. The first part of the essay presents Benjamin's theory of the artistic aura, a phenomenon which has its origins in magical practices and doctrines. It is the aura which gives traditional works of art—be they religious or autonomous—a supernatural, transcendent quality, whose esoteric truth content is accessible only to elites (priests or connoisseurs). To be sure, up to this point in Benjamin's analysis there is little that would distinguish his essay as a genuinely materialist study and much to suggest that he had merely carried over motifs from his theological period and attempted to fit them into a materialist framework. On the other hand, the second half of the study consists of an unqualified endorsement of de-auraticized, mechanically reproduced arts such as film, with the last vestiges of speculative sentiment having been thoroughly purged. Somehow it is assumed—though the precise nature of the link is never specified—that the esoteric promise that is stored in the aura will be redeemed exoterically by mechanically reproduced art; a premise which suggests that there exists an essential *continuity* between these two species of art, and that the emancipatory potential of mechanically reproduced art is somehow dependent on its capacity to make good the utopian claims of auratic art. The interlacing of speculative and materialist motifs in the essay is thus much more thoroughgoing than it would appear initially—which suggests how little even in his most explicitly materialist studies Benjamin's thought was capable of parting definitively with metaphysical principles. When Scholem pointed out the glaring contradiction between the two parts of the essay to Benjamin in the late 1930s, he could only respond: "The philosophical unity you deem lacking between the two parts of my essay will be more effectively provided by the revolution than by me."[9]

Hence, Benjamin's relationship to historical materialism was constantly fraught with tension, but at the same time it was precisely *because of* the "experimental" nature of this relationship rather than despite it that many of his essays in materialist criticism of the 1930s—especially the works on Leskov, Proust, Fuchs, and the second Baudelaire study—stand out as models which in many ways have yet to be surpassed. Marxism for Benjamin was therefore never a creed to be adopted *in toto,* but a way of thinking which represented an indispensable corrective to his earlier criticism, a vital confrontation with the idea that all facts of life are simultaneously sociohistorical facts, and that whoever elects to ignore this truth is living a life of illusion. Thus, while there is no reason to question the essential sincerity of his commitment to materialist principles of research, one finds nevertheless scattered throughout his letters and papers remarks such as the following, which point to the fundamental insufficiency of the Marxist world view taken by itself and the inevitable need to enhance it with a "metaphysical orientation":

I have found the strongest propaganda imaginable for a materialist perspective not in the form of communist brochures, but rather in the "representative" works which have emerged in my field—literary history and criticism—from the bourgeois camp in the last twenty years. I have had as little to do with what has been produced in the academic ranks as with the monuments which a Gundolf or an [Ernst] Bertram have erected; and in order to separate myself early and clearly vis-à-vis the loathsome odes of this official and unofficial bustle [*Betrieb*], I did not find Marxist ways of thinking necessary—these I became acquainted with only later—rather this I owe to the basic metaphysical orientation of my research.[10]

Nowhere was the problematical character of his attitude toward the standpoint of historical materialism more evident than in the "Theses on the Philosophy of History," his last extant writing and an autobiographical statement which itself represented the consummate "Dialectical Image" of his later thinking in its entirety: for in these Theses he located his own thought in a monadic, shock-charged Dialectic at a Standstill, in which the ultimate boundaries were established by the extremes of Marxism and theology. The "Theses" were originally intended to serve as the "theoretical armature" to the second Baudelaire essay, as Benjamin remarks to Horkheimer in a letter of February 1940; but as the accompanying notes and drafts demonstrate, what Benjamin had ultimately planned was a much more intricate and developed critique of the idea of "progress" in general—in both its Enlightenment and materialist variants.[11] As was often the case with his more intimate, meta-theoretical reflections, Benjamin had no intention of publishing the "Theses": "They would open the gate wide for enthusiastic misunderstanding."[12] Nevertheless, their overwhelming significance for understanding his work as a whole is illustrated by his remark that they were something he had "kept to himself for twenty years."[13]

It is above all, the first Thesis—the by now famous parable about the chess-playing "puppet in Turkish attire"—which represents the ultimate allegorical confession by Benjamin concerning his own theoretical relationship to the twin extremes of Marxism and theology:

The story is told of an automaton constructed in such a way that it could play a winning game of chess, answering each move of an opponent with a countermove. A puppet in Turkish attire and with a hookah in its mouth sat before a chessboard placed on a large table. A system of mirrors created the illusion that this table was transparent on all sides. Actually, a little hunchback who was an expert chess player sat inside and guided the puppet's hand by means of strings. One can imagine a philosophical counterpart to this device. The puppet called "historical materialism" is to win all the time. It can easily be a match for anyone if it enlists the services of theology, which today, as we know, is wizened and has to keep out of sight.[14]

The imagery of Benjamin's metaphor is highly revealing. According to this imagery, in order for the puppet "historical materialism" to be victorious it must enlist the services of theology—the little hunchback who is charged with the *ultimate* responsibility of pulling the strings and thus dictating the movements of the historical materialist "puppet." By way of this parable Benjamin seeks to call attention to the fact that historical materialism—especially in face of its manifest failure to meet the threat of fascism in the 1930s—remains in and of itself incapable of providing humanity with the full range of wisdom and understanding necessary to surmount the realm of historical necessity. This explicit return to the Messianic philosophy of history of his early work—as I have noted earlier, the content of the "Theses," though more detailed, is nearly identical with that of the "Theologico-Political Fragment" of the early 1920s—signifies not a hasty appeal, made in an hour of historical despair, to a suprahistorical redeemer, but instead an acknowledgement of the fact that in its reliance on the

Enlightment myth of historical progress, historical materialism has remained a prisoner of the same logic it wanted to transcend. For in its Panglossian trust in the *historical necessity of socialism*, it has neglected the *negative, dark, and destructive side of the revolutionary process*, a side which evaporates in the forever optimistic prognosis concerning the imminent demise of the capitalist system. It is Benjamin's conviction therefore that Marxism has been lulled and seduced into a false sense of security based on the erroneous assumption that the forces of history are on its side; and thus he seeks to mobilize, in opposition to this fatal historical naïveté, the elements of distrust and pessimism, the powers of *"revolutionary nihilism,"* for the side of the revolutionary struggle. For this is an enemy whose diabolical nature it would be impossible to *over-estimate*. And thus in the fragments and sketches for the "Theses" Benjamin provides the following relfections on the relationship between destruction, history, and redemption:

The destructive powers release those which lie in the idea of redemption.

Three moments must be made to penetrate the foundations of the materialist view of history: the discontinuity of historical time; the destructive power of the working class; the tradition of the oppressed.

The destructive or critical element in historiography receives its validity in the explosion of historical continuity. Authentic historiography does not select its object carelessly. It does not grasp it, it explodes it from the historical continuum. This destructive element in historiography must be understood as a reaction to a moment of danger which threatens equally the recipient of tradition *as well as* what is handed down [*dem Uberlieferten*]. . . . In authentic historiography the redemptive impulse is as strong as the destructive impulse.[15]

Benjamin's relevance for a nondogmatic and critical understanding of historical materialism therefore lies neither in the 1935 version of the theory of Dialectical Images nor in his advocacy of a technologically advanced, committed art, but instead in the "materialist theory of experience" whose consummate expression is the 1940 "Theses on the Philosophy of History." The theory of Dialectical Images advanced here has renounced the mistaken tendency of the Arcades Exposé to view the Dialectical Image as a "dream" and returned to the original, authentic version of the theory as elaborated in *One-Way-Street*. Moreover, in the materialist theory of experience developed in the late 1930s Benjamin had come round to correcting a crucial misconception of his Brechtian period, insofar as he now realized that for any materialist understanding of culture that seeks to be of value, it is essential to recognize that the contents of tradition contain a utopian claim, a *promesse de bonheur,* and are not therefore something to be negated abstractly in a surfeit of revolutionary zeal. Thus, in the "Theses on the Philosophy of History" and related studies Benjamin reversed this earlier one-sided judgment against tradition. He realized that the erosion of the last remnants of tradition with the onslaught of rationalization and the capitalist fetishization of *nouveauté* resulted in the catastrophic destruction of unrenewable meaning potentials; meaning potentials that had been sedimented in the "great" works of culture, but also in the not so great—the forgotten allegories of the baroque era, Baudelaire's lyric versification of urbanism, and the stories, dances, and songs that for ages represented the mainstays of a vital popular culture. In these fragile relics of tradition the collective desires of unfree humanity found expression in the hope that one day some future generation would redeem the promises of a better life that it had been denied. As Benjamin states in a passage that is crucial for understanding his later materialist theory of experience: "The past carries with it a temporal index by which it is referred to redemption. There is a secret agreement between past generations and the present one. Our coming was expected on earth. Like every generation that preceded us, we have been endowed with a *weak* Messianic power, a power to which the past has a claim. That claim cannot be settled cheaply."[16]

It is precisely the *temporal index of redemption* encoded in the products of tradition, in which the guarantee of our "secret agreement" with past generations has been inscribed, that Benjamin sought to resuscitate and preserve in his final writings. As the nightmare of German fascism threatened to efface all remnants of tradition from the face of the earth, his task became more urgent and his tone all the more exhortatory—culminating in the apocalyptic pitch of the "*Geschichtsphilosophische Thesen.*" The powers of *redemptive criticism* were needed once again. Benjamin therefore sought to transpose his earlier esoteric theory of experience into an immanent, historical setting. He saw his mission as a historical materialist as one of redeeming endangered semantic potentials from the fate of oblivion that seemed ready at any moment to descend on them once and for all. It was the task of historical materialism to blast "now-times"—moments of a "Messianic cessation of happening"—out of the homogeneous and profane continuum of history; which meant "a revolutionary chance in the fight for the oppressed past"—"blasting a specific life out of the era or a specific work out of the lifework."[17] "Cultural history" (Ranke, Dilthey, etc.) knows history only as the history of the victors, as progress in domination and oppression. Benjamin's theory of now-times seeks to break with this conception of progress in order to establish a *unique* relation to the past—i.e., one in which the rare and endangered images of redeemed life are separated out from the historical flow of eternal recurrence and allowed to shine forth on their own. For it is precisely in such now-times that the key to the redemption of the *historical past in its entirety* is enciphered. As Benjamin observes: "To be sure, only a redeemed humanity receives the fullness of its past—which is to say that only for a redeemed humanity has its past become citable in all its moments. Each moment it has lived becomes a citation *à l'ordre du jour*—and that day is Judgment Day."[18]

For the later Benjamin, then, the concept of redemption, so paramount for his early work, has once again become central. In "Some Motifs in Baudelaire" it was the *correspondances* of Baudelaire's poetry that provided indications of how to recapture a long repressed *auratic* relation to nature. In "The Storyteller" the fluid continuum of experience characteristic of the world of the story was contrasted with the fragmented nature of experience in advanced industrial societies. And in the "Theses on the Philosophy of History" the task of the historical materialist becomes that of redeeming now-times from the oblivion of forgetting that incessantly threatens them. In these essays Benjamin no longer speaks of the *Aufhebung* of traditional bourgeois culture, an idea he entertained in "The Work of Art" essay and his commentaries on Brecht; rather it is the effort to preserve and render exoteric the secret utopian potential embedded in traditional works of culture that Benjamin views as the preeminent task of materialist criticism. The esoteric phraseology of his earlier conception of redemptive criticism has been cast aside in favor of a quasi-Marxian vocabulary, but in essence the two approaches are parallel. Nor could one say unequivocally that his later exercises in materialist criticism were possessed of a less abstruse or hermetic structure than his earlier studies of *Elective Affinities* or *Trauerspiel*. The materialist writings too were composed for a very select audience. The theme that unites these later studies in materialist criticism is the idea of *remembrance* (*Gedächtnis, Eingedenken*). For in face of the boundless and irrepressible triumph of the forces of rationalization in the modern era and the concomitant destruction of all traces of premodern, traditional life, Benjamin's great fear was that along with all remnants of tradition the all-important index of redemption which the past provides would also fall victim to the oblivion of forgetting—resulting in the most hollow and defective civilization imaginable, a civilization without origins, without memory. It was precisely the danger of this brave new world without tradition that he sought to counteract through the employment of the method of "*rettende Kritik*" in a new historical and exoteric context. For it is in the increasingly remote recesses of past life that the secret of redemption is inscribed. In 1940, Benjamin expresses this insight as follows:

We know the Jews were prohibited from investigating the future. The Torah and the prayers instruct them in remembrance, however. This stripped the future of its magic, to which all those succumb who turn to soothsayers for enlightenment. This does not imply, however, that for the Jews the future turned into empty homogeneous time. For every second of time was the strait gate through which the Messiah might enter.[19]

I would like to suggest that Benjamin's relevance for historical materialism is to be found in this late attempt to secularize the notion of redemptive criticism. His relevance lies precisely in the *reverential* attitude he assumes toward tradition, a position which to be sure stands in sharp contrast to most Marxist accounts. Benjamin's appreciation of the contents of tradition, his deep fears

concerning the irretrievable decay of the semantic potentials embodied therein, serves therefore as a decisive corrective to the
customary *devaluation* of the meaning of tradition characteristic
of Marxist doctrines. That denigration of tradition echoes clearly
in the standard Marxian dichotomy between "history" and "prehistory," which implies that all history before the advent of socialism would stand convicted of insubstantiality. One might go
a step further. Perhaps the central conviction of revolutionaries
from Robespierre to Lenin and beyond—that the idea of revolution implies the necessity to recast totally *all* elements of tradition
(which are all, by definition, contaminated by the deficiencies of
the *ancien régime*)—has been responsible for the totalitarian excesses
which today seem inseparable from the very concept of "revolution."

While the idea of socialism as representing a decisive *break*
with the historical past is certainly one that Benjamin would en-
dorse, in the usual Marxist accounts the contents of tradition seem
less dialectically preserved in the process of *Aufhebung* than merely
cancelled and *suppressed*. The Marxist disdain for tradition is also
evident in the unreflective employment of the method of ideology
critique, in which cultural expressions are deemed illusory and
valueless in and of themselves, mere epiphenomenal reflections
of the economic infrastructure. Benjamin realized, however, that
the lore of tradition stakes claims that the present can choose to
ignore, but from which it will never be able to escape—for there
is already too much of the past in us, and thus to deny the past
is to deny part of ourselves. By such an understanding, he refutes
these views. His studies in redemptive criticism demonstrate that
the cultural remnants of tradition are in no way reducible to the
status of epiphenomena, but contain a *promesse de bonheur* which
future generations must preserve and redeem.[20]

It is surprising that the importance of Benjamin's thought for
the Frankfurt School has remained so greatly neglected.[21] There
is no question, though, that during Benjamin's lifetime their relationship was at times strained. On two occasions the editorial
board of the Institute for Social Research felt compelled to tone
down the overly explicit Marxist rhetoric of essays submitted by

Benjamin ("The Work of Art in the Age of Mechanical Reproduction"; "Eduard Fuchs: Historian and Collector"); and on a
third occasion ("Paris of the Second Empire in Baudelaire") his
work was rejected outright. I think it would be correct to conclude
as Scholem has that Benjamin never truly felt committed either
intellectually or temperamentally to the critical theory of the Institute in the 1930s. Theirs was largely a relationship of conven-
ience: while the Institute recognized Benjamin's brilliance and
sought to provide him with a forum to express his views, and
Benjamin was dependent on the stipend he received from the
Institute for means of support during the last six years of his life,
a genuine intellectual bond between them cannot be said to have
existed. Nevertheless, Benjamin remained philosophically close
with Adorno, who became a member of the Institute only in 1938.

The link between critical theory and Benjamin was only really
developed after Benjamin's death in 1940. Shortly before his death,
Benjamin left instructions that his *"Geschichtsphilosophische Thesen"*
manuscript be sent to Adorno in New York. The "Theses" were
then published by the Institute in a small memorial volume in
1942. The influence they exerted on the two leading members of
the Institute, Horkheimer and Adorno, was immeasurable. For
many of their premises were then incorporated into the Institute's
major work of the 1940s, *Dialectic of Enlightenment* (written jointly
by Horkheimer and Adorno), which represents critical theory's
fundamental statement on matters of philosophy of history and
social evolution.

Dialectic of Enlightenment is penetrating work of incredible
scope. It seeks on one level to account for Germany's descent into
barbarism in the Nazi era; but its more far-reaching goal is an
understanding of the hidden *Bildungsprozess* of civilization, whereby
the most laudable breakthroughs of reason and culture seem inextricably intertwined with regressive elements—i.e., new relapses
into myth and repression. Prima facie, Horkheimer and Adorno's
argument is much more indebted to Freud's pessimistic philosophical anthropology than to any of Benjamin's views. They
claim that man, for the sake of individuating himself in face of
his primordial, total bondage to external nature, is forced to submit to an inordinate level of instinctual repression in order to

attain the level of social organization necessary to combat nature—and thereby as it were raise himself above this prehistorical, un-individuated stage. The initial triumphs in this process of man-kind's coming to self-consciousness as a species are expressed in the new world views of magic and myth, which serve the function of organizing principles vis à vis a hostile and alien cosmos. A higher stage in the process of self-individuation is reflected in the cunning of Odysseus—for Horkheimer and Adorno, the proto-typical bourgeois man—who combines an ethic of self-renuncia-tion and rational calculation in order to outwit the Olympian deities, who are in essence personifications of the forces of nature. The teleology of rational self-preservation reached its peak in the modern age of Enlightenment, where reason was enthroned as the absolute means through which the last vestiges of myth, un-reason, and superstition would be forcibly expelled from the face of the earth. Twentieth-century positivism has sought to inherit the legacy of the Enlightenment. It espouses a doctrine of unre-mitting scientism as a result of which "meaningful" discourse is identified with empirically verifiable discourse—the "protocol statements" of Carnap and Russell. The end result of the dialectic of enlightenment is the fact that the *Nous* of Plato, the *Raison* of the French *philosophes,* has ultimately been divested of all *substan-tive* claims; it has shrunk to the concept of *technical* or *formal reason,* which the social engineers of today employ to erect a world in which considerations of "freedom and dignity" are anathematized as "pre-scientific."

Horkheimer and Adorno thus claim that the measures of self-denial and repression which the species was forced to endure for the sake of individuating itself vis-à-vis the *ur*historical world in which natural alienation reigned unchecked were of necessity so harsh that once the initial objective of raising mankind above the level of utter thralldom to nature was achieved, the ultimate *telos* of the process—the pacification of the *struggle* for existence, the creation of a harmonious and free social environment—was lost sight of, and the means to this goal, the methods of rational calculation and control, were enthroned as ends in themselves. The fact which the dialectic of enlightenment has always neglected to take into account is that man too is part of nature, so that once this ruthless apparatus of domination and mastery has been un-leashed against nature, man himself is ultimately caught up in the gears of the mechanism. The repression to which mankind has submitted in order to construct civilization has been so relentless and severe that the ego, once it has achieved a firm measure of control over instinct, has simultaneously been rendered so thoroughly inflexible that it proves incapable of enjoying the fruits of its triumphs. In the authors' words:

In class history, the enmity of the self to sacrifice implied a sacrifice of the self, inasmuch as it was paid for by a denial of nature in man for the sake of domination over non-human nature and other men. This very denial, the nucleus of all civilizing rationality, is the germ-cell of a pro-liferating mythic irrationality: with the denial of nature in man, not merely the *telos* of outward control of nature but the *telos* of man's own life is distorted and befogged. As soon as man discards the awareness that he himself is part of nature all the aims for which he keeps himself alive—social progress, the intensification of all his material and spiritual powers, even consciousness itself—are nullified and the enthronement of the means as an end, which under late capitalism is tantamount to open insanity is already perceptible in the prehistory of subjectivity.

The *ratio* which supplants mimesis is not simply its counterpart. It is itself mimesis: mimesis until death. The subjective spirit which cancels the animation of nature can master a despiritualized nature only by imitating its rigidity and despiritualizing itself in turn.[22]

In this way Horkeimer and Adorno seek to account for the defective logic of civilization, in consequence of which moments of enlightenment seem unavoidably interwoven with instances of regression. They believe they have discovered the key to this logic in the identitarian reduction of other to self which is said to reside a priori in the very process of human ratiocination itself, from its earliest expressions in magic and myth to its most sophisticated and lethal manifestations in modern systems of technical-scientific reason.

The reflections on the philosophy of history sketched in Benjamin's "Theses," when divested of their theological trappings, can be seen to play an essential role in the theory of social evolution elaborated in *Dialectic of Enlightenment*. It is above all his conception of the continual relapse of historical development into new forms of *myth*—such that the entire modern spirit of demythologization or *Entzauberung* can be read as the fabrication of new myth—that Horkheimer and Adorno adopt in their book.[23] In the history of the development of critical theory, *Dialectic of Enlightenment* represents a crucial new phase, the point at which a definitive break was made with the Enlightenment doctrine of progress as perpetuated in the thought of Hegel and Marx. No doubt the dire nature of contemporary historical circumstances influenced significantly this rejection of the naïve Marxian faith in the intrinsically benevolent character of the forces of historical development. But it was Benjamin in his "*Geschichtsphilosophische Thesen*" who was the first to make this important break and develop its implications. For Horkheimer and Adorno, "Angelus Novus," Benjamin's "Angel of History," became the "Angel of Reason." Hence, Benjamin's conception of history as essentially mythic, as the eternal recurrence of the always-the-same, was taken up by the authors of *Dialectic of Enlightenment*. In their eyes too, the storm of historical progress led not to utopia, but to renewed barbarism.

The prospects for remedying the dilemmas of enlightenment suggested by Horkheimer and Adorno also reveal profoundly Benjaminian overtones. These prospects revolve around the restoration of a symbiotic relation between man and nature which would be actualized not in the form of regression, but on a higher, civilized plane. What civilization has attempted concertedly to suppress in its advanced, enlightened stage is the memory of that insufferable, *ur*historical state of undifferentiated unity with nature, for the sake of whose abolition civilization has endured such self-sacrifice and denial. For Horkheimer and Adorno, only reflection on that lost immediate state of oneness with nature could provide the leverage necessary to divert enlightenment from the course of disaster toward which it seemed uncontrollably headed. Only the restitution of the lost capacity for a *mimetic* relation to nature could alter the irrational rationality of progressive mastery over both external and internal nature—to the point where under late capitalism no aspect of life remains safe from the all-dominant apparatus of technical control. It should be clear that themes from

Benjamin's "On the Mimetic Faculty" and his theory of *correspondances* echo strongly in their arguments, for the utopian ideal of restoring the long forgotten mimetic relation between man and nature figured prominently in his work. For Horkheimer and Adorno the concept of *remembrance* became the central means through which the spell of domination might be broken, an idea which was also of fundamental importance in Benjamin's work. "All reification is a forgetting,"[24] as Adorno once remarked in a letter to Benjamin, and he viewed it as the task of theory to set in motion the process of reflection which alone could release humanity from the collective psychosis that threatens at any minute to result in total annihilation:

Every progress made by civilization has renewed together with domination that prospect of its removal. . . . the realization of this prospect is referred to the notion, the concept. For it does not merely, like science, distance men from nature, but as the self-reflection of the thought that in the form of science remains tied to the blind rule of economics, allows the distance perpetuating injustice to be measured. By virtue of this remembrance of nature in the subject, in whose fulfillment the unacknowledged truth of all *Kultur* lies hidden, enlightenment is universally opposed to domination.[25]

In his Hegel critique in *Negative Dialectics* Adorno recapitulates the "negative" philosophy of history developed in Benjamin's "Theses" and *Dialectic of Enlightenment* in the following passage:

Universal history must be construed and denied. After the catastrophes that have happened, and in view of the catastrophes to come, it would be cynical to say that a plan for a better world is manifested in history and unites it. Not to be denied for that reason, however, is the unity of the control of nature, progressing to rule over men, and finally to that over men's inner nature. *No universal history leads from savagery to humanitarianism, but there is one leading from the slingshot to the megaton bomb.* It ends in the total menace which organized mankind poses to organized men, in the epitome of discontinuity. It is the horror that verifies Hegel, [i.e., his philosophy of history—R.W.] and stands him on his head.[26]

One might seriously inquire as to whether Benjamin's conception of history as the eternal recurrence of "myth," or Adorno's analogous notion of universal history as a "spell" (*der Bann*), would be of more than metaphorical value. Recently, this negative philosophy of history has been challenged in the work of Jürgen Habermas. Habermas expresses himself quite succinctly on this point: to condemn the entirety of history as vacuous and unful-filled—as the history of domination—runs the risk of simulta-neously cancelling those essential (albeit incremental) advances in the course of historical development—advances in the spheres of universal ethics, jurisprudence, and scientific knowledge—which would not only constitute the prerequisite for every emancipated society of the future, but without which civilization as we know it would relapse entirely into the Dark Ages.[27]

The undeniable components of truth to Habermas' assertion notwithstanding, it was the polemical intention of Benjamin and Adorno to indicate the repressed (and not so repressed) capacity for violence and destruction that lurks beneath the civilized veneer of culture. Habermas rightly detects a potentially fatal undercur-rent of nihilism in this aspect of Benjamin and Adorno's thought, an undercurrent which could foreseeably give rise to a quietistic and defeatist political outlook, and it is precisely this dimension of their philosophy of history that he seeks to combat. To be sure, the historico-philosophical outlook of Benjamin and Adorno was in a large measure conditioned by the horrors of the Nazi era—horrors whose full extent Benjamin did not live to see but which he clearly anticipated. Nevertheless, their view of the essentially *mythic* character of history and modernity is worth preserving and in more than a merely metaphorical sense. For it seeks to illustrate the degree to which domination in the modern era has become both universalized (spatially) and internalized (psychologically)—to the point where it assumes the guise of a "second nature" (Hegel/Lukács) that is as relentless and implacable as the original nature symbolically represented in the world of myth. The mod-ern can be said to revert to prehistory insofar as the all-dominant ideology of commodity exchange comes to assume the same un-reflected, nature-like opacity in the lives of men that the power of myth had in the world of primitive man. Moreover, as Adorno points out, under late capitalism the apparatus of ideological he-gemony wages an all-out, systematic campaign of psychological domination—the "colonization of consciousness"—which divests the associated individuals of bourgeois society of the capacity for autonomous self-reflection, the indispensable subjective prerequisite for initiating a generalized process of social criticism and change. In his own work, Habermas has fully acknowledged the thesis of "the end of the individual,"[28] a process whereby the technocratic-functionalist imperatives of *system integration* take precedence over the normative-communicative requirements of *social integration*. To equate the dynamic of history with the eternal return of myth is therefore more than just a metaphor; it is also a substantive index of the determinate state of unfreedom which masquerades today in the guise of natural necessity, a measure of how much ground must first be traversed before a reconciled world might truly begin to come into its own.

I began these concluding remarks by speaking of the inconsummate character of Benjamin's lifework. The failures of his life however—his failure to habilitate, the failure of his work to get the reception it deserved among his contemporaries, his failure to complete his *Hauptwerk* on the Paris Arcades—were largely circumstantial in nature. There is also the admittedly ambivalent resolution of his general philosophical project itself: the attempt to combine the methods of materialism and metaphysics, to force the absolute to step forth from an unmediated constellation of material elements. The pre-Marxist *Trauerspiel* book exemplifies Benjamin's greatest achievement in this direction; one, however, whose idealist basis seemed incompatible with a truly exoteric, generalizable theory of experience. It was ultimately the weight of historical circumstances which compelled him to abandon this approach and seek a theory of knowledge that was consistent with materialist principles. Yet, in its traditional, scientistic versions, Marxism was diametrically opposed to the very substance of Benjamin's theoretical inclinations. Benjamin wished to downplay his originality, the initial genius he had shown as a literary critic, for the sake of more pressing political concerns, or at least to assimilate that originality to these concerns. It was, to be sure, a form of self-sacrifice, a self-sacrifice through which he sought at the same time to gain meaning for his life. Yet, this transformation of methodological focus also entailed a tacit and on occasion lethal subordination of theory to practice, a subordination which led to the problematical character of many of his later works. Yet, to desire for him to have lived or written in any other way would be to attempt to evade the real historical problems with which he found himself confronted. In *Negative Dialectics* Adorno has, in a polemical spirit, raised the by no means otiose question as to whether it would still be possible to write poetry in good conscience after Auschwitz. In a somewhat analogous manner, Benjamin came to view the critic's preoccupation with the ethereal realm of belles lettres as morally irresponsible in face of the impending threat of fascism. The philosophy of history penetrated the heart of his self-understanding as a theorist.

There is at the same time an "unaccountable" dimension of Benjamin's thinking which reveals great affinities with the concept of freedom. It is that aspect of his thought that is "nameless," that aspect which defies all traditional rubrics of intellectual categorization. A cursory glance at his writings of the 1930s would testify to the difficulties of assimilating his views in any organic way to the traditional concepts of Marxism. The same claim could easily be made for his speculations concerning the theory of knowledge or the realm of theology. In all these fields Benjamin's convictions remained staunchly heterodox. There is, to be sure, an ever-present danger in a mode of thought that is so thoroughly sui generis, a danger that originality and fancy will themselves turn into fetishes. Yet, Benjamin prevented his thinking from tumbling into sheer arbitrariness or solipsism insofar as he simultaneously displayed a profound *veneration* for the authority vested in tradition; a veneration, however, in which tradition is not treated as a power before which one must submit blindly, but as a now-time which enters into a unique relation to the present. The magical quality of his writing lies in the fact that the semantic potentials of tradition reappear not as something merely "transmitted," but as something transfigured and thus *actualized*. As Adorno has observed, "Everything which fell under the scrutiny of his words was transformed, as though it had become radioactive."[29]

A longing for happiness was the profound desire animating the entirety of his work: "Everything Benjamin said or wrote sounded as if thought, instead of rejecting the promises of fairy tales and children's books with its usual disgraceful 'maturity,' took them so literally that real fulfillment itself was now within sight of knowledge."[30] As Benjamin once wrote in his essay on Proust: "Cocteau recognized what really should have been the major concern of all readers of Proust. . . . He recognized Proust's blind, senseless, frenzied quest for happiness"[31]—words which one could apply equally to his own writing. The more happiness seemingly withdrew from immediate reach, the more fervently he renewed his quest. Benjamin's thought exhibited a unique sensibility for those objects and texts which through their sheer uselessness, their "intentionlessness," display a great affinity with the idea of emancipation; a world which would transcend the distortion of a society of universal being-for-other, in which things would be allowed to express their own inherent meanings, their being-for-self. As such his essays attain an exemplary status; they are models which because of their uniqueness can never be duplicated. They possess a fragile, autonomous existence, whose secret can never be divined by way of imitation, but only in an effort of concentration on the part of the reader that equals them in rigor. As with any truth worthy of the name, the understanding of the truth content of his thought must never be "an unveiling which destroys the secret, but a revelation which does it justice."[32] The attempt to furnish an image of the absolute consistent with the Enlightenment principle of rational autonomy presented itself as a central concern to philosophers and men of letters in the age of German classicism. It was this very antinomy which preoccupied the lifework of Walter Benjamin, "Whose genius united the insight of the Metaphysician, the interpretative power of the Critic, and the erudition of the Scholar."[33] Today, the ruins of this lifework still radiate more brilliantly than the triumphs of other men and women. He was to be sure "A l'écart de tous les courants."[34]

NOTES

Preface

   1. These have been collected in Walter Benjamin, *Über Haschisch*.
   2. Cf. Charles Rosen, "The Ruins of Walter Benjamin."
   3. Gary Smith, "Walter Benjamin: A Bibliography of Secondary Literature," *New German Critique,* "Special Walter Benjamin Issue" (Spring 1977):
75–82.
   4. The title of Susan Sontag's essay on Benjamin.
   5. The recent work of two American scholars in particular, Susan Buck-
Morss and Irving Wohlfarth, stands out as a notable exception to the often rather
arbitrary and journalistic appropriation to which Benjamin's writings have been
exposed in North America. See their entries in the Bibliography.
   6. Theodor W. Adorno, *Prisms,* pp. 227 ff.
   7. Conversely, interpreters who have made great strides in comprehending
the logic of Benjamin's early development are Sandor Radnoti, Rolf Tiedemann,
and, despite his own pronounced discomfort with certain aspects of Benjamin's
alleged esotericism, Bernd Witte.
   8. The question of Benjamin's relationship to Marxism in the 1930s has
been in general the source of the most rancorous controversies in the secondary
literature to date. Specifically, first Helmut Heissenbüttel in *Merkur* (July 1967)
and then the editorial staff of the West Berlin publication *Alternative* (November
1967 and April 1968) have questioned the integrity of the Frankfurt executors
of Benjamin's estate (above all, Adorno) in editing Benjamin's work. Their basic
charge is that Adorno somehow attempted to suppress documents supportive
of Benjamin's later commitment to Marxism. Hannah Arendt, in her article on
Benjamin in *Merkur* (nos. 1, 2, 3, and 4, 1968; a revised version of her Introduction to *Illuminations*), also seems to have jumped on the bandwagon, accusing
Adorno, in his capacity as editor, of having sought to perpetuate to his own
advantage the intellectual disagreement between him and Benjamin the 1930s.
However, what little substance there is in any of these charges is lost, firstly,
amid the uncontrolled vitriol with which Adorno is personally attacked, and,
secondly, in light of the fact that it was Adorno (and now his former student

Rolf Tiedemann, who has assumed the major responsibility for producing an exquisite, six-volume edition of Benjamin's *Gesammelte Schriften*) who was singularly responsible for having rescued Benjamin's work from a state ot total oblivion by publishing in 1955 (along with his wife Gretel) a two-volume selection of his *Schriften* (Frankfurt am Main). The *Alternative* editors have suggested, on the basis of some extremely flimsy evidence, that Adorno had engaged in a *systematic* effort to alter Benjamin's texts in accordance with his own interpretations of them. Adorno did in fact once authorize the omission of the final sentence from Benjamin's 1930 article "Theorien des deutschen Faschismus" (a review of Ernst Junger's *Krieg and Krieger*), which announced the need to turn the coming war into a civil war (an English translation of the essay can be found in *New German Critique* 17). Other than this one instance, however, *Alternative* bases its case on the fact that back in the 1930s the Institute for Social Research, recently transplanted from Europe to New York, was forced to tone down Benjamin's flamboyant employment of Marxist rhetoric in the case of two articles he had submitted for publication to the Institute's literary organ ("Edmund Fuchs: Collector and Historian" and "The Work of Art in the Age of Mechanical Reproduction"); for the inner circle of the Institute in exile feared the very real possibility of reprisals in the rather unsympathetic political climate of their new home. What the *Alternative* editors fail to mention, however, was that the treatment of Benjamin's essays was in no way *selective,* but rather was merely in line with an editorial policy of self-censorship which was applied *equally* to the many Marxist thinkers within the Institute's own ranks; a policy of which Benjamin was well aware and with which he sympathized. See especially his letter to Max Horkheimer of March 29, 1936 (reprinted in Benjamin, *Gesammelte Schriften* 1(3):1012), in which he remarks, "You know that I have never lacked an awareness of the special limits which the *Zeitschrift für Sozialforschung* is obligated to respect in regard to its work"—in a statement of solidarity concerning the editorial changes required for his "Work of Art" essay. Thus the editors of *Alternative* suspect Adorno of having perpetuated such censorship in his more recent editorial work; whereas in fact the editorial discrepancies that do exist between earlier and later variants of Benjamin's writings are exceedingly rare and insubstantial. Yet, the most scurrilous of the various accusations raised by *Alternative* was the claim that Benjamin's *financial* dependence on the Institute in the late 1930s also entailed an *intellectual* dependence. On the contrary, all available evidence suggests that there were absolutely no strictures of a substantive nature placed on Benjamin's literary activites by the Institute for Social Research, nor did their dealings deviate in any respect from what would be considered a normal relationship between writer and editor. For more on this dispute, see the rejoinders to *Alternative* by Adorno, "Interimsbeschied," *Über Walter Benjamin* (Frankfurt am Main, 1970), pp. 91–95 and Tiedemann, "Zur 'Beschlagnahme' Walter Benjamins oder Wie man mit der Philologie Schlitten fährt," pp. 74–93. For an excellent summary of the debate, see Pierre Missac, "Du nouveau sur Walter Benjamin?" pp. 681–98.

1. Origins

1. Walter Benjamin, "A Berlin Chronicle," *Reflections: Essays, Aphorisms, Autobiographical Writings*, Edmund Jephcott, trans. Peter Demetz, ed. (New York: Harcourt, 1978), p. 11.

2. As Benjamin boasts, "If I write better German than most writers of my generation, it is thanks largely to twenty years' observance of one little rule: never use the word 'I' except in letters. The exceptions to this precept that I have permitted myself could be counted." *Ibid., p. 15.*

3. *Ibid.*, p. 28.

4. *Ibid.*, p. 6.

5. *Ibid.*, p. 13.

6. *Ibid.*, p. 5.

7. For more on the Youth Movement see Walter Z. Laqueur, *Young Germany, A History of the Youth Movement.*

8. George L. Mosse, *The Crisis of German Ideology: Intellectual Origins of the Third Reich*, pp. 171–89.

9. *Ibid.*, p. 185 ff. For another discussion of Benjamin's relation to the Youth Movement and Wyneken's group in particular, see Theodor W. Adorno, "A l'écart de tous les courants," pp. 96–99. Benjamin's own relation to the expressionist movement in general was complex. As one learns from Gershom Scholem's book *Walter Benjamin: Die Geschichte einer Freundschaft*, p. 85, Benjamin greatly admired expressionist painters such as Kandinsky, Franz Marc, Chagall, and Paul Klee, and was attracted to the mystical aspects of Kandinsky's treatise (*Über das Geistige in der Kunst*). On the other hand, he appears to have been unimpressed by expressionism as a literary current. As Adorno has noted, "That trait of Benjamin's which one might call objectivistic set him from the beginning in a certain opposition to expressionism." See "A l'écart de tous les courants," p. 96.

10. Bernd Witte, *Walter Benjamin: Der Intellektuelle als Kritiker*, pp. 15–22.

11. Walter Benjamin, *Briefe*, 1:86–87.

12. *Ibid.*, p. 66.

13. Benjamin, *Gesammelte Schriften*, 2(3):842. Hereafter cited as GS.

15. Benjamin, *Briefe* 1:93.

16. Cf. Immanuel Kant, *Critique of Practical Reason*, p. 66: "Whether [philosophers] placed this object of pleasure, which was to deliver the supreme concept of the good, in happiness, or in perfection, in moral feeling, or in the will of God—their fundamental principle was always heteronomy, and they came inevitably to empirical conditions for a moral law. This was because they would call their object, as the direct determining ground of the will, good or bad only according to its exclusively empirical relation to feeling. Only a formal law, i.e., one which prescribes to reason nothing more than the form of the universal law as the supreme condition of its maxims, can be a priori a determining ground of practical reason."

17. Benjamin, "Der Moralunterricht," *GS* 2, 1, p. 50.

18. G. W. F. Hegel, *Phenomenology of Spirit*, pp. 383 ff.

19. Cited in Benjamin, *GS* 2(1):48.

20. *Ibid.*, p. 49.

21. "In keiner einzelnen empirischen Beeinflussung haben wir das Gewahr, wirklich den sittlichen Willen als solchen zu treffen." *Ibid.*

22. There is a fine, yet essential, distinction at work when one says that the moral law cannot be "rationally demonstrated." On the one hand, since the sphere of freedom embodied in the moral law belongs to the intelligible world, and for this reason we can have no empirical intuition corresponding to it, it can not be "known"—i.e., in the strict, Kantian sense—by the faculty of human reason. On the other hand, as Kant shows in the Second *Critique*, the faculty of reason is nevertheless capable of demonstrating on a priori grounds that it would be impossible to consider ourselves as free, morally responsible subjects without reliance on the idea of moral law. Hence, the moral law is a transcendental constitutive condition of our existence as ethically acting subjects. In this sense it is permissible to say that whereas one can "demonstrate" (or appeal to) the necessity of thinking it, it would be impossible, given the constitutive boundaries of the human understanding, factually (i.e., empirically) *to prove its existence*.

23. Kant, *Critique of Practical Reason*, pp. 117 ff.

24. Benjamin, *Briefe* 1:89.

25. For a provocative critique of Kant's moral philosophy, see Theodor Adorno, "Freedom," in *Negative Dialectics*, pp. 211–99.

26. For a classical discussion of inadequacy of the merely formal posture of the moral consciousness when confronted with the hard realities of concrete existence, see George Lukács, "On the Poverty of Spirit," pp. 371–85. See also the moving commentary on this work by Agnes Heller, "Georg Lukács and Irma Seidler," pp. 74–107.

27. Benjamin, "Der Moralunterricht," *GS* 2(1):50.

28. Cf. Werner Fuld, *Walter Benjamin: Zwischen den Stühlen*, pp. 44 ff.

29. Benjamin, "Erfahrung," *GS* 2(1):54.

30. His remarks about the play, published in the August issue of *Der Anfang*, are reprinted in *GS* 2(1):56–60.

31. *Ibid.*, p. 81–82.

32. Cf. Gershom Scholem, *Walter Benjamin: Die Geschichte einer Freundschaft*, p. 27: "There was something sacrosanct about the death for him, which was recognizable in Benjamin every time he spoke of Heinle."

33. Benjamin, "Berlin Chronicle," *Reflections*, p. 17.

34. Benjamin, *Briefe* 1:121–22.

35. Cf. Fritz Ringer, *The Decline of the German Mandarins*.

36. Michael Löwy, *Georg Lukács: From Romanticism to Bolshevism*, p. 30. Cf. Ringer, *Decline of the German Mandarins*, pp. 3, 13, 86–90.

37. George Lukács, *The Theory of the Novel*, p. 21.

38. *Ibid.*

39. The disastrous consequences of this position from a theoretical stand-

point for Lukács's own later development can be seen in his voluminous 1953 work *Die Zerstörung der Vernunft*, in which the totality of nineteenth- and twentieth-century German philosophy from Schelling to Heidegger is dismissed as irrationalist and thus latently or avowedly fascistic. Adorno later remarked appropriately that the book was much more indicative of the state of the author's own reason than of those whom he condemned in its pages.

40. Paul Piccone, "Why Did the Left Collapse?", *Telos* (Winter, 1981) 46:96.

41. The early Lukács, particularly in *Soul and Form*, remained highly indebted to Kant; and while he mentions in the 1962 Preface to *The Theory of the Novel* that the latter work represented, so to speak, his "turning from Kant to Hegel," he also fully acknowledges that its methodological approach essentially derived from the method of synthetic abstraction characteristic of Dilthey and the *Geisteswissenschaften* school (pp. 12–13). For a discussion of the young Lukács's reception of Kant, see Andrew Arato and Paul Breines, *The Young Lukács and the Origins of Western Marxism*, p. 40.

42. Kant, *Critique of Pure Reason*, A 240, B 299. In the *Critique of Judgment* Kant admittedly credits the faculty of aesthetic judgment with the capacity to surmount the sensory limitations imposed upon the faculty of pure reason and gain access to the supersensible. Nevertheless, even here aesthetic judgment is granted this capacity only *subjectively*—or "for itself" and not really "in itself"— and objectively—to express the character of the deficiency of Kant's argument in Hegelian terms. Moreover, insofar as the pleasure which the object of aesthetic judgment provokes is necessarily "disinterested"—i.e., it refers only to the formal character of the object, the work of art, and never to its content or cognitive status—the possibility of a relation between art and *conceptual* truth of any type is necessarily foreclosed from the outset according to the Kantian schema. Thus, in opposition to Kant, the emphasis on the *cognitive* character of aesthetic judgment by the twentieth-century thinkers with whom we are concerned is more consistent with the Hegelian *Aufhebung* of Kantian aesthetics.

43. For an excellent discussion of the early Lukács's oscillation between a sociological and existentialist explanation of the crisis of modernity, see Gyorgy Markus, "The Soul and Life: The Young Lukács and the Problem of Culture."

44. Lukács, *History of Modern Drama* (Budapest, 1911), pp. 100–101; cited in *ibid.*, pp. 101–2. This statement shows unequivocally the early Lukács's profound indebtedness to the social theory of George Simmel—above all, his reliance on Simmel's theory of the "tragedy of culture"—a process whereby the forms and institutions of human social life inevitably develop according to an autonomous, alienated logic, ultimately turning hostilely against their creator, man himself. For Simmel's main work concerning the unprecedented level of social alienation under capitalism, see his *The Philosophy of Money* (London, 1978). For an important statement concerning the general contradiction between men and their institutions, see his "On the Concept and Tragedy of Modern Culture," in Simmel, *The Conflict and Tragedy of Modern Culture*, pp. 27–46.

45. Lukács, *Soul and Form*, pp. 152–53.

46. Lukács, The Theory of the Novel, p. 64.

47. Ibid., p. 88.

48. Cf. the important elaboration of this idea in Ibid., pp. 74–75. My discussion of The Theory of the Novel, is heavily indebted to the work of Arato and Breines; see note 41.

49. Lukács, The Theory of the Novel, p. 72.

50. Ibid., p. 80.

51. Arato and Breines, The Young Lukács and the Origins of Western Marxism, p. 51.

52. An informed treatment of this important distinction in Benjamin's thought is in Sandor Radnoti, "The Early Aesthetics of Walter Benjamin," pp. 81–82.

53. Cf. Arato and Breines, The Young Lukács and the Origins of Western Marxism.

54. Lukács, The Theory of the Novel, pp. 152–53.

55. Arato and Breines, The Young Lukács and the Origins of Western Marxism, p. 51.

56. Ernst Bloch, Geist der Utopie, pp. 251 ff.

57. Ibid., p. 204.

58. Heinz Pätzold, Neomarxistische Ästhetik, pp. 122–23.

59. Bloch, Geist der Utopie, p. 207.

60. Ibid., p. 151.

2. The Path to Trauerspiel

1. Walter Benjamin, The Origin of German Tragic Drama, p. 182.

2. Jürgen Habermas, "Bewusstmachende oder rettende Kritik—die Aktualität Walter Benjamins," pp. 185–86.

3. Benjamin, "Goethes Wahlverwandtschaften," in GS 1(1), 125.

4. Benjamin, Briefe 2:505.

5. Benjamin, GS 2(1):157.

6. Ibid., p. 160.

7. Ibid., p. 159.

8. Ibid., p. 158.

9. Ibid., p. 159.

10. Immanuel Kant, Critique of Pure Reason, B 20.

11. Ibid., B xvi.

12. For a more detailed discussion of Benjamin's theory of knowledge, see chapter 3.

13. The degree to which "Über das Programm der kommenden Philosophie" anticipates the Kant-critique of Horkheimer and Adorno in Dialectic of Enlightenment is especially striking.

14. Ernst Bloch, Geist der Utopie, p. 219.

15. Benjamin, GS 2(1):162.

16. Ibid., p. 164.

17. For a more sympathetic appraisal of the neo-Kantian movement, see Andrew Arato, "The Neo-Idealist Defense of Subjectivity," pp. 108–64; and Thomas E. Willey, *Back to Kant.*

18. Benjamin, *GS* 2(1):164.

19. *Ibid.*, p. 159.

20. *Ibid.*, p. 168.

21. Cf. Rychner's reminiscences in Adorno et al., *Über Walter Benjamin* (Frankfurt am Main, 1968), pp. 24–29.

22. Gershom Scholem, *Walter Benjamin: Die Geschichte einer Freundschaft*, p. 158.

23. For a biography of Scholem, which also takes up the question of his relationship to Benjamin in some detail, see David Biale, *Gershom Scholem: Kabbalah and Counterhistory.*

24. In his "Theses on the Philosophy of History" Benjamin cites Karl Kraus' maxim "Origin is the Goal" as the motto for Thesis XIV—in reference to the French Revolution's emulation of ancient Rome as a model for its republican ideals. This use of the concept of "origin" represents a secularization of its original employment in *Origin of German Tragic Drama*, in keeping with Benjamin's later interest in historical materialism.

25. Scholem, *The Messianic Idea in Judaism*, p. 23. The allusion to the 'shells which dam up and choke life' refers to the doctrine of the "breaking of the vessels" which according to the lore of Lurianic Kabbalah is responsible for the original influx of evil in the world.

26. In *Die Geschichte einer Freundschaft* Scholem reports (pp. 118–19) having discussed Abulafia's philosophy of language with Benjamin in connection with the linguistico-philosophical interests of his planned *Habilitationsschrift* on *Trauerspiel.*

27. Scholem, *Major Currents in Jewish Mysticism*, pp. 132–33.

28. *Ibid.*, p. 133.

29. Benjamin, *Briefe* 1:329. See also his letter of December 28, 1917, to Ernst Schoen, where he remarks: "Above all: questions concerning the essence of knowledge, law, art, are for me connected with the question of the origin of all expressions of the human spirit in the essence of language"; *Briefe* 1:165.

30. Benjamin, *Reflections*, p. 322.

31. *Ibid.*, p. 323.

32. *Ibid.*

33. *Ibid.*, pp. 326–27; Benjamin, *GS* 2(1):152.

34. *Ibid.*, p. 327.

35. The precise nature of the link between the appearance of Kabbalistic motifs in Benjamin's work and the specific texts from which Benjamin might have derived these motifs still remains very much of a mystery. Certainly, much of his information concerning Kabbalah came from Franz Joseph Molitor's magnum opus *Philosophie der Geschichte oder über die Tradition* 4 vols. (Münster, 1827); indeed, Scholem reports that this work for "many years occupied a place of honor in his library" (Scholem, "Walter Benjamin," *On Jews and Judaism in*

Crisis, p. 192). Since the period in which Benjamin's interest in Kabbalah was keenest (1916–1924) roughly coincides with the beginning of Scholem's own researches in this realm of scholarship, it is very likely that for Benjamin (whose many attempts to learn Hebrew repeatedly came to naught) conversations with Scholem represented an equally important source of insight concerning Kabbalistic matters. As Scholem explains, in these years the two were "on very close terms" and the "problem of Judaism and its discussion occupied a central place in [their] relationship" (*Ibid.*, p. 172).

On the other hand, in a letter to the author of November 27, 1980, Gershom Scholem has indicated another important source for Benjamin's views on philosophy of language: the linguistic theories of Johann Georg Hamann. In "On Language as Such and the Language of Man," Benjamin enthusiastically quotes Hamann's remark: '*Language, the mother of reason and revelation, its alpha and omega*' (p. 321). Other direct references to Hamann in his essays and letters are, however, notably scarce. Nevertheless, there is one *profound* similarity in their views on the philosophy of language which would seem to confirm Scholem's suggestion admirably: namely, for both men the essence of language is to be found not in the semantic content of individual words, but rather in its *expressive capacity;* that is, both are interested in language not primarily as a means of communication, but instead in its formal, nonsignifying side. However, at the same time, Hamann's own speculations on the philosophy of language, scattered throughout his texts and letters, are themselves *largely derived from Kabbalistic sources.* In this way, one can speak of the work of Hamann as a prism through which the teachings of Kabbalah exerted a profound, if indirect, influence on Benjamin's thought. For both men look toward the linguistic doctrines of the Kabbalists in an attempt to evoke an antifunctional, noninstrumentalist vision of language as pure expression. For a book that probes Benjamin's theory of language in relation to Hamann with results that are quite impressive from a philological standpoint, see Winfried Menninghaus, *Walter Benjamins Theorie der Sprachmagie*, especially pp. 21–33 and 205–215. See also the discussion of Benjamin's essay "On the Mimetic Faculty" in chapter 7.

36. Benjamin, *GS* 1(1):1–122.
37. Benjamin, "'Der Idiot' von Dostojewskij," *GS* 2(1):237.
38. *Ibid.*, p. 238. Emphasis added.
39. *Ibid.*, p. 239.
40. Benjamin, *Illuminations*, p. 70.
41. Bernd Witte, *Walter Benjamin: Der Intellektuelle als Kritiker.*
42. Benjamin, *GS* 2(1):240.
43. Scholem, *Die Geschichte einer Freundschaft*, p. 66.
44. All in all, Witte is put off by what he considers the "elitist" qualities of Benjamin's early work (through the *Trauerspiel* book); he is therefore much more sympathetic to Benjamin's later alliance with Brecht and self-conception as a "strategist in the literary struggle."
45. Scholem, *On Jews and Judaism in Crisis*, p. 193.
46. In his Introduction to the two-volume edition of Benjamin's *Schriften*

(Frankfurt am Main: Suhrkamp Verlag, 1955), Adorno discusses the problem of fragmentariness in Benjamin's work in the following historico-philosophical terms: "Just as modern music, in its uncompromising representatives, no longer values 'completion,' nor the difference between theme and development, and instead, every musical idea, even every tone, stands equally close to the center, so too is Benjamin's philosophy 'a-thematic.' It represents a dialectic at a standstill insofar as it knows no internal time of development, but instead receives its form from the constellation of individual statements. Thus its affinity with the aphorism." Reprinted in Adorno, *Über Walter Benjamin*, p. 46

47. It would perhaps be a more accurate way of characterizing the utopian dimension of works of art to say that their magical power consists in their straddling of *two worlds:* they overstep the boundaries of the given empirical world in order to attain a vision of a transcendent not-yet-being (Bloch), and then return to the empirical world in order to present that vision of transcendence in reality.

48. Benjamin, "Theses on the Philosophy of History," *Illuminations*, p. 257.

49. *Ibid.*, p. 251.

50. Benjamin, *GS* 2(1):75.

51. Benjamin, *Illuminations*, p. 263.

52. *Ibid.*, p. 261.

53. *Ibid.*, p. 255.

54. *Ibid.*

55. Cf. *Origin of German Tragic Drama*, p. 109, where Benjamin describes the fate of the tragic hero in the following terms: "what appears before the public is not the guilt of the accused but the evidence of speechless suffering, and the tragedy which appeared to be devoted to the judgment of the hero is transformed into a hearing about the Olympians in which the latter appears as a witness and, against the will of the gods, displays the honour of the demi-god. The profound Aeschylean impulse to justice inspires the anti-Olympian prophecy of all tragedy. . . . 'in tragedy pagan man realizes that he is better than his gods, but this realization strikes him dumb and it remains unarticulated.'" The analysis of classical tragedy in the *Trauerspiel* study is profoundly indebted to two sources. The idea of the 'speechlessness' of the tragic hero once he has realized himself to be superior to his gods derives from Franz Rosenzweig's *The Star of Redemption*, pp. 209–11. The idea of tragedy as *the* art form historically appropriate to mankind's once-in-history conquest of myth (in ancient Greece) derives from Lukács's early essay "The Metaphysics of Tragedy," in *Soul and Form* pp. 152–74. Cf. Rolf Tiedemann, *Studien Zur Philosophie Walter Benjamins*, pp. 94–98.

56. Habermas, *Zur Aktualität Walter Benjamins*, p. 188.

57. Benjamin, "Fate and Character," in *Reflections*, p. 307.

58. *Ibid.*, p. 308.

59. Benjamin, *Origin of German Tragic Drama*, p. 109.

60. *Ibid.*, 182.

61. *Ibid.*, Benjamin, *GS* 1(1):358.

62. Friedrich Schlegel, *Schriften und Fragmente*, pp. 21–42.

63. Benjamin, "Drei Lebensläufe," in *Zur Aktualität Walter Benjamin*, p. 46.

64. Benjamin, *GS* 1(1):158–64.

65. Hannah Arendt falls victim to this line of reasoning when she argues against the inclusion of the *Elective Affinities* essay in *Illuminations* on the erroneous grounds that it "consists to a large extent of a polemic against Friedrich Gundolf's *Goethe*" (*Illuminations*, p. 265).

66. Benjamin, *GS* 1(1):135.

67. *Ibid.*, p. 130.

68. *Ibid.*

69. Where Kant defines marriage as the "union of two people of different sexes with a view to the lifelong mutual possession of each other's sexual attributes." Cf. Kant, *Die Metaphysik der Sitten*, Part 1, #24.

70. Benjamin, *GS* 1(1):130.

71. *Ibid.*, p. 138.

72. *Ibid.*, p. 139.

73. *Ibid.*, pp. 139–40.

74. *Ibid.*, p. 200.

75. *Ibid.*, p. 201.

76. J. W. Goethe, *Elective Affinities*, p. 299.

77. In his *Walter Benjamin—Der Intellektuelle als Kritiker*, Bernd Witte, in the context of an informed discussion of the *Elective Affinities* essay, suggests Benjamin's unorthodox treatment of the figure of Ottilie derives from an allegorical reading in terms of an unrequited love for Jula Cohn—to whom the essay was dedicated. Cf. pp. 61–63.

78. For the difficulties that have arisen in trying to date this important fragment (Adorno claims Benjamin had read it to him as a work in progress in 1938; Scholem contends it dates from the early twenties, and that the "materialist" Benjamin, by representing it as a current work, was merely trying to test his gullibility) see *GS* 2(3):946–49.

79. Benjamin, *Reflections*, p. 312.

80. *Ibid.*

81. *Ibid.*

82. Benjamin, *Illuminations*, p. 257.

83. Benjamin, *Origin of German Tragic Drama*, p. 55. The term *Kunstwollen* or "will to art" was developed by the German art historian Alois Riegl in his *Die spätrömische Kunstindustrie* (Munich, 1901)—a work Benjamin later claimed had influenced him greatly.

84. Scholem, *The Messianic Idea of Judaism*, p. 10.

85. Benjamin, *Reflections*, p. 313.

86. Benjamin, *Illuminations*, pp. 257–58.

87. Scholem, *The Messianic Idea in Judiasm*, pp. 10 and 12.

88. Benjamin, *Origin of German Tragic Drama*, p. 62.

89. Benjamin, "Drei Lebensläufe," in *Zur Aktualität Walter Benjamin*, p. 53.

90. *Ibid.*, p. 46.

91. Cf. Benjamin, "Goethes Wahlverwandtschaften," *GS* 1(1):194–96, where Benjamin develops the concept of *das Ausdrucklose*.

92. *Ibid.*, p. 126. See also, Anson Rabinbach's informed discussion of this motif in Benjamin's thought, "Critique and Commentary/Alchemy and Chemistry," *New German Critique* (Spring 1979) 17:3–14.

93. Benjamin, *Origin of German Tragic Drama*, p. 176.

94. *Ibid.*, p. 166; Benjamin, *GS* 1(1):343. Cf. the very important preliminary outline of the difference between historical and tragic time in the 1916 "Trauerspiel und Tragödie," *GS*, 2(1):133–37: "The time of history is infinite in every direction and unfulfilled in every moment. That means there is no empirical event conceivable that would have a necessary relation to the determinate juncture at which it occurs. For the empirical occurrence, time is only a form; however, what is more important, an unfulfilled form. The occurrence does not fulfill the formal nature of the time in which it lies. For to be sure, one must not think that time is nothing but the standard with which the duration of a mechanical change is measured. This time is indeed a relatively empty form; to conceive of its fulfillment is meaningless. The time of fulfilled history is something different from that of mechanics. . . . This idea of fulfilled time appears in the Bible as its dominant historical idea: Messianic time. In each case the idea of fulfilled historical time is not however to be thought of as the idea of an individual time. It is this definition, which naturally entirely changes the meaning of fulfillment, which differentiates tragic time from Messianic time. Tragic time relates to the latter as individually fulfilled time relates to divinely fulfilled time." Consequently, tragic time appears as an intermediary between historically unfulfilled time (the time of *Trauerspiel*) and "divinely fulfilled time" (Messianic time). Tragedy represents fulfillment, yet only symbolically, limited to an individual moment—in terms of the philosophy of history, the moment of man's coming to self-consciousness in face of his *ur*historical bondage to the domination of myth. Whereas the allegorical structure of *Trauerspiel* knows only the infinite heaping of ruins upon ruins proper to the state of interminable decline that distinguishes history as natural history.

95. Cf. Ernst Bloch's very significant remarks concerning the utopian content of the symbol and the relation between art and utopia in general, in *Das Prinzip Hoffnung*, pp. 199–203 and 929–82.

96. Benjamin, *Origin of German Tragic Drama*, p. 167.

97. *Ibid.*, p. 175.

98. For an excellent discussion of the significance of allegory in Benjamin's *Trauerspiel* study, see Hans Heinz Holz, "Prismatisches Denken," in T. W. Adorno et al., *Über Walter Benjamin*, pp. 62–110. For a general discussion of the relationship of allegory and symbol as modes of aesthetic representation, see Hans-Georg Gadamer, *Truth and Method*, pp. 63–73.

99. Benjamin, *Origin of German Tragic Drama*, p. 184.

100. *Ibid.*, p. 183–84.

101. *Ibid.*, p. 178.

102. *Ibid.*, p. 216.
103. *Ibid.*
104. *Ibid.*, p. 233.
105. *Ibid.*, pp. 233–34.
106. *Ibid.*, p. 232–33.
107. Cf. Arnold Hauser, *The Social History of Art*, 4:166–259, *passim*.
108. Benjamin, *Origin of German Tragic Drama*, p. 235.

3. Ideas and Theory of Knowledge

1. Walter Benjamin, *Origin of German Tragic Drama*, p. 28.
2. Benjamin, *Briefe* 1:347.
3. *Ibid.*, p. 372.
4. *Ibid.*, p. 375.
5. Cited in Benjamin, *GS* 1(3):895–96.
6. Gershom Scholem, *Walter Benjamin: die Geschichte einer Freundschaft* (Frankfurt am Main, 1975), p. 185.
7. Cf. Max Rychner, "Erinneringen," in T. W. Adorno et al, *Über Walter Benjamin* (Frankfurt am Main, 1968), p. 25: "Benjamin asked me whether I began to read the book from the beginning, namely with the Introduction. I responded affirmatively, since it is my customary practice to read books from the beginning; however, he told me that one should do the opposite of what I did, for the introduction could be understood only if one were familar with the Kabbalah."
8. Benjamin, *Briefe*, 1:374.
9. *Ibid.*, pp. 321–22.
10. *Ibid.*, p. 323.
11. Benjamin, *GS* 1(1):227; *Origin of German Tragic Drama*, p. 47.
12. Rolf Tiedemann, *Studien zur Philosophie Walter Benjamins*, pp. 18–19.
13. Theodor W. Adorno, "Der Essay als Form," in *Noten zur Literatur* 1:21–23. This essay, and Adorno's thought in general, represents the fulfillment of many of the motifs concerning the relation of the essay form to the theory of knowledge originally developed by Benjamin and the young Lukács.
14. Benjamin, *Origin of German Tragic Drama*, p. 28.
15. Georg Lukács, "On the Nature and Form of the Essay," in *Soul and Form*, p. 15.
16. *Ibid.*, p. 3.
17. At the same time the essay has become in a certain measure capable of standing on its own (free of its former dependency on "books or poets"). This is a primary symptom of its having become problematic. Cf. Lukács, "On the Nature and Form of the Essay," in *Soul and Form*, p. 15.
18. Benjamin, *Origin of German Tragic Drama*, p. 27.
19. Lukács, "On the Nature and Form of the Essay," *Soul and Form*, p. 16.
20. *Ibid.*, pp. 16–17.
21. Cf. Adorno's essay of the same title in *Noten zur Literatur* 3:152–88.

22. Benjamin, *Origin of German Tragic Drama*, p. 30.
23. *Ibid.*
24. *Ibid.*, p. 31.
25. Benjamin, *GS* 1(1):211; *Origin of German Tragic Drama*, p. 31.
26. *Ibid.*
27. Benjamin, "Der Begriff der Kunstkritik in der deutschen Romantik," *GS* 1(1):69.
28. *Ibid.*, p. 72.
29. Benjamin, "Theorie der Kunstkritik," *GS* 1(3):835.
30. Adorno, "Einleitung zu Benjamins 'Schriften,'" in *Über Walter Benjamin*, p. 36.
31. Adorno, "Vorrede" to Tiedemann, *Studien zur Philosophie Walter Benjamins*, p. 9.
32. Benjamin, "Ursprung des deutschen Trauerspiels," *GS* 1(1):208; *Origin of German Tragic Drama*, p. 29.
33. Adorno, *Minima Moralia*, p. 247.
34. Benjamin, *Origin of German Tragic Drama*, p. 34.
35. *Ibid.*
36. *Ibid.*
37. *Ibid.*
38. *Ibid.*
39. Cf. Adorno, *Zur Metakritik der Erkenntnistheorie*.
40. Benjamin, *Origin of German Tragic Drama*, p. 36.
41. *Ibid.*, p. 33.
42. *Ibid.*
43. Benjamin, *GS* 1(1):215; *Origin of German Tragic Drama*, p. 35.
44. Cf. Adorno, *Ästhetische Theorie*, p. 208.
45. Benjamin, *Origin of German Tragic Drama*, p. 36.
46. Cf. Tiedemann, *Studien zur Philosophie Walter Benjamins*, pp. 59–66.
47. Benjamin, *Origin of German Tragic Drama*, p. 45.
48. Benjamin, "Nachträge zum Trauerspielbuch," *GS* 1(3):953–55.
49. Benjamin, "Einleitung" (original draft of the "Erkenntniskritische Vorrede" to *Ursprung des deutschen Trauerspiels*), *GS* 1(3):935. For more on Benjamin's concept of "origin," see Tiedemann, *Studien zur Philosophie Walter Benjamins*, pp. 76–84.
50. Benjamin, *Origin of German Tragic Drama*, p. 46.
51. *Ibid.*, pp. 45–46.
52. *Ibid.*, p. 46.
53. Benjamin, *GS* 1(1):225; *Origin of German Tragic Drama*, p. 44.
54. *Ibid.*, pp. 227–47.
55. Benjamin, *Origin of German Tragic Drama*, p. 47.
56. *Ibid.*
57. *Ibid.*, p. 46.
58. *Ibid.*, p. 47.
59. *Ibid.*, p. 48.

60. *Ibid.*, p. 37.
61. Adorno, *Minima Moralia*, pp. 151–52.
62. Benjamin, *Origin of German Tragic Drama*, p. 47.
63. *Ibid.*, p. 37.
64. *Ibid.*, p. 36.
65. *Ibid.*, p. 37.
66. Benjamin, *GS* 1(1):216; *Origin of German Tragic Drama*, p. 36.
67. Benjamin, *Origin of German Tragic Drama*, p. 36.
68. Tiedemann, *Studien zur Philosophie Walter Benjamins*, p. 52.
69. Cf. Karl Marx, "Theses on Feuerbach," in *Writings of the Young Marx on Politics and Society*, p. 400.
70. Hans Heinz Holz, "Prismatisches Denken," in T. W. Adorno et al., *Über Walter Benjamin*, pp. 98–99.

4. From Messianism to Materialism

1. "Paris of the Second Empire" and "Some Motifs in Baudelaire" are contained in Walter Benjamin, *Charles Baudelaire: A Lyric Poet in the Era of High Capitalism;* "The Work of Art in the Age of Mechanical Reproduction," "The Storyteller: Reflections on the Work of Nikolai Leskov," "Theses on the Philosophy," "Kafka," as well as "Some Motifs in Baudelaire," can be found in Benjamin, *Illuminations;* "Edmund Fuchs: Historian and Collector" appears in Benjamin *The Essential Frankfurt School Reader;* "On the Mimetic Faculty" is in Benjamin, *Reflections: Essays, Aphorisms, Autobiographical Writings;* and "The Author as Producer" can be found in Benjamin, *Understanding Brecht,* as well as in *Reflections* and *The Essential Frankfurt School Reader.*

2. Virtually every contribution to the ever-growing voluminous secondary literature on Benjamin has felt compelled to take one side or the other in this debate. For more concerning it, see the Preface to this book.

3. In her essay on Benjamin, Hannah Arendt attempts to read the whole of Benjamin's life in terms of the allegory of the "hunchbacked dwarf," the omnipresent cause when things go wrong according to German children's lore; perhaps the American equivalent would be Mr. Nobody; cf. the concluding section of *Berliner Kindheit um Neunzehnhundert,* "Das buchlichte Männlein," 4(1):302–4. However, Arendt goes too far in suggesting that Benjamin consciously willed his own misfortune. Moreover, her attempt at a neoconservative reading of the significance of his work leaves the sincerity of his left-wing political convictions totally unaccounted for. Cf. Arendt, Introduction to *Illuminations.*

4. Benjamin, *Briefe* 1:381. Benjamin makes this remark in a letter to Scholem in which he confides he has reached the plateau of 1000 in his carefully kept list of books read, which he had begun while preparing his dissertation on the German romantics in the late 1910s. The final steps were: Thomas Mann's *Der Zauberberg,* the Lukács book, and Paul Valéry's *Eupalinos ou l'architecte.*

5. See the discussion of Benjamin's involvement in the Youth Movement in chapter 1.

6. Gershom Scholem, *Walter Benjamin: Die Geschichte einer Freundschaft*, p. 36.

7. Benjamin, *Reflections*, pp. 277–300. Benjamin had been introduced to Sorel's *Réflections sur la violence* in the course of conversations with Bloch and Hugo Ball during his stay in Switzerland in 1919. See Scholem, *Die Geschichte einer Freundschaft*, p. 109.

8. Scholem, *ibid.*, p. 103.

9. *Ibid.*, p. 104.

10. Sandor Radnoti, "Benjamin's Politics," p. 66.

11. To be sure, the liberal reprieve of Weimar represented a climate of relative tolerance in which Jews were afforded an unprecedented opportunity to play an active role in the shaping of cultural and political life. Peter Gay has treated the Weimar period from this point of view in his *Weimar Culture: The Outsider as Insider*. Yet, the difference between "native" and "assimilated" Germans by no means vanished overnight; and for an acutely sensitive spirit such as Benjamin, a sense of impending catastrophe was not difficult to discern.

12. Benjamin, *Briefe* 1:310.

13. Cf. Arendt, Introduction to Benjamin, *Illuminations*, pp. 24–25; see also Bernd Witte, *Walter Benjamin: Der Intellektuelle als Kritiker*, p. 140.

14. In a letter to Scholem of February 19, 1925, Benjamin laments: "Above all what worries me in the event of the successful completion [of his *Habilitation* efforts] is, first of all Frankfurt [where Benjamin would be teaching], then lectures, students, etc., things which would murderously consume my time."

15. An account of Benjamin's activity as a *Publizist* can be found in Witte, *Walter Benjamin: Der Intellektuelle als Kritiker*, pp. 137–85.

16. His reviews have been collected in GS 3.

17. Benjamin, *Briefe* 1:351.

18. In her memoirs, *Revolutionär als Beruf: Berichte über proletarisches Theater, Brecht, Benjamin und Piscator*, Lacis boasts of having single-handedly changed Benjamin's mind concerning his plans to emigrate to Palestine (pp. 45 ff.).

19. Benjamin, *Briefe* 1:355; emphasis added. Scholem, who at this point had secured a teaching position in Jerusalem, was of course quite taken aback by this new turn in his friend's thinking; and he recalls in his reminiscences that "communism in its Marxist form represented the precise antithesis to the anarchist convictions in which Benjamin and I had found agreement on the political plane until then"; *Die Geschichte einer Freundschaft*, p. 155.

20. Cf. Georg Lukács, *History and Class Consciousness*, pp. 83–222. For an in-depth discussion of *History and Class Consciousness* see Andrew Arato and Paul Breines, *The Young Lukács and the Origins of Western Marxism*, pp. 113–60.

21. Benjamin, "Über das Programm der kommenden Philosophie," GS 2(1):157–70.

22. A detailed discussion of Lukács's complex argument in *History and Class Consciousness* unfortunately falls outside the scope of the present study. In all fairness to Lukács, however, he avoids a purely metaphysical deduction of the role of the proletariat in *History and Class Consciousness* through his reliance on

the Weberian category of "objective possibility." See Arato and Breines, *The Young Lukács and the Origins of Western Marxism*, p. 114.

23. Radnoti, "Benjamin's Politics," p. 66.

24. Benjamin, *Briefe* 1:425–26.

25. Benjamin, "Theologico-Political Fragment," *Reflections*, p. 312.

26. Although both works are available in translation in *Reflections*, only selected aphorisms from *One-Way Street* have been included. My references will therefore be to the German original, *Einbahnstrasse*, GS 4(1):108 ff.

27. *Ibid.*

28. Benjamin, *The Origin of German Tragic Drama*, p. 152.

29. Benjamin, GS 4(1):103.

30. For a classical study of the rise and fall of "bourgeois publicity," see Jürgen Habermas, *Strukturwandel der Öffentlichkeit*.

31. Cf. Herbert Marcuse, "The Affirmative Character of Culture," in *Negations*, pp. 88–133. In the last book published before his death, Marcuse criticized the position of his early study by arguing for the necessity of preserving *autonomous art*, instead of recommending the *integration* of culture and life as he had in *An Essay on Liberation* as well as the 1936 essay. Cf. *The Aesthetic Dimension*. For a good discussion of Marcuse's aesthetics in light of Benjamin's work, see Heinz Pæstzold, *Neo-Marxistische Ästhetik* 2:102–37.

32. Cf. Benjamin's discussion of the *feuilleton* in *Charles Baudelaire*, pp. 29–31; see also Hauser, *A Social History of Art* 4:16–19, 121–24.

33. Benjamin, "Eduard Fuchs: Historian and Collector," in *The Essential Frankfurt School Reader*, p. 233. The same remark reappears in the 1940 "Theses on the Philosophy of History," in *Illuminations*, p. 256.

34. Ernst Bloch, *Erbschaft dieser Zeit*, pp. 367–71. According to Bloch's reminiscences, Benjamin reacted favorably when Bloch, at a Berlin café where they often met in the late twenties, handed him a review which compared Benjamin's book to a "store-opening, with the newest spring fashions in metaphysics in the display window." Cf. Adorno et al., *Über Walter Benjamin* (Frankfurt am Main, 1968), pp. 22–23.

35. *Ibid.*, p. 17.

36. Benjamin, GS 4(1):101.

37. Cf. Marcuse, *Eros and Civilization*, p. 47. Benjamin and Scholem had in 1915 scorned Buber and others for their glorification of the war "experience." Cf. Scholem, *Die Geschichte einer Freundschaft*, p. 14.

38. Benjamin, GS 4(1):122.

39. Lukács, *History and Class Consciousness*, pp. 43–85, *passim*.

40. This fact has also been noted by Radnoti, "Benjamin's Politics," p. 72.

41. Benjamin, "Theses on the Philosophy of History," in *Illuminations*, p. 258.

42. Adorno, "Benjamins Einbahnstrasse," in *Über Walter Benjamin*, (Frankfurt am Main, 1970), p. 53.

43. Benjamin, GS 4(1):143. Emphasis added.

44. Benjamin, "Zentralpark," GS 1(2):682. For an excellent discussion of

Benjamin's theory of Dialectical Images, see Rolf Tiedemann, *Studien zur Philosophie Walter Benjamins*, pp. 155–159; also see Tiedemann, "Bild, dialektisches," p. 919.

45. Benjamin, *Briefe* 1:(390).
46. Benjamin, "Paris, Capital of the Nineteenth Century," in *Charles Baudelaire*, pp. 9–101. The Arcades Exposé will be discussed at length in chapter 6.
47. André Breton, *Manifestoes of Surrealism*, pp. 10–11.
48. Adorno, "Benjamins 'Einbahnstrasse,'" *Über Walter Benjamin* (1970), pp. 53–54.
49. *Ibid.*, p. 54.
50. In *One-Dimensional Man*, pp. 67–70, Marcuse analyses the political significance of avant garde aesthetics in terms of its preservation of the moment of *non-identity* in the midst of an advanced industrial society that is totally administered. As such its dream-like language preserves the "Great Refusal" vis-à-vis the dominant reality principle. One might also note that the book closes with a moving tribute to Benjamin as someone who remained, in the tradition of critical theory, loyal to the principle of the Great Refusal: "The critical theory of society possesses no concepts which could bridge the gap between the present and its future; holding no promise and showing no success, it remains negative. Thus it wants to remain loyal to those who, without hope, have given and give their life to the Great Refusal. At the beginning of the fascist era, Walter Benjamin wrote: '*Nur um der Hoffnungslosen ist uns die Hoffnung gegeben.* It is only for the sake of those without hope that hope is given to us.'" Actually, this citation was the concluding sentence to the *Elective Affinities* essay, which was completed in 1923.
51. For a good summary of the issues in this debate, see Maurice Nadeau, *The History of Surrealism*, pp. 169–190. See also Breton's *Manifestoes of Surrealism*, pp. 117–93.
52. Benjamin, *Briefe* 1:446.
53. *Ibid.*, p. 455.
54. *Ibid.*, p. 663.
55. Louis Aragon, *Paysan de Paris*, pp. 18–19.
56. See Adorno's recollection of Benjamin's oral description of the methodological focus of the Arcades Project in Tiedemann, *Studien zur Philosophie Walter Benjamin*, p. 147n.
57. Benjamin, *Briefe* 2:489.
58. *Ibid.*, p. 491.
59. Cited in Adorno, Foreword to Tiedemann, *Studien zur Philosophie Walter Benjamins*, p. 8.
60. Benjamin, "Zentralpark," *GS* 1(2):681.
61. Benjamin, *Briefe* 2:654.
62. Benjamin, "Zentralpark," *GS* 1(2):671.
63. *Ibid.*, p. 683.
64. *Ibid.*
65. Benjamin, *Briefe* 2:496.

66. Benjamin, "Surrealism: The Last Snapshot of the European Intelligentsia," in *Reflections*, p. 179. The "Snapshot" of the subtitle is meant to be the "Latest" rather than "Last" ("*Letzte*"); the photographic imagery of the title immediately suggests affinity with the concept of Dialectical Images.

67. *Ibid.*, p. 178.

68. *Ibid.*, p. 182.

69. *Ibid.*, p. 189.

70. See Benjamin's comments on these experiments, "Die politische Gruppierung der russischen Schriftsteller" and "Zur Lage der russischen Filmkunst," *GS*, 2(2):743–50. These two pieces, as well as a longer essay, "Moscow" (*Reflections*, pp. 97–130) were the fruits of a two-month visit to the Soviet Union in late 1926 and early 1927.

71. Benjamin, *Reflections*, p. 179.

72. Scholem, *Die Geschichte einer Freundschaft*, p. 169.

73. Benjamin, *Reflections*, p. 189.

74. *Ibid.;* Benjamin, "Surrealismus," *GS* 2(1):307.

75. Benjamin *Reflections*, pp. 188–89.

76. Breton, *Manifestoes of Surrealism*, p. 14.

77. Benjamin, *Reflections*, p. 191; *GS* 2(1):308.

78. Benjamin *Reflections*, p. 191.

79. *Ibid.*

80. The seriousness with which Benjamin approached the role of radical polemicist in the late twenties and early thirties can only fully be appreciated upon examination of his more than 200 reviews and literary notes from this period, originally published in the *Literarische Welt* and the *Frankfurter Zeitung* and now available in *GS* 3. Also see the very important section of *Einbahnstrasse* entitled "The Technique of the Critic in Thirteen Theses" (omitted from the American edition) in which Benjamin presents his conception of the role of the critic in the "literary struggle." In this section one finds, for example, the following claims:

no. 5) "Objectivity must always be sacrificed to the spirit of the Party if the thing which the struggle concerns is of any value.

no. 7) "The critic's colleagues are the most important court of judgment. Not the public. Above all, not posterity."

no. 9) "Polemics means to destroy a book in a few sentences. The less one studies it the better. Only the one capable of destroying it can criticize it."

no. 11) "Enthusiasm for art is alien to the critic. In his hands the work of art is a polished weapon in the battle of intellects."

no. 12) "The art of the critic *in nuce:* to coin slogans, without betraying ideas. The slogans of an inadequate critique sell out thought to fashion."

81. Benjamin, *Reflections*, p. 192.

82. Peter Bürger, *Theorie der Avantgarde* (Frankfurt am Main, 1974), p. 66 ff.

83. See Hauser, *The Social History of Art* 3, *passim*.

84. Immanuel Kant, *Critique of Judgment*, pp. 42–44.

85. Cf. Burkhardt Lindner, "Aufhebung der Kunst in der Lebenpraxis?" *"Theorie der Avantgarde": Antworten auf Peter Bürgers Bestimmung von Kunst und bürgerlicher Gesellschaft*, W. M. Lüdke ed. (Frankfurt am Main, 1976), pp. 72–104.

5. Benjamin and Brecht

1. Hannah Arendt, Introduction to Walter Benjamin, *Illuminations*, pp. 14–15.

2. Benjamin, *Understanding Brecht*, p. 108.

3. A fact confirmed to me in a conversation with Herbert Marcuse in May 1976.

4. Rolf Tiedemann, *Studien zur Philosophie Walter Benjamins*, p. 112n.

5. Benjamin, *Understanding Brecht*, p. 110.

6. *Ibid.*, p. 114.

7. See for example Klaus Völker, *Brecht: A Biography*.

8. Gershom Scholem, *Walter Benjamin: Die Geschichte einer Freundschaft*.

9. Tiedemann, *Studien zur Philosophie Walter Benjamins*, p. 112n.

10. Cf. Benjamin, *Illuminations*, pp. 217–51.

11. Tiedemann, *Studien zur Philosophie Walter Benjamins* p. 112n.

12. Bertolt Brecht, *Arbeitsjournal*, p. 16.

13. Scholem, *Die Geschichte einer Freundschaft*, pp. 199, 198. However, both Scholem and Hannah Arendt (see note 1 above) are in error when they attempt to view the influence of Horkheimer and Adorno—like that of Brecht—as having pushed Benjamin further toward a Marxist point of view. Above all, this claim fails to differentiate between the rather orthodox (if not at times vulgar) appreciation of Marx displayed by Brecht and the philosophical renewal of Marxism which characterized the outlook of critical theory—a difference of night and day. For more on critical theory's appropriation of Marx, see Martin Jay, *The Dialectical Imagination*, pp. 41–85.

14. Cited in Scholem, *Die Geschichte einer Freundschaft*, p. 198.

15. Benjamin, *GS* 3:280–81.

16. Bernd Witte, *Walter Benjamin: Der Intellektuelle als Kritiker*, p. 149.

17. Benjamin, *GS* 2(2):743–47.

18. Benjamin, "Neue Dichtung in Rußland," *GS* II, 2, p. 756.

19. Benjamin, *GS* 2(2):747.

20. Cf. Witte, *Walter Benjamin*, p. 170.

21. I have attempted to pursue the links between anti-aesthetic tendencies and modernism in connection with Adorno's aesthetics in my essay "The De-Aestheticization of Art: On Adorno's *Aesthetische Theorie*," pp. 105–27.

22. Cited in Benjamin, "Bert Brecht," *GS* 2(2):661.

23. Cf. Arnold Hauser, *The Social History of Art* 4:94–98.

24. Cited in Benjamin, *GS* 2(2):661.

25. Theodor W. Adorno, *Ästhetische Theorie* (Frankfurt am Main, 1970) pp. 49–50.

26. Benjamin, *GS* 2(2):665.

27. A fact which came to the fore clearly in the great rupture of the late 1920s over the movement's position vis-à-vis the Communist Party, with Breton, on the one hand, and Aragon and Naville, on the other, as the chief protagonists.

28. Benjamin, *Illuminations,* p. 69.

29. Benjamin, *Briefe* 2:534–35.

30. Benjamin, "What is Epic Theatre" (1st version), in *Understanding Brecht,* p. 4.

31. *Ibid.,* pp. 4–5.

32. *Ibid.,* p. 7.

33. Bertolt Brecht, *Brecht on Theatre,* p. 38.

34. *Ibid.,* p. 44.

35. Cited in Arendt, Introduction to Benjamin, *Illuminations,* p. 38.

36. Benjamin, "What is Epic Theatre" (2nd version), in *Understanding Brecht,* p. 19.

37. For two important discussions of the monumental effect the idea of montage has had on contemporary art, see Hauser, *The Social History of Art,* 4:226–259; and Peter Bürger, *Theorie der Avantgarde* (Frankfurt am Main, 1974), pp. 98–116.

38. Brecht, *Brecht on Theater,* p. 70.

39. *Ibid.*

40. *Ibid.,* p. 48.

41. Benjamin, "What is Epic Theatre" (2nd version), p. 21.

42. At the same time, as Tiedemann has noted, there is no small measure of irony in the fact that while Brecht vehemently rejected the Benjaminian theory of the decline of the aura, it was largely on the basis of Brecht's own discussion of the superseding of 'glowing religious art' by technically structured art that Benjamin had developed this theory in the first place. Cf. Tiedemann, "Nachwort" to Benjamin, *Versuche über Brecht,* p. 193.

43. Cf. Benjamin, *GS* 2(3):1461.

44. Benjamin, *Briefe* 2:609.

45. Both the Kafka essay and an important letter to Scholem concerning the theoretical grounding of the essay (titled "Some Reflections on Kafka") can be found in Benjamin, *Illuminations,* pp. 111–46.

46. Benjamin, "The Author as Producer," in *Understanding Brecht,* p. 86; "Der Autor als Produzent," *GS* 2(2):685.

47. *Ibid.* "Author," p. 87; *GS* 2(2):685.

48. *Ibid.* "Author," p 87; *GS* 2(2):686.

49. *Ibid.,* "Author," pp. 87–88.

50. Brecht, *Gesammelte Werke* 7:212.

51. Benjamin, "The Author as Producer," p. 93.

52. *Ibid.,* p. 88.

53. *Ibid.,* p. 88; *GS* 2(2):687.

54. Benjamin, "The Author as Producer," p. 94. In light of Benjamin's plea for the *Umfunktionierung* of artistic media, it is of interest to note the error

of H. M. Enzensberger. The author, in what is purportedly one of the first attempts to apply Benjamin's findings to the mass media in the postwar era, (*The Consciousness Industry*, pp. 96–128) claims that to effect political change it would be sufficient for leftist intellectuals *to take over the mass media as such*—i.e., without first refunctioning them. In this connection, see the pertinent critique of Enzensberger's position in Jean Baudrillard, *For a Critique of the Political Economy of the Sign*, pp. 164–84.

55. *Ibid.* "Author," pp. 102–103; *GS* 2(2):701.

56. See Benjamin's important letter to Brecht of February 1931, announcing his resignation. In it he describes his own interpretation of the original intention of the journal—which he felt had been betrayed—as follows: "The journal was planned as an organ in which specialists from the bourgeois camp should attempt to present the crisis in science and art. This was to have been brought about through the intention to show to the bourgeois intelligentsia that the methods of historical materialism would be dictated to them through their own inmost necessities—necessities of spiritual production and research as well as necessities of existence. The journal was to have made use of the propaganda of dialectical materialism *through its application to questions which the bourgeois intelligentsia is forced to acknowledge as those which are to it most pertinent.*" Cf. Benjamin, *Briefe* 2:521.

57. Adorno, "Commitment," in *Aesthetics and Politics*, p. 187. For an interesting examination of the relationship between Brecht's political convictions and his artistic credo, see Henry Pachter, "Brecht's Personal Politics," *Telos* (Summer 1980), 44:35–48.

58. Benjamin, *Understanding Brecht*, p. 28.

59. Tiedemann, "Nachwort" to Benjamin, *Versuche über Brecht*, pp. 176, 178.

60. Benjamin, "Conversations with Brecht," in *Understanding Brecht*, p. 119.

61. Brecht also composed the following poem, "On the Suicide of the refugee W. B." in Benjamin's honor:

I'm told you raised your hand against yourself
Anticipating the butcher.
After eight years in exile, observing the rise of the enemy
Then at last, brought up against the impassable frontier
You passed, they say, a passable one.

Empires collapse. Gangleaders
Are strutting about like statesmen. The peoples
Can no longer be seen under all those armaments.

So the future lies in darkness, and the forces of right
Are weak. All this was plain to you
When you destroyed a tortuable body.

Brecht, *Poems: 1918–1956*, p. 363.

6. The Adorno–Benjamin Dispute

1. Walter Benjamin, *Baudelaire: A Lyric Poet in the Era of High Capitalism*, pp. 9–101.
2. Benjamin, *Briefe* 2:523.
3. Benjamin, *Reflections: Essays, Aphorisms, and Autobiographical Writings*, pp. 239–73.
4. Adorno, *Aesthetics and Politics*, p. 131.
5. For a good account of the biographical background of the debate, see Susan Buck-Morss, *The Origin of Negative Dialectics*.
6. Adorno, *Aesthetics and Politics*, p. 127.
7. Cf. Adorno, "Erinnerungen," *Über Walter Benjamin* (Frankfurt am Main, 1968).
8. This thesis is explored in detail in Buck-Morss' work.
9. Adorno, *Gesammelte Schriften* 1:345.
10. *Ibid.*, p. 346.
11. *Ibid.*, pp. 354–55. Emphasis in the original.
12. *Ibid.*, p. 357.
13. *Ibid.*
14. Cf. Jürgen Habermas, "Bewusstmachende oder rettende Kritik: die Aktualität Walter Benjamins," in *Zur Aktualität Walter Benjamins*, pp. 207–15.
15. Adorno, *Gesammelte Schriften* 1:325. English translation: "The Actuality of Philosophy," p. 120.
16. Adorno, *Gesammelte Schriften*, 1:336–39; "The Actuality of Philosophy," *Telos* 31, pp. 127–129.
17. Adorno, *Kierkegaard: Konstruktion des Ästhetischen*. For Benjamin's review of Adorno's book, see "Kierkegaard: Das Ende des philosophischen Idealismus," *GS* 3:380–83.
18. Benjamin, *Briefe* 2:663.
19. *Ibid.*, p. 662.
20. Benjamin, *Charles Baudelaire*, p. 159, Benjamin, "Paris, die Hauptstadt des XIX. Jahrhunderts," pp. 171–72.
21. *Ibid.*, pp. 159–60, 164–65.
22. Adorno, *Aesthetics and Politics*, p. 112.
23. *Ibid.*, p. 111.
24. *Ibid.*, p. 113. Emphasis added.
25. *Ibid.*
26. *Ibid.*, p. 114.
27. *Ibid.*
28. Rolf Tiedemann, *Studien zur Philosophie Walter Benjamins*, p. 158.
29. Adorno, *Aesthetics and Politics*, pp. 115–16.
30. *Ibid.*, p. 114.
31. Benjamin, *Illuminations*, p. 242.
32. *Ibid.*, p. 218.
33. Benjamin, *Briefe* 2:690.

NOTES TO PP. 186–198 297

34. *Ibid.*, p. 695.
35. *Ibid.*, p. 700. Elision in the original.
36. Benjamin, *Illuminations*, pp. 223–24.
37. *Ibid.*, p. 222.
38. *Ibid.*, p. 223.
39. *Ibid.*, p. 224.
40. *Ibid.*, pp. 220–221.
41. *Ibid.*, p. 223.
42. Cf. Adorno's remarks on the role of technique in art in *Ästhetische Theorie*, pp. 56–57, 94–96, and 316–26.
43. Adorno, *Aesthetics and Politics*, p. 126.
44. *Ibid.*, pp. 121–22.
45. Though Mallarmé, especially because of his theory of *poésie pure*, was a very important figure for Benjamin, the study suggested by Adorno never materialized. For an excellent study of Mallarmé which, although written from a post-structuralist perspective, would have fulfilled many of Adorno's desiderata, see Julia Kristeva, *Révolution du langage poétique*.
46. As Adorno remarks at one point: "I find it disquieting—and here I see a sublimated remnant of certain Brechtian motifs—that you casually transfer the concept of the magical aura to the 'autonomous work of art' and flatly assign to the latter a counter-revolutionary function." *Aesthetics and Politics*, p. 121.
47. *Ibid.*, p. 124–25.
48. *Ibid.*, p. 124.
49. Cf. Andrew Arato's Introduction to part 2 of *The Essential Frankfurt School Reader*, pp. 185–219.
50. In fact, as a comparison of the two works would easily demonstrate, "The Fetish Character of Music and the Regression of Listening" later served as the methodological basis of "The Culture Industry: Enlightenment as Mass Deception" a chapter of *Dialectic of Enlightenment*, which Adorno wrote with Max Horkheimer in 1944. This chapter thus in many ways represents the real conclusion of the Adorno-Benjamin debate. At this point in history, for Adorno and Horkheimer, now living in Hollywood, which "moment" of the debate had, at least temporarily, won out, no longer remained in question.
51. Adorno, "The Fetish Character of Music and the Regression of Listening," p. 274.
52. *Ibid.*, p. 278.
53. *Ibid.*, p. 287.
54. *Ibid.*, p. 296.
55. Adorno, *Aesthetics and Politics*, p. 123.
56. Cf. Andrew Arato, "Antinomies of the Neo-Marxian Theory of Culture," pp. 3–24.
57. Cited in Benjamin, *GS* 1(3):1067.
58. *Ibid.*, p. 1091.
59. The importance of the *correspondances* for Benjamin's thought wll be discussed in detail in chapter 7.

60. Benjamin, letter to Adorno of July 7, 1937, cited in *GS* 1(3):1070.

61. Cited in Benjamin, *GS* 1(3):1091.

62. *Ibid.*

63. Adorno, *Aesthetics and Politics*, p. 127.

64. *Ibid.*, p. 128.

65. *Ibid.*, p. 129–30.

66. *Ibid.*, 130.

67. Benjamin, *Charles Baudelaire*, pp. 107–54. This work will be discussed in detail in the following chapter.

68. Benjamin, *Aesthetics and Politics*, p. 137.

69. *Ibid.*, p. 136. Benjamin, *Briefe* 2:793. The allusion to "San Remo" refers to the cite of the last meeting between Benjamin and Adorno, which occurred earlier in 1938. Elisions in the original. Emphasis added.

70. Habermas, "Bewusstmachende oder rettende Kritik," p. 208.

71. Benjamin, "Theses on the Philosophy of History," in *Illuminations*. p. 255.

72. Benjamin explicitly uses the term "Janusgesicht" to refer to the theoretical oscillation in his later years between metaphysical and materialist points of view. Cf. Gershom Scholem, *Walter Benjamin: die Geschichte einer Freundschaft*, pp. 274–75.

73. Cf. Benjamin, *Briefe* 2:613.

74. *Ibid.*, p. 792.

75. Cf. Scholem, *Die Geschichte einer Freundschaft*, pp. 274–75.

76. Benjamin, *Illuminations*, pp. 257, 264.

77. Leo Lowenthal, *Literature, Popular Culture, and Society*, pp. 14–18.

78. Adorno, *Ästhetische Theorie*, p. 9.

79. It is worth noting in this context that Adorno studiously avoided the term "mass culture," because it implied that the so-called masses were themselves in some way responsible for the cultural commodities which in reality were foisted on them by the forces of industry; thus his preference for the more accurate designation "culture industry." Cf. Adorno, "The Culture Industry Reconsidered," p. 12.

80. Adorno, *Ästhetische Theorie*, p. 356.

81. Sandor Radnoti, "Mass Culture," private manuscript, p. 27.

82. *Ibid.*, pp. 36, 33–34. Nevertheless, Radnoti errs seriously when in conclusion he attributes an emancipatory potential to contemporary administered mass culture in terms of the latter's retention of the capacity to produce "other worlds." In truth, these so-called "other worlds" deal solely in images which are fully compatible with the existing world. Their end is adjustment, not emancipation.

7. *Benjamin's Materialist Theory of Experience*

1. At the same time, it should be noted that in the two most important studies of his early years, *Origin of German Tragic Drama,* and the "*Elective*

Affinities" essay, Benjamin's polemical aim was directed against the conventions of neoclassicist aesthetics. In the former work, by relying on the category of allegory, be sought to discredit the notion of the organic, self-contained, *beautiful* work of art; and in the latter study, he sought to expose the fallacies of an author-oriented aesthetic of genius through a critique of Friedrich Gundolf's biography of Goethe.

2. Walter Benjamin, "Eduard Fuchs: Collector and Historian," p. 233.

3. *Ibid.*, p. 234.

4. *Ibid.*, p. 227.

5. Benjamin, *Briefe* 2:793.

6. For more on Schleiermacher and the origin of modern hermeneutics, see Hans-Georg Gadamer, *Truth and Method*, pp. 162 ff.

7. Benjamin, "Theses on the Philosophy of History," in *Illuminations*, p. 254.

8. Benjamin, *Illuminations*, p. 83.

9. *Ibid.*, pp. 83–84.

10. George Lukács, *The Theory of the Novel*.

11. Benjamin, *Illuminations*, p. 84.

12. *Ibid.*, p. 85.

13. *Ibid.*, p. 86.

14. *Ibid.*, p. 87.

15. *Ibid.*

16. *Ibid.*

17. *Ibid.*, p. 92.

18. *Ibid.*, p. 87.

19. *Ibid.*, p. 89.

20. *Ibid.*

21. *Ibid.*, p. 90.

22. *Ibid.*, p. 99.

23. Cf. Gershom Scholem, *Walter Benjamin: Die Geschichte einer Freundschaft*, p. 104.

24. Lukács, *The Theory of the Novel*, p. 56. In a letter to Scholem in 1928, Benjamin refers to what appears to have been an early draft of the Leskov essay, "Romane lesen," as the beginnings of "a new 'Theory of the Novel.'" Cf. Benjamin, *GS* 2(3):1276.

25. Lukács, *The Theory of the Novel*, p. 62.

26. Cited in Benjamin, *Illuminations*, p. 99.

27. Benjamin, "The Image of Proust," *Illuminations*, p. 202.

28. Benjamin, *Illuminations*, p. 101. Needless to say, it would be extremely unjust to restrict the significance of the novel as a genre to the cathartic function of providing vicarious enjoyment. As a vehicle of knowledge, much more important is its role as the unconscious writing of history of the bourgeois epoch; it chronicles the consolidation of the idea of the bourgeois individual in the eighteenth century, then ultimately the decline and demise of that same individual in the nineteenth and twentieth centuries.

29. Benjamin, *GS* 2(3):1277.

30. Benjamin, "The Storyteller," p. 83.

31. Benjamin, "Some Motifs in Baudelaire," in *Charles Baudelaire: A Lyric Poet in the Era of High Capitalism*, p. 121.

32. *Ibid.*, p. 132.

33. Cf. Benjamin's long citation from Engels' *The Condition of the Working Class in England*, which reads in part: 'they crowd one another as though they had nothing in common, nothing to do with one another, and their only agreement is a tacit one, that each is to keep to his own side of the pavement, so as not to delay the opposing stream of the crowd, while it occurs to no man to honour another with so much as a glance. The brutal indifference, the unfeeling isolation of each in his private interest, becomes the more repellent and offensive the more these individuals are crowded together within a limited space.' Cited in *ibid.*, p. 121.

34. *Ibid.*, p. 123.

35. Cited in *ibid.*, p. 114.

36. *Ibid.*, p. 117. Emphasis added. For a discussion of the relationship between *Erinnerung* and *Gedächtnis* in Benjamin's thought, see Irving Wohlfarth, "On the Messianic Structure of Walter Benjamin's Last Reflections," pp. 148–212.

37. Benjamin, *Charles Baudelaire*, p. 111.

38. *Ibid.*, p. 113.

39. Cf. Charles Baudelaire, "Le Soleil," in *The Flowers of Evil*, p. 326.

40. Benjamin, *Charles Baudelaire*, p. 117.

41. Benjamin, "Addendum to 'The Paris of the Second Empire in Baudelaire,'" in *Charles Baudelaire*, p. 104n.

42. Benjamin, *Charles Baudelaire*, pp. 116–17.

43. Baudelaire, *Paris Spleen*, pp. ix–x.

44. Benjamin, *Briefe* 2:752.

45. Cited in Rolf Tiedemann, "Nachwort" to Benjamin, *Charles Baudelaire*, p. 202.

46. *Ibid.*, p. 203.

47. Benjamin, "Konspekt" for the Baudelaire study, *GS* 1(3):1151.

48. Benjamin, *Charles Baudelaire*, p. 134.

49. Karl Marx, *Capital*, pp. 455–639.

50. Benjamin, *Charles Baudelaire*, p. 133.

51. Perhaps at this point a brief note on the subtle terminological differences that exist between "rationalization" and "reification" would be in order. By rationalization we mean the process first observed by Max Weber whereby all personal and affective considerations are eliminated from the operation of social organizations (e.g., business concerns, politics, the legal sphere); instead social action is governed by predictable, clearly defined sets of rational and calculable formal rules. By reification we intend the etymological (*verdinglichen*: literally, to turn into a thing) and Marxian ("social relations among men turning into relations between things") definitions; in contrast, for example, to the pioneer-

ing, yet too general, use to which the term is put in Lukács *History and Class Consciousness,* where reification (for Lukács, synonomous with the Marxian notion of "commodity fetishism") is deemed the "central structural principle of capitalist society." Therefore, in our employment, reification can be deduced from rationalization, whereas the contrary proposition does not necessarily hold. Thus, the phenomenon of bureaucracy, for example, is an outgrowth of "rationalization" which gives rise to "reified" relations between persons; here reification is merely a *result* rather than a prime mover.

52. Benjamin, *Charles Baudelaire,* p. 133.

53. *Ibid.,* p. 133–34. For a description of the Poe text referred to here ("The Man of the Crowd"), see *ibid.,* pp. 126–28.

54. *Ibid.,* p. 132.

55. *Ibid.,* pp. 134–35.

56. Baudelaire, "Le Jeu," *Flowers of Evil,* p. 341.

57. Benjamin, "Some Motifs in Baudelaire," *Charles Baudelaire,* p. 113.

58. See also the discussion in the following chapter.

59. Benjamin, *Charles Baudelaire,* p. 141.

60. *Ibid.*

61. *Ibid.*

62. *Ibid.*

63. Quoted in *ibid.,* p. 140.

64. *Ibid.,* p. 139.

65. *Ibid.,* p. 148.

66. *Ibid.,* p. 145.

67. *Ibid.,* p. 146.

68. *Ibid.,* pp. 146–47.

69. Cf. Benjamin, *GS* 2(3):950–55 for a thorough account of the *Enstehungsgeschichte* of the two 1933 fragments on the theory of language.

70. *Ibid.,* p. 950.

71. Walter Benjamin and Gershom Scholem, *Briefwechsel: 1933–1940,* p. 71.

72. Scholem, *Die Geschichte einer Freundschaft,* pp. 79–80.

73. Benjamin, "On the Mimetic Faculty," in *Reflections,* p. 333.

74. *Ibid.*

75. Cited in Benjamin, *GS* 3:456–57.

76. Benjamin "Das Ornament . . ." (sketch for "Lehre vom Ähnlichen"), *GS* 2(3):958.

77. Benjamin, "On the Mimetic Faculty," in *Reflections,* p. 334.

78. Benjamin, "Der Augenblick der Geburt . . ." (sketch for "Lehre vom Ähnlichen), *GS* 3(3):956.

79. For an important discussion of the relationship between mimesis, art, and expression, see Adorno, *Ästhetische Theorie,* 168–78. The degree to which Adorno's treatment of the concept of expression is indebted to Benjamin's discussion in "On the Mimetic Faculty" is striking.

80. Benjamin, "On the Mimetic Faculty," *Reflections,* p. 335.

81. *Ibid.*

82. Hans Heinz Holz, "Philosophie als Interpretation," p. 235.

83. Benjamin, *GS* 2(3):956.

84. Cf. Benjamin, "On the Mimetic Faculty," in *Reflections*, p. 336.

85. Benjamin, *Reflections*, p. 336.

86. Benjamin, "Lehre vom Ähnlichen," *GS* 2(1):208; English translation: "Doctrine of the Similar," *New German Critique* (Spring 1979) 17:65–69.

87. Benjamin, *Reflections*, p. 335.

88. Benjamin, *Briefe* 1:126–27. It was on the basis of similar linguistic concerns that Benjamin renounced the Buber-Rosenzweig Bible translation. Cf. Martin Jay, "Politics of Translation," pp. 3–24.

90. Benjamin, "On Language as Such and On the Language of Man," in *Reflections*, p. 314; "Über die Sprache uberhaupt and über die Sprache des Menschen," *GS* 2(1):140–41.

91. Holz, "Philosophie als Interpretation," p. 235.

92. Scholem, *Die Geschichte einer Freundschaft*, p. 260. In the same context—a description of his last meeting with Benjamin in 1938—Scholem describes the essential unity of Benjamin's writings on language as follows: "The distinction between word and name, which he had established twenty years earlier in his 1916 work on language and developed further in his Prologue to the *Trauerspiel* book, was still alive for him, and in his sketch on the mimetic faculty even the faintest reference to a materialist view of language was lacking. On the contrary, matter appeared here only in a purely magical frame of reference." *Ibid.*

93. Benjamin, *Briefe* 2:524.

94. Holz, "Philosophie als Interpretation," p. 242.

95. Benjamin, *Briefe* 1:170.

8. "*A l'Écart de Tous les Courants*"

1. This thought was first expressed by Benjamin in a letter to Florens Christian Rang of January 1924, cf. Benjamin, *Briefe* 1:327, and was later reiterated verbatim in "Einbahnstrasse" *GS* 4(1):107.

2. Benjamin, *Illuminations*, pp. 144–45.

3. Gershom Scholem, *On Jews and Judaism in Crisis*, p. 178.

4. Cited in T. W. Adorno, "Vorrede" to Rolf Tiedemann, *Studien zur Philosophie Walter Benjamins*, p. 8.

5. Benjamin, *Charles Baudelaire*, p. 263.

6. *Ibid.*, p. 263.

7. Adorno, "Commitment," in *Aesthetics and Politics*, p. 194.

8. Jürgen Habermas, "Modernity versus Postmodernity," p. 10.

9. Gershom Scholem, *Walter Benjamin: die Geschichte einer Freundschaft*, p. 258.

10. Benjamin, *Briefe* 2:522.

11. The supplementary materials are available in Benjamin, *GS* 1(3):1228–66.

12. *Ibid.*, p. 1227.

13. *Ibid.*

14. Benjamin, *Illuminations,* p. 253.

15. Benjamin, *GS* 1(3):1246–47. For an excellent discussion of the general importance of the category of "destruction" in Benjamin's work, see Irving Wohlfarth, "No-Man's-Land," pp. 47–65.

16. Benjamin, *Illuminations,* p. 254.

17. *Ibid.,* p. 263.

18. *Ibid.,* p. 254.

19. *Ibid.,* p. 264.

20. For an important study of the inadequacies of the traditional Marxist relationship to the past, see Christian Lenhardt, "Anamnestic Solidarity," pp. 133–54.

21. A laudable exception to this tendency is Susan Buck-Morss's *The Origin of Negative Dialectics.*

22. Max Horkheimer and Theodor W. Adorno, *Dialectic of Enlightenment,* pp. 54, 57.

23. More recently, the view of modern administered culture as a "mythological phantasmagoria" has received extremely fruitful expression in the semiology of the late Roland Barthes; see his *Mythologies.*

24. Adorno, *Über Walter Benjamin,* p. 159.

25. Horkheimer and Adorno, *Dialectic of Enlightenment,* p. 40.

26. Adorno, *Negative Dialectics,* p. 320. Emphasis added.

27. Cf. Jürgen Habermas, *Zur Rekonstruktion des Historischen Materialismus;* partial English translation: *Communication and the Evolution of Society.*

28. Cf. Habermas, *Legitimation Crisis* (Boston, 1974), pp. 117–29.

29. Adorno, "A Portrait of Walter Benjamin," in *Prisms,* p. 229.

30. *Ibid.,* p. 230.

31. Benjamin, "The Image of Proust," *Illuminations,* p. 203.

32. Benjamin, "Ursprung des deutschen Trauerspiels," *GS* 1(1):211.

33. Gershom Scholem, "Dedication" to *Major Trends in Jewish Mysticism.*

34. The title of Adorno's final commentary on Benjamin; Cf. Adorno, *Über Walter Benjamin,* pp. 96–99.

BIBLIOGRAPHY

Adorno, Theodor W. "The Actuality of Philosophy." *Telos* (Spring 1977) 31:120–33.

—— "A l'Écart de Tous les Courants," in *Über Walter Benjamin, q.v.*

—— *Ästhetische Theorie.* Frankfurt: Suhrkamp Verlag, 1970.

—— "The Culture Industry Reconsidered." *New German Critique* (Fall 1975) 6:12–19.

—— "The Fetish Character of Music and the Regression of Listening." In A. Arato and E. Gebhardt, eds. *The Essential Frankfurt School Reader.* New York: Urizen, 1978.

—— *Gesammelte Schriften 1: Philosophische Frühschriften.* Rolf Tiedemann, ed. Frankfurt: Suhrkamp Verlag, 1973.

—— *Kierkegaard: Konstruktion des Ästhetischen.* Frankfurt: Suhrkamp Verlag, 1974.

—— *Minima Moralia.* E. Jephcott, trans. London: New Left Books, 1974.

—— *Negative Dialectics.* E. B. Ashton, trans. New York: Seabury Press, 1973.

—— *Noten zur Literatur.* 4 vols. Frankfurt: Suhrkamp Verlag, 1958–1974.

—— *Prisms.* Translated by Samuel and Sherry Weber. London: Neville Spearman, 1967.

—— *Über Walter Benjamin.* Rolf Tiedemann, ed. Frankfurt: Suhrkamp Verlag, 1970.

—— "Vorrede." Rolf Tiedemann, *Studien zur Philosophie Walter Benjamins,* pp. 7–11. Frankfurt: Suhrkamp Verlag, 1973.

—— *Zur Metakritik der Erkenntnistheorie.* Frankfurt: Suhrkamp Verlag, 1970.

Aesthetics and Politics. R. Taylor, translation ed. London: New Left Books, 1977.

Aragon, Louis. *Le Paysan de Paris.* Paris: Gallimard, 1926.

Arato, Andrew. "Esthetic Theory and Cultural Criticism: Introduction." In A. Arato and E. Gebhardt, eds. *The Essential Frankfurt School Reader,* pp. 185–219. New York: Urizen.

—— "Introduction: The Antinomies of the Neo-Marxian Theory of Culture." *International Journal of Sociology* (Spring 1977) 7(1):3–24.

—— "The Neo-Idealist Defense of Subjectivity." *Telos* (Fall 1974) 21:108–64.

Arato, Andrew and Paul Breines. *The Young Lukács and the Origins of Western Marxism.* New York: Seabury Press: 1979.

Barthes, Roland, *Mythologies.* A. Lavers, trans. New York: Hill and Wang, 1972.

Baudelaire, Charles. *The Flowers of Evil.* New York: New Directions, 1955.

—— *Paris Spleen.* Louise Varèse, trans. New York: New Directions, 1947.

Baudrillard, Jean. *For a Critique of the Political Economy of the Sign.* C. Levin, trans. St. Louis: Telos Press, 1981.

Benjamin, Walter. *Briefe.* 2 vols. Gershom Scholem and Theodor W. Adorno, eds. Frankfurt: Suhrkamp Verlag, 1966.

—— *Charles Baudelaire: A Lyric Poet in the Era of High Capitalism.* H. Zohn, trans. London: New Left Books, 1973.

—— "Drei Lebensläufe." *Zur Aktualität Walter Benjamins.* Siegfried Unseld, ed. Frankfurt: Suhrkamp Verlag, 1972.

—— "Eduard Fuchs: Collector and Historian." In A. Arato and E. Gebhardt, eds., New York: Urizen, 1978. *The Essential Frankfurt School Reader,* pp. 225–53.

—— *Gesammelte Schriften.* 6 vols. Rolf Tiedemann and Hermann Schweppenhäuser, eds. Frankfurt: Suhrkamp Verlag, 1972– .

—— *Illuminations.* Hannah Arendt, ed. H. Zohn, trans. New York: Schocken Books, 1969.

—— *Origin of German Tragic Drama.* J. Osborne, trans. London: New Left Books, 1977.

—— "Paris, Die Hauptstadt des XIX. Jahrhunderts." In *Illuminationen.* Frankfurt: Suhrkamp Verlag: 1977.

—— *Reflections: Aphorisms, Essays and Autobiographical Writings.* Peter Demetz, ed. E. Jephcott, trans. New York: Harcourt, Brace, Jovanovitch, 1978.

—— "Theories of German Fascism." *New German Critique* (Spring 1979) 17:120–28.

—— *Über Haschisch.* Tillman Rexroth, ed. Frankfurt: Suhrkamp Verlag, 1971.

—— *Understanding Brecht.* A. Bostock, trans. London: New Left Books, 1973.

Benjamin, Walter and Gershom Scholem. *Briefwechsel: 1933–1940.* Scholem, ed. Frankfurt: Suhrkamp Verlag, 1980.

Biale, David. *Gershom Scholem: Kabbalah and Counterhistory.* Cambridge: Harvard University Press, 1979.

Bloch, Ernst. *Erbschaft dieser Zeit.* Frankfurt: Suhrkamp Verlag, 1962.

—— "Erinnerungen." *Über Walter Benjamin.* With contributions by Theodor W. Adorno et al. Frankfurt: Suhrkamp Verlag, 1968. pp. 16–23.

—— *Geist der Utopie.* Frankfurt: Suhrkamp Verlag, 1964.

—— *Das Prinzip Hoffnung.* 3 vols. Frankfurt: Suhrkamp Verlag, 1959.

Brecht, Bertolt. *Arbeitsjournal.* 2 vols. W. Hecht, ed. Frankfurt: Suhrkamp Verlag, 1973.

—— *Brecht on Theatre: The Development of an Aesthetic.* J. Willet, ed. and trans. New York: Hill and Wang, 1964.

—— *Gesammelte Werke.* Vol. 7. E. Hauptmann et al., eds. Frankfurt: Suhrkamp Verlag, 1967.

—— *Poems: 1918–1956.* J. Willett and R. Manheim, eds. New York: Methuen 1976.

Brenner, Hildegard. "Die Lesbarkeit der Bilder." *Alternative* (June 1968) 59–60: 48–61.

Breton, André. *Manifestoes of Surrealism.* R. Seaver and H. R. Lane, trans. Ann Arbor: University of Michigan, 1974.

—— *Nadja.* R. Howard, trans. New York: Grove Press: 1960.

Buck-Morss, Susan. *The Origin of Negative Dialectics: Theodor W. Adorno, Walter Benjamin and the Frankfurt Institute.* New York: Free Press, 1977.

Bulthaup, Peter, ed. *Materialien zur Benjamins Thesen "Über den Begriff der Geschichte."* Frankfurt: Suhrkamp Verlag, 1975.

Bürger, Peter, ed. *Seminar: Literatur und Kunstsoziologie.* Frankfurt: Suhrkamp Verlag, 1978.

Davies, Ioan. "Time Aesthetics and Critical Theory." In John O'Neill, ed. *On Critical Theory,* pp. 58–77. New York: Seabury Press: 1976.

Enzensberger, H. M. *The Consciousness Industry.* New York: Seabury Press, 1974.

Fehér, Ferenc. "Is the Novel Problematic?" *Telos* (Spring 1973) 15:47–74.

Fekete, John. "Benjamin's Ambivalence." *Telos* (Spring 1978) 35:193–99.

Friedrich, Otto. *Before the Deluge: A Portrait of Berlin in the 1920's.* New York: Harper and Row, 1972.

Fuld, Werner. *Walter Benjamin: Zwischen den Stühlen.* Munich: Hanser Verlag, 1979.

Gadamer, Hans-Georg. *Truth and Method.* New York: Seabury Press: 1975.

Gay, Peter. *Weimer Culture: The Outsider as Insider*. New York: Harper and Row, 1968.

Goethe, J. W. von. *Elective Affinities*. R. J. Hollingdale, trans. Middlesex, England: Penguin, 1971.

Habermas, Jürgen. "Bewusstmachende oder rettende Kritik: Die Aktualität Walter Benjamins." *Zur Aktualität Walter Benjamins*. S. Unseld, ed. Frankfurt: Suhrkamp Verlag, 1972.

—— *Communication and the Evolution of Society*. T. McCarthy, trans. Boston: Beacon, 1979.

—— "Modernity versus Postmodernity." *New German Critique* (Winter 1981) 22:13–14.

—— *Strukturwandel der Öffentlichkeit*. Neuwied and Berlin: Luchterhand, 1962.

—— *Zur Rekonstruktion des Historischen Materialismus*. Frankfurt: Suhrkamp Verlag, 1976.

Hauser, Arnold. *The Philosophy of Art History*. Cleveland and New York: World Publishing, 1963.

—— *The Social History of Art*. 4 vols. Stanley Godman, trans. New York: Vintage, 1951.

Hegel, G. W. F. *Aesthetics*. 2 vols. T. M. Knox, trans. London: Oxford University Press, 1975.

—— *Phenomenology of Spirit*. A. V. Miller, trans. Oxford: Oxford University Press, 1977.

Heissenbüttel, Helmut. "Von Zeugnis des Fortlebens in Briefen." *Merkur* (March 1967) 228:232–44.

Heller, Agnes. "Georg Lukács and Irma Seidler." *New German Critique* (Fall 1979) 18:74–106.

Hillach, Ansgar. "The Aesthetics of Politics: Walter Benjamin's 'Theories of German Fascism.'" *New German Critique* (Spring 1978) 17:99–119.

Holz, Hans Heinz. "Philosophie als Interpretation." *Alternative* (October–December 1967) 56–57:235–42.

—— "Prismatisches Denken." In *Über Walter Benjamin*. With contributions by Theodor W. Adorno et al. Frankfurt: Suhrkamp Verlag, 1968.

Horkheimer, Max and Theodor W. Adorno. *Dialectic of Enlightenment*. Translated by J. Cummings. New York: Seabury Press, 1972.

Jameson, Fredric. *Marxism and Form: Twentieth Century Dialectical Theories of Literature*. Princeton: Princeton University Press, 1971.

Jay, Martin. *The Dialectical Imagination: A History of the Frankfurt School and the Institute for Social Research, 1923–1950*. Boston: Little, Brown, 1973.

—— "The Politics of Translation: Siegfried Kracauer and Walter Benjamin on the Buber-Rosenzweig Bible." *Yearbook of the Leo Baeck Institute* (1976):3–24.

Kandinsky, Wassily. *Concerning the Spiritual in Art.* M. T. H. Saunders, trans. New York, 1977.

Kandinsky, Wassily and Marc, Franz. *The Blaue Reiter Almanac.* K. Lankheit, ed. New York: Viking, 1974.

Kant, Immanuel. *Critique of Judgement.* James C. Meredith, trans. London: Oxford University Press, 1973.

—— *Critique of Practical Reason.* Lewis White Beck, trans. Indianapolis, New York: Bobbs-Merrill, 1956.

—— *Critique of Pure Reason.* N. K. Smith, trans. London: Macmillan, 1970.

Kristeva, Julia. *La révolution du langage poétique.* Paris: Editions du Seuil, 1974.

Lacis, Asja. *Revolutionär im Beruf: Berichte über proletarisches Theater, Brecht, Benjamin, Piscator.* H. Brenner, ed. Munich: Rogner and Bernhard, 1971.

Laqueur, Walter Z. *Young Germany: A History of the Youth Movement.* London: Basic Books, 1961.

Leibniz, G. W. von. *Discourse on Metaphysics.* P. G. Lucas and L. Grint, trans. Manchester: Manchester University Press, 1965.

—— *Monadology and Other Philosophical Essays.* P. and A. M. Schrecker, trans. Indianapolis: Bobbs-Merrill, 1965.

Lenhardt, Christian. "Anamnestic Solidarity: The Proletariat and Its Manes." *Telos* (Fall 1975) 25:133–54.

—— "The Wanderings of Enlightenment." In John O'Neill, ed. *On Critical Theory,* pp. 34–57. New York: Seabury Press, 1976.

Lethen, Helmut. "Zur Materialistischen Kunsttheorie Walter Benjamins." *Alternative* (October–December 1967) 56–57:225–34.

Lindner, B. and W. M. Lüdke, eds. *Materialien zur Ästhetischen Theorie Theodor W. Adornos.* Frankfurt: Suhrkamp Verlag, 1979.

Lowenthal, Leo. *Literature, Popular Culture and Society.* Palo Alto: Pacific Books, 1961.

Löwy, Michael. *Georg Lukács: From Romanticism to Bolshevism.* Patrick Camiller, trans. London: New Left Books, 1979.

—— "Interview with Ernst Bloch." *New German Critique* (Fall 1976) 9:35–45.

Lüdke, W. M., ed. *"Theorie der Avantgarde": Antworten auf Peter Bürgers Bestimmung von Kunst und bürgerlicher Gesellschaft.* Frankfurt: Suhrkamp Verlag: 1976.

Lukács, Georg. *History and Class Consciousness.* R. Livingstone, trans. Cambridge: MIT, 1971.

—— "On the Poverty of Spirit: A Conversation and a Letter." *The Philosophical Forum* (1972) 3(3–4):371–85.

—— *Realism in Our Time.* J. and N. Mander, trans. New York: Harper Torchbooks, 1974.

—— *Soul and Form.* A. Bostock, trans. Cambridge: MIT, 1974.

—— *The Theory of the Novel.* A. Bostock, trans. Cambridge: MIT, 1971.

—— *Die Zerstörung der Vernunft: Der Weg des Irrationalismus von Schelling zu Hitler.* Berlin: Augbau Verlag, 1953.

Marcuse, Herbert. *The Aesthetic Dimension.* Boston: Beacon, 1978.

—— *Counterrevolution and Revolt.* Boston: Beacon, 1972.

—— *Eros and Civilization.* Boston: Beacon, 1962.

—— *An Essay on Liberation.* Boston: Beacon, 1969.

—— *Negations.* J. J. Shapiro, trans. Boston: Beacon, 1969.

—— *One-Dimensional Man.* Boston: Beacon, 1964.

Markus, Gyorgy. "The Soul and Life: The Young Lukács and the Problem of Culture." *Telos* (Summer 1977) 32:195–216.

Marx, Karl. *Capital.* Ben Fowkes, trans. New York: Vintage, 1977.

—— *A Contribution to the Critique of Political Economy.* Moscow: Progress Publishers, 1971.

—— *Writings of the Young Marx on Philosophy and Society.* L. Easton and K. Guddat, trans. and eds. Garden City, N.Y.: Doubleday, 1968.

Menninghaus, Winfried. *Walter Benjamins Theorie der Sprachmagie.* Frankfurt: Suhrkamp Verlag, 1980.

Missac, Pierre. "Du Nouveau sur Walter Benjamin?" *Critique* (August–September 1969) 267–68:681–98.

—— "Walter Benjamin: de la rupture au naufrage." *Critique* (April 1980) 395:370–81.

Mosse, George L. *The Crisis of the German Ideology: The Intellectual Origins of the Third Reich.* New York: Universal Library, 1964.

—— *Germans and Jews: The Right, the Left and the Search for a "Third Force" in Pre-Nazi Germany.* New York: Howard Fertig, 1970.

Nadeau, Maurice. *The History of Surrealism.* R. Howard, trans. New York: MacMillan, 1965.

Pætzold, Heinz. *Neomarxistische Ästhetik.* 2 vols. Düsseldorf: Schwann Verlag, 1974.

—— "Walter Benjamin's Theory of the End of Art." (Translation of Chapter 2 of *Neomarxistische Ästhetik.*) *International Journal of Sociology.* (Spring 1977) 8(1):25–75.

Pfotenhauer, Helmut. *Ästhetische Erfahrung und gesellschaftliches System: Untersuchungen zu Methodenproblemen einer materialistischen Literaturanalyse am Spätwerk Walter Benjamins.* Stuttgart: J. B. Metzler, 1975.

Piccone, Paul. "Why Did the Left Collapse?" *Telos* (Winter 1980–81) 46:92–97.

Plato. *The Collected Diologues.* E. Hamilton and H. Cairns, eds. Princeton: Princeton University Press, 1973.

Radnoti, Sandor, "Benjamin's Politics." *Telos* (Fall 1978) 37:63–81.

—— "The Early Aesthetics of Walter Benjamin." *International Journal of Sociology* (Spring 1977) 7(1):76–123.

—— "Mass Culture." Unpublished manuscript.

Ringer, Fritz. *The Decline of the German Mandarins: The German Academic Community, 1890–1933.* Cambridge: Harvard University Press, 1969.

Rosen, Charles. "Walter Benjamin and His Ruins." *The New York Review of Books* (October 27, 1977) 24(17):31–40; (November 17, 1977) 24(18):30–38.

Rosenzweig, Franz. *The Star of Redemption.* Boston: Beacon, 1972.

Rychner, Max. "Erinnerungen." *Über Walter Benjamin.* With contributions by Theodor W. Adorno et al. Frankfurt: Suhrkamp Verlag, 1968. pp. 24–29.

Sartre, Jean-Paul. *Literature and Existentialism.* B. Frechtman, trans. New York: Citadel Press, 1949.

Schiller, Friedrich. *On the Aesthetic Education of Man.* New York: Frederick Ungar, 1954.

Schlegel, Friedrich. *Schriften und Fragmente.* Ernst Behler, ed. Stuttgart: Alfred Kröner Verlag, 1956.

Scholem, Gershom. *Kabbalah.* New York: New York Times Publishing, 1974.

—— *Kabbalah and Its Symbolism.* New York: Schocken Books, 1965.

—— *Major Trends in Jewish Mysticism.* New York: Schocken Books, 1974.

—— *The Messianic Idea in Judaism.* New York: Schocken Books, 1971.

—— *On Jews and Judaism in Crisis.* New York: Schocken Books, 1976.

—— *Walter Benjamin: Die Geschichte einer Freundschaft.* Frankfurt: Suhrkamp Verlag, 1975.

Simmel, Georg. *The Conflict in Modern Culture and Other Essays.* K. P. Etzkorn, trans. New York: Teachers College Press, 1968.

—— *The Philosophy of Money.* T. Bottomore and D. Frisby, trans. London: Routledge and Kegan Paul, 1978.

Sontag, Susan. "Walter Benjamin: The Last Intellectual." *The New York Review of Books* (October 12, 1978) 25(15):75–82.

Tiedemann, Rolf. "Bild, dialektisches." *Historisches Wörterbuch der Philosophie,* pp. 919–20. Basel, Stuttgart: Schwabe, 1971.

—— "Nachwort." Walter Benjamin, *Charles Baudelaire: Ein Lyriker im Zeitalter des Hochkapitalismus,* pp. 189–212. Frankfurt: Suhrkamp Verlag, 1973.

—— "Nachwort." Walter Benjamin, *Versuche über Brecht.* Frankfurt: Suhrkamp Verlag, 1978.

—— *Studien zur Philosophie Walter Benjamins.* Frankfurt: Suhrkamp Verlag, 1973.

—— "Zur 'Beschlagnahme' Walter Benjamins oder Wie man mit der Philologie Schlitten fährt." *Das Argument* (1968) 46:74–93.

Völker, Klaus. *Brecht: A Biography.* J. Nowell, trans. New York: Seabury Press, 1978.

Wiesenthal, Liselotte. *Zur Wissenschaftheorie Walter Benjamins.* Frankfurt: Athenaum Verlag, 1973.

Willey, Thomas E. *Back to Kant.* Detroit: Wayne State University Press, 1978.

Witte, Bernd. "Benjamin and Lukács: Historical Notes on their Political and Aesthetic Theories." *New German Critique* (Spring 1975) 5:3–26.

—— "Festellungen zu Walter Benjamin und Kafka." *Neue Rundschau* (1973) 84:480–94.

—— *Walter Benjamin: Der Intellektuelle als Kritiker. Untersuchungen zu seinem Frühwerk.* Stuttgart: J. B. Metzlerische Verlagsbuchhandlung, 1976.

Wohlfarth, Irving. "No-Man's-Land: On Walter Benjamin's 'Destructive Character.'" *Diacritics* (June 1978) 8(2): 47–65.

—— "On the Messianic Structure of Walter Benjamin's Last Reflections." *Glyph* (1978) 3:148–212.

—— "The Politics of Prose and the Art of Awakening: Walter Benjamin's Version of a German Romantic Motif." *Glyph* (1980) 7:130–48.

—— "Walter Benjamin's Image of Interpretation." *New German Critique* (Spring 1979) 17:70–98.

Wolin, Richard. "The De-Aestheticization of Art: On Adorno's *Aesthetische Theorie.*" *Telos* (Fall 1979) 41:105–27.

INDEX